DENTALES

BA CALLAOS.

la vermuda.

CANCER

Lisboa

Canarias

R de loro
G Blanco.
Verde

ESPA
Mexico
Aca pulco

Cuba
Prico
Domin...
Jamaica

MAR (DEL NORTE)

Honduras
Tierra firme
Cora
Dominica
Trinidad

Y. de cocos.
Panama

90.   800   Prico 70   R. Pasao 60   R. de las Amazones   40   20   40

Y. de galapagos.

PERU

C de S Agustin

DEL SVR

Callao
Arica

BRASIL

C. Frio

B. de. Vicente.

P. de chile.

R. de plata   C de S Maria
C. Blanco.

P. de baldivia

Prouincia deletrecho

C. de las birgenes.

Estrecho de Magallanes.

MERIDIANO DE LA DE MARCACION POR LA PARTE O CIDENTAL.

...les de la Antonio de Herrera, Madrid, 1730.

To

Andy with many

thanks - from

Paula

Delhi 1948.

SALVADOR DE MADARIAGA

THE FALL
OF THE
SPANISH AMERICAN
EMPIRE

LONDON
HOLLIS & CARTER
1947

Liberty is a condition, a way of being, not a real and positive being, and that is why we see how a civilisation which takes liberty as its creative principle without troubling about anything else, leads to no result or to negative results.

from the Catalan of
Bishop Torres y Bages
La Tradicio Catalana

Licet arma vacent cessentque doli,
Sidunt ipso pondere magna
Ceditque oneri Fortuna suo.
Seneca : *Agamemnon*, 87-90.

PRINTED IN GREAT BRITAIN AT THE CHAPEL RIVER PRESS, ANDOVER, HANTS,
FOR HOLLIS AND CARTER, LTD., 25 ASHLEY PLACE, LONDON, S.W.1
First Published in 1947
10.47

TABLE OF CONTENTS

PART I

THE SOUL OF THE INDIES

PART II

INTERNAL ORIGINS OF THE SECESSION

PART III

EXTERNAL ORIGINS OF THE SECESSION

v

LIST OF ILLUSTRATIONS

ACKNOWLEDGMENTS

My thanks are due above all to the Bodleian Library and its staff; to the London Library and to the British Museum. I am especially indebted to the Public Record Office for their kindness in putting at my disposal papers which had been " evacuated " owing to the war. I thank Miss S. England for her co-operation in this.

Many of the books consulted had to be acquired here or in other cities overseas. In this, a difficult task in war times, my best help came from my brother César, exiled in Bogotá; and next to him Don Justino de Azcárate, exiled in Caracas, and the two Spanish-American scholars D. Vicente Lecuna and " Cornelio Hispano." A number of personal friends in the London diplomatic corps have been most generous with their private libraries—notably Sres Bianchi, Cárcano, Carnevali and Paz Castillo. The Duke of Alba, always ready to put history above politics, has sent me the three volumes of Gondomar's letters. My thanks are due to all these friends. My wife has advised me on the English text and when it goes wrong it can only be because I have not taken her advice.

The actual preparation of an MS. of such dimensions with an original text in both English and Spanish, and copious notes in several other languages demands intellectual gifts far above the common : I wish to record my gratitude to Mrs. Rauman for having so generously put hers at the service of this work.

I am indebted to Mr. Julian Duguid for the frontispiece; and to the Peruvian Ambassador, my friend Don Fernando Berckemeyer, for allowing me to reproduce the sketches of Lima life by Pancho Fierro.

PART I

THE SOUL OF THE INDIES

Chapter I

THE SPANISH ROOTS : THE CONQUEROR AND THE FRIAR

A N objective and comparative examination of the New World between 1500 and 1800 destroys the popular and all too often accepted view of the Spanish Empire. And yet the men who led the struggle for emancipation were neither fools nor knaves. They were for the most part men of outstanding intellect, capable of sacrifice, and fully deserving the name of *patriots* which they proudly bore. These men often used as projectiles loose facts or half facts or pseudo-facts. But the patriots were not lying. They were shooting in the heat of battle with words and ideas, or giving vent to pent-up passions, the depth and even the origin of which were often unknown to them. To take all they said as sober truth and set it down as history is fatal for history. If we are to understand what happened between 1800 and 1830 in the Spanish world we must seek the roots of events in that subsoil of the human soul from which events draw their substance. We must try to understand the soul of the Indies.

It was impressive in its vastness. Even to-day, when, drained of much of its power and originality, divided within itself and severed from its Spanish roots, it is no more than a shadow of its old self, we can perceive its historical size; for the Spanish-American, under his seemingly facile and superficial life, conceals a far subtler and more shaded " soulscape " than that of all but exceptional North-Americans. The vastness, splendour and variety of the world in which it lived, the wide range of cultures, states of civilization, racial colours and origins that went to its making, the complex system of tensions which arose between its men, colours, classes, climates and kingdoms, the vivid presence of far-off influences, that of the King of Spain and his grandees and Councils, and that of the Lord of Heaven and his Saints, the ups and downs of fortune caused by storms, earthquakes, pirates, savage Indians, the Inquisition, official justice or injustice, the king's favour or wrath ; and finally all this inner unsteadiness seething within

3

a world kept in a thrice secular peace and security from European wars, everything contributed to make the soul of the Indies something strange and rare, almost unique in the annals of the human spirit.

*   *   *

Three strains composed its stock.   But in most of the Indies each of these three strains entered into the life of the whole in a way of its own : the Indian strain was rooted in the soil ; the African strain had been transplanted from overseas, and later became also rooted in the soil, partly directly, partly through the Indian ; the Spanish strain had been grafted into the Indian and into the African, and only through them did it gain access to the soil of its new fatherland.

This fact stands at the basis of the human history of the Indies.   Unless it be grasped, many of the events of the wars of emancipation must remain unintelligible.   The spiritual evolution of each of the three strains and of the collective soul which they made up is determined by the fact that the Indians went on growing on their own soil, while they had to share this soil with the Blacks and to give up their sun to the Spaniards ; that the Blacks came from a different continent, and, though taking root on the American soil, felt in the roots of their being the pull of their African memories ; and that the Spaniards, in touch with the New World only through the Indians, or even through the more circuitous channel of the Blacks, remained till the eve of the war of emancipation mentally and morally rooted in Spain even though warmed by the sun of the Indies.

But reality was even more complicated.   For within every one of these three strains there arose differences and tensions of the most baffling complexity.   It is time to throw some light on these inner differences and to illustrate how the rich and unexpected life of the Indies brought together the three simple colours and the many more combined colours which resulted from their mixture, in ways which differ as much from the generally accepted descriptions as a picture of Tintoretto from a crude coloured print.

*   *   *

The prototypes of the Spanish strain were the *conquistador*
and the friar.   The *conquistador* is safe in his epic greatness.
No man in human history has attempted, no man has achieved,
greater things.   Men of the stamp of Cortés, Pizarro, Quesada,
Orellana, Soto, Belalcázar, Balboa or Cabeza de Vaca stand
in History as a race of epic giants, hewing History into shape
with the well tempered steel of their massive wills.   Above all,
they had style—that style which comes from a creative spirit,
and shows itself in the actions of a Cortés as clearly as in the
play of a Shakespeare or in the symphonies of a Beethoven.
Cortés " burning " his ships, Pizarro drawing a line across his
path with his sword, Balboa falling on his knees on seeing the
SouthSea, and many more of this kind, are scenes which remain
in the memory of man with the dramatic force of perfection.
When Almagro made ready to cross the Andes into Chile
through passes no man had ever dared cross in winter, his
Inca friends warned him that such a thing was impossible.
But Almagro argued that the discoverers and conquerors of
Peru were men " whom the earth and other elements were
bound to obey and Heaven to favour."   Such was the faith
which lived in them.   It is illustrated in a perfect scene whose
hero was not a Spanish, but a Greek *conquistador*.   When
Pizarro and his thirteen companions, after years of privations
and perils across unknown seas and treacherous coasts, arrived
in Túmbez or Tumpiz, they wondered whether, being only
fourteen men, they would dare explore a city which looked so
large and powerful.   " In this confusion "—writes Garcilaso—
" Pedro de Candía came forward with virile courage and with
the faith and trust of a Christian and said: ' I shall go on my
own to see what there is in this valley ; if they kill me, all you
will have lost will be one companion ; if I succeed, our victory
shall be the greater.'   Saying which he donned a coat of
mail which reached down to his knees, a steel helmet of the
most elegant they had, a steel buckler, a sword at his girdle,
and in his right hand a wooden cross longer than a yard, in
which he put more trust than in his weapons, being the sign of
our Redeemer.   Pedro de Candía was very tall, so I was told,
for I never saw him, but a son of his who was a student with me
when I was learning the a.b.c. showed by his corpulence what

his father must have been, for though he was only eleven or twelve he was twice as big as his age warranted. So, Pedro de Candía left his companions, asking them to recommend him to God. He went to the city, step by step, showing a grave and lordly face, as if he were the lord of all that province. The Indians, who on seeing the ship were all agog, became far more excited when they saw so big a man, covered with steel from head to foot, with a beard on his face, a thing which they had never seen or imagined. Those who saw him crossing the fields ran away sounding alarms. When Pedro de Candía arrived in the city, he found the fortress and the square full of people ready to fight. They all were astounded at such a strange sight and knew not what to say and dared not do him any harm, wondering whether he was a divine thing. To make an experiment of it, the chiefs decided to set on him a lion and a tiger (which Huayna Capac had asked them to keep) so the beasts should destroy him ; and so it was done. [. . .] The two fierce animals, seeing the Christian, and what is more certain, the sign of the Cross, went to him, having lost all their natural fierceness, and as if they were two dogs bred by him, they caressed him and lay at his feet. Pedro de Candía, considering the marvel which God Our Lord had performed, and drawing more courage from it, stooped to pass his hand over the head and back of the animals, and laid his Cross on them, letting those gentiles understand that the virtue of that sign softened and took away the ferocity of the beasts ; whereby the Indians were confirmed in their belief that he was a son of the Sun, come from Heaven."

This is marvellous enough, but what follows is perhaps more marvellous : " With this belief they went to him and by common consent worshipped him as the son of their god, the Sun, and took him to their temple which was covered inside with thick plates of gold, so that he might see how his father was honoured in their land. After showing him the temple, the vessels and other ornaments and wealth which they had for the god's service, they took him to see the royal house of his brothers the Incas, whom they also held to be sons of the Sun. They took him about so that he should see all the halls, rooms and apartments, tapestries of gold and silver which they had. They showed him the table service for the Inca, which was of gold and silver down to the pots and pans and pitchers, water-jars and water barrels. They took him to the garden, where Pedro de Candía saw trees and other smaller plants, grass, animals and other smaller reptiles and insects which, as we have said, they had in their gardens made of gold and silver in imitation of their natural shapes ; at all of which, the Christian remained in greater admiration than the Indians had been at seeing so marvellous and strange a person as he was."(1)

*   *   *

The men who, on the threshold of the New World, met with such marvels as gardens of gold and silver, brought their own imagination aflame with the marvels of the books of Chivalry then at the apex of their success. In their eyes, every knight had the right to expect that the tree of fate, at the first stroke of his spear, should let fall a kingdom at the feet of his horse. And what kingdoms! Suns of gold, moons of silver, temples walled with thick plates of the two precious metals, emeralds, amethysts, all the metallic and mineral splendour of the books of knight-errantry and adventure, till then a tale conjured out of dusty folios by the magic of the printed word, had taken bulk and substance and stood, tempting and provocative, behind yonder hills or shores which challenged their stout hearts and hungry eyes.

Now, these men were the scions of a nation of fighters who for centuries had grown used to acquiring wealth with the sword. Most of these conquerors had been born before the fall of Granada (1492). From about 800 till their own generation, the men of Spain had been born and bred in a society in which gentlemen lived by the spear, and by the spear conquered their estates and kept them safe against constantly recurring attacks. In these seven centuries, their mental processes had acquired two definite and deeply ingrained trends : (i) a man of quality, by fighting, acquires wealth more honourably and more quickly than a meaner man by work ; and (ii) a man of quality does not rest on his wealth but goes on fighting as a matter of course, for of infidels to destroy, of wealth to acquire and of honour to reap, there is no end.

These men, therefore, were as goldthirsty as any other men of their age, or of ours. But they were not merely goldthirsty. Not one of them was content to store his gold and live on the sweat of his Indians. " For this was a common habit "— writes Garcilaso—" not only of those who went to that particular campaign, but also of all the noble soldiers of Peru, to refuse any pay or money help, and to be offended if it were offered them, for they put their honour in serving without immediate gain, and only for the royal favours to come, and if one of them out of dire need accepted money, he never did so by way of pay or help, but only as a loan, considering himself bound to return it to H.M.'s Treasury as soon as he was able to ; and so they did with the utmost punctiliousness, for they put their honour in fulfilling a soldier's promise." These words from a half-caste chronicler who knew many of the soldiers in question personally, throw a light not usually seen on the character of the *conquistadores*. They came of a breed of men who could discriminate between money and leisure, and between leisure and sloth, as their native proverbs reveal. *Treasure goes to treasure, and to the knight, leisure* : i.e., the nobleman need not have anything to do with menial activities, which are but a poor sort of endeavour ; yet, lest it might be imagined that the leisure of a nobleman is to be spent in idleness, here is another sentence from the people of Castille : *The worldly man, a spinning wheel in his bosom, a sword in his hand.* None of your worldly men, therefore, who are but women disguised as men. A true man must seek a life of high endeavour.(2)

" The Spaniards "—writes Garcilaso—" after discovering the New World, were so eager to discover new lands and ever more new lands, that, although many of them were rich and prosperous, not content with what they owned, nor weary of their hardships, hungers, dangers, wounds, illnesses, bad days and worse nights spent by sea and land, undertook new conquests and greater endeavours, to achieve higher exploits which should make their names famous for eternity." And so he reminds us how rich and famous Pizarro was when he threw his comfort and wealth to the winds in order to discover Peru. Pedro de Alvarado is another case in point. This man, whose memory stands stained for ever by the massacre of Mexico and by the torture he inflicted on the king of Tetzcuco, the latter merely to wrench gold from the wretched king, the former, in part at least, under the temptation of wealth, this man can nevertheless by no means be dismissed as a mere goldthirsty adventurer. " As he was in peace and very prosperous governing Huahutimallan and Chiapa [. . .] he sought a charter from the emperor to go and discover and populate in Quitu of Peru, famous for its wealth, in lands where there were no other Spaniards. And so, in 1535 he armed five ships in which, and in two others which he took in Nicaragua, he embarked 500 Spaniards and many horses. He landed in Puerto Viejo : went to Quitu : suffered much cold, thirst and hunger on the way." He there met with the other conquerors, sold them his ships and artillery and " returned rich and content to Huahutimallan." " There he did not rest, as he might have done, since he was rich and prosperous, full of trophies and exploits which from his early youth he had achieved. But the greater his deeds, the greater was his spirit and ambition to seek greater ones still, till he found death in them." He undertook further exploits with the Viceroy Mendoza, and in the course of an expedition to put down a rebellion in Azatlan, he was killed fighting to lend a hand to a local Spanish captain (June, 1541), having been thrust down a precipice by a huge rock which an Indian had hurled down from the top of a hill. His stout frame fought with death for several days. " When asked where he ached, he always answered : ' In my soul.' "(3)

This answer provides the dimension in depth which most of the conquerors possessed. Alvarado's evil deeds (possibly exaggerated by envy, as Garcilaso points out) would not lead us to expect the moral elegance of some of his actions. To judge by what we know of him, he was by no means always a morally elegant man. He bargained with Almagro over the head of his followers ; and his dealings with the Viceroy of New Spain, as Garcilaso says, " without regard for Cortés' interests, and the ingratitude they implied towards Cortés to whom he owed all he was," are unsavoury. But when not wealth but life was at stake, his nobility shone untarnished.

As is often the case with Spaniards, his virtues were extolled after his death more freely than while he lived. In his childhood, Garcilaso heard high praise " of his kindness and virtue " ; and " that when they went to Peru they suffered greatly from thirst at sea, so much that on arriving in Tumpiz, many of them were sick with thirst-fever and unable to land. Don Pedro de Alvarado, having landed, and as water was brought to him, he refused to touch it, though as thirsty as the thirstiest, but sent it to the ships for the sick, and he did not drink till all had been quenched."(4)

Nor are such scenes isolated. Far from it. They express a norm of behaviour, cheek by jowl with others no less frequent of wanton rebellion or lack of faith. Gonzalo Pizarro, already rich and powerful, left the delights of Quito to go and discover what turned out to be the Amazon basin. Three hundred leagues down and four hundred back of sheer horror, during which, confronted by the wilderness and the mighty river, the Spaniards, decimated by hunger and sickness, built a ship. Technique was improvised, for when the aim was high enough, the Spaniard could overcome his dislike of technique. They made nails with shoes of the horses they had eaten ; charcoal with the trees of the forest which encircled them ; sheds to make charcoal under a roof in a rainy climate, and to build their forges dry ; tar with gum from some trees they discovered ; tow with their decayed clothes. " Gonzalo Pizarro, like the great soldier he was, was the first to cut wood, to hammer iron, to make charcoal, or work at any other craft, however low, to give an example to the others." His second, Orellana, sent down to explore the river in the ship, left him in the lurch and went down all the way to the Atlantic and Trinidad, building bigger and bigger ships as the rivers became deeper and wider. Gonzalo Pizarro had to return, exploring another way which turned out to be even worse ; four hundred leagues of it. When at last the eighty men who remained out of the original four hundred and over, arrived in Quito, they had no clothes, and hardly a spot on their skin which was not bitten, cut or burnt. Quito did its best to help them. But the city, in the throes of civil war, could send clothes for no more than six men along with a dozen horses and some food. " Gonzalo Pizarro and his captains and soldiers received the gifts and relief with due gratitude ; but, seeing that there were clothes and horses only for the captains, they refused to dress or ride, so as to keep the strictest equality, as good soldiers ; and in such a guise they entered Quito city one morning, going straight to the church to hear Mass and thank God who had rescued them from so many hardships."(5)

The scene illustrates yet another feature of the conquerors : self-esteem, which implies a high level of performance. This feature often took a competitive aspect. Garcilaso tells one or two stories of Alvarado : one in which at the top of the tower of Seville Cathedral, provoked by another man who had preceded him in the exploit, he walked on a plank ten or twelve feet out over the abyss, turned round and came coolly back ; another one in which the future lieutenant of Cortés, seeing some peasants leaping over a wide well, leapt also, but feigned not to have gone far enough, touched the edge with his toes and leapt back. Both stories may be legends, growing out of the famous " leap of Alvarado " on the night in which Cortés' army fled from Mexico, a leap which may also be a legend. But the fact remains that the conquerors were most exacting as to their endurance and achievements and often disregarded the advice of the Indians as to what was possible or impossible.(6)

*   *   *

This self-esteem often acted as a check on greed, and love of immediate gain. When Pizarro decided to honour the treaty made on his behalf by Almagro with Alvarado, and to pay Alvarado the agreed 100,000 *pesos* to buy him out of Peru, his more short-sighted followers strongly advised him against such a course, urging all kinds of utilitarian reasons ; all of which he silenced, signifying to his men that " he would not accept any advice given him to the benefit of his wealth and to the detriment of his honour."(7)

This word, honour, had for the conquerors a complex meaning and content. It comprised both individual and social elements, and was at times a feeling born of the self, defined and defended by the self, and not open to discussion by others on objective grounds. At other times, it took on a social value ; and then was apt to imply status and authority granted by the only source there was for such things : the King of Spain. As an example of the first, we have the answer of Garcilaso de la Vega (the chronicler's father) to his soldiers after many months of hardships during an expedition across wild country in Peru : " that he had seen for many days what they told him about the difficulties of that discovery and conquest, and that within two months of having entered those mountains, he would have tried to retrace his steps ; had it not been the respect he felt for the honour of all of them, which had egged him on to further endeavours. And that even then, it impelled him to push on stubbornly ; lest their rivals should taunt them saying they had come back to their fat sheep in Peru, and the delights of their homes. So he entreated them not to turn their backs on hardships, for the greater the hardships of the past, the higher the honours of the future."(8)

As a transition, here is another scene. Almagro receives in Chile hundreds of thousands of ducats worth of gold which the Indians put at his feet. And then, " seeing the wealth of the land which had fallen to his lot, holding it as his own, he showed his joy with a magnificent gesture ; to win honour and fame, of which he was very fond, and to bind his companions to himself, he drew out in their presence the bonds and cognizances of the monies which he had lent them towards the expenses of that expedition, which amounted to over 100,000 ducats, and tore them up one by one." This same Almagro, however, supplies a good example of the social meaning which the word honour was apt to take in those days. It is admirably put by Garcilaso. " While Almagro was waging war in Chile, Juan de Herrada arrived with the letters-patent granting him a governorship [of the southern part of Peru] brought over [from Spain] by Hernando Pizarro ; which, though they were to cost him his life, caused him more joy than all the gold and silver he had won, for he was greedy of honour." This is the position constantly met with in the Indies : the stout conquerors who discover and then conquer the land never dream that their high deeds entitle them to a full sovereignty over their conquests. They are overjoyed when the distant monarch, who, worried and absorbed by European cares, follows their adventures with a distracted eye, scrawls an imperial signature over a paper granting to their campaigns the honour of State recognition.(9)

For in fact what the conqueror sought was not wealth, nor even power, but greatness. Not that greatness which is handed down from father to son, but the greatness which the great man himself founds. They were founders of blazon, not heirs to it. They felt they belonged to an aristocracy, yet one rooted in the people, for they only rose to it by their own exertions. This was a living tradition in them, one which inspired the proverbs of their country and shaped its laws. " And for these reasons "—say the Laws of the Seven Parties— " in the days of old, in order to make knights, [our ancestors] chose them from the hunters of the hills, who are men who can suffer much hardship, and carpenters, and smiths, and stone-cutters, for they are used to striking hard and are strong-handed. And also from the butchers, because they are used to killing living things and to spill blood. And they also took care in choosing them that they should be well proportioned in their limbs, so that they should be tough, strong and swift."(10)

The greatness, therefore, which the conquerors sought was first and foremost that of their own great deeds. They felt the world was theirs, and that their vigour was robust enough to conquer it. This was sheer vanity in those among them who happened to be mean ; but magnanimity in those whose soul was worthy of the age and of the occasion. Their background was not so much history as destiny. The Spaniard to whose lot fell the huge golden sun in the Inca temple of Cuzco gambled and lost it that very night. Garcilaso knew him personally, and goes on to say that " later, as the *Cabildo* of the city saw how this son of its own was wasted owing to gambling, it elected him as *alcalde* in ordinary. And he took the service of his country so much at heart, for he had many good parts as a gentleman, that he did not touch a playing card in the whole year. The city, seeing this, elected him again and again," and so finally " he gave up gambling and hated it." Very Spanish, this idea of rescuing a desperate gambler by granting him the chief judicial responsibility of the city.(11)

At the height of his power, Pizarro gave away gold quietly with a peculiar grace of his own. Garcilaso tells a story—one among many, he asserts—of a soldier whose horse had died (which in those days and in the Indies was a disaster for even richer men than soldiers) and whom Pizarro wanted to comfort with a gift of a gold nugget ten pounds in weight. He brought it down to his tennis court, where he expected to find the soldier, but had to hide it under his coat, accept a game and play with the gold hidden and his coat on, till three hours later, the soldier turned up ; when Pizarro took him aside, gave him the gold and said : " I would have given you three times as much rather than carry it these three hours."(12)

Such was greatness, for the conquerors. It demanded simplicity, good manners, comradeship and generosity. Garcilaso describes these virtues as he depicts Gonzalo Pizarro's way of living, which he observed personally " almost six months and most of those days I was in his house, and saw his personal ways in and out of it. Everyone honoured him as a man of a higher rank, and accompanied him wherever he went, on foot or horseback ; and he treated everybody, settlers or soldiers so amiably, and so like a brother, that no one com- plained of him ; I never saw anyone kiss his hand, nor did he offer it to those who asked to kiss it out of deference ; he took off his cap to all most modestly, and no one deserving it did he ever forget to address as ' Your Mercy.' [. . .] He ate always in public ; at a long table, for at least one hundred men ; he sat at the head, and on either side two seats were left empty ; after which, all the soldiers who so wished sat at meals with him ; captains and settlers ate at home."(13)

*   *   *

To achieve this aim, noble in its way, if limited to the ambit of the self, most of these men of the Conquest were ready, not merely to risk their lives, but—and this is perhaps their chief shortcoming—to crash through every rule of co-operation, friendship, alliance, to upset any concerted plan, to skirt round every agreement, to seize every opportunity, to take any short cut to forestall the others in the race towards power. Keen judges of men, they could behave when strongly led. Under Cortés, a born leader, intrigue, conspiracy, rebellion, withered ; while under Pizarro, already relatively old when he attempted the conquest of Peru, and who became somewhat easy-going and perhaps too trusting after his initial struggles in Peru had been crowned with success, the conquest gave rise to a series of civil wars to which he fell the first victim. Garcilaso has left us a vivid account of these wars, in which, under cover of defending the true royal authority, every captain who could amass some money and gather together a few scores of men and horses, took the field and fought against his kith and kin under the bewildered eyes of the Indians. They fought heroically, and dealt with the conquered, at times magnanimously, other times with unbelievable cruelty.

These civil wars were Spanish anarchy at its most active and lively, for, despite the show of legal respectability most captains sought to put up, the chief impulse behind all but a handful of leaders was personal ambition, when it was not personal vengeance. There is an episode in them which illustrates this point at its best. On the eve of one of the bloodiest of these civil battles, that of Salinas, Hernando Pizarro, who commanded one side, sent a challenge to Rodrigo Orgoños, who commanded the other, " saying that he and his second would go into battle wearing coat and armour breast-plates ; and over them they would don jackets of slashed orange-coloured velvet, and he let him know, in case he, Orgoños, or any other, had in mind to seek him out, so that he might recognize him. This was the message Hernando Pizarro sent, because he had a grievance owing to things done to him while in gaol, which he thought beneath his person. Orgoños took it as a field challenge," and with his second, donned white leather jackets, sought his enemy and through the battle carried out a personal civil war within the general civil war.(14)

*   *   *

How are we to reconcile so much greed with so much generosity ; so much anarchy with so much fidelity to the King, so many seemingly contradictory features of these conquerors, one of the sturdiest roots of the human tree of the Indies ? The answer must be found in the Spanish character. Strongly polarized in the self and the universe, at the two ends of the gammut of man's interests, the Spanish character neglects the middle stretches, where grow the political, social and municipal virtues. It follows that the Spaniard is apt to be more genuine when serving his own self and mankind in the widest sense than when applying his energy to any intermediate activity between these two extremes. His services to society tend to become instruments of his two chief interests—self and universe, or a combination of the two. Society and what it can give become ornaments of the self, his " honour." Government is best assured by choosing a good man who in his honour's interest will see that the country is well governed. The imperial seal on the paper one can brandish to assert one's own authority, is a personal asset—honour. But moreover, this honour comes from the Emperor, i.e., the temporal monarch of the universe, whose title to the New World is vouched for by the Pope, the spiritual monarch of the universe. The Catholic faith came thus to strengthen the individual trend with a vigour borrowed from the universal trend. This explains why, despite the misdeeds of many a *conquistador* against the Indians, and even against his fellow-Christians, the *conquista* was and ever remained inspired in a universal spirit which made of the Indians and of the Blacks fellow-men of the Whites. All too frequently this fellowship showed itself in no charity whatsoever. Cruelty stained the conquest at every step, in the lesser men, only rarely in the greater ones. The treatment of the Indian auxiliaries, beheaded at the slightest occasion, sometimes merely for purposes of convenience, that of Indian workers and Black slaves in later days, were shameful and terrible. But these failings of human nature did not discriminate as to race and colour, and the Spaniard was a wolf to the Spaniard as easily as to the Indian or the Black.(15)

*   *   *

The religious side of the mighty adventure was kept alive by the wonderful activity of the friar. The friars were the second prototype of the White strain in the Indies. They

were not, of course, fundamentally different from the conquerors. They were in fact conquerors *a lo divino*, as the
phrase went in Spain in those days. They stood more for
the universal than for the individual pole of Spanish psychology,
but this was a matter of degree and of stress rather than of
nature ; and the two types merged easily into each other.
Many conquerors became friars. Las Casas was first a conqueror, later a settler, finally a friar. He is a case in point,
for no one ever espoused the cause of the universal spirit with
more ardour and zeal ; and yet, no one put into his crusade
a stronger individual and opinionated stubbornness. The
sense of daring, of sacrifice, of achievement, which we found
in the conquerors also animates the friars. While the conquerors strove hard to rise and acquire honour and greatness,
the friars strove hard to humble themselves. " The Indians
marvelled at the fortitude of the preachers, and more so at
seeing them so averse to gold and silver of which the secular
Spaniards made so much "—writes a contemporary author.
This example was at first the only language in which the friars
could convey their faith to the natives, and they spoke it even
to the risk of death. " And so we lost Fr. Martín de Valencia,
out of sheer penitence," writes Juan de Samano in 1537 ;
while the Viceroy Velasco reports to Philip II.(1554) : " And
as the friars of this order of St. Dominic eat no meat and always
go on foot, their hardships are intolerable and they do not live
long." They made a point of living as modestly as the humblest Indians, " they go about poor and barefoot as we do "—
said the Indians of them—" they eat what we do, sit down
among us, speak to us mildly." There were several cases of
martyrdom, and one perhaps more significant than martyrdom,
the case of Fr. Antonio de Roa, who, not content with imitating
the poverty of the Indians the better to win their confidence,
and finding they did not yet realize the horror of sin, used to
have himself lashed during his sermon, and, to demonstrate
that the body is a slave, he branded himself with a torch. One
day, to prove to his native flock how unbearable Hell must be,
he threw himself on a bed of burning coals and stayed on it
for a while, showing that it could not be borne for long by
men alive, though infinitely milder than the fire of Hell.(16)

Such were the methods whereby the spiritual conquest of the Indies was achieved, or at any rate attempted. And it was of all this labour of love that *Motolinia* was thinking when he, who had thundered against the greed of many conquerors and their ill treatment of the Indians for the sake of gold, wrote a notable page on the triumph of the conquest which had spread the name of Christ far and wide in the New World : " The Lord also pours the virtue of His Holy Name so freely that even in the parts that are not yet conquered and where no cleric, no friar, no Spaniard has penetrated, His Holy Name is to be seen painted and worshipped. It is multiplied in this land to such an extent, either written or painted over churches and temples, in gold and in silver, in feather-work with gold, [. . .] in such great numbers ; and over the houses of people and over many other parts, carved in wood with ornaments ; and every Sunday and every feast day, they deck it with roses and compose it in a thousand ways with roses and flowers." The good friar, who had re-named himself *Motolinia* because it meant *poverty* in the language of his new flock, then bursts into joy : " And why should not the men of the earth rejoice, before whose eyes God brings forth these things, and more so those who came over and conquered so many provinces with a good intention, so that God should be known and worshipped in them ? And even though they may have had sometimes a cupidity for wealth, let us believe it was by the way and not directly. For men whom God endowed with reason and who saw themselves in such hardships and dangers of death, so many and so many times, who would not believe that they would form and re-form their consciences and intentions, and that they would be ready to die for the faith, and to enhance it among the faithful, and that such would be their chief and main objective ? And these conquerors and all the Christians who are friends of God must rejoice deeply seeing such an accomplished Christendom achieved in so short a time, and prone to so much virtue and kindness ; wherefore I pray all those who may read this that they praise and glorify the Lord in the innermost of their souls."(17)

CHAPTER II

THE WHITE ELEMENT

THIS friar and this conqueror are the roots of what was later to be known as the " Spaniard," the " Creole," or the " American Spaniard." The prototypes and these other forms evolved from them present a number of common features which are the framework of American-Spanish psychology. The chief of them is a certain " vertical " attitude which strives at the utmost by the self, and is therefore unwilling to bend to daily tasks and weave itself into social patterns with others. A feature, of course, transplanted from Spain. It gives to the Spanish collective tissue—whether in Spain or in America—that grating and rasping consistence which makes it both so tough and so difficult to handle, as well as so static. These men, when the urge to conquer or to convert died down in them, were apt to feel somewhat helpless, and they relaxed into mere being, leaving the doing to others. Next to conquest and conversion, no action seemed worth while in their eyes. The middle stretches of life had no hold on them, and for the most part, they let them lie fallow, waiting for more stimulating tasks and days. Some found this stimulus in commerce, perhaps because in those days storms and pirates turned commerce into something so near gambling. Others found it more straightforward, and simpler also, to gamble at the green table, and it was even possible to come across blends of commerce and gambling. " It sometimes happened "— says Garcilaso—" that a Spaniard gambled with another one a debt owed him by a third person who was away, and it was enough for him to say to the winner : ' Tell So-and-So that the debt he owes me must now be paid to you ' and that was enough for the winner to be believed." Nearly all gave themselves to the even more hazardous gamble of love, then highly spiced with death. And then, of course, there was civil war.(1)

This feature, deeply ingrained in the Spanish character, had been duly noted down by Bodin, though with that awkward way of interpreting Spanish psychology often to be found in

French observers : " The Spaniard is marvellously lazy,
outside arms and commerce." It was exacerbated by the
conquest. "Along with other favours granted him by the
Imperial Majesty "—writes Garcilaso—" Don Francisco Pizarro brought a commission to raise two dozen halberdiers as a
bodyguard and to enhance the authority of his position. As
soon as he took Tumpiz, he desired to choose them, so as to
enter the land with more dignity ; but he found no one who
would accept such an office, though he made great promises ;
which is no small smartness and pride on the part of the
Spaniards, especially those who arrived in that land, for,
humble as they may be, as soon as they see themselves there,
they feel a new generosity and a new greatness in their souls.
Only two accepted the halberds [. . .] good soldiers
[. . .] both died at the hand of their enemies [. . .] I
shall not give their names out of respect."(2)

Even trade, however, came to take on a certain knightly
colour, as the same *mestizo* chronicler relates, with the insight
into Castillian character which he owed to his father's blood.
" In time of peace many soldiers, very knightly and noble, in
order not to remain idle, took a part in this trade of coming
and going to and from Potosí with coca-herb and cloth for
the Indians, selling it wholesale and not in retail ; and in this
way, it was seemly for men, however noble, to trade with their
own wealth ; but it could not be done with cloth from Spain,
which is sold by the yard and in regular shops. Many liked
to travel with their goods, and so as not to ride in step with the
sheep [the *guanacos* loaded with the goods] they took with them
a couple of falcons and some retrievers and hounds, and an
arquebus, and while the animals plodded along with the
goods, they would stray on one side or the other of the road
and hunt ; by the evening they had killed a dozen partridges,
or a wild *guanaco* or *vicuña* or some other kind of game ; for
the land is wide and long and abounds in everything. And so
they went on disporting themselves there and back, there
being more sport than trade in it ; and the rich and powerful
citizens were most grateful to the noble soldiers for it."(3)

No laziness in all this. A different tendency of the human
spirit. That is all. But the effects of climate and wealth

must be taken into account. " Those who are born over here "
—writes Father Vetancurt in 1698—" are shrewd and profound
in every kind of science, although most of them when they
reach the age of forty flag in their studies, and only work
while young." We have heard this before. We shall hear it
again. And every time with a different explanation. That
given by our Mexican friar is worth noting : " because the
various amusements lead them astray, and as there are not
always rewards for so many, they get discouraged, and what
makes thoughtful people wonder most is that the capacity for
reasoning should dawn so soon in children, and that they should
all have such high-spirited souls that few are those who incline
towards the mechanical arts and crafts of their elders, the
reason being that the climate, abundance and wealth of the
land raises their spirit and ennobles their thoughts." The
trend upward should be observed. · But it would be absurd to
read it in our present-day, class-war context. The ambition
to rise to knightly leisure warmed every breast with democratic
equality. Here is the way the same author describes it with
unrivalled vividness, as the pageant of social vanity of viceregal
Mexico passes under his eyes : " the gala, the lustre is considerable, and the cleanliness and adornment of both the wealthy
and the workers ; those of lesser means, even if they are
workers, wear ruffs and black cloaks, go about in carrosses or
ride horses ; no doubt it is greatness, but he who would see
all these men in a gathering, with no difference to distinguish
the rich knight or heir from the craftsman, may think it bad
policy, yet it is a gallantry of the land, which imparts lordship,
makes humble hearts bigger and destroys mean conditions."(4)

All this has nothing to do with laziness. In a way, it is
universal. The skilled worker of Mexico under the Spanish
rule was prosperous enough to wear a ruff and ride a horse,
just as his Californian comrade of our days is prosperous
enough to wear a white collar and to drive a car. In essence
also there was in it something more specifically Spanish : an
instinct which seeks to defend the person of the individual
from the collective gear. The machinery is the insidious
master which, under the disguise of a slave, takes hold of men
and makes them its own, reducing them to wheels and levers

in a huge world factory. Technique is the no less insidious power of the new tyrant. Hence the true nature of the disinclination of the Spaniard towards technique, and of his love of leisure, which other peoples, less aware of these states of mind and moods, mistake for laziness. A tendency to be rather than to do ; to live to-day, and as a tree which gives forth fruit and lets it fall regardless of whether it rots or fructifies, rather than as a bridge between yesterday and tomorrow trodden by the traffic of hum-drum life. This disharmony between the upward, static tendency of the Spanish soul, and the onward, dynamic tendency which western affairs took on gradually, was in later days to be one of the deepest causes of the wars of secession.

*   *   *

Meanwhile a gentleman must live, and the natural way of living for the White, who had no more new lands to conquer, was on the labour of the native. Hence the feeling of resentment and injustice which, from the end of the sixteenth century, began to rise in the heart of the Creole population owing to the policy followed by the Crown in the granting of *encomiendas*. In their legal essence, after a number of initial experiments, limited on the one hand by the anxiety of the Crown to protect the Indian, on the other by the resistance of the Whites in the Indies against having the Indians too well protected, the *encomiendas* were reduced to the mere right given to a particular person to cash and make his own the personal tribute of a number of Indians ; but in practice it meant a considerable amount of sway over such Indians. The grant enabled the beneficiary to live like a gentleman. But the Crown limited all *encomiendas* to two lives, that of the person to whom it was granted and that of his heir. After which, the *encomienda* lapsed, reverted to the Crown and remained practically in the giving of the Viceroy.(5)

Now, the royal will had always been that, in the granting of *encomiendas*, the sons of the conquerors should be preferred to all others. It seemed natural that once they had been granted this reward for their deeds, the privilege accorded to the conqueror should remain for ever in the family. Many

prominent men, from Cortés to Solórzano Pereira, advocated
this solution. But the Crown was averse to it, for reasons
which were not always the same as time elapsed. At first,
the limitation to two lives was but a trace of the reluctance
with which the Crown had accepted the system of *encomiendas*
altogether, a system in which it rightly saw a thinly disguised
slavery. Later, however, another consideration is mentioned :
that the very wealth and power which perpetual *encomiendas*
might bestow on the privileged might beget disloyalty in some
of the American-Spanish magnates ; for, as Solórzano Pereira
puts it, " it is a consideration which must be borne in mind
most carefully in every province, but most particularly in
those of the Indies which are so remote from the royal
presence." Finally, the system adopted was perhaps the best in
theory, though as bad in practice as any other would have
been, since it was corrupted by the foibles of the men who had
to live it : in effect, the Viceroy and the Crown gave away
the lapsing *encomiendas* to whomsoever they pleased. The
principles were that the sons of conquerors were to be preferred ; next to them the settlers ; finally the " pacifiers," or
men who, in home or foreign emergencies, had enlisted under
the royal standard ; and at the end of the list came those
who had obtained a royal *Cédula* to that effect, which could
hardly be wider as a loophole. Frequent royal letters to the
Viceroys enjoin them to use their powers in this respect with
justice and good sense, and in particular insist on the priority
to be given to conquerors' sons (i.e., Creoles). Yet Solórzano
Pereira himself has to record the breakdown of the system,
" considering that most of them, and the best, have been given
to lords and ladies of Spain and to others who neither reside
nor will ever reside in the Indies, nor have any merit nor
rendered any services in the conquest of them."(6)

*   *   *

Meanwhile, the superabundant energy of the Spanish people
in the New World had to manifest itself in some way. Trade
was enough in warm, pleasant climates. A constant fight
with wild Indians took much time and strength in a number
of places, particularly at the northern end (Texas and Cali-

fornia) and at the southern end (Chile) of the Empire. Hot countries gave rise to a languorous civilization, given over to the enjoyment of *la vida sabrosa*. Potosí rejoiced in civil war.

These civil wars of Potosí deserve attention, because they reveal some of the psychological tensions which arose within the bounds of the White community, showing how far more complex and unexpected they were than is generally assumed. The civil wars or " *bandos* " (partisanships) began almost with the founding of the town and as a natural development of the civil wars of the Pizarros. The Silver Hill of Potosí was discovered in 1545 ; the same year the town was founded. In 1546 there was already some fighting in it, connected with one of the Pizarros' rising. But the first entry of the chronicler of Potosí in which we perceive the true flavour of these famous feuds is under 1548. " This year there were several fights between the nations from Spain settled in Potosí, and more than forty men were killed in them." How they were divided, we do not know. Not till 1564 does any light on the subject appear in the annals : " This year there were innumerable fights between Castillians and Andalusians on the one side and on the other Portuguese and *Extremeños* ; and in various battles there died of the one and of the other side twenty-three men and there were fifty wounded." This is an invaluable entry, for it shows how the true origin of the trouble was not this or that " enmity " or " hatred," whether fostered or not by the Creoles, but sheer love of battle and civil war. In 1564 the sons of the conquerors were very young. The Creole generations were not yet in full bloom. Not a word about them in this fight which divides the Spaniards from overseas somewhat oddly into Castillians and Andalusians on the one hand and Portuguese and *Extremeños* on the other.(7)

Yet another generation, and a new " nation " appears which will soon take a leading part in the civil wars. " 1582. This year there were cruel feuds between the nations ; and in one fight between *Extremeños* and Basques, there died 18 men on both sides ; and amongst them, the Chief Constable of the city and Diego Aumeta, *Alcalde* in Ordinary who both were always at the origin of these troubles." The Basques enter the stage—perhaps as the men who, though in authority, provoke the disturbances ; for that Aumeta must have been a Basque, to judge by his name.   In the following year, a Basque captain was killed in a game of reeds " and thereupon [the Basques] set fire to the houses and quarter of the *Extremeños*, in search of the aggressor, who was of this nation ; and eight houses were turned into ashes ; the damage would have been much bigger had not the town-dwellers rushed to put out the fire." This again is an entry full of information.   To begin with, no news yet of the Creoles.   Whether they stood by or entered the lists under the " nation " to which their fathers happened to belong, we do not know.   What we do know is that fifty years after the conquest, the tensions which lead to civil war in Potosí develop, so as to oppose, not the American Spaniard to the European Spaniard, but certain European Spaniards to other European Spaniards, in groupings, moreover, which are apt to change from year to year. This entry also reveals that the Basques were apt to be spirited and high-handed, since, for one life lost, they burnt down a whole quarter of the opulent city.   Finally, the several " nations " seem to have settled each in a separate quarter of Potosí, thus reproducing in the Silver City the sectionalism of their native Spain.(8)

Then, in 1587, the Creoles enter the lists.   The text is not clear ; but it seems that in this first set of fights, they stood by themselves against all the European-born together : " As the Creoles caused several fights in the city of Potosí, and all of the nations of Europe which were in the city, there was a cruel battle in the month of August ; and after many men had died on both sides, the Creoles withdrew to a house near that of the *corregidor* ; their enemies set it on fire ; and as a strong wind was blowing at the time, the whole quarter was burnt out."   But lest we be tempted to date from this year the enmity of the late eighteenth century which set the Creole against the European-born, here comes the entry of 1588 : " This same year, in the course of a battle between on the one hand Andalusians, *Extremeños* and Creoles of the cities of Peru ; and on the other Basques, Navarrese, Gallegos, and other Spanish nations, 85 men killed each other."   Now in 1564 the Andalusians and the *Extremeños* had fought on opposite sides ; and in 1587, the Creoles had faced a combination of all the European-born. It is evident that the alliances, if not altogether capricious, were apt to change considerably, even within twelve months, and that moreover the line separating Creoles and Europeans was by no means harder or clearer than that which separated any other two Spanish " nations."(9)

Soon, however, a tension appears explicitly noted down by the annalist. Here are his words : " 1593. This year there were bloody battles between the Basques and the *Extremeños*, these last being helped against the Basques by the young men native of this country, that is by the Creoles of Potosí, of whom there were already some who had reached the age of eighteen or sixteen. The Creoles of Potosí always felt antipathy against the Basques. Of whom 16 died ; many *Extremeños* died." This again is full of news. There is a constant antipathy between Creoles and Basques ; but so far it shows itself in help given by the Creoles to another European-Spanish nation, the *Extremeños*, who happen to have a feud with their co-Europeans the Basques. But stay. None of your anachronisms ; none of your theories about separate nationhood, a more active race, less romanized, a race of healthy mountaineers who kept their ancestral faith and simple life pure from the corruption of modern life and so forth. Let us read on, and, from the cold facts set down by the annalist, try to see the tension between Basques and Creoles as it grew in its own native earth. " 1600. This same year the city being governed by General Don Alvaro Patiño [. . .] during a bullfight in his honour [evidently in the square of the city] Martín de Igarzábal, a Basque, owing to certain love claims, threw a young man of Potosí, Nicolás Enriquez, from a balcony down to the square ; his father saw it, a man from the kingdoms of Spain ; he went up to the balcony to the flat where hidden in a bed he found Igarzábal ; and with many stabs, took his life. The square was in turmoil ; the servants and ministers of the *corregidor* came upon the scene, as well as the friends of Enriquez, who were Andalusians and *Extremeños*. The Basques shouted : ' Death to the criminal ! ' They went at each other and there was a cruel battle." This scene allows us to witness the work of the tensions, the oddity of the alliances, the dramatic and altogether apolitical character of the feuds.(10)

No event born of Spanish life can be adequately understood when it is reduced to merely political or economic terms. The essence of Spanish life is neither political nor economic, but human. Our annalist provides constant examples. " This year "—he writes under 1605—" took place that memorable battle between eight Basque and eight Andalusian knights for the sake of a maid." And under 1604 : " This year there were in Potosí lamentable feuds and fights between Basques and Andalusians and Creoles, and at dawn many men from both sides were found in the streets and squares dead and quartered." And even when wealth is involved, it is not wealth as such that is at stake, but the attitude and behaviour which it provokes. " 1602. From this year on, the Basques began to come forward in a considerable manner, helped by their good luck, which favoured them in arms, wealth and official positions ; for out of 132 mills on the river, 80 belonged to that nation ; and so was fortune raising them that their fall, caused by their excessive pride, should be the bigger." This way lie, not economic and political arguments and struggles, but human tragedies, dramas, novels.(11)

In 1608 the city of Potosí witnessed gorgeous festivals in which horsemanship and the thousand gleams and splendours of metals, silks and precious stones wove themselves into movement and beauty : " and the motive was that the Basques made the young Creole gentlemen observe that they were not very expert at governing a horse in their sports ; and that they were not capable of imagining or of organizing entertaining games. The Creoles rightly grew indignant," and they set up such festivals as could only fit the Arabian nights. But, as in the famous Spanish play, " the reeds turned into spears," and out of the tournament there grew a Shakespearean tragedy. " This same year, after the festivals, Don Nicolás Saulo Ponce de León, one of those who took part in the game, with the help of Bernardo Cortés, also born in Potosí, both on horseback, wrenched by force of spear from the hand of Don Sancho de Mondragón and of more than one hundred Basque knights, the lady Margaret, daughter of the *Factor* Bartolomé

Astete de Ulloa ; who was to be married to Mondragón, the maid being forced thereto by her parents ; for as for her feelings, she and Saulo had promised each other love unto death. They took her from Mondragón in the very square ; and having put Margaret behind him on his horse, Saulo and his friend fled towards Chuquisaca. Don Sancho de Mondragón armed himself and together with six other Basques they overtook Saulo two leagues out of Potosí and gave him a cruel battle ; Mondragón and another Basque were killed by Saulo and Cortés, and although Saulo had seven wounds, he rode on with Margaret, and with her arrived in Chuquisaca, where, four days later, being in part recovered, they were married. One night the friends of the dead Mondragón arrived in Chuquisaca and as the newly married couple were in bed the Basques entered the room : Saulo defended the door with great courage ; Cortés came from outside to help him ; Saulo was wounded ; a cousin of Margaret entered the bedroom ready to cut Margaret's head off with a Moorish sword ; she wrestled with him and with his own Moorish sword wounded him, cutting him from the nose to the forehead ; the Basque fell ; Margaret came out to help her husband and the two men and the woman fought against the five Basques, mortally wounded two of them, not counting the one who was breathing his last in the bedroom. The magistrates turned up ; Saulo, Margaret and Cortés fled through the orchard ; crossed the valleys ; recovered from their wounds ; were found out by the police ; ran away to Cuzco ; and finding that they were not in safety there, finally went to Lima . . ." and the Viceroy closed the novel ordering them " to consider the city of Lima as their prison."(12)

Bias against the Basque ? Perhaps. But read on. The very next line. The same year. " This year there was a fierce fight between the Creoles and the Portuguese on the one hand and the Basques on the other. [The Governor] General Mejía was most partial to the Basques, and therefore, he punished the Creoles and the Portuguese but not the others ; and so, there was a general challenge in which twenty Creoles and thirty Portuguese fought against sixty Basques, killing between these two nations fifty-two Basques, although twelve

Creoles and seven Portuguese died." In 1612 this Governor
was "called to Madrid to answer for complaints sent by the
Creoles." But it does not seem that the change of Governor
brought any advantage to them ; for in 1614, another Governor, says the annalist, " was possessed of such a passion against
the Creoles, the Andalusians and the Portuguese," that he
egged on the Basques to challenge the other three nations and
even fought at the head of the Basques, under a disguise, being
the first to fall dead. The battle cost their lives to seventy
Basques and twenty of the other nations. So far, it should be
noted, the line is not one between Creoles and Europeans, but
between Basques and a number of other nations, which is apt
to vary and often, though not always, includes the Creoles.
In 1617 we find yet another *corregidor* favouring the Basques
against the Creoles who this time were in alliance with the
Castillians. " The *corregidor*, most partial to the Basque nation,
arrested Don Alonso Yáñez, a Castillian, the standard bearer
Flores, a Creole of Potosí, the standard bearer Zapata, a
Gallego, Captain Moreno and other Creoles, beheading them
and putting their heads on the pillory. The Creoles and
Castillians, being aware that all this had been done at the
instigation of the Basques, killed upwards of fifty of them in
several attacks." The Castillians took refuge in the crypt of
a church and then fled to Lima. Little by little these feuds
take shape and become one of the civil wars, later to be
described as one of the forerunners of the wars of secession.
But meanwhile, this survey of the endemic disturbances of
Potosí will have shown that the deepest cause of the wars of
secession themselves is to be found, not in any political
antagonism, but in the Spanish tendency to dissension and
civil war, for the sake of dissension and civil war.(13)

*   *   *

This tendency to widen gaps instead of bridging them over,
and to turn a split into a ditch, a ditch into a gulf, is primal
and permanent in Spanish psychology. It will seize upon
anything which happens to be handy, in order to satisfy
itself. And just as in the cold, warlike climate of Potosí, it
played so tragically for years on the largely imaginary differ-

ences between groups of " nations " from metropolitan Spain,
it was sooner or later bound to find an outlet in the more real
differences between American-born and European-born Spaniards.   Deep down, the core of the difference was already one
between the son of the land and the newcomer ; for the Creole
stood on his rights as the conqueror's heir.   Nothing indeed
is more constant in the records than this proud identification
between the conqueror and the Creole ;   as against the
European-born who comes belatedly to build his career upon
the heroic endeavours of the Creole's ancestors.   The difference takes two lines, at bottom closely connected.   A scion of
the conquering race, the Creole feels that he is of a better
blood than the European-born Spaniard ;   a man therefore,
unused to work, and who, by his noble birth, should be above
labour, he looks down upon the European-born Spaniard as
an upstart.   Both lines are intertwined in many observations
of the day, just as they appear in the following sonnet by an
unknown Creole author, and ·which I give in a translation,
though bad enough, no worse than the original :

> Across the salty sea, there comes from Spain
> A rough-hewn man with neither friends nor health,
> Who, poor in wit, in manners and in wealth,
> Here settles in our Mexican domain.
> And as he plucks some courage and some gain,
> His friends crown him in barbarous commonwealth,
> With laurel and with oak, by scheme or stealth,
> Cæsar and Virgil of the Spanish Main.
> While he, who pins and needles hawked at home,
> Dresses with rank and wealth his native loam,
> And pours contempt on those his friends of yore
> Who taught him how to live when, still uncouth,
> He came fresh from the harbour of his youth
> Where he dragged fishing boats on to the shore.(14)

The author of the *Annals of Potosí* gives no less than four
cases in one page which illustrate this cantankerous sonnet :
two Andalusians and two (to judge by their names) Castillians,
who from humble beginnings, such as begging, or selling
needles, rose to owning considerable fortunes ; and his com-

ment is the more valuable for the fact that his general trend is partial to the Creoles : " I write so that, not without wonder, the greatness of Potosí may be noted, as well as the good fortune of the Spaniards who know how to save their earnings, instead of spending them all in one day, as do the Creoles, whose prodigality is such that what they spend in one day in a picnic is enough for a Spaniard to eat very well for a whole year." Nor was this tendency to spend the only cause of the impoverishment of the Creole. For the conqueror's son often held it beneath his dignity to have recourse to manual work when he had lost more glamorous ways of living. Yet here care should be taken not to generalize. For instance, on this precise point of the attitude of the poor Whites to manual labour, considerable differences were observed between Quito and Lima by Ulloa and Jorge Juan. Here is Quito. " The name of *Spaniard* there "—we are told—" has a different meaning from that of *Chapetón* or *European,* which actually mean *a person who descends from Spaniards and who has no mixture of blood.*" This settled, the position is described as follows : " It is easy to see that as between these four kinds of people [Spaniards, *Mestizos*, Indians, Castes], the Spaniard is the highest in rank, but also proportionately the unhappiest, poorest and most miserable ; for the men do not adapt themselves to any of the crafts, which they think beneath their quality, i.e., the fact that they are not Blacks, Husky or Toasted." And now here is Lima : " The Negroes, Mulattoes and their offspring [. . .] carry on all the work of the crafts, though the Europeans also practise them, without the objections which in Quito prevent them from doing so. This is due to the fact that, as everybody is keen on making money, as this is done in Lima in many ways, they do not find it an obstacle that the same craft is also practised by other craftsmen who are coloured ; for material interest is above all other considerations."(15)

The Crown sympathized with this latter tendency rather than with the aristocratic tendency of Quito. Solórzano Pereira recommends that " all those who people and inhabit the provinces of the Indies, even though they may be the stiffest men from Spain, should work there and should lend the shoulder to the burden and the hand to the plough, without expecting everything from the labour and sweat of the Indians.   For, as I heard it from the lips of the Viceroy, Marqués de Montesclaros, who was a wise and excellent governor in New Spain and in Peru, and understood these matters well, the happiness and growth of the Indies depended on the fact that the Spaniards should make up their minds to work and keep working."   This was precisely the attitude of the Crown also.   On May 16th, 1609, Philip III wrote to the same Montesclaros recalling that " there were many Spaniards in those provinces, both arrived from here and Creoles born there, and yet, though many are poor and humble, they are not willing to work in the fields, in the mines or on other useful work, nor to serve other Spaniards, for they think it beneath their worth, and so there are too many idle persons and all the work and service of the Spaniards falls on the Indians ; " he therefore requests the Viceroy that " with great skill and by the means you may devise, you must try to introduce some Spaniards into the work of the land and mines and other public work ; so that through their example others may follow and get used to work."(16)

But the Whites with noble memories and claims resisted all these endeavours, and tried to seek honour and leisure either in property or in Church or State posts.   The Indies had to carry the deadweight of a host of poor Whites, the stagnant dregs of sickness, laziness and vice, which fell from the upper classes, and the scum of worthless immigrants who smuggled into the New World as stowaways.   These Whites looked down on manual work, lacked ability for trade or the professions, and had to drag a miserable existence, embittered by a suffering which for them was even worse than poverty—rubbing elbows with the castes of mongrels, Blacks and Indians on a footing of practical equality, and even, when it came to food and lodging, of actual inferiority, when they did not have to depend on the charity of the Blacks.

Here again, this feature of the society of the New World was by no means exclusive of the Spanish Empire.   In Barbados, this class of idle Whites was extremely numerous as late as the 1820's, and often had to depend also on the charity

LADIES OF LIMA, OUT FOR FUN,
DISGUISE THEMSELVES

CREOLE WOMAN RIDER

from " Types and Customs of Old Lima," by Pancho Fierro

ELEGANT LADIES DRESS THEIR CHILDREN
AS FRIARS

BUTCHERS RIDE AROUND SELLING THEIR
MEAT

of coloured people. The poor Whites of Barbados had secured legislation whereby " every estate is obliged to maintain a certain number of Whites in proportion to its extent. [. . .] They owe no fealty to the landlord, make him no acknowledgment, and entertain no kind of gratitude towards him." The Anonymous Visitor adds that " with the exception of that service [the militia] the greatest part of them live in a state of complete idleness, and are usually ignorant and debauched to the last degree. They will often walk half over the island to demand alms, and if you question them about their mode of life and habits of daily labour, they stare in your face as if they were actually unable to comprehend the meaning of your discourse. The women who will work at all, find employment in washing and mending the clothes of the negroes, and it is notorious that in many cases whole families of these free Whites depend for their subsistence on the charity of the slaves. Yet they are as proud as Lucifer himself, and in virtue of their freckled ditchwater faces consider themselves on a level with every gentleman in the island." " The lower Whites of that island "—he adds—" are without exception the most degraded, worthless, hopeless race I have ever met with in my life." And another English observer dismisses them declaring that they are " wholly ignorant and regardless of any laws human or divine."(17)

Chapter III

MORE ON THE WHITE ELEMENT

THESE facts from the English New World show that there were universal human features in the attitude of the Whites towards manual labour in the Spanish New World. In the Spanish world the poor Whites do not seem to have been so numerous or so lamentable as in Barbados. This may well be because they found refuge in *encomiendas* and other privileges in earlier times and government posts in later years. This led, of course, to a rivalry between Creoles and Europeans for the possession of any advantage which enabled a gentleman to live and shine without work ; a rivalry which was to become one of the causes of the enmity or tension between American-born and European-born Spaniards, even though this tension had first emerged as just one more between any two Spanish " nations." The same forces prevailed in the field of civil and ecclesiastical appointments. We need waste no time on the oft repeated accusation that " of the 166 Viceroys and 588 Captains-General, Governors and Presidents who had held office in the Colonies, in all 754, only 18 were Creoles." This kind of argument is worthless. No Canadian has ever been Governor-General of Canada, no Australian of Australia, no Anglo-Indian (let alone Indian) has ever been Viceroy of India. And the first South African (though born in Scotland) to be Governor-General of South Africa died but the other day. It is in the nature of things that such leading posts should not be given to local persons. The Viceroy was forbidden to take a meal with anyone but the members of his family—a clear sign of the aloofness and impartiality which was expected of him. How could Creoles be expected to achieve such aloofness and impartiality in the midst of their kith and kin ? But even leaving aside the highest officials, enough remains to make a good case for the Creoles, and to explain how the tension between Creoles and Europeans increased owing to the fact that too many Government and Church posts were given to Spaniards from the mother country.

Of course, even here there might often be good reasons for abstaining from appointing Creoles. " There is nothing which raises the heat of local partisanships more than the circumstance that the two heads of a province, the civil and the ecclesiastic, are both Creoles," write Ulloa and Jorge Juan in an analysis of this matter which, like nearly everything they wrote, is admirably objective. The author of the *Annals of Potosí* records how the twenty-fourth *corregidor* of Potosí, a European Spaniard, eager enough to make money, yet it seems a good ruler, lost the sympathies of the influential Creoles not because of his cupidity, but because of his " good zeal and good work," and in particular, his endeavour to bring down prices which had been raised by powerful monopolists. The first man with whom he came into conflict in this attempt at economic justice was " Don Luis Paniagua, an illustrious gentleman of Potosí, a Creole, who had been *corregidor* in three provinces, and was at the time *Alcalde* in Ordinary. This gentleman, believing that the Count [the new *corregidor*] arrived indebted like most *corregidors* who come to govern this city, made no scruple of presenting him with money ; he sent him 500 *pesos*, requesting him to distribute them among his servants ; and without more ado, the *corregidor* sent them back with one thousand vituperations." The insolent Creole was indignant, and behaved accordingly. We hear again from O'Higgins that the priest of the parish of Querobamba, " a man born in Lima, wholly ignorant of the Indian language, kept the church in a state of unseemly neglect thinking of nothing but acquiring gold from his parishioners."(1)

This, of course, by no means proves that the Creoles were any worse than the European-born Spaniards as civil or ecclesiastical authorities. Indeed it is likely that they were often better, but it does show that Creoles in authority were not a rarity ; and that they were not always good. Reliable observers, moreover, and as objective as Ulloa and Jorge Juan, were inclined to argue that American-born authorities found it more difficult to keep above local feuds, which on the face of it is sound enough. The law was final. The sons of " Spaniards " born in the Indies were to be preferred for

State and Church benefits and posts.   But the actual application of the law was not easy ; and at first attempts were even
made to deny to the Whites born in the New World their
right to the very name of Spaniards.   A Creole born in Lima,
elected Prior of the Monastery of St. Augustine in Naples, a
post reserved to Spaniards by the foundation, had to go to the
Courts at the Vatican to defend his right to the post against
those who asserted that he was not a Spaniard.   For a time, a
regular separatist campaign raged against New World
Spaniards.   It was waged by Spanish friars with the charitable
aim (charity begins at home) of keeping the plums of the
Church for themselves.   There was even a bishop in Mexico
who refused to ordain Creoles till the Council of the Indies
forced him to do so.   The campaign was backed by all kinds
of pessimistic theories on the character and intelligence of
the Creoles, some based on the effects of the climate, some on
the influence of their Indian nurses—all of which Solórzano
Pereira stoutly condemns with sound common sense and an
almost modern scientific outlook.   "Although I do not
forget that the ways of men, like those of plants, usually
respond to the manner of being and the temperament of the
country in which they grow, and that there are vices which
would appear to be particularly widespread in some countries,
[. . .] it can be readily denied that the American countries
give forth so completely and absolutely the many vices
attributed to them, since, covering as they do as much as or
more than the rest of the world [. . .] they cannot all have
equal features nor can all Creoles be measured with the same
yardstick or weighed in the same scales."(2)

This was the view which ultimately prevailed, even though
often the European-born felt that the Creole was not quite up
to the mark.   "The Creoles of these provinces "—wrote an
official of the Inquisition of Lima in 1757—" are not fit for
the administration of justice."   But Solórzano Pereira argued
that, at any rate, the Creoles " must surely be more apt for
such administration of justice [than the European-born] owing
to the fact that they surely feel more love towards the land and
country in which they were born."   Well-educated Creoles
do not seem to have found any difficulty in rising to State

and Church posts. Many brilliant State and Church careers
are described in the well-informed books of the Chilean
historian José Toribio Medina. Feijóo, who provides a
crushing answer to those who claimed that the Creoles were in
any way less apt than the Europeans, incidentally gives a
number of cases in support of his argument : Fray Antonio
de Monroy, Archbishop of Santiago, José de los Ríos, of the
Council of Finance, the Marquess of Villarocha, President of
Panama, " a great mathematician and familiar with every
kind of good literature," the Marquess of Casa-Fuerte, Viceroy
of Mexico, the Captain-General of the Fleet, Don Pedro
Corvete, the Inquisitor of Toledo, Ovalle, the Marquess del
Surco, tutor of the King's sons, Don Nicolás Manrique and
Don José Munive, of the Council of War, Don Miguel Núñez
of the Council of Orders—all quoted off-hand, not as proof of
the fact that Creoles rose high, but of the fact that Creoles
remained mentally vigorous till a ripe old age. This argues
that the list, on another basis, would have been longer, and
shows that American-born Spaniards could easily rise to high
positions of State in Spain.(3)

No doubt American-born Spaniards are not found in high
positions, particularly in the New World, as often as might
proportionally be expected. They became canons, bishops,
rectors of Universities, inquisitors, often also *oidores*, as well as
regidores, *alcaldes* and *corregidores*. (One even rose to the
highest position the Church can give : that of a saint : Saint
Rose of Lima.) But needless to say, a strict distributive
justice would have reserved for them all the posts of their
own countries without exception, so that however often they
might be successful, they could never be successful often
enough, and the grievance remained alive.

In the course of centuries, the tension between American
Spaniards and European Spaniards increased owing to this
rivalry. It acquired a singular bitterness in the provision of
the posts of Provincials, or Heads of Districts for certain
communities of friars. This was by no means due to any
vying in zeal to convert Indians or to preach the Gospel ;
but to the fact that " the rent of these Provincialates is so
substantial that they are far more desirable in those lands and

more likely to lead to strife." Since the Provincials were elected by the friars of the province, two parties gradually emerged : Creoles v. Europeans ; whose campaigns, chicanery and even violence were a scandal to all. A compromise had been reached whereby the province should be ruled in alternating periods of three years by a Creole and by a European. Ulloa and Jorge Juan favoured this solution, on the ground that the Creole period would give rise to abuses which the European period would probably set right. This argument reads at first as if, for once, the two objective observers had dropped their impartiality. But what they mean is that since, as a matter of fact, the incredible corruption and licentiousness of the religious orders in the Indies in the eighteenth century was unknown in Europe, " it was only natural that the European Provincial should keep the ways of his noviciate and original province." In which they were probably optimistic. Both sides struggled valiantly under the system of alternatives. Some of the Orders managed to get rid of it during a Creole period, by refusing to ordain Europeans, or to admit them into their ranks. To prevent the recurrence of such cases, some Orders enacted from Europe that even when there would be no one but a lay brother available at the beginning of a " European " period, he was to be ordained and elected. As for true qualifications for the post, no one seems to have troubled about the matter. The case of the Provincials is typical of the high tension which by 1740 was raging between Creoles and Europeans in the Indies ; and also of the predominance of this kind of feud over any other objective consideration of the collective interests of the country on the part of either American or European Spaniards.(4)

*   *   *

One thing is certain. The Creoles who resented being left out of *encomiendas* in the early days and of official posts in later times, did so, not on behalf of their Spanish-Indian fellow-citizens at large, but exclusively on behalf of the American-born Whites, the men whom they called " Spaniards." This word was still laden with the meaning

it had had at the beginning of the conquest, i.e., the Spaniard as
distinct from the native. No Spaniard in those days ever
dreamt that it was unjust to keep the native out of office. The
outlook throughout was definitely aristocratic, and while, of
course, the " European," i.e., the Spain-born Spaniard, was
entitled to his coat of arms (if any), the fact of descending
from the conquerors was in itself in the Indies an excellent
claim to aristocracy. " At the rebuilding of this City "—
writes Gage, referring to Mexico—" there was a great
difference betwixt an Inhabitant of *Mexico*, and a Conquerour ;
for a Conquerour was a name of honour, and had lands and
rents given him and to his posterity by the king of *Spain*, and
the Inhabitant or onely dweller payed rent for his house. And
this hath filled all those parts of America with proud *Dons* and
Gentlemen to this day ; for everyone will call himselfe a
descendent from a Conquerour, though hee bee as poore as
Job ; and aske him what is become of his Estate, and fortune,
hee will answer that fortune hath taken it away, which shall
never take away a Don from him. Nay, a poore Cobbler, or
Carrier that runs about the Countrey farre and neere, getting
his living with half a dozen Mules, if hee bee called *Mendoza*,
or *Guzman*, will sweare that hee descended from those Dukes
houses in *Spain*, and that his Grand-Father came from thence
to Conquer, and subdued whole Countries to the Crowne of
Spain, though now fortune have frowned upon him, and
covered his ragges with a thredbare Cloake."(5)

This aristocratic prejudice, which lived in the Creole at
least as much as in the European Spaniard, led to a number
of consequences. The first was that the chief positive feature
of the royal policy to limit the *encomiendas* to two lives was
often lost. The privilege of drawing a valuable income from
the tribute of a number of Indians was wisely limited to two
lives, during which, the conqueror's line (or the settler's or
pacifier's), sheltered from immediate want, could build up
some economic basis to gain independence of royal favours
and become useful to the community. This happy evolution
must have occurred oftener than is generally believed, for
otherwise the economic fabric of the new kingdoms would
have collapsed. Happy people have no history, and those

we hear from are the disgruntled gentlemen whose ancestors, having squandered their too easily begotten income during those two lives, left them, the third life and the rest, to vegetate as they could as parasites of the Viceroy. It is of these that Solórzano Pereira writes deploring " the great poverty and misfortune to which, owing to this cause, many well-deserving and ancient conquerors and settlers have been reduced, and the laments with which they express their grief and sadness at seeing themselves forgotten and needy in their own lands, while those of other countries enjoy and use the fat and the honour of them."(6)

The second was a keen competition for government offices and honours which increased the dependence of the Creole on the Crown, fountain not merely of salaries but of distinction. The " lances, Arquebuses and Halberdiers," set up by the first Marquess of Cañete in 1554 as a bodyguard for the Viceroy of Peru were avowedly an institution devised to compensate conquerors' sons for the loss of the *encomiendas*. Their salaries, relatively modest, came from the rent of the vacant *encomiendas*, and they strove to obtain certain favours reserved for noblemen : they were gentlemen and sat on the benches of the nobility during the sittings of the *Audiencia*, " which "—adds Solórzano Pereira—" is a considerable privilege." In fact, under the Viceroyalty of Prince Esquilache, in 1619, they offered to serve for no salary at all on condition that their military privileges should be preserved, and in particular that " in both civil and criminal cases they should have to answer only under military law, and before the Viceroy in person and his legal adviser, as Captain General."(7)

This privilege, which was granted, was bound to create a defensive state of mind ; for a privilege, by its mere existence, sets up forces which tend to abolish it, and against which it must assert itself. Now, the class of Creoles stood on two grounds : colour and wealth ; and this double basis of its social position explains the complex attitude and tensions which developed between American and European-born Whites. In point of wealth, the American Spaniard could nearly always look down upon the newcomers from Spain—

since wealthy Spaniards seldom emigrated. In point of colour he could not ; for, as we know, there never was complete certainty as to the whiteness of an American-Spanish family, however noble. Indeed, the nobler the shadier, since nobility in the Indies hailed back to the conquerors, and many conquerors had married native women during the first two generations, and many more had had *mestizo* offspring, who, whether legitimized or not, bore their names. Hence the situations described by Ulloa and Jorge Juan.(8)

The two distinguished observers clearly saw that the tension between Creole and European could not adequately be described as one of mere " hatred." They noted how even though " the Europeans or *Chapetones* who arrive in those countries are generally of low birth in Spain or of little known lineages, with no education or any other merit to recommend them," " the Creoles, without discrimination, treat them all with friendship and on an equal footing : it is enough that the newcomers are from Europe for the Creole to treat them as persons of rank, so that even in the families who think most of themselves, they seat the lower sort at their table, though their guests may be servants, and though their guests' masters be present at table also. [. . .] The Creoles have no other foundation for this practice than that the newcomers are white. [. . .] The reason is that, as, overseas, the families with a true right to the name of white are rare, for generally speaking only the most distinguished enjoy this privilege, the fact of being white takes the place of quality with them." This makes all Whites from Spain bold enough " to seek the hand of the highest ladies of the country." The Creoles in their turn, " much as they rant against the Europeans, out of envy for their successes, have made it an honourable thing in the Indies to give their daughters to these Europeans in marriage, and they avoid marrying the girls to the Creoles, whose family blemishes and personal defects are notorious to them, and so they try to spare their daughters these draw-backs, by marrying them to Europeans, even though they be, as they say, ragged." Then comes the trouble. At the slightest quarrel the humble origin of the son-in-law from Spain is thrown in his face. " But the fault is with the Creoles, for if they dealt in trade in bulk, having as they have capital enough for it, they would not lose their wealth in less time than a European needs to make his own. If the Creoles forsook their vices and kept their wives in honour and esteem, they would not give cause to the women of their countries to turn away from them ; and if they lived a sound and regular life, they would draw to themselves the approval and esteem which now go to outsiders ; but as nothing of this fits their character, there remains a root of envy to twist their feelings, forgetting that it is they who give the Europeans all the consideration, authority and advantages which these outsiders enjoy."(9)

True the two men who wrote this were Spaniards. But they wrote objectively, so objectively indeed that their strictures against their own countrymen have been almost as widely exploited against Spain as those of Las Casas. Their testimony must be duly weighed. They maintain that, at any rate in the towns inland, not so much on the coast, it was the European Spaniards who kept trade going, and by their industry and good services to the community, were early elected to local government offices and became leading members of their cities. The description which Ulloa and Jorge Juan give of the tension between Creoles and European Spaniards is acute and sounds true ; they rightly emphasize the complexity of the situation and the interplay of economic factors and colour considerations which entered into it. It follows that the attitude of the white Creole towards the European cannot be fully explored until the attitude of the *mestizo* has been analysed. The fact is important, since it accounts for much which would otherwise remain incomprehensible in the wars of secession.(10)

This same fact explains the stress on distinction and nobility so typical of the Whites. Nobility was their strong point. And it somehow strengthened by implication their less sure claims to pure White blood. " For a number of years "— writes Humboldt at the beginning of the nineteenth century— " the Ministry in Madrid had thought it profitable to make even the smallest appointments in the colonies : nevertheless, the Viceroy's recommendation remains most important for the applicant, particularly if what is wanted is a military post, or a title of nobility (*titulo de Castilla*) which the American Spaniards covet generally more than the European Spaniards." A similar motive acted behind the general request for military honours. " It is not the military spirit of the nation "—writes Humboldt again—" but the vanity of a small number of families whose heads seek the titles of Colonels or Brigadier-Generals, which has fostered the creation of militia-forces in the Spanish Colonies." Ulloa and Jorge Juan confirm this when they suggest that more honours should be granted to them : " To remunerate them with some stimulating reward, a number of posts of honour should be assigned to those Provinces, which with no outlay to the Royal Treasury, are yet very much esteemed by them, such as Field-Master, Chief-Sergeant, Cavalry-General, and others which might be granted them of those that exist in Spain, which the nobility of those lands would hold in as much esteem as the few which they now display, for the vanity for such distinctions is great in them, and in order to obtain these titles, particularly if they were posts of honour without effective employ, such as those that exist in the Royal Household, the persons of greatest lustre would vie with each other to win such grants for themselves." And Humboldt pens a picturesque sketch of the results of the wholesale concession of such honours which developed when vanity in the Indies came out to meet need of money in Madrid : " The fever for titles which everywhere is characteristic of the beginning or of the end of a civilization [he forgot the middle period] has made this traffic extremely lucrative. When one travels along the chain of the Andes one is surprised to see over the back of these mountains, in small provincial towns, all the tradesmen transformed into Colonels, Captains and Sergeants-Major of the militia. As the rank of Colonel entails the style or title of *señoría*, which is constantly repeated [even] in familiar conversation, it may be imagined that it is that which contributes most to the happiness of domestic life, and that for which the Creoles are ready to make the most extraordinary sacrifices of fortune. One sometimes sees these militia officers, in gala uniform and wearing the royal order of Charles III, sitting gravely in their shops, busy with the smallest details of the sale of goods ; a singular mixture of ostentation and simplicity which surprises the European visitor."(11)

He was surprised, because he misunderstood the attitude of the decorated merchants. There was no ostentation in it. The merchant's uniform and his order were in his mind a dress and a badge which stamped him as belonging to the American-Spanish Whites. Hence it was that the Whites of the Indies remained attached to the Crown far longer than might have been expected considering the acerbity of the feuds between American and European Spaniards. Yet, the feature carried within it the germs of its own disappearance. For if, as Humboldt rightly says, " in the colonies, the real outward mark of this nobility is the colour of the skin," an undercurrent of equality was soon bound to set in within the White strain. *Todo blanco es caballero*, became an axiom in the Indies. Humboldt says that since " the truth of this axiom has been recognized in Spain for a long time by a people justly famous for their loyalty, their industry and their national spirit," for " every Biscayan calls himself a nobleman," the Basque in the Indies contributed not a little to spread the principle of equality within the white community of men.(12)

It is therefore one of the many paradoxes of the history of the Indies that these very Biscayans, or as we now say Basques, whom Humboldt rightly praises for their virtues and for their equalitarian spirit, should have been the cause of so much bloodshed for their " haughty ways and intractable manners " against the Creoles.(13)   But then, everything in the Indies was intricate and made up of folds within folds of feelings and counterfeelings. Out of this picture of the tensions and forces which were to prepare the white population of the Indies for an era of republican equalitarianism, it is easy to see how complex, how delicately shaded, how unsteadily poised on a set of contradictory trends, was this opinion and attitude of the American-Spanish Whites. To all these complexities must be added that opposition between sword and gown which is one of the sturdiest psychological features taken over by the Spaniards to the Indies, where to this day it thrives, adorns, deforms and even stifles the constitutional life of many a

State.   The conquerors were mostly of peasant or at any rate
country stock.   This was traditional in Spain.   *The good
soldier, from the plough-holder*, says a Spanish proverb.   And
the peasant, rich or poor, held the legal man in abomination,
no doubt due to dire experience.   Castille is full of proverbs
against lawyers high and low.   The general tenor of them
may be drawn from this one : *If the case is clear, let no lawyer
come near ; if the case is not clear, no lawyer will come near.*   But
there is more symbol and fancy in the following pretty conceit,
where the paper, the ink, the fingers and the pen of the scrivener
are transmuted into peasant values : *A dead white field, black
seed to spare, and five oxen to drive but one plough-share.*   Behind this
grace shines the contemptuous purity of the straightforward
producer for the crooked barren parasite, a feeling that deeds
are swift and noble, while words are just obstacles for action.
Where mean folk abound, the Council sits the whole year round.   And
even beyond that there is a general condemnation of the city
slick arts and vile crafts by the fresh-air community which
grows the wheat for the nation.   Here is its outspoken
expression : *The Court clerk, the barber and the slut graze on the
same pasture and tread the same rut.*

This antipathy between sword and pen, blood and ink,
turns out, therefore, to be one of the deepest tensions in the
Castilian soul, as it was at the time in most other European
souls.   The knight and the soldier stood for the countryside
way ; the lawyer (and often the friar, for the two gowns were
often but one) stood for the city and the law.   The first stood
for straight, expeditive, forceful, clear methods ; the second
for slow, careful, complex, patient procedure.   The first, for
privilege ; the second, for equality.   The swordsmen acted
first, then justified their actions by appealing to honour.   The
penmen sought first to justify their future actions by law and
precedents, and only then acted upon the results of their study.
The norm of the one was honour, that of the other, virtue.
Hence, as we know since Montesquieu, the man of cape and
sword and the peasant were the core of the monarchist faith ;
while in every lawyer, as well as in most friars, there lurked
a republican.

Such are the psychological forces which explain the tension

between swordsmen and gownmen within the white community in the Indies, and which too often have been considered only as petty quarrels over precedence. They responded to forms of life inherent in the Spanish character, both in its European and in its American variety, and their interplay will add zest to the struggle for secession and to the struggles within that struggle. It was, moreover, inextricably mixed with the general tension between American Spaniard and European Spaniard. Thus everything in the Indies took on a peculiar colour and complexity of its own. Aristocratic prejudice was based on colour rather than on actual tradition of nobility ; equality was limited to the bounds of the white stock, and therefore based on a wider inequality ; sense of superiority was lined with what nowadays we should describe as an inferiority complex ; the budding separatist tendency was often but the obverse of a desire to incarnate the royal authority of Spain in a more direct and executive way ; and the seemingly republican fire of many a patriot was but the monarchist trend of a sword-and-cape man eager to get rid of the republican rule of friar and lawyer.

CHAPTER IV

THE INDIAN ELEMENT

WHILE the Whites hailed from Europe and the Blacks from Africa, the Indians were in the Indies the only human stock rooted in the continent. The name, of course, is utterly arbitrary, and merely perpetuates Colón's delusions as to the new world which he discovered by accident, if not by mistake. Moreover, nothing but an arbitrary name, superimposed by strangers, could have bestowed on the aborigines of the New World a unity which they never possessed. This is a remarkable though often overlooked fact. Colón's error provided a name, which in its turn created the thing it designated. " Indians " were for the Spaniards all those men who inhabited the New World before their arrival. For them, they were all one, very much as for some Englishmen all " foreigners " are one. But these men themselves had never thought of each other at all, let alone as one people. They had never known each other, nor existed for each other before the Conquest. They were never in their own eyes one single people, nor have they spontaneously been one single people even since. " In each province "—writes a close student of the Indies in the sixteenth century—" there is a great difference in everything, and even in many *pueblos* there are two or three different languages, and they do not hold any intercourse or know each other, and this, I am told, is general all over the Indies." The first trace of any solidarity between Indian and Indian turns up in Garcilaso Inca de la Vega, when, before quoting a description of Mexico by another chronicler, he writes : " Allow me to write what he says, for, as an Indian, I am fond of the greatness of that other Rome in its days." But Garcilaso was a *mestizo*. Indians proper had no solidarity, not even within the closer areas of their territories, let alone the vast continent of whose very existence they had but a vague notion. What we now know as Mexico, the New Spain of the Spaniards, was a core of Aztec organization, the Anahuac, surrounded by a galaxy of independent or semi-

47

independent tribes, speaking different languages, worshipping different gods and living in different ways. The Chibcha of New Granada were a congeries of loosely organized tribes, surrounded by savage and mutually independent hordes of cannibals and sodomites. And as for Peru, we know that the Incas spent centuries reducing to a passing obedience tribes of widely different natives, and that when the Spaniards arrived the task was both in process of decay and unfinished. These were the only three centres of a more or less advanced organization. Beyond and around them, the continent seethed with human beings in a state far too primitive even to dream of unity or solidarity of any kind.(1)

*   *   *

This is then the starting point of any enquiry on the natives of the New World. " Indians " is a double misnomer. It does not fit them because the New World is not India, and it bestows upon them a unity which they do not possess. This, of course, leaves open a possible actual unity of origin, at any rate for some of the tribes. The Jesuit, Blas de Valera, gives a Mexican origin to some of the most bloodthirsty tribes of the Andes, and there are other signs of common origin, such as the patterns on textiles, and the habit of wearing fillets round the head, which could be used as slings. But even if such a unity of origin existed, it certainly did not reach the level of consciousness in any of them. The memories and traditions which are at the roots of a people's consciousness of itself are for the most part entirely different and mutually unconnected. The peoples of the Anahuac lived on a mixture of two traditions : that of Tetzcatlipuca-Witchilo-pochtli, bloodthirsty deities which demanded and obtained an appalling tribute in human blood every month of twenty days ; and that of Quetzalcoatl, a kind of archaic Christian preacher who brought them the arts and graces of a better civilization, but ultimately perished, submerged by a counter-attack of the old worships. In Peru, the Incas gradually spread their worship of the sun and moon over the wilder and more primitive tribes they mastered. They seem to have had in Pachacamac an inkling of a more universal deity, though this is not certain, having come down to us through Garcilaso, who, as a Christian, may have unwittingly coloured the beliefs of his mother with those of his father. But strangest of all, the Incas had added to their Olympus another god whom they named Viracocha, whose description as he appeared to the heir to the throne, exiled by the reigning emperor, reads singularly like that of the Aztec Quetzalcoatl. "Lord"— said the prince to his father—" you must know that as I was at mid-day, I cannot say whether asleep or awake, leaning back under a big rock such as can be found in the Chita pastures, where, by your orders, I keep the sheep belonging to our father the Sun, a strange man stood before me, with a figure and garments different from ours, for he had a beard longer than a hand, and his frock was long and loose, and covered him down to his feet ; and he brought an unknown animal tied by its neck." Here is now Torquemada's description of Quetzalcoatl : " They say that he was a white man, tall in body, with a white forehead, big eyes, black and long hair, a long and round beard." In both these descriptions there is so strong a likeness to the men of the white race that one might be tempted to attribute both to some retrospective legend grown after the Conquest. The more so as in Mexico, Cortés was taken for Quetzalcoatl or his emissary ; and in Peru the Indians gave the Spaniards the name of Viracocha.(2)

But the facts are well established : the two traditions were old enough and strong enough when the Spaniards arrived to have played a not inconsiderable part in the conquest of both Mexico and Peru. Moreover, in both cases, the changes which these two new mythical persons bring to the life of the natives concerned, even though vague enough, are not unlike a foretaste of Christian civilization, culture and ideals. Our knowledge of the human soul, individual or collective, is not deep enough to allow us either to accept or to reject the view that Quetzalcoatl and Viracocha were divinations or pre-visions of what was coming on the part of the Indian communities most directly concerned ; the first impact of a future, ever present in the timeless essence, on the collective beings whose life it was so powerfully to alter to their depths. In any case, these two haunting traditions of Incas and Aztecs are the only traces (with the possible exception of Pachacamac) of any spiritual, as distinct from animic mood, in the vast field of New World native beliefs.

*　　*　　*

This is an important fact in the life of the New World aborigines, before the Conquest, and one which might well have to be related to the two almost universal features which they present to all observers : cannibalism and drunkenness. Enough data have been provided to establish how widespread, almost omnipresent, cannibalism was in the Indies. Whether limited to religious ceremonies, merely given a religious colour to cover a wider use, or finally frank and open without any necessary connection with sacrifices to the gods, the habit of eating their like was general among the natives of the New World ; even the Incas who, if we are to believe Garcilaso, fought steadily against it, met with it in most of the campaigns they launched against the surrounding Indian peoples and were not always able to stamp it out. We have it on the authority of one of the most competent and impartial, in fact pro-Indian, Spanish students of the New World natives, the Jesuit Blas de Valera, that, even late in the sixteenth century " those who live in the Andes eat human flesh, are fiercer than tigers, have no god nor land, and possess no idea of virtue ; nor do they worship any idols or any such thing. [. . .] If they make any captive at war, or otherwise, should he be a man of low condition, they quarter him and give the flesh to their friends and servants, for them to eat or sell at the butcher's ; but if the captive is noble, the foremost members of the tribe with their women and children, ministers of the devil, undress him and tie him alive to a stake, and with flint knives cut slices out of him, without disjointing him, but just taking the flesh from the limbs where there is plenty of it, such as the calves, thighs and seat, and the arms, and with his blood they rinse their own limbs, men, women and children ; and they eat the flesh very quickly, without allowing it time to be well cooked or roasted ; they eat it biting at it, so that the wretched victim sees himself eaten alive and buried in their bellies. The women, more cruel than the men, smear

their nipples with the blood, so that their children drink and
suck it with their mothers' milk. They do all this as a
sacrifice, with great joy and elation, till the prisoner dies.
Then, they eat up all that remains, no longer in a mood of
festivity and delight, but as a matter of worship, for from then
on they hold that flesh in deep veneration, and eat it as sacred.
Should the victim during his torment show any sign of suffering
in his face or body, or utter a sob or sigh, after eating his flesh
and entrails, they break his bones and with much contempt,
throw them away over the field or in a river ; but if throughout
his ordeal he remains strong, steadfast and ferocious, once they
have eaten him up, they dry his bones and sinews and set them up
on hilltops and hold them as gods and offer them sacrifices."(3)

Father Valera adds that this cruel tribe had come from
Mexico and had spread over Panama, Darien and New
Granada. They seem to have been the fiercest kind of
American native. They were by no means typical. In fact,
variety is the chief law in the Indies ; but this type and others
less, but hardly less savage, described by equally well-informed
authors, provide a corrective against the general tendency to
imagine the Indians of the Southern continent as softer and
milder than those of the North. As late as the beginning of
the nineteenth century, the Observant Fathers reported in
their letters : " Our Caura River Indians say when they come
to confession that they fully understand that to eat human
flesh is sinful ; but they ask to be allowed to shake off the
habit gradually ; they suggest eating human flesh once a
month, then once in three months, till the habit tapers off
without their noticing it."(4)

* * *

Drunkenness was also a universal feature of the Indian
peoples all over the continent, and the theme recurs constantly
under the pen of secular and church authors. Here is a
typical example, from a *mestizo* proud of his Indian blood.
Garcilaso is describing one of the festivals of the Incas : " After
the repast, drinks were served in very great abundance, for
this was one of the outstanding vices that these Indians had,
though nowadays, by the Lord's mercy, and owing to the

good example the Spaniards have given them in this respect, no Indian gets drunk, but rather abhors and despises it as an infamy ; for if in all vices the example had been as good, the Spaniards would have been apostolic preachers of the Gospel." Three centuries later, Stübel reports during his travels in the late nineteenth century : " As we arrived in Huila, the *Gobernador* (in Indian villages the chief authority) and other persons were heavily drunk with *Chicha* (beer of maize)." Between these two dates, numerous observations record the universality and permanency of the evil. (5)

In spite of the flattering testimonial which Garcilaso extends to the Spaniards in this matter, with regard to Peru, there is sound evidence for the view that, at any rate in Mexico, the tendency to drink had been better checked by the authorities of the Aztec Empire than it was later by the Spanish authorities. The *Oidor* Zorita stoutly maintains that in pre-Cortesian days there was little or no drunkenness because the laws repressing it were most severe. " Drunkenness was most hated among them, and they held as infamous those who indulged in it." The drunkard's house was demolished. " The young man who drank too much wine "—says another witness, Father Vetancurt—" was taken to prison and there knocked to death ; women who drank were stoned like adulterous women ; the nobleman lost his office and his honour, those of a meaner sort were shorn of their hair, and their houses were demolished. In Tetzcuco, the nobleman was hanged, and his body thrown into the river, so that it should drink its fill of water, having drunk so much wine on earth ; while the man of the people was sold for a few years, and the third time he was drunk, he was hanged."(6)

The very severity of these laws confirms the force of the evil they were meant to repress. But the responsibility of the Spanish authorities in what amounted to a reversion of this policy cannot be disputed. The favourable opinion of Garcilaso and the unfavourable report of men such as Zorita and Vetancurt may well be but correct observations of two different phases : one in which the Spaniards, singularly self-controlled in matters of drink, influence the Indians into a sobriety based on self-repression rather than on State-repression ; and a later stage in which corruption sets in, and the State looks on and even profits by a shameless exploitation of this Indian foible on the part of drink traffickers. As usual, the most outspoken, courageous and concrete criticism comes from Spanish authors. Zorita is eloquent in his report to the king. Vetancurt, in his *Teatro Mexicano* prints a *Manifesto of the Zeal of a Religious Minister of the Natives on the state of the Indian Commonwealth owing to the consumption of Pulque, and how they are destroyed thereby.* In this statement, probably his own, a scathing indictment of the Spanish authorities, the author shows how, though at the beginning of the Spanish rule, " drunkards were punished with imprisonment and flogging," what with " the greed of selling them the wine of Castille and their own proclivity to drink and get drunk," a disastrous situation had been brought about in the capital. In smaller places, he avers, the Indians hold themselves better because " they fear and revere the magistrates and the religious ministers more " ; but in Mexico, the publicans keep *pulquerías* " which they keep much cleaner and better swept than the church," " and in order to attract the Indians, they put them in the hands of women managers and saleswomen, the most beautiful and clean, most useful for making their souls and consciences dirty, and though I should not like to offend the chaste ears of the virtuous, I feel bound to say that it is held for certain that to attract customers these publicans have a provision of persons of both sexes for evil commerce ; the price of this public dissolution has risen so much that the licensees have given as much as ninety thousand *pesos* per year, apart from what they earn for themselves and what they distribute to so many watchmen who register who comes in." The good friar says that " in the City of Mexico, two thousand *arrobas* [of wine of the land] enter every day, and especially on Tuesdays and Saturdays, more than fifteen thousand." " There is no quarter, no street, without a public house in which liquor is sold to the music of guitars, harps and other instruments, with rooms in which Negroes, Mulattoes, *Mestizos* and many Spaniards meet." Finally, the publicans had come to enjoy an exorbitant privilege : " No royal minister of Justice is allowed to enter the public-house to arrest or to expel a delinquent."(7)

This state of affairs was due in part to corruption, and in part to Treasury needs and bad practices, for the *pulquerías* were a solid item of revenue. "The sum provided by the licensees is already embodied in the royal finances," says our author, who bases thereon his scepticism as to the possibility of mending matters. The heavy responsibility of the Spanish State and system is therefore patent. But the point now at issue is the natural proclivity of the Indians to drink. And it is obvious that it was there before the Spaniards arrived or exploited it. It obeyed deeper causes than any let loose by the Conquest.

*　　　*　　　*

In both cases, therefore, that of cannibalism and that of drink, the facts are well proved. But no explanation has so far been provided. Now, in part, or in some cases, drunkenness may well spring from some lack of balance in a particular body or in the supplies which are being furnished to it by its material environment ; but in most cases it answers a psychological need. The state of inebriation is the only way in which people rigidly held by the forces of the earth can escape from their heavy grip. Alcohol is not needed by those who enjoy other means of evasion from the donkey work of life. The animistic Indian, held to the ground by his close adherence and submission to the forces of the earth, was constantly in the presence of the self, or dragged down towards animals and plants, or haunted by the demons of treacherous forest and angry cloud. He could find relief only in strong liquor, which raised him above himself or made him sink below, but in any case broke the monotonous continuity of his existence.

That is why, despite the endeavours of the friars, even away from the allurements of worldly centres such as Mexico City, the Indians were unable to give up drinking even after conversion. For in reality a complete and thorough conversion must have been a rare spiritual occurrence with them. To this day, many Indian communities remain isolated and unrelated to the Christian world in which they are set, as flint fossils in chalk cliffs. Even in those which have been strongly influenced by Christianity, the influence is apt to be skin-deep and does not seem to illumine the depths, at any rate not enough to quench the craving for stimulants. Drink and religion, moreover, were always closely connected in the Indian consciousness as in that of many men of other lands. Towards the end of the seventeenth century, Vetancurt, who seems to have had first-hand knowledge of the ways of the Indians, wrote of their " idolatrous " ways in relation to the making of *pulque*. " When they sow their magueys and when they prune them, they use superstitious ceremonies, as well as when they drink the new *pulque* ; idolatrous forms, for they meet in a festival and offer the first pitcher to their god *Tezcatzoncatl*, who is Bacchus, when one of the old men rises, goes several times round the fire, and saying a few set words, throws some new *pulque* on the fire, and then the others, before drinking, spill some of their own drink as a sacrifice on the fire."(8)

This connection between drink and religion was by no means dissolved with the advent of Christianity. Drunken orgies have become a traditional, indeed the most important traditional fixture of religious " Christian " festivities in modern Indian communities. " The Indian "—writes a French visitor to some native districts of Ecuador in 1904— " has a true mania for religious festivities. He celebrates them with much solemnity, but in a wholly external manner and without any Christian spirit. [. . .] They are for him mostly an occasion for drinking. Every one, particularly the most important, Holy Week and Easter, Corpus Christi, Christmas, All Saints and the local festivity of *la Merced*, is followed by an orgy of eight days [. . .] which is the true festivity, the only one which counts for the Indians, the *función* or *obligación*, as they say. [. . .] This *obligación* is for the Indians a sacred duty. An Indian who fails to attend is cursed."(9)

A similar impression can be gathered from the descriptions of the German Stübel. " By means of church festivals which often last several days "—he writes—" the Indians try to forget the misery of their being in an inebriation of *Chicha*." And he describes one of those festivals, a Corpus Christi procession, in which men and women, masked and dressed-up, went singing and dancing with a fantastic mixture of Spanish and Indian styles and traditions, stopping now and then just the second they needed to swallow a draught of heady *chicha* offered them by the faithful. All this shows that Christianity, grafted on the Indian stem and root, produced new human forms, even more at variance with the forms come from Europe than these were from their original inspiration which had come from Palestine. Not in vain did Voltaire say that if God had made man in His image, man had returned the compliment.(10)

In Stübel's days, 1870, " Bolivian doctors " used to travel all over South America, from Panama to Patagonia, " curing " the sick with a mixture of Christian miracles and Indian magic and old wives' herbs. They " almost without exception, wore on the chest a silver Crucifix, richly decorated, often a foot long." And it is probable that the faith which cured their patients was as naïve a mixture of Christian and Indian belief and gullibility as the faith that cures any of us is a mixture of scientific notions and prejudices and old wives' experiences. Christianity was not always received by the Indians willingly. Indeed it often gave rise to determined opposition, at times armed and brave, more often of the indirect, sly nature, which so admirably suits the Indian character. To this day, the place where the chief idols of the main *teocalli* of Mexico were hidden on Cortés' second arrival in the city, remains a carefully guarded secret among the Indians of Mexico—which argues a certain underground persistence of the ancient cults. Native priests and *caciques* fought for ages against the friars, spreading the absurdest rumours about them among the terrified Indians ; and a current of pessimism set in from the earliest days as to the efficacy and actual virtue of the conversion of the Indians, particularly when it took, as it often did, wholesale forms. The fact that the Observant Fathers of Caura should have admitted to confession Indians who still ate human flesh shows that conversion was not always strictly defined. To this day, in Mexico, incense is offered to a stone fish by fishermen to obtain good catches, and idols are found behind images in Christian churches.(11)

No hasty conclusions should be drawn from these facts. The view has been put forward that the Indians have evolved a religion of their own, a kind of " mixed " or " intermediate " religion. There is something to be said for this view. Some of the superstitions of the " converted " Indians are of Spanish origin ; but a study of the religious tenets and practices of the Indians of our day reveals a mixture of the two beliefs ; and there are tribes for which the Catholic priest is but a sorcerer, somewhat less efficient than the pagan one. It is doubtful, however, whether all this amounts to a new composite religion ; nor is it certain that the existence of Indians wholly conquered by the religion of Christ can be roundly denied. Those are tempted to do so who see in some parts of South America, particularly in Ecuador, whole communities of Indians, prosperous and happy, but absolutely severed from the Whites, with whom they have no intercourse whatsoever, not even when they see them passing through their thronged market places. But the chief fact should not be forgotten that in the Spanish New World the area of the Church reached out further than that of the State, owing to the stubborn resistance of the friars against teaching Spanish to the natives, whose language they preferred to learn. We know little about the deeper layers of the Indian soul. While it is difficult to say how deep the light of the Christian faith has penetrated into this abyss it can hardly have done so without taking on the colour and direction of the new medium it was invading.(12)

*   *   *

Drunkenness general, cannibalism widespread, would thus be but forms or symptoms of a deeper need, a lack, or at any rate, a weakness, of some kind of faculty for rising to the perception of spiritual values. This feature of the Indian character is perhaps the most important of all, and the only one which might provide a certain psychological unity to the whole continent. Throughout the pages left by eye-witnesses, earlier or later, one feels this kind of *listlessness* ; a forlorn, passive, silent, sullen state, relieved only by bouts of drunkenness, or, if provoked, by the excitement of war. This negative, passive, closed attitude of the Indian, has sometimes been attributed to the Conquest. The explanation does not resist even a cursory reading of the first-hand authorities. The two only well developed Empires of pre-Spanish days, the Aztec and the Inca, had no idea of the outer world, not even of each other ; and it was the Spaniards who discovered them, not they the Spaniards, which after all means something in psychology. So, passivity was there enthroned even at the summit of these two otherwise brilliant centres of Indian life. But then, even under the Aztecs and the Incas, the mass lived in a state of complete submission ; in the northern kingdom, accepting without a murmur a system of human sacrifices which took heavy toll of its own blood ; and in the southern, living a life admirably regulated by its Inca masters, but little better than that of kindly-treated though scantily-fed animals ; for they owned nothing and had no liberty to move about or change their mode of life.(13)

This conclusion is confirmed by a study of the pre-Columbian art of the Indian aborigines. A remarkable feature of it is the contrast between its rich colour and the poverty-stricken quality of the design, which on its constructive side never rises higher than the elementary *poncho*, an ordinary square of cloth with a hole for the head ; and on its ornamental side rarely ventures beyond a repetition of a few geometric figures. The Indian never " sculpted " his garments. His sleeves never were more than bare prolongations of his back and front, in their turn, mere folds of the same piece. This passivity before the material reappears in the parallel or repetitive form of most of his designs, as well as in the very poise and shape of his human and animal figures.(14)

The repetitive form of the activity of the Indian mind can be perceived in literary works known to us in the translations of modern Mexican scholars. Here is, for instance, a fragment of the preface to the history of the Conquest of Mexico, written towards 1600 in Nauatl by a pure Indian, translated from a literal Spanish version : " Truly, here is the entreaty made to whomsoever [be] the reader of this book : that you may know, that you may understand, oh you, whosoever you may [be], oh you book-reader that I therefore with much humility, I courteously beg you, that all the things the author is writing thereon, its end, its perdition, its termination of the State of the Mexicans, when the boiling sea [of war] was in order, when the Captain Hernando Cortés, Marqués del Valle, conquered them, when he came to enter, when he again to that effect here entered anew, in Mexico-Tenoxtitlan ; when here entered His divine light, His divine glow our Lord, He the only one, God, Jesus Christ, His faith which of Him was had, His news which of Him was gained, the preaching of His divine faith ; for not many know of it [the Conquest], for nowhere inhabits, lives, is born [he who knows], and those who are still to live shall be born when this over there [in their time] will be seen, truly it will not sound as it happened, for those who were already old when in their presence, when in their time, it happened, are now quite dead, dead are those who saw it, those who won honour with the things which happened in their time, for truly they are no longer here for they are gone to the place named Ximouayan, for the Lord was good enough to conceal them, and this book truly shall for ever be springing up, germinating for ever, and for ever living, that so many things may be seen and admired which no one saw and no one fully understands yet." This repetitive style may in part be deliberate ; as a means for helping illiterate hearers to memorize the texts. Such methods are familiar to students of primitive literatures. But, even allowing for this consideration, the page quoted enables us to glance into the Indian mind. Complicated and if not wholly form-less, painfully seeking form. This by no means implies that the Indians were incapable of thought or action. Far from it. On this point, the testimony of objective Spanish observers is most favourable, at any rate for the Indians of Mexico and Peru. Father *Motolinia* saw the value of the mind behind the quiescent, passive façade, and put it most felicitously : " They have a quick understanding, drawn to itself and calm, and not proud nor spilt over things as other nations " ; an admirable tribute from one coming from the " other nations " hinted at. The good friar extols the abilities of his flock in whole pages rich with experience and stories. He recalls how an old friar had taught the Indians to sing, read and write music, with great success, even though at the beginning of his course he could only address his class in Spanish, which they did not understand ; " and now there are many of them who are so proficient that they lead chapels, and as they are quick-witted and of good memory, most of what they sing, they know by heart." Motolinia adds that "an Indian of these singers of Tlaxcala has composed an entire Mass, set down out of his own invention, and belauded by good singers of Castille who have seen it." Another detail provided by him is relevant. "They learnt to write in a short time, for in very few days they are able to imitate whatever their masters show them, and if their masters alter the hand, [. . .] the students at once alter it also and take on the new form shown by the master." This fact, directly observed, strengthens the observation independently made by another first-hand observer, the *mestizo* Garcilaso : "They are men of little or no invention of their own ; but on the contrary, keen imitators of everything they see made."(15)

*   *   *

All this suggests a "lean-to" psychology, a character used to relying on forces outside itself. And the observation is confirmed by other features noted down, for instance, by Garcilaso who repeatedly states that the Indians of Peru are given to flattery and, in order to please the Spaniards, are apt to simulate. Garcilaso contradicts the statement made by other Spanish historians that the practice of confession existed in Peru before the arrival of the Spaniards, "which is a false story made up by the Indians to flatter the Spaniards and ingratiate themselves with them answering questions according to the wish they guess in the questioner and not according to truth " ; and he also relates how the Indians made the Spaniards believe that they had erected a statue in honour of Viracocha, taller than that of the Sun, to make them think that Viracocha was the highest god of all, which they calculated would flatter the Spaniards, whom they had also given that name. This feature became a serious obstacle in the law courts : " Everyone "—says Solórzano Pereira—" can prove whatever he likes with Indian witnesses, owing to their pusillanimity." In Mexico, there is a traditional story, dating from the earliest days, of an Indian who went to confession and upon the friar asking him (rather insidiously) " how many gods are there ? " he answered : " Two." Anger of the friar, depicted in his frown. " Three," says the Indian.

The frown darkens. " Four " . . .   And the scene continues,
till the willing Indian, having bidden by leaps and bounds up
to fifty, is expelled from the church by the irate friar.   At the
church door, he meets another Indian entering to confess.
" How many gods are there ? "—he asks.   " One "—answers
the newcomer.   " Don't go in to that friar with your one god.
I offered him fifty and he was not content."(16)

Many authors are scathing about the lying habits of the
Indians. But this does not go deep enough. The chief
feature of the Indian is his apathy. Lying requires a certain
effort, and, therefore, is only to be found in active men. If
the Indian lies it can only be to guard his peace with that tiny
amount of endeavour which his lie demands. The Indian,
therefore, cannot be a born liar. What he is is subservient,
lacking in initiative when it means leaving the bed on which
his life flows ; though endowed with considerable inertia for
remaining in his own line of flowing. When confronted with
other men of a more pushing nature, he yields—for the time
being. In the long run, his inertia will win. The tyrannous
rule under which he had always lived before the Spaniards
came had already inured him to dissimulate. But meanwhile
yield he must. And if he yields without inner acquiescence,
he will, of course, bridge over the distance with a lie. Yet
he can yield with faith also, as shown by Garcilaso. And
then, he is not only truthful but loyal to the death.(17)

CHAPTER V

MORE ON THE INDIAN ELEMENT

ALL this tallies perfectly. The Indians are intelligent and active when led ; dull and passive when left without leadership. The idea is indirectly, yet clearly, expressed by Father Valera (undersigned as usual by Garcilaso) : " The domestic animals which God gave the Indians of Peru fitted the soft condition of the Indians ; for they are so mild that any child will take them where he wishes." Garcilaso himself says of his mother's countrymen that " in general they are so weak that any threat is enough for them to reveal all they know." And a like thought is expressed by Humboldt speaking of " the copper-coloured race in its timid mistrust and mysterious impassivity." Their fortunes depend, therefore, on the lead which turns up. Modern observers confirm this diagnosis. " The Indians "—writes Stübel in 1869— " are not without political opinions, but they are mostly guided by the personality of their leader ; when he knows how to handle them, they are true and brave soldiers ; for the rest, they are peace-minded and they find it irksome to carry arms." This subservience to leadership was noted by Humboldt even among the Indians hardly absorbed by European nations : " In the Amazon and the Río Negro, the Indians of neighbouring villages on either side of the Spanish-Portuguese border, detest each other. These poor people speak only American languages ; they do not know what happens ' on the other side of the ocean, beyond the big salty pond ' ; but the frocks of their missionaries have a different colour and that is most unpleasant to them."(1)

Garcilaso often refers to the feeling of surrender, submission and desire to serve aroused in the Indians by either the industry or the valour of the Spaniards : " The Indians of Peru in those days, and even at the time the Spaniards came, were so simple that it was enough for a man to invent something they had never seen, for them to surrender and recognise as the child of the Sun the one who had done it." And again :

" Every time the Spaniards produce some new thing which they have never seen, they say that the Spaniards deserve that the Indians should serve them." This subservience went to the uttermost limits when they had been beaten in a fight. " The Indian who had surrendered and was taken prisoner in war [by the Spaniards] considered himself more a subject than a slave "—writes Garcilaso—" believing that the man who had conquered him was his god and his idol, and as such, he was bound to obey and respect him, to serve him and be faithful to him to the death, and never to deny him either for his fatherland, or for his relations, parents, children or wife. In this belief, he put his own kith and kin behind his Spanish master's health, and if necessary, should his master wish it, he sold them all, and he acted as spy and watchman for the Spaniards."

At the other end of time, in the eighteenth century, Ulloa and Jorge Juan, in the course of a narrative about a tyrannous priest, who had slanderously accused a *cacique* of rebellion because the honest and brave native chief had sought to defend his people against the exactions of the infamous cleric, say that considering the circumstances, which were most favourable for a rebellion, " there is no doubt that if they did not rebel it was merely because they are so quiet and loyal [. . .] How are we then to believe "—they ask—" that cruelty and ill-treatment are to foster loyalty and love for the King, and that good treatment would make rebels of them, when they are a people who love affection and kindness so much, that they take it as the highest favour that their masters give them the remainder of their own food, and care more for a morsel of bread bitten by their masters, or to be allowed to lick the plates in which their masters had eaten, than a portion of meat untouched by them ? They take it as a proof of esteem to be asked to sit close by their masters, or to be allowed to lie on the floor by their masters' beds." And the two Spanish authors go on to remark how loyal to the King the Indians always are despite the ill-treatment they receive from the King's white subjects, both American and European.(2)

*   *   *

This kind of psychology could only lead to societies controlled by military force. In so far as the New World was organized at all, before the Spaniards came, it was so in the form of military dictatorships, no doubt widely different in character, yet similar in their essence in that both were built on authority backed by force, in its turn backed by courage. The Aztec Empire was ruled by a warrior class not altogether closed, since admittance to it could be gained by courage in the field. The Inca Empire was ruled by an aristocracy so hermetically closed that to ensure its purity, the reigning monarch had to be the son of both a son and a daughter of the preceding monarch, so that reigning Incas had to marry their own sisters. The plebs under the Incas remained sunk in ignorance. Among the sayings of the great Inca Topac Yupanqui, culled by Father Blas de Valera, we read : " It is not meet that the sons of plebeians should be taught the sciences reserved for the great ; for they are low people and should not be allowed to grow pride which would impoverish the republic ; it is enough for them to learn the craft of their parents, for governing and commanding is not a thing for the common man." We know that in Mexico the system had led to a ruthless oppression of the surrounding peoples, a circumstance which greatly eased the Conquest, owing to the consummate ability with which Cortés exploited it. Garcilaso, an Inca himself, painted a much better picture of the Inca system. But how could an aristocratic authoritarian system without a balancing power work otherwise than to the disadvantage of the underdog ? At any rate, when the Spaniards arrived, Atahuallpa, a half-breed as Incas went, had usurped the throne and put to death the whole royal family—hundreds of them—thus destroying the aristocratic principle on which the system rested.(3)

*   *   *

The Spanish society then grafted on to these native communities was also aristocratic. Its principle was more like the Aztec than the Inca. The tendencies to quality and to equality, both strong in the Spaniard, usually led to a generous allocation of titles and honours to all and sundry.

INDIAN FRUIT MARKET

INDIAN FESTIVAL IN PERU

from " Types and Customs of Old Lima," by Pancho Fierro

OLD JESUIT COLLEGE, LA PLATA—in Upper Peru, now Bolivia

[Facing page 6

The imitative Indians followed suit. Garcilaso says that in the days of the Conquest the use of " Don " before the Christian name " was not so general among noblemen as it is now [*circa* 1610] when everybody uses it, so much that the Indians of my country, whether noble or not, realising that the Spaniards style themselves so to show their rank, don it themselves and get away with it." We perceive here one of the *joints of the graft*, where the tissue of the Indian stump links up with that of the Spanish stem. Indian social inequalities merged into Spanish ones. The somewhat elementary picture of a society ruled by Spaniards on top with an Indian crowd below, even though in the main and roughly correct, reveals richer and more complicated shades when those who actually saw it live are consulted, and as usual, the bird of reality evades all ready-made cages.(4)

" In Potosí "—writes Garcilaso—" about 1554 or 1555, there was a popinjay of the kind known as parrot, so talkative that he addressed all Indian passers-by with the name of the provinces to which they belonged, never making a mistake, for he called out Colla, Yunca, Huayru, Quechua, &c., as if he knew the differences between the several head-dresses which in the Inca days were worn to that effect. One day a beautiful Indian woman passed by, followed by three or four servants, and showing off as a lady *Palla*, i.e., a lady of the royal blood. As soon as he saw her, the popinjay began to shriek in derision, screeching : Huayru, Huayru, Huayru, which is a nation more vile and less esteemed than others. The Indian woman went by full of shame, for there were people present, as the popinjay always was surrounded by a crowd of Indians listening to him ; and as she passed close to the bird, spat towards him and called him *cupay*, which means Devil. That was also the opinion of the Indian onlookers, since he had recognised the woman's true station, though she went about parading as a *Palla*."(5)

*   *   *

Once this inequality within the Indian community is understood, many things become clear, in particular the fact that the poor Indians suffered at times from the corrupt

c

practices and oppression of their own more powerful brethren
as well as from that of unscrupulous white officials or settlers.
This evil was not born of the Conquest. It was widespread in
the New World when the Spaniards arrived. Some of its
old forms lingered on ; it took new ones as well. One was
the exploitation of the royal tribute. Martín Cortés writes to
Philip II that, of 8,000 *pesos* of tribute which a *pueblo* of Indians
yielded over and above that which was due to him, " I found
that four or five hundred had been spent by the friars and the
rest drunk by the chiefs, *alcaldes* and *regidores* [Indian of course]
without leaving over a single *real*." Martín Cortés crudely
suggests that the institution of " tribute surpluses and community property was an invention of those who wanted
something they could plunder." It is only fair to recall that
the *oidor* Zorita in his " Brief and Summary Relation " to
Philip II points out that " it is general in all this land that
those who hold these posts of *regidores*, *alcaldes*, *alguaciles*,
escribanos or *fiscales*, are officials brought up amongst Spaniards
or in their service, or who have been their slaves, or have
held intercourse with them for a long time, and they are very
sophisticated and slick."(6)

Zorita describes how the Indian *alguaciles* exploit the Indian
peasants who come to town, taking them to prison for drunkenness, whether true or not, and in connivance with " the
court-clerk and the *alcalde* of the prison, all Indians," make
them pay jail fees and other expenses ; they even pretend to
have been assaulted, and then, " the *oidor* orders doctors to
see the *alguacil*, and as all are at one to squeeze money out of
the prisoner, the doctors say he is ill ; and if the *oidor* sends
another, a Spaniard this time, to see the sick *alguacil*, he
simulates illness, for they know very well, how to do it, rubbing
themselves with some ointments they know of, to seem very
much weakened." Similar abuses arose from the power
which local Indian magistrates had to choose the Indians
sent to serve in the houses and farms of Spaniards, a power
which they turned into money with much waste of labour and
much injustice inflicted on the poorer Indians ; and it is a
curious sidelight on the system that Zorita believes that,
contrary to what was constantly asserted by the settlers,

labour would have been more easily obtainable under a wholly voluntary system.(7)

Throughout the three centuries of Spanish rule this tendency of the Indian to ill-treat and exploit the Indian may be observed alongside the exactions caused by the still more powerful White. Humboldt has observed it from the wilderness of the Missions to the most advanced industrial districts. "We found at San Fernando"—he writes of his travels in the Upper Orinoco—"dainty vicarages covered with creepers, surrounded with gardens. [. . .] During our walks, the Father President related to us the raids they make in the Guaviare river. He reminded us how eagerly the Indians of the Mission look forward to these expeditions undertaken ' to conquer souls.' All, even women and old men, desire to take part in them. Under the vain pretext of pursuing the neophytes who have deserted the village, children of over eight or ten are kidnapped and distributed among the Indians of the Missions as serfs or *poitos*. The diaries of these expeditions, communicated to us by Father Bartholomé Mancilla, contain geographical material of the highest value." This man-hunting war disguised under the Gospel led at times to cases of unbelievable cruelty. Humboldt relates one which had remained almost legendary in the district. "The missionary of San Fernando had led the Indians to the banks of the Guaviare, on one of those hostile raids equally forbidden by religion and by the Spanish laws. They found in an Indian cabin a *Guahiba* mother with three children two of which were not yet adult. [. . .] All resistance was impossible ; the father having gone to fish, the mother tried to run away with her children. Hardly had she reached the plain when the Indians of the Mission who go man-hunting, as the Whites and the negroes in Africa, succeeded in seizing hold of her. The friar sitting in his bark waited the result of this raid the dangers of which he did not share. Had the mother made too lively a resistance, the Indians would have killed her ; all is allowed when one goes conquering souls (*a la conquista espiritual*), and it is above all children one wants to catch to keep in the mission as *poitos* or slaves of the [Indian] Christians." Humboldt relates at length the adventures of this heroic mother and how time and again, beaten, tied, ill-treated by the Indians under the cold eye of the missionary, she escaped towards her children, from whom she had been separated, covering in one case 25 leagues of forest no Indian man would have dared to traverse. All in vain. " We urged the missionary to tell us whether the *Guahiba* had at last enjoyed in peace the happiness of remaining with her children, whether at last her persecutors had repented of their excessive cruelty. He would not satisfy our curiosity ; but when we came back to Río Negro, we learnt that the Indian woman was not given time to recover from her wounds [caused by flogging], that she had again been separated from her children and sent to a Mission in the High Orinoco, where she had died refusing all food as do savages in their great afflictions." Meanwhile the missionary would recite his *Ave Maria* as usual in worship of the Mother of Jesus.(8)

As for the civilized end, as late as 1803, Humboldt has also noted a clear case of Indian exploited by Indian, this time with a lesser influence from the Whites. When he visited textile factories in New Spain, he pointed out that this industry, founded in 1592 by the Viceroy Velasco II, in Tetzcuco, had " gradually passed into the hands of the Indians and *mestizos* of Queretaro and Puebla." How did these native owners treat their workers ? " A visitor to the works is unpleasantly struck not only by the extreme imperfection of the technical processes [. . .] but by the unhealthy conditions which prevail and the ill-treatment meted out to the workers. These men are free. Indians and coloured men are seen mixed up with felons which the authorities distribute in the mills to make them work on daily salaries. They are half naked, covered with rags, thin and haggard. Every mill resembles a dark prison : the doors, which are double, are always kept shut and no worker is allowed to leave ; those who are married are only allowed to see their families on Sundays. All are flogged ruthlessly at the slightest breach of the rules of the factory." This among many more examples that might be quoted shows what indeed was evident at the outset : that it would be far too simple to imagine life in the Indies as a kind of class and caste war in which all privilege,

power and oppression was on the White side and all suffering
on the native side of the line of colour.(9)

*   *   *

And yet when all shades of life are added to the picture for
the sake of truth and mental honesty, the broad fact remains
that the discovery and conquest of the New World dispossessed
the Indian aborigines of the free and sovereign possession of
their continent, brusquely deflected their historical evolution,
mixing it inextricably with that of an utterly alien lineage of
men, and in the process caused them a psychological shock of
incalculable gravity.

The conquerors and friars who overran the Indies in the
sixteenth century were for the most part unaware of all this.
Their faith was simple. The conquerors held that a line
scratched with their sword on the ground was as good as a
title deed. The friars believed that, by the mystic virtue of
the Holy Ghost, a few drops of holy water on an Indian head
made that Indian a Christian, and therefore one of the flock
shepherded by the Spanish King. But gradually the shrewder
among them began to see how much inevitable harm went
with the Conquest and even with the conversion. On the
material side, the chief cause of the trouble seems to have been
that the Spaniards, under a get-rich-quick impulse, did not
stop to realize the relative physical weakness of the Indian.
In his admirable report, Zorita maintains that, though there
was much compulsory work among the Indians before the
Conquest, this was done easily and " with much joy " because
things were organized to suit the soft Indian ways, " for they
are people fit for little work man for man, [. . .] six *peons*
will not work as much as one Spaniard, for just as their food
is little, so is their yield." And then he shows how the
Spaniards short of, indeed lacking labour, made the Indians
work far more than they could bear, and rightly fustigates
the greed, heartlessness, and cruelty of the mine-owners,
encomenderos and others who, for personal gain, overworked
their men when they did not actually torture them to extract
secrets of gold hoards.(10)

The actual impact of the new men, more powerfully built,
more daring, more enterprising, more ruthless, must perforce

have bruised the Indian soul. We need not limit the issue to its ethical aspect. We need not even imagine that all was black everywhere. Far from it. Here, as is often the case, one hears more readily of the scandalous abuses which raise a foam than of the smooth running of happily solved relations. There were abundant cases of happy Indian life. Many have been noted down above. Many can be gathered from routine descriptions. Here is Tunja in 1610 : " Crop-growing and breeding of animals are too costly and unprofitable owing to the excessive salaries paid to the Indians, and the little yield obtained." Here is Nombre de Dios in 1608 : " There are no *repartimientos* and no *encomenderos*, because the Indians pay tribute to nobody. [. . .] In the lands known as ' the bad country ' there are allotments for the Indians. More land than they can till. Everyone owns a piece of land with water, in which he can sow his corn, and they also have their kitchen gardens. [. . .] Those who work on the farms are paid five or six *pesos* a month, and some more. [. . .] A yearling bull is worth one *peso* and a half ; a three year old four *pesos*. [. . .] An Indian who goes as a guide for a Spaniard is paid for himself and his horse (for no one will travel on foot) four *reales* per day. [. . .] At the beginning of the year every group or nation [of Indians] elects its mayor, *regidor* and *topile*, i.e., constable." Here is Hambato, in Peru : " The Indians are tall, well made, of a handsome face, big eyes. They go about dressed in a cloak and a woollen shirt, but those who are better off dress in cotton and silk."(11)

And yet the pages of many a Spanish idealist bleed for the Indian, made to suffer untold hardship at the hands of heartless Spaniards. " And I heard it said in the Kingdom of New Granada "—writes Zorita—" that from there to the Government of Popayán one could not go astray, because the road was marked by the bones of dead men." And he adds : " And let us not speak of how they [the Spaniards] took the Indians in yokes, and the ill-treatment they meted out to them on the way, and how if the Indian man or woman was tired out owing to the load carried, they cut his head off rather than take the trouble of undoing the chain, and they distributed the load on to the others." In vain, he adds, the King writes letters upon letters ordering that the Indians be well treated. Zorita, who had been an *oidor*, is sceptical about the law, and frankly thinks the Indians were happier before the Conquest because " they had but few laws in their time, and so few that they all knew them by heart. [. . .] And so they were well governed, their numbers grew, and they lived in peace and happiness." The arrival of the Spaniards, he claims, upset this order as well as the classes and powers of the native State with disastrous results for all.(12)

The consequences were grave for the Spaniards, whom fate doomed to three centuries of unlimited dominion over other kinds of men. The moral effects of such a situation were incalculable. Ulloa and Jorge Juan, having described the abominable cruelties inflicted on the Indians in the *obrages* or textile works, paint an equally dismal picture of what went on in the *haciendas* or country estates. There were three men in authority : the steward, the assistant and the foreman. " This last one, being an Indian, does not usually punish the others, but to uphold his authority, it is understood that he must, like the two former, carry a cowskin as the insignia of his function. [. . .] Upon the slightest mistake or oversight, the Indian is made to lie face down on the ground, stripped of the light drawers which are all he wears, and is lashed and forced to count the lashes. After which, as they have been taught to do, they go to kneel before the man who has punished them, kiss his hand and say ' may God reward you for it,' thus forcing the Indian's trembling lips to thank God for the lashes—nearly always unjust—he has suffered." The two Spanish authors report that women, children and *caciques* were also punished in this fashion, and not merely by overseers but even by private persons and negro slaves, " for no other reason than that of their own caprice."(13)

Ulloa and Jorge Juan report a curious psychological consequence of this lamentable state of affairs, and one not without interest for the understanding of both the Indian and the Spanish characters. The Indians became so used to punishment that they lost all fear of it, and even missed it when it was not forthcoming. " The little Indians brought up by the priests and by other persons will grow sad, and even run away when too much time goes by without their being punished ; and when they are reproached for their moody ways or for their flight, innocently answer that they do not appear to be loved since they are not punished. This is not due to simplicity [. . .] but to the fact that, used to such a treatment since the Conquest, they have come to think that the Spaniards are people whose love and caresses are knocks and lashes, since after a punishment, even the most inhuman, they always explain to the Indians that they punish them because they love them, and the simple Indian has taken this barbarous explanation to the letter." This is illuminating, for without attenuating the cruel nature of the ill-treatment, its evil effect on the Indian, and on the Spaniard, it shows that in the midst of all this inhumanity there was a closeness between the two human strains perhaps not to be found elsewhere.

The responsibility of the " Spaniard " was not the lesser for that. The consequences for the development of a common human heritage in the Indies must have been disastrous. " The fear which the name ' Spaniard ' or *Viracocha* (which includes every kind of human being who is not an Indian) causes in the Indians is so great that when they want to frighten their little ones or make them stop crying or drive them to hide in their huts, it is enough to say that the *Viracocha* is coming, for the children to run and hide in terror. When little Indians keeping herds or working in the fields see a Spaniard coming, they leave herds and fields and run for the most dangerously broken land to keep out of sight of the Spaniards who, they fear, will not fail to ill-treat them."(14)

*   *   *

Yet, bad as all this was, it was not the worst. Ill-treatment, tyranny, oppression may stimulate the soul of a people ; and in any case the Indians before the Conquest lived, practised and suffered much of the worst which the worst Spaniards inflicted on them. It was, moreover, mostly individual suffering. The worst was the collective suffering inflicted on the whole people of the Indies by the mere fact of the Conquest, both political and spiritual. For the Indian the worst was not the Spaniard at his worst, but the Spaniard at his best ; not the Spaniard who revealed himself as a more barbarous man than the Indian of heathen days, but the Spaniard who brought to the Indian a vision of life which the Indian felt desirable and yet so alien and distant that he could never hope to attain it without untold spiritual effort. The Conquest brought with it a human environment so different from the original one that it put the Indian in a permanent state of tension and of inferiority. This was not precisely due to Christianity. Indeed the point has been put time and again by the friars that, so far as actual living went, the Indians were much nearer Christian perfection than the Spaniards. " In truth, they are men so lacking in greed and self indulgence and so content with living moderately that if their way of life was due to a free choice and not merely to habit and nature, we should say that it is a life of great perfection ; and not a little apt to receive with profit the doctrine of the Gospel." This is an opinion amongst many. The Christian attitude which was strangest to them was that urge forward, that sense of action which the West owes perhaps to the Jewish myth of the ever-unfulfilled promise, and which has set mankind on the march towards something ever shining and ever receding on the horizon. The Spaniard was not the worst sufferer from this disease of the West. Perhaps he was the least. But in comparison to the Indian, who was wholly free from it, he was seething with activity and even with turbulence. One is struck in the pages of Garcilaso by the vast chorus of Indians who, silent and passive, though not altogether indifferent, share in the ups and downs of the civil wars between Spaniards the stake in which was their own country. And next to this sense of activity, there was the zest of western individualism, so distant from the spiritual collectivism of the more-than-eastern Indian. The Spaniards were comparable to a gas, every molecule of which moves freely in a wide, empty space, regardless of the others ; the Indians to a viscous liquid, in which every molecule is sunk in the mass.(15)

This deeper violence of one character over the other was the worst form of oppression which the Indian suffered as the result of the Conquest. It was the graver, the more penetrating in its effects for being unexpressed, unrecognized, unseen ; inflicted by the best Spaniards, by the saintly or well meaning friars, with the best good faith, indeed with enthusiasm ; by the best Viceroys and *oidores*, with the most statesmanlike sense of right ; accepted even by the most enlightened Indians as the highest possible gift the Whites could bring them. And yet, who doubts but that, looking at things from an adequate distance, these Whites were usurpers of destiny, like the Whites in Africa, like the English in India, the French in Indo-China and later, by a curious recoil of history, the English in Spanish Trinidad and Jamaica, the Americans in Spanish New Mexico, Texas and Puerto Rico, usurpers of the land, twisters of the natural course of things, meddlers with an evolution which, to judge by the state of the Inca and Aztec cultures, might and probably would have led the natives of the New World to meet European civilization on a footing of lesser inequality a few centuries later.

No one is at fault. It is all part of the human tragedy which we call History. Few minds were then great enough to see " the pity of it " ; one of them, Sahagún, has left a page of singular and penetrating wisdom. " As for the fact that they [the Mexican natives] were in the old days apter for the government of their commonwealth and for the service of the gods, the reason is that their government was suitable to the needs of the people, and that is why boys and girls were brought up with the utmost rigour till they were of age. [. . .] This way of ruling was very much in accordance with natural and moral philosophy, because the temperate climate and the abundance of this land and the constellations which rule over it all help human nature to be vicious and idle and to give itself over to sensuous vices ; and moral philosophy taught these natives by experience that, for them to live in a moral and virtuous way, rigour, austerity and constant occupations for the common good were indispensable. As all this ceased with the coming of the Spaniards, who destroyed and uprooted all the ways and manners of ruling these natives had, and wished to reduce them to the manner of living of Spain, both in divine and in human things, thinking them idolatrous and barbarous, all their governing system was lost ; it was found necessary to destroy all idolatrous things and buildings, and even the habits of the republic, which were all mixed up with idolatrous rites and accompanied with ceremonies and superstitions [. . .] and that is why it was necessary to upset everything and to turn them over to another kind of culture, so that nothing should remain of their idolatrous ways.   But as we now see that this new way makes them very vicious and gives them bad leanings and very bad behaviour [. . .] we shall have to find a remedy for it all ; and we all believe that the chief cause of it is drunkenness, for, as the rigour with which it was punished by death ceased, even though drunkards are now punished with whipping, shearing and being sold as slaves for years or for months, this is not enough to stop them from drink. [. . .]   But I think it is a great shame to us that these native Indians of old, so wise and prudent, were able to find a remedy for the evils this land causes in those who live in it, meeting natural causes with antagonistic practices ; while we follow the current of our evil inclinations, and so breed people, both Spanish and Indian, who are intolerable to rule and most difficult to save. [. . .]   At the beginning, as we found in their old republic that they brought up boys and girls in their temples where they were disciplined and taught to worship their gods and to obey their commonwealth, we adopted that style of bringing them up in our houses [. . .] where we even taught them to discipline themselves by night and to pray mentally ; but, as they took no bodily exercise, as they used to and as is required by the nature of their vigorous sensuousness, and as they also fed better than they used to in their old days, for we applied to them the softness and charity usual among us, they began to feel sensuous desires, and to turn to lascivious matters ; and so we turned them out of our houses and sent them to sleep with their parents, and they came in the morning to our schools to learn reading, writing and singing, and that is the practice now."(16)

No better description could be given of the effects of the impact of one people upon another.   There is no doubt that this *bruise* caused in the core of the Indian soul by the Conquest and the conversion was, and still is, the chief psychological feature of the Indies.

CHAPTER VI

THE NEGRO ELEMENT

THE Indian was the original inhabitant of the New World. He was there. The Spaniard gate-crashed into it. He went there. The negro was not there and did not want to go there. He was kidnapped into it, to serve as a slave. The idea was well meant. There were negro slaves in Spain. Some passed over to the New World with their masters. But as a wholesale measure, the idea was put forward by the uncompromising advocate of the Indians—Las Casas. In his ardent wish to reduce to a minimum the violence done to the Indians, he proposed another violence, possibly worse : he brought the negro slave.

How procured ? Labat will tell us. There are four kinds of persons, he says, apt to become slaves. The first is that of criminals sentenced to death by their " kings " in Africa ; the kings commute this sentence to perpetual exile and sell them to the foreign slave-dealer. Next come prisoners of war, a war between African tribes which " has no other object than this human booty or kidnapping of persons, done by surprise without hardly ever coming to open war." The third category is that of Blacks who were slaves in Africa and are sold by their masters to the White dealers. " The fourth, lastly, who are the most numerous, are those who are kidnapped, now by order or by consent of the Princes, now by certain thieves known as Merchants," who are " in fact highwaymen who do nothing but rob everywhere, especially by night ; if they find some-body, and if they think themselves stronger, they throw them-selves on him, hold his hands behind his back, and put a gag on his mouth, if it is a man or a woman, to prevent the victim from crying ; if children, they put them in a sack ; and as night falls, they take them to the factories of the Europeans, who forthwith brand them, and have them transported to their ships."(1)

The unhappy creatures thus violently torn from their home and land, had then to go through the ordeal of a crossing in torrid seas, chained in pairs by their ankles, and suffering hunger and thirst, in the dark and pestilential hulls of their floating prisons, now and then seeing a child, a woman, even a man succumb to their atrocious suffering. " It is supposed " —writes Moreton—" that about one hundred thousand slaves are yearly exported from Africa ; several of these poor wretches, when they get sickly on the Guinea coast, are thrown overboard alive to save insurance ; and from their being stowed so close together, about sixteen thousand are computed to die during their voyage ; about thirty thousand die in the seasoning." Many harboured in their souls that fear of being eaten by the Whites which seems to have tortured the Blacks, a pertinacious tradition which led many of them to die at once, throwing themselves overboard.(2)

What happened when they arrived in harbour ? Here is Moreton's account of a reception of a slave-ship in one of the English Antilles : " Until the day of sale they are kept on board in the harbour ; during which time, the master, mate and doctor (for every ship has a quack on board) use every art to set them off to the best advantage ; the grey hairs and beards of the old men and women are cut and shaved, and not only their skins but that of the whole cargo, are rubbed with palm and other oils : so that a person who is not a judge may purchase an old slave for a young one, a distempered boy or girl for one healthy and stout. About eight or nine o'clock every morning they are mustered on deck and are obliged to jump and dance and roar loudly for half an hour, obedient to the sailors, who chastise those who are sick or lazy. Several of those poor creatures, heartbroken at their fate, die daily ; and lest any report should circulate of the cargo's being sickly, to hurt the sale, the dead bodies are concealed in the hold until night, and given to the sharks, which devour them in a trice : when there are many ships in the harbour, the fish fare well."(3)

As for those who remain and land, here is one of the scenes they had to live, described by an English eyewitness as he observed it in Jamaica : " In this place, it is certainly proper to observe that a mode of selling negroes is sometimes practised which ought to be abolished by a law of the islands where it prevails, as being repugnant to decency, and, *in some measure* to humanity.   The custom I mean to reprobate is the selling a cargo of slaves by what is called a *scramble*.   This is shutting them up in the merchant's house or the area adjoining, and, at the beat of a drum, or some other signal, all those who intend to become purchasers *rush on suddenly* or, to use a *military* phrase, *dash* upon the astonished and frightened negroes, and endeavour to get hold of or to incircle in a cord, as many of them as they can.   Although the negroes are generally prepared for this by being preinformed of what is to happen, yet some of the *women and children have been known to expire* from an excess of terror, which is incited by a scene of such confusion and uproar. Nor is it uncommon for the purchasers themselves to go by the ears and quarrel about the objects of their choice."   And Dickson, who copies this, adds : " Such is the language even of an *apologist* for negro slavery."(4)

*   *   *

The memories of the fatherland were bound to remain the more vividly engraved in the soul of the transplanted Blacks for all this violence.   Their native land pulled at their roots and drew them often to commit suicide, " holding a prejudice that after their death they are to return to their country."   So writes Labat, who lost one of his young slaves in this way. " When I scolded him because he wanted to die, he began to weep and said that he loved me, but that he wanted to return to his father."   The French friar relates how a Major Crips, of St. Christopher's Island, succeeded in arresting an epidemic of suicides among the slaves : " As this man was very rough to them [. . .] the number of his slaves dwindled down every day ; they hanged themselves continually.   At last he was warned by one of his staff that all his negroes had resolved to run away the following day to the wood, and there hang themselves all in a company, to go back together to their country. [. . .]   He instructed his White servants [. . .] to load on carts the boilers of the sugar and rhum factories with all the gear of the mill, and to follow him.   He went to the wood and found his negroes preparing their ropes to hang themselves ; he walked towards them with a rope in his hand,

told them to fear nothing, for he had learnt of their decision
to return to their country, and he wanted to go with them also,
for he was going to set up a sugar mill there, where they would
all be much apter for the work than other negroes who had
never been in a sugar factory ; but he warned them that, as
he would no longer fear that they might run away, he would
make them work there the whole night and would not give
them either Saturday or Sunday." The cunning Englishman
spoke so convincingly, having first chosen his own tree and
branch, that the negroes surrendered and agreed to remain.
He refused to allow those who had hanged themselves on
previous days to come back, and laid it down that if only one
hanged himself, he would hang all the others to go and work
in Africa.(5)

*　　　*　　　*

Men less virile and vigorous than the African negro might
have succumbed to this, no, not inhuman, but all too human
violence. If the negroes were able to withstand it, indeed to
live down the initial uprooting and later sufferings of slavedom,
they owe it to the sterling virtues of their stock. Physically,
they are a superb kind of men : " I have never seen in any
place of America where I have been "—writes Labat—" any
negro who was hunchback, lame, one-eyed, cross-eyed or
maimed by birth." And he adds : " I have seen negroes and
negresses who ought to have been painted, marvellously beautiful. Their skin is extremely fine and there is no velvet like it."
Labat is an excellent authority for refuting an often heard
accusation against the negro. " As the pores of their skin are
more open than the pores of the white skin, they perspire more,
and smell ill if they neglect to wash themselves. They rarely
give an occasion for reproaches on this account if they live
near the sea or near a river ; for they are by nature like
ducks."(6)

Morally, the negroes are a strong, self-possessed and active
kind of men. Labat speaks highly of their fortitude, which
makes them withstand physical pain without murmur, even
though they are sensitive and delicate, which, he explains,
comes from " a certain greatness of soul, and an intrepidity
that makes them contemptuous of pain, dangers and even

death." And he adds : " I have seen some of them broken alive without a single cry. One was burnt at Fort Royal in Martinique, without uttering a word." Hence, he says, " a courage which is natural to them."(7)

The circumstances of their exile and of their life in their new land bred a feeling of solidarity among them. " They love each other very much, and help each other willingly in their need. It often happens that if one of them commits a fault, they all come in a body to ask for his reprieve." And Labat adds : " They are most loyal to each other and will undergo the hardest punishment rather than betray each other." Despite their condition as down-trodden and op-pressed people, their spirit does not seem to have flagged at all. Labat has left several vivid stories to show that they held their own even against the master race. " It is the custom of all the negroes to attribute to the Whites all the bad qualities likely to make a person contemptible, and to say that it is owing to their rubbing shoulders with the Whites that the negroes become spoiled." And of their own black sheep (white, they would say, I suppose) they said : " He is a miserable man, who swears like a White, who gets drunk like a White, who is as much of a thief as a White, etc." " I once found our negro carpenter much puzzled "—writes Labat— " for he could not master the cutting of a dove-tailed tenon [. . .] I took his rule and compasses, I drew the work and had it cut, and my cut fitted perfectly." Now the good Abbé used to explain to his slaves : " In the days when I was a negro I served my master with so much diligence that owing to that I became a White." The carpenter thanked Labat for his help by saying : " I never believed that you had been a negro, but now that I see this work, I am convinced ; for no White would have had the wits to do it."(8)

Vanity, concludes Labat. Perhaps. But a defensive vanity, much needed to keep the slave erect. Other signs of this spirit can be gleaned in his writings, in particular the tendency of the negroes to make sport of the foibles of the Whites, giving them nicknames, and poking fun at their masters in African language. They were proud. Labat says of his negro boy, that the slightest " word of contempt was more painful to him

than if he had been skinned alive." To be called "a poor
negro boy" drove him to despair. " He then took the liberty
to tell me that only the Whites were poor, that no negro ever
begged for alms, for they had too much heart for that." So
that, if perchance a White beggar came to call for alms,
" there were as many people to come and tell me as I had
servants in the house, and especially my Black boy, who never
failed to come and tell me with a most pleased and satisfied
air : ' My father, there is a poor White at the door begging
for alms.' This was the summit of joy for him."(9)

The negro boy used to add alms of his own to those of his
master, which made him feel superior to the White beggar.
So says Labat, and no doubt it was so in this case. But the
genuine character of the charity of the Blacks towards the
poor Whites cannot be doubted. There are both English and
Spanish documents which prove it. " The women who will
work at all "—writes an English visitor to Barbados in 1825,
referring to the poor Whites—" find employment in washing
and mending the clothes of the negroes, and it is notorious
that in many cases whole families of these free Whites depend
for their subsistence on the charity of their slaves." No mean
virtue considering these degraded Whites thought themselves
privileged to mutilate or kill any negro they wished, sure of
impunity provided there was no *White* witness of their deed.
As for the Spanish Indies, when the stowaways who landed in
Cartagena, having failed to join the convoy of some merchant
going inland, succumbed to the misery of the first weeks of
hunger and destitution, and fell ill with the *chapetonada* or
disease of the new Spaniards, Ulloa and Jorge Juan explain
that " here is the point when the charity of those people can
be observed, for out of compassion, the free negresses and
mulatas receive them in their houses where they nurse and cure
them at their own expense with as much affection and care
as if it were their duty to do so : if the man dies, they have
him buried by charity, and they even have some masses said
for his soul." This, they point out, often ended in marriage,
whereby of course, according to the prejudices of the time, the
woman rose and the man fell. But the two authors add :
" They are so disinterested that they should not be suspected

of exercising charity with the aim of getting married, for it is very often the case that they will not accept them either as husbands for themselves or for their daughters, for they do not want them to lose caste thereby ; on the contrary, they try to find for them some person who will take them in his service away inland."(10)

This charity, moreover, is in keeping with all we hear of the character of the negroes. For all authors are agreed on their good humour and feelings, their love of children and old people, their readiness to lend a helping hand, and even their loyalty to their masters, provided they found in them men and not fiends. "If one is good to them, ever so little, and with a good grace, they love their masters infinitely, and will brave any danger to save their masters' lives, even risking their own." And here is a fresh detail from the same observer : "They will often do without food to be able to help or treat those of their own country who come to visit them and who happen to be in need."(11)

*   *   *

As for their ability, the authorities are all favourable. They are acute and capable of putting their case well and of listening to reason. "They are naturally eloquent "—writes Labat— "and most able to make use of this talent wherever they have something to ask for from their masters. [. . .] If the request is feasible, as it generally is [note the tribute to the reasonableness of the negro] it should be always granted forthwith, and with a good grace ; and if it cannot be done, good reasons should be given and they should be sent away pleased with some slight concession."(12)

This general capacity showed itself notably in arts and crafts. "It cannot be denied "—writes another observer of the time—"that the negroes, when put to a trade which happens to coincide with the bent of their genius, become as good, and sometimes better artificers, than white men." And he adduces concrete examples of excellent negro craftsmanship in carpentry and watchmaking. "To these instances of African capacity"—he writes—"I shall add two remarkable ones. 'Wanted to purchase two negro carpenters, one of *which* must be *able to carry on business by himself*' &c., *Barbadoes Gazette*, March 1st, 1786.—'To be sold two valuable negro carpenters, one of *which* is a *compleat wheel-wright*, WIND-MILL, *and house carpenter*,' &c., *Barbadoes Mercury*, October 21st, 1786. Would not an European carpenter who could, with any propriety, be said to be *compleat* in these three branches, be accounted rather an ingenious man ? " The same author provides the following detail : " Of nine negro ship-carpenters, now in His Majesty's yard at Antigua, three can read very well, four read in the Bible, and two in the spelling-book."(13).

*   *   *

The special aptitude of the negro for the arts is well known Poetry and music come naturally to his buoyant yet wistful nature ; and he is a born dancer. In all these gifts, he was on common ground with the Spaniard, also a born and spontaneous poet and musician. The powerful rhythm of both Spanish and negro music, though very different, could harmonize in a way which we understand and enjoy to-day better than could the Frenchman Labat in 1700 : " Their music is not agreeable, and their accords have not got much sequence. Nevertheless there are people who prize this harmony as much as that of the Spanish and Italian peasants who all have guitars and play very badly on them. I do not know whether they are right." Haenke, who describes the instruments of the negroes of Lima towards 1800, including " handfuls of bells and tambourines, a flute played with the nose, and the jaw of a horse or an ass," also condemns their music as " noisy and unpleasant."(14)

This inner rhythm which manifests itself in song and dance was due to the buoyancy of the negro. Humboldt is constantly struck by what he calls the turbulent gaiety of the Blacks. Turbulence is a word that often occurs under the pen of authors writing on the negroes. While the Indians suggest passivity and quiescence, the Blacks impress the observer as turbulent. In either case, the type of man observed is not in a free and normal, but in a subjected state. The features observed are therefore not necessarily those which the man in question would evolve in freedom. It is nevertheless noteworthy that under conditions which, though different, were parallel, both living as subject peoples to a third, the Indians manifest listlessness and the negro turbulence as their chief characteristic.   The turbulence of the negro suggests a natural trend to activity which turns aimless for lack of a co-ordinated free object to absorb it.   So the chief difference between the Indian and the Black under pressure turns out to be that the first falls into indifference, the second bubbles over with dance and song.(15)

Due note must be taken, however, of the fact that, in the Spanish New World, the free negro population increased very rapidly owing to the strong tendency towards emancipation, not only in law but in the practice of magistrates and private persons.   This circumstance brought in a difference within the black strain in the population of the Indies : the slaves differed from the free in a number of ways.   But there was yet another difference within the Blacks : that between Creole and *Bozal*.   It was for the Blacks what the difference between " Spaniard " and " European " was for the Whites. The Creole Black was the American-born negro.   The *Bozal* Black was the African-born.   The consequences were not so subtle as in the case of the Whites.   With the Whites they varied in the course of time, but were always complex.   The mutual attitude which resulted was the outcome of many subtle feelings, due to differences in wealth, education, family-pedigree, colour-pedigree and alertness ; so that it is impossible to say that the Creole was above the European or the European above the Creole.   With the Blacks, the *Bozal* was more of a slave than the Creole, less " one of us."   He brought his language, was fresh from his heathen ways, more of a stranger. The Creole negroes were more often to be found in the homes of the Whites, entering, mostly by way of the nursery, into the intimacy of even the wealthiest families.   " These slaves "— writes Haenke—" and domestic servants always endeavour to adorn themselves and live in such a luxury as to be not a little injurious to the way of living and to the interests of their masters, and, rendered vain by the excessive trust which their mistresses put in them, they aim at becoming their equals in language and in pleasures, and to a certain extent, they set the fashion." So the Creole Blacks influenced the Whites and at the same time absorbed culture and civilization from them. But there were many *Bozals* in the city also, taking on the rough work for salaries on part of which they lived, paying over the rest to their owners. Black women, slave and free, were seen in the cities working for their living, or selling fruit and sweets, with their children on their backs, to whom they passed a plentiful breast, long enough to be served at meal times under the arm or over the shoulder of the busy mother.(16)

The Black was distinctly more of a city man than the Indian, even though there were many Black slaves in the plantations. A number of city crafts were in their hands. They mixed more easily with the Whites, to whom they seem more akin than the New World aborigines. Haenke has described the ways of the Blacks in the city of Lima. There were ten tribes, which seem to have remained conscious of their several origins. They were organized mostly for religious worship. Each of the ten tribes elected representatives, who together with the leaders or *capataces*, chose by ballot the two *caporales mayores*, whose function, once elected, lasted for life. These elections of the negroes took place in the chapel of Our Lady of the Rosary, which was kept at their expense in the Monastery of Santo Domingo. The several assemblies and committees of the ten tribes, their links together, and the work they carried out for purposes of worship, sports and burials, were a model of order, democratic discussion and good administration. These gatherings took place in rooms which the negroes had bought and were known as the *Cofradías*; all points, from those of financial accounts to those of social precedence (on which the Blacks were very pernickety), were discussed with a sense of dignity and of justice which excite the admiration of the author. As soon as business was over, the fun began and the buoyancy and the turbulence of the negroes gave themselves free play. They became " excited at the sight of some grotesque figures they have on the walls, representing their original kings, their battles and rejoicings." Possibly this " grotesque " of Haenke may be another case of the incapacity of the period to understand negro art, like

Labat's condemnation of negro music along with Spanish and Italian popular music. Who can say but that if, re-discovered to-day, those " grotesque figures " would not draw crowds to our art galleries and make art critics pour rivers of refined ink. But the point to note is that the pictures, grotesque or not, represented " their original Kings."(17)

*   *   *

There seems to be a closer affinity between the White and the Black (and the East-Indian) than between this group and the New-World-Indian, more akin perhaps to the yellow stock. Thus the negro seems to have had an easier access to the Christian faith than the Indian, even though the inducement thereto was sometimes singular. Labat reveals that conver-sion was apt to be stimulated by making the negro believe that the status of the Christian was higher than that of the heathen so that Christian negroes could neither eat at the same table nor sleep in the same room with heathen negroes ; " and as they are of a very proud nature, they constantly prod their masters and their priests to have themselves baptized."(18)

In the Spanish territories the religious education of the negro with a view to his conversion seems, however, to have been taken seriously, to judge not merely by Spanish but by non-Spanish visitors. One gathers from these descriptions that there was a closer intimacy in actual life between the Whites and their Black slaves than in other lands of the New World—a fact which would naturally lead to an easier absorp-tion into the pious atmosphere of Spanish families. A contemporary description of Lima (*circa* 1629) depicts how the market occupied the centre of the big square, " in which everything pertaining to fruit and other foods is sold by negresses and Indian women in such numbers that the square looks like an ant heap ; and so that on fete-days all this crowd should not remain without hearing Mass, a Mass is said for them on a balcony or corridor on the façade of the main church, which commands the whole square." " Among the most amiable traits of the Creolian character "—writes an English observer of Buenos Aires in 1806—" there is none more conspicuous [. . .] than their conduct towards their slaves. Often a witness to the harsh treatment of those fellow mortals in the West Indies, of the total indifference to their religious instruction there so universally prevalent, I was instantly struck with the contrast between our planters and those South Americans. These unhappy exiles from their own country are no sooner purchased at Buenos Aires, than the master's first care is to instruct his bond-servant in the native language of the place, and in the general principles as well as the creed of his own faith. This sacred branch is committed to a priest, who reports when his scholar " is fit for baptism. " The owners were [. . .] equally attentive to their domestic morals. Every morning before their mistress went to Mass, she assembled the females in a ring upon the floor, both young and old, to whom needlework or knitting was assigned, according to their capacities. All seemed cheerful, and I doubt but admonition too entered their circle. Before and after dinner, and also at supper, one of these ultimately was introduced to implore a blessing, and to return thanks, which they were taught to think as duties of pre-eminence, and they always performed them with solemnity."(19)

The sceptical Englishman comments on the tuition and baptism of the negroes in terms of typical wisdom : " although this process at best must be superficial, still it has a tendency to inspire a sense of dependence upon a Supreme Being, it enforces a serious deportment, tranquillizes the temper, and reconciles those sufferers to their lot." In the end, as we now see it, the process of Christian tuition and conversion was above all one of assimilation by a new society. This is illustrated by the next sentence in our author's page : " Until thus naturalized "—he says most aptly, meaning ' converted and baptized '—" the negroes from Africa, and their brother-natives of America, are stigmatized by the vulgar as infidels and barbarous." No bigotry. Just natural instinct which demanded assimilation. How deep could this assimilation go ? Labat thinks not very, and provides amusing examples of negroes returning to their native faith even long after the Christian society had tried to absorb them by conversion.(20)

All this seems to show that despite the transplantation of

which he had been the victim, and despite his conversion to Christianity—almost certainly deeper, more sincere and less laborious than that of the Indian—the negro remained closely attached to the root feelings and traditions of his African motherland. This circumstance, buried in the depth of the soul of the Indies, on its negro side, was bound to tell in the course of time. The more so as soon the traffic, both open and illicit, gave rise to a growing importation of negroes who did not come straight from Africa to the Spanish domains, but passed first a shorter or longer period in English-held territories. Often the slaves sold to Spanish territories were men who had proved undesirable in either English, French or Dutch territories, or even runaway slaves, *maroons* as they came to be called, caught napping by adventurous and unscrupulous merchants of human flesh. In any case, the mere fact that the negro population of the Indies was constantly being fed from new African blood acted also in the same sense. All these elements came to add to the life of the Indies one of its most baffling complexities—a people, strong, active, united and with an allegiance to itself, but none whatever to Spain.(21)

When in 1795 the King of Spain granted coloured people access to what the Creoles described as " the public offices fit for White people," the Creoles protested in the following terms : " How is it possible for the Crown to entrust the safety of the nation and the defence of its Whites to men who, far from looking to Spain as the centre of their happiness, perforce will look to the dark inhabitants of Africa, whence they come, to protect them and make them rise in revolt against the Spaniards against whom they say they have a grievance ? "(22)

CHAPTER VII

THE *MESTIZO* ELEMENT

THE Indian, the White and the negro were the three pure colours in the human palette of the Indies. In the course of time, they came to be combined in every possible proportion ; and as, over and above the bodily blends, life brought the three types into constant intercourse, it may be said that the key to the Indies and the true representative type of their life was the Mixed-Blood. Whatever the statistics, the soul of the Indies was essentially of a *mestizo* character.

The three colours blended readily. Yet there is perhaps a tendency to over-simplify the attitude of the Spaniard towards the Black and the Indian, and to contrast it with that of the Anglo-Saxon as an absence of colour-bar. After all, there are Eurasians in British India, and mulattoes in the West Indies and in the United States ; while the Spanish New World affords many an instance of colour prejudice. The very word " colour-bar," even though it may serve its purpose to define Anglo-Saxon facts, is not suitable for Spanish facts. The two attitudes differ too deeply to be merely opposed in contrast. They are not just on opposite sides of a line, both on the same plane. They are on different planes altogether.

The reason springs from the general laws of the two national characters : the English, predominantly collective ; the Spanish, predominantly individual. The sense of group rules English feelings and attitudes. The sense of self rules all Spanish life. Hence, in the Anglo-Saxon, a group-distance towards Blacks and Indians, which separates less a given man from a given man than a whole colour from a whole colour. Moreover, when, as in the present day, the colour bar is criticized, those who raise their voices against it do so in the name of collective interests, such as imperial collaboration and other reasons of political import. The relation between the individual Black and the individual White is not direct, but passes by the nation.

With the Spaniard, the psychological springs under the

position are reversed. Relations between two men, whatever their colours, are a matter for the two men concerned. The idea that Blacks and Indians are men beyond the pale does not come to the Spaniard. The Conquest was made on the explicit basis that all men were the offspring of Adam and Eve. Conquerors and conquered treated each other as brothers—i.e., often abominably, generally with indifference, at times with charity, exceptionally with intelligent affection, but never on the assumption that colour made of a man something less than a man. However dastardly a Spaniard may have treated an Indian or a Black, he never inflicted an insult or an injury on a coloured man which he would not have inflicted on a brother Spaniard in the same circumstances.(1)

Two of the emissaries sent by Gonzalo Pizarro to the provinces to announce and follow up his victory of Huarina committed abominations : Diego de Carvajal, in Arequipa, raped two Spanish women, who poisoned themselves, unable to survive their dishonour ; Espinosa " stole all he found, more than 60,000 ducats ; in Arequipa he killed two Spaniards, and in the town of La Plata, he hanged an alderman and a constable because they had fought on the other side ; and on his way back to Cuzco, he burnt alive seven Indians because they had warned some Spaniards of his coming "— all this much to the displeasure of Gonzalo Pizarro, " who did not like such cruelties." Note how the lawless behaviour falls with equal harshness on Indian and Spaniard alike. Note, moreover, the sequel. The two adventurers were presently caught by the other side and hanged, " particularly " —says Garcilaso—" because of the burning of the seven Indians, burnt alive for no fault of theirs, which closed to them the door of their superiors' mercy."(2)

" During the summer of 1830 "—writes Captain Alexander —" the [Dutch] Governor of Surinam issued a proclamation, similar to those that have been promulgated from time to time, enjoining that no negro should smoke, or sing, or whistle in the streets of Paramaribo ; that on approaching a white man within five yards the negro must uncover his head ; that no negress is permitted to wear clothes above the waist, the breasts are to be exposed, and a petticoat from the waist to the knee is the only covering allowed. There are a few of our countrymen in Surinam, and even at their tables my informant said he was shocked to see the negresses in attendance with what ought to be sacred and concealed exposed—their bosoms."(3)

"This is most disgraceful"—cries out the Englishman, rightly indignant. But a similar attitude was observable in the British West Indies ; and the Frenchman Labat noted it carefully, though he himself was apt to take on a similar point of view when, discussing the economics of a sugar factory and mill, he speaks of Blacks as he would of cattle. The fact is that this attitude comes naturally to the rationalist. Grahame speaks of Blacks and Indians as " the two degenerate races." It is all part of the scientific, physical outlook on life, which set in with the eighteenth century and gave its masterpiece in Darwin's great book. Spanish thinkers looked upon these matters in a different light—which was not in the end less scientific. Sahagún's shrewd remarks, quoted in a previous chapter, on the influence of food on customs should be remembered. Blas de Valera, who did for Peru what Sahagún had done for Mexico, is no less impartial on the Indian, indeed one might suspect him of partiality to the Indian. As for skill and ability, he declares them outstanding, " since, though having no alphabet, they were able to understand many things the Egyptians, Greeks and Chaldeans understood thanks to it." He points out that they quickly learnt all European art and crafts, and adds : " We are duller in understanding the system of their books than they in understanding ours, for we have been dealing with them these seventy years and more, and are not able to disentangle the system and rules of their knots and accounts [*quipus*] while they in a short time are able to read our letters and reckon by our figures—which proves much ability." Finally in point of memory he also gives the prize to the native over the Spaniard. As for arms and the art of war, he is no less uncompromisingly favourable to the Indian. " For give me the most famous captains French or Spanish, without horses, harness, armour, with neither spear nor sword, neither guns nor other firearms, just with a shirt and a loincloth on, a sling for a girdle, and on the head, neither helmet nor vizor, but garlands of flowers or feathers, barefoot over bushes, rocks and thorns, for food nothing but grasses and roots, for a buckler a yard of matting on the left hand," and if in these circumstances, the French or Spanish captains won, " then should we be able to grant them the fame of valiant men among the Indians." (4)

Nor would the conquerors dissent from the friar's generous award, as many pages in Garcilaso testify. Four Spaniards were riding after a battle, " when they saw seven Indians appear over a small hill, handsome men, ready with their bows and arrows, who came to battle much beplumed and in gala array. Who, upon seeing the Spaniards, dispersed themselves so as to divide their enemies, and got ready to fight ; and though the Spaniards signalled to them not to fear, for they did not intend to fight, but be friends, the Indians refused any parley and joined issue with much spirit and bravery." Now mark these words : " The Spaniards, as they later explained, were ashamed and abashed to meet seven Indians on foot and barefoot, without defensive arms, while they were four horsemen well armoured and spear in hand." The Indians fought bravely and each Spaniard killed one Indian, though they had to fight hard for it, and when the three remaining Indians left the field, the Spaniards preferred not to follow them nor to celebrate the victory of having killed four Indians, " deeming it unworthy of them." (5)

The Spanish conqueror was often led to admire the Indian as a fighter. Garcilaso has recorded a splendid scene. After a battle between Indians and Spaniards, the Indians being defeated, " only a few captains remained fighting, preferring to die in the presence of their Inca rather than run under his eyes." A Spanish knight attacked one of them. The Indian seized the Spaniard's spear, wrenched it from his hands and left him disarmed. " Another gentleman, whom I also knew, who had been watching this singular battle, in which, since the Indian fought single-handed, he had abstained from intervening, seeing the Spaniard unspeared attacked the Indian with his spear. The Indian shook it off with the one he had in his hand, let this go, seized the second and held it as his own to defend himself against the two Spaniards whose names I omit out of deference for their descendants, one of whom studied grammar with me. Gonzalo Pizarro, who had been fighting elsewhere and had put his enemies to flight, happened to come close by, and seeing what was going on rushed in, shouting : ' Out of the way ! Out of the way ! ' for he saw the two Spaniards were closing on to the single Indian ; and they, recognizing Gonzalo Pizarro, stood aside, to see whether he would fare better or worse than they. The Indian stood up on the first spear, and with the second in his hand, received the Spaniard and struck the horse on the face, which made the horse rise on his hind legs and might have caused the rider to fall backwards. Seeing his foe thus embarrassed, the Indian let go his spear and seized that of Gonzalo Pizarro, to wrench it from him as he had done with the others. Gonzalo Pizarro passed his spear to his left hand, and drew with his right to cut off the Indian's hands. The Indian, seeing the sword, stooped to get hold of one of the spears. Upon which, the two Spaniards who were standing by, thinking ill of the Indian's daring, attacked him to kill him. Then Gonzalo Pizarro shouted again : ' He deserves no harm, but much honour and praise.' This made the two gentlemen stop, and the Indian, realizing that he had been saved by Gonzalo Pizarro, let go the spear which he had raised from the ground to signify his surrender, came forward and kissing Pizarro's right leg said : ' You are my Inca and I am your servant.' And henceforth he served him most loyally, and Gonzalo Pizarro loved him as his son."(6)

We know how strong was this link for a beaten Indian. As for the conquering Spaniard, here is what Garcilaso has to say in the course of his narrative of the disastrous expedition to the Amazon valley. " The hardships and hunger which Gonzalo Pizarro and his men had to undergo were so terrible that the four thousand Indians who took part in this discovery died of starvation, and among them, the Indian beloved of Gonzalo Pizarro who had seized two spears from two Spaniards as told above ; whose death Gonzalo Pizarro felt and wept as if he had been one of his brothers, and so he said many a time." Nor did this relationship between Indian and Spaniard necessarily spring from such chivalrous and soldierly feelings. In his parallel between Francisco Pizarro and Almagro, Garcilaso provides yet another anecdote which makes this clear. "Both were fond of favouring their servants and friends, and of enriching them and fostering their station and protecting them from danger. But the Marquess [Francisco Pizarro] was so eager in this that once, as they were passing a river known as the Ravine, the strong current swept away an Indian of his service, and the Marquess threw himself swimming behind him and brought him out of the water by the hair, in which he faced such a danger of the fury of water as no one in his army, whatever his youth or courage, would have dared to risk. And as some of his captains reproached him for his excessive daring, he answered that they did not know what it was to love a servant dearly."(7)

*　　*　　*

These facts should be remembered when trying to appraise the attitude of the Spaniard to the Indian. Unless such individual experiences are brought into the picture, the general view must fail to reflect the life of a people as individualistic as the Spaniard. There were in all this the elements of an easy blend of the two stocks of men. The blend began early, since the conquerors did not bring their wives with them. A considerable number of *mestizos* must have resulted everywhere from the first meeting of the two human strains—an offspring obscurely begotten and born, left to the care of their neglected mothers ; but this first wave of white blood must have passed finally into the native stock, for these children, left behind in most places by their adventurous fathers, would mate with natives, and recede into Indiandom. We know, however, of not a few cases in which the captain or soldier kept his children's mother and took his paternal responsibilities in earnest. In Peru, where the Inca or royal family constituted a more definite and exclusive aristocracy than in Mexico, there were many marriages of Spanish conquerors with *Coyas*, or women of the royal blood ; and, at least one in which an Inca man married a Spanish woman. This was Don Carlos

Inca, a grandson of Huaina Capac, who married Doña María Esquivel, born in Pizarro's birthplace, Truxillo, in Extremadura. We also know of conquerors, high and low, who honoured their concubines as if they were their wives, short of marrying them, which they abstained from doing only out of ambition and in the hope of a better marriage in Spain. Some of these Indian women were the founders of great Spanish families, such as Doña Elvira, the daughter of Maxiscatzin, one of the four *tlatoanis* of the Republic of Tlaxcala, whose daughter by Alvarado married into the highest Spanish nobility ; Doña Inés, the ex-concubine of Francisco Pizarro, whose marriage with Ampuero gave rise to the premier family of Peru ; the granddaughter of Manco Capac, who by her marriage with Oñes de Loyola (a nephew of St. Ignatius) was the stem of the noble family of Oropesa, and many others whose records are well ascertained.(8)

During those first days, many *mestizos* were therefore at the apex of society, even when illegitimate, as was often the case. After the murder of Francisco Pizarro, Diego de Almagro junior was declared Governor of Peru by all the " Almagrist " Spanish faction, then in the ascendancy, without anyone even thinking of objecting on the ground that he was not only a *mestizo*, but an illegitimate son, and the son of an Indian woman of Panama and not of Peru. Garcilaso, himself a *mestizo*, says of Diego de Almagro junior that he had been " the best *mestizo* born in the whole New World. He was a handsome man on a horse, in either style of riding." We gather from Garcilaso how in those early days the cities of the Indies saw the first crop of *mestizos* of noble blood, often illustrious also on their mother's side, and how carefully these youths were educated by their soldierly fathers. They came to be a kind of kernel of aristocracy. We see them acting collectively : " In 1581 the *mestizos*, sons of those Spaniards [killed in the battle of Salinas] and of Indian women, transferred the remains of their fathers to the City of Cuzco, and had them buried in a hospital where many Masses were said for their souls, and they gave many alms and performed many other pious works."(9)

*　　*　　*

As for the attitude of the Indians towards the Spaniards, it is no less complex. Feelings of both attachment and aversion were simultaneously generated by victory, oppression and ill-treatment. We know this from human nature in general, and from Garcilaso's Indian blood in particular. The Spaniards never found any difficulty in recruiting thousands of men for their hazardous discoveries and for their deadly civil wars. Sometimes, we read of Indians robbing Spaniards in unsavoury circumstances, such as during the night which followed the battle of Salinas, or worse still after the battle of Chupas, when many wounded died of exposure, having been despoiled of their armour and clothes by the Indians, who also killed many fugitives. But, all things considered, and since the strange and domineering people were indulging in civil war in the country which till then the Indians had enjoyed as their own, this behaviour of some of the less scrupulous Indians is easy to understand. The battle of Salinas, moreover, provides a valuable sidelight on the relations between the two peoples. The Indians had a plan : to wait till the end of the battle, and then fall upon the winning side and kill victors and vanquished indiscriminately. This plan failed because the Indians had no leader ; but also " because the Indians who were familiar servants of the Spaniards, owing to the natural loyalty they felt towards their masters, did not agree that they should die. [. . .] Owing to this contradiction, the ill intention which the non-familiar Indians had conceived had to be given up." These words, " familiar," " non-familiar " are revealing, for, taken in conjunction with the noble behaviour of the familiar Indians, they show the cordial relations which must have existed between Spanish master and Indian servant.(10)

These early days were perhaps the highwater mark of the intimacy between Spanish and Indian. After the first inrush of healthy and vigorous men, who seized their women where they found them—a period of obscure *mestizos*—the class rises to the top because all conquerors, no matter their origin, were ennobled by both deeds and booty ; and they sought their women at the top of the Indian society. As for the women, they seem to have entered into these alliances, though most of them were irregular, not only without constraint but even with eagerness. Garcilaso speaks of one, Juan de la Torre, a captain who "had married an Indian woman, the daughter of a *curaca* [chief]. The Indians, seeing themselves favoured by this relationship with a Spaniard, which they valued more than all their treasures, revealed to him a sepulchre of one of their ancient lords, containing more than 150,000 ducats worth of gold and fine emeralds." This was a regular marriage. But mere concubinage was a more frequent case. In at least one case, that of Francisco Pizarro, matrimony was blocked for political considerations, which can be perceived through the discreet phrases of his descendant Don Fernando Pizarro y Orellana in a "Memorial" to Philip II. "The Marquess left two children, by Doña Ines Toaillas, or Yupangui, daughter of the great lord of that empire, Guainacap, Don Gonçalo and Doña Francisca Pizarro. He was content to have them legitimized by a royal letter, not wanting the marriage to be celebrated in order to avoid all suspicion which those envious of his good fortune might conceive seeing him married to the heiress to those kingdoms." After Pizarro's death, his daughter Doña Francisca married her uncle Hernando Pizarro, "a prisoner in those days in the tower of Medina del Campo, for having carried out the death sentence on Don Diego de Almagro." And after Hernando's death, his *mestizo* widow married a scion of an old noble family, don Pedro Arias, son of the Count of Puñonrostro.(11)

Garcilaso (whose father was one of those who preferred to marry a Spanish heiress, though his concubine was of Inca blood, and who had therefore left his *mestizo* son illegitimate), writes on the subject with bitterness, but with accuracy ; and revealing important sidelights in a vivid and picturesque scene. When Pedro de Alvarado, himself the father of *mestizo* children by his concubine Doña Elvira, came back from Spain wealthy and powerful, married to a noble relative of Charles V's principal secretary of State, " he brought with him many noble women to marry them to the conquerors." He was received in Guatemala with much rejoicing, and festivals were offered him everywhere. During one of these

D

festivals, " it happened that, as all the conquerors were sitting in a big hall watching an evening entertainment, the ladies were looking from a door which commanded the whole length of the hall ; they stood behind the door, out of modesty, and because they did not want to be seen.   One of them said to the others : ' They say we are to marry these conquerors.' And another one : ' What !   These rotten old men ?   Not me, for sure.   Let the devil take them, for they all look as if they had run away from hell, all battered and broken, some lame, some one-armed, another one earless, another one with but one eye left, some with half a face, and the best off has it slashed about once, twice or even more times.'   Said the first : ' We are not going to marry them for their beauty, but so as to inherit their Indians, for, to see how old and tired they are, they will soon die, and then we shall be able to choose young men to suit ourselves, just as one changes an old pot for a new one.'   An old gentleman who happened to be close by, unnoticed by the ladies, whose eyes were on the hall, overheard the whole conversation ; and unable to stand any more of it, castigated the ladies for their good intentions, and told the men what he had heard. [. . .]   Then he went home, summoned a priest, and married an Indian noble-woman by whom he had two children, whom he legitimized so that they should inherit his Indians, and not the young man the lady would have chosen later, keeping his own children as servants."(12)

The voice of the disgruntled *mestizo* can already be heard in this tale.   Garcilaso goes on to say : " There have been some in Peru who have done the same, and married Indian women ; but they are few.   Most of them have justified the plans of that lady.   It is for their [*mestizo*] children to say whether they were right or not, for, from the hospitals in which they live, they see the children of others enjoy what their fathers won and their [Indian] mother and relations helped to win.   For in those early days, when the Indians saw an Indian woman who had just had a boy by a Spaniard the whole Indian family met to respect and serve the Spaniard as their idol, for having mixed with them ; and such Indians were of much help in the Conquest of the Indies.   One of the

Orders in Council on the conquerors of the New World was
that they were to enjoy their *repartimientos* for two lives, their
own and that of one son ; failing which the wife was to inherit
in preference to any natural son, as if these [women from
Spain] had done more than the [Indian] mothers to win the
land.   This was the reason why the lady was ready to marry
an old man in order to change him for a younger one
eventually."(13)

No clearer outline could be wished of the evolution which
led the *mestizos* from the height of society as the aristocracy
of the New World to the wilderness of poverty and illegitimacy.
We see them moving in the streets of Cuzco, as the scions
of the noble class, in many pages of Garcilaso ; going to
school at Canon Cuellar's, who " read grammar to the *mestizos*,
sons of noble and rich men of the city " ; being, in great
occasions, the object of special distinctions : " I ate twice at
his table, upon his command "—says Garcilaso, referring to
Gonzalo Pizarro. " His son Don Fernando, his nephew
Don Francisco, son of the Marquess, and I with them, ate
standing, the three of us, in that space which was left empty
between him and his guests, and he gave us off his plate what
we were to eat."   We can see the three *mestizo* boys (" I was
nine ") envied and looked up to by all present.(14)

But the position was undermined by a mixture of economic
and aristocratic considerations which Garcilaso describes.
His own is a case in point. " As my father's ' second life '
died early, we the remaining brothers were left without any
provision."   At the time he writes his history, he mentions
one " Francisco de Loaysa, who now lives in Cuzco, one of
the few conquerors' sons who enjoy the *repartimientos* of their
fathers " ; and though he does not explicitly say that Loaysa
is a *mestizo*, the context allows us to guess he was.   The third
phase, in which the Spanish women had the better over the
native, lasted for generations.   But the attraction of the
Spaniard to the Indian women soon returned, as Montesclaros
points out in 1612 (about the time Garcilaso wrote).   This
time, he says, the attraction was due not to scarcity but to a
surfeit of Spanish women.   There seem to have been other
reasons than those Montesclaros gives, for Don Andrés Hurtado

de Mendoza sent to Spain several married gentlemen who had their wives there, " though it is true that it was not their fault, but their wives' ; for though some of them had asked them to come and sent them much money for the voyage, they refused to obey their husbands so as not to leave Seville which is bewitching for all who know it, rather did they try to force them by law to come to Spain ; for rather than go to Peru, three of these wives, with whose husbands I was acquainted, lost the *repartimientos* which they would have inherited, worth more than one hundred thousand ducats a year ; and I could give the names were it fair to betray their honour and reputation."(15)

Whatever the reasons, the Spaniard came back to the Indian woman and this attraction was not always satisfied out of wedlock. " This year "—says the annalist of Potosí (1579)—" there came to govern Potosí Don Martín de Loyola, a nephew of St. Ignatius, who was married to an Indian princess, an heiress of Peru." But in general, the *mestizo* was losing ground and prestige, and even reputation ; and both official reports and historians begin to attribute all kinds of defects to him. They become, so we are told, the instruments of the white oppressors of the Indians. " Your Excellency must bear in mind "—writes Montesclaros to his successor— " that every one of these negroes, mulattoes and *mestizos* is worse than lightning towards the Indians, hence they are forbidden to live and converse with them, not only owing to the ill treatment, but also to the low habits which they communicate to the natives." Ulloa and Jorge Juan describe them as " haughty and very lazy people, full of vices and very ill inclined." In the course of an argument in defence of the Indians against those who accuse them of laziness in order to impose forced labour laws and practices on them, the two authors go further : " If to shun work and to be inclined to leisure and laziness were to be punishable by the *mita*, no one would deserve it more than the many *mestizos* who swarm in those countries, and who are useless, particularly when they have no definite craft. These half-castes deem it dishonourable to till the soil or do other humble work, and, therefore, the cities and townships are but a crowd of them, living on what they steal, or busy on such abominable doings that the paper should not be sullied by recording them." Solórzano Pereira is no more favourable : " Most of them turn out men of vicious and depraved ways, and it is they who cause the greatest harm and vexations to the Indians." And he backs his opinion with that of Father Joseph Acosta, as he might have done with nearly every author of the time.(16)

*   *   *

But surely there is no natural law which condemns the *mestizo* to be necessarily worse than any other kind of man ; even though this was believed to be the case by many other authors : " On these men "—writes Solórzano Pereira— " falls the blemish of the mixed colour and other vices which are as it were natural to them and sucked with their milk." At the time when the aptitude of the *mestizos* for religious orders was still a matter of discussion, a Chilean Bishop wrote to Philip II (January 20th, 1590) how out of " a number of *mestizos*, natural sons of noble conquerors of Chile, who had studied church matters, [. . .] three or four were ordained, all able men and of good example." And he praised them in another letter as " very virtuous and of good example, and proficient in the language of the natives ; persons of whom no one could say anything derogatory, and would to God that all the priests we have here were as good as they !" While in the same letter he wrote : " The persons whom I find most unworthy of the priesthood in this land are the Creoles and sons of owners of Indians, because they grow up very viciously, are inclined to evil and most unreliable."(17)

The fact was that most of the defects and vices attributed to the *mestizos* were the inevitable consequence of the social conditions in which they were bred. At the top, illegitimacy was the rule. Besides the many cases we have recorded, here is Solórzano Pereira's explicit statement : " The most frequent case is that they are born of adultery, or of other illicit and punishable alliances, for few honourable Spaniards marry Indian women or negresses, which defect makes them infamous, at any rate *infamia facti*." But it often happened that at the lower levels there was a good deal of illegitimacy also. This was an indirect result of the laws, and even more so of the practice with regard to forced labour, the burden of which fell on the poor Indians only. " From which abuse flows the fact that many Indian women forsake their Indian husbands and loathe their children and leave them helpless, when they see them submitted to tributes and personal services ; they desire love and treat better those they beget outside of wedlock by Spaniards or even by negroes, for they see them altogether free and exempt." And Solórzano Pereira comes very near stating that all *mestizos* and mulattoes are illegitimate, when, contrasting the fate of the Indian, subject to the *mita* and other personal and financial tributes, with the half-breeds, who are free, he argues : " Lasciviousness should not be more privileged than chastity, but rather the reverse ; those born in wedlock should be more favoured and privileged than illegitimate bastards."(18)

* * *

Illegitimacy, therefore, quite apart from colour, was an important feature of the society of the Indies. The illegitimate son is born with a grievance, not merely against both his parents, but against the society in which he is a misfit. The part played by illegitimate sons in human history deserves study. It would probably be found that a number of subversive, revolutionary men, those particularly whose urge was rather to destroy existing forms than to evolve new ones, were illegitimate sons. To be sure, there came to be so many illegitimate sons in the Indies that the social stigma attached to their irregular birth must have been somewhat blunted. But other circumstances came to set off this cause of appeasement. To begin with, the illegitimate son is generally brought up in a fatherless home, and this in itself was bound to produce incalculable effects on the *mestizos*, rich or poor, and therefore on a society in which there were so many of them. Nor can these effects have been limited to those every family man or woman would expect in such a situation ; for in this case, the absent father was of a different colour and blood and of a different class from the mother ; his orders, news, ways, were bound to be received as coming from a different world ; from a world, moreover, towards which the secret resentments of the outcast children were bound to converge. As in nearly every case there were legitimate sons as well, enjoying all the advantages of family, social prestige, class and colour, denied the *mestizo*, the knot of psychological tensions thereby created must have been particularly rich.

Nothing is more complex than the soul of a *mestizo*. Compared with it, the subtlest soul of a pure blood—white, black or Indian—is as transparent as water. The typical feature of the *mestizo* soul is its swift-changing hue, calling to mind those iridescent tinctures or shot silks which change from green to blue and react to the slightest movement in the incidence of light. This feature has often been put to the debit of the *mestizo* as shiftiness and unreliability. " Pray, be seated, *gentlemen* "—a South American President is said to have requested the Minister of a neighbouring republic known for its predominantly *mestizo* population. " But, I am alone, Mr. President." " Oh "—smiled the President—" you people of your country, you are always each at least two." Now, the President meant it in a neighbourly, i.e., in a poisonous way. But he was right, though not in intention. The *mestizo* is always at least two : a White and an Indian.

This means a world of possible swift changes, because there is in him a world of possible attitudes. The *mestizo* carries with him the vigour of the conqueror, the leisurely pride of the settler, the creative charity of the early friar, the vicious, lascivious epicureanism of the later friar, the greed of the *corregidor*, the barbarous contempt of the brutal priest for the passive and long-suffering Indian ; the tacit assertion of the right to rule which the abler stock of men assumes towards its subjects, all the virtues and vices of the Spaniard. But he does not carry them in their natural and spontaneous state. All these features in him live constantly under the inner opposition from his other self, the Indian, object and often victim of them. The Indian in him is just as rich and complex as the White. He is subservient and faithful to that White who has conquered him ; ready to flatter him and to shape himself and truth and the world to please the White ; and he is proud of his own native blood and history, which in Mexico and Peru had given rise to two great well-ordered empires ; he is aloof, contemptuous of the White intruders who came to occupy the land in which he, the Indian, was rooted ; distant, strong in his superoriental capacity for suffering, and in his patience to weave a destiny out of threads too long and thin for a Spaniard to see ; at times he is wildly resentful ; grateful at times ; now confiding and credulous, like a child, now as immovable in his perennial wisdom as the oldest of men. The tension within the soul of the *mestizo* between the two strains of men living together under his skin in the closest intimacy could not be more acute. But it was a rich tension, vibrating with the mutual attractions and repulsions of powerful opposites. And it might have resolved itself into something wonderful if left to mature in a healthy moral climate. Unfortunately, the moral climate was unhealthy. The two men, the White and the Indian, come to live together from those two continents of the spirit so distant from each other, had to breathe a social air which challenged them both, humiliated them both, by setting them socially aside, always as half-castes, often also as bastards. Under this pressure and this challenge, the complex tensions within the *mestizos* soon turned aggressive. They answered challenge with counter-challenge, and kept a kind of permanent warfare against the environment, as a matter of habit, whatever the environment might be. Indian to the White, the *mestizo* was white to the Indian. But in both these attitudes, he benefited from the advantages and suffered from the handicaps of his other blood. Indeed, the *mestizo* was an Indian who, at war with the White, was in alliance with a White ; and a White who, at war with the Indian, was in alliance with an Indian— alliances which nothing could break, since the two allies co-existed within the same skin.

Much of what we hear or read about the *mestizos* becomes clear in this light ; much, for instance, that we read in the chronicles of the early *mestizos*, such as Garcilaso or Fernando de Alvarado Tezozomoc, or of those of the middle period, such as Don Fernando de Alva Ixtlilxochitl, or again in those of the *mestizos* who preached emancipation. The evident satisfaction with which Don Fernando de Alva tells the story of his ancestor, the turbulent Prince of Tetzcuco, is in this early *mestizo* tempered and balanced by an equal pride in his Spanish blood ; *mestizos* can always be harsh in their account of Spanish misdeeds against their Indian kinsmen, yet are always proud of the high and noble deeds of the Spaniards ; a combination due less to impartiality than to a succession of strongly felt passions on different watersheds of their split souls. Garcilaso, for instance, now proudly asserts that he was an Indian, now betrays the contempt of a Castillian for the Indian rabble : "They made their Indians and negroes ride on their horses, giving them spears and halberds, and formed them in a regular squadron, and so that the enemy should not realise that they were a rabble, they put in the vanguard three or four rows of Spaniards, the best armed, to hide the negroes and Indians."(19)

In the later *mestizo* writers, the anti-Spanish passion pre-dominates along with a tendency to idealise the Inca civiliza-tion which is characteristic of the epoch. Here is a typical page from a Mexican *mestizo*, Fernando Pimentel Ixtliulxuchitl, dated October 25th, 1821 : "The glory most sublime, the truly singular and peerless, the invaluable among many, whereof the robbery ill-disguised with the name of conquest despoiled the Americas, undoubtedly was the truly paternal government which, achieving the complete happiness of everyone of the individuals of the Inca empire, brought about the happiness of the empire itself, preserved it for at least five centuries, and would still prevail had not Atahuallpa dared conquer Quito by force, and had not the robbers arrived on the occasion which that Inca's disorders afforded them." Note the passion, the superlatives heaped on top of each other, glory *most* sublime, the *complete* happiness of *everyone* ; the robbery and the robbers. Note the contradictions : the Inca empire would have gone on being happy—he was going to say—if the Spaniards had not conquered it, but his Indian pride does not let him admit this, and so he hints that had Atahuallpa behaved, the Spaniards would not have conquered ; but then, his whole construction crashes, since the most sublime glory of the Inca empire gave forth Atahuallpa's bloodthirsty reign without any foreign interference. Our fiery *mestizo* is unaware of the contradiction. He is not thinking. He is feeling. He is feeling Indian emotions with the heat of a Spanish temperament. In the strong Spanish saying, he is breathing through his wound.

Note, moreover, that this fierce *mestizo* of Spaniard and Mexican, as he stoops to gather stones from his motherland to throw at his fatherland, carefully choses them from the Inca, and not from the Aztec, ruins. A tacit confession of his belief that the Aztec civilization was not such as to stand his extraordinary claims. So that, unknown to him, this Ixtlilxuchitl who stoops to gather stones against Spain is pushed thereto by the Pimentel in him, who, as a good Spaniard, is longing for a civil war, and finds a good pretext in the different colour and shape of eyes he borrows from the Ixtlilxuchitl who lives with him inside the same skin. And so both Pimentel and Ixtlilxuchitl sign this paper, in which one can read further : " Now is the time to recall the greatness, the knowledge which was to be found among our most lovable Indians before the iniquitous Conquest, to restore true happiness to some, and impart it to the rest, the more so as we all love the divine religion of the Crucified One, the only One Who can perfect what otherwise could not have attained its full perfection." A statement which of course again destroys his hot accusation about the robbery ill disguised as a conquest, to which he owed not only whatever white blood he had, but that religion he loved and thought indispensable to fulfil the " complete " felicity of the Inca rule.(20)

Such were the contradictions in which the soul of the *mestizo* was apt to live. Towards the Indian, they must outwhite the White. " They declare themselves vassals of the king of Spain "—write Ulloa and Jorge Juan—" and though *mestizos*, they take pride in being Spaniards and in descending from Indians, in such a curious way that, though they have an equal share of both, they are most bitter enemies of the Indians, who are their own blood." This enmity towards the Indian was not born merely of a desire to assert his white blood and status over the downtrodden and conquered people ; but also of an equally ardent desire to avenge on the beaten people the humiliation of the defeat which the

Indian within the *mestizo* felt more bitterly than the pure Indian by all the Spanish blood in him. Similarly, when he took up a challenging attitude against the Spaniard, as, despite Ulloa and Jorge Juan's optimistic report, the *mestizo* often did, both individually and collectively, what animated him was not merely his desire to assert his Indian blood and to restore to it its pre-conquest proud and independent stature —a desire stiffened and stimulated by his own Spanish impulses—but also the urge to avenge on the Spaniard the humiliation of the Spaniard within him, a misfit of a conqueror, and a mean exploiter and tormentor of Indians.(21)

The two sides of his soul acted thus upon each other like the two plates of an electric condenser, raising each other's pitch, and therefore the tension between the two. The somewhat shallow and wilful enmity of the white Creole against the European Spaniard was enriched and deepened in the *mestizo* by all the unfathomable injuries and memories of the repressed and oppressed Indian, while the passive aloofness of the pure Indian borrowed a passion and a purpose from the Spanish blood which flowed together with his own in the veins of the half-caste.

It is easy to see to what a rich gamut of states of mind, feelings and emotions this set of inner tensions could lead, according to the individual condition of mind and character, the upbringing and social rank, the ups and downs of fortune, and the thousand petty incidents of life, when the subtle and complex soul of the *mestizo* came into friction or collision with a subtle and complex society as variegated as that of the Indies. The chief feature of this psychological situation was its extreme mobility and instability : no relation to the turbulence and gaiety of the negro, to the energy of the mulatto, still less to the impassivity of the ever silent pure Indian. The mobility and instability of the *mestizo* are all inward. They are due to a constant ebb and flow between the opposite currents in his life blood, and to the ever unexpected way in which they will react to outer challenges. Now fiercely pro-Indian, now contemptuous of the native, at one time as proud a Spaniard as a pure Castillian, at another a violent opponent of the Spanish tyranny, the *mestizo* will be the tortured and twisted stem in which the sap from the new earth rises through the Indian to meet the sunrays from the Spanish foliage in the grafted tree of that complex life ; the centre of all the ideas, feelings, emotions, movements for or against everything, the only spirit wide enough, tormented enough, fully to incarnate the history of the Spanish New World.

Chapter VIII

THE MULATTO ELEMENT AND THE CASTES

ILLEGITIMACY was even more frequent among mulattoes than among *mestizos*. The Indian, after all, drew some prestige from the imperial houses and Courts, which the Spaniards saw in the light of their European, knightly experience. The negroes of the New World were all actual or enfranchized slaves. Sin was therefore the origin of all half-colours between White and Black. But when did sin ever stand in the way of man's desires ? The rich Creoles soon discovered the outstanding qualities of the negro woman as a priestess of Venus. Beauty, rhythm, and all those mysterious magnetic forces which draw men to women had in this case to triumph over forbidding social barriers. It follows that, in the nature of things, only outstanding negro women could hope to win in the struggle ; and therefore that the mulatto was the outcome of a process of natural selection on the maternal side. " It is a mistake "— writes Labat—" to believe that we understand negro beauty to consist in the deformity of their face, their thick lips, their flat noses. If this kind of taste was ever fashionable in Europe, it was never so in the Islands ; there, one asks for regular features. The Spaniards, above others, look closely into the matter, and they will not haggle over a few hundreds of dollars in order to secure a beautiful negress."(1)

The blend was apt to make the Anonymous Visitor, a good connoisseur of feminine beauty, wax lyrical. " Coloured women here [Martinique], as in St. Lucía and Trinidad, are a much finer race than their fellows in the old English islands. The French and Spanish blood seems to unite more kindly and perfectly with the negro than does our British stuff. We eat too much beef and absorb too much porter for a thorough amalgamation with the tropical lymph in the veins of a black ; hence our mulatto females have more of the look of very dirty white women than that rich oriental olive which distinguishes the haughty offspring of the half blood of French or Spaniards. I think for gait, gesture, shape and air, the finest women in the world may be seen on a Sunday in Port of Spain. The rich and gay costume of these nations sets off the dark countenances of their mulattoes infinitely better than the plain dress of the English."(2)

There was in any case a lesser distance between the White and the Black than between either and the Indian. The beauty and lasciviousness of the negress was too much for the White—whether Spanish, French or English. "The attire of this baser sort of people of *Blackmores* and *Mulatta's* is so light, and their carriage so enticing, that many *Spaniards* even of the better sort (who are too prone to Venery) disdaine their Wives for them." So wrote Gage of Mexico ; while Labat wrote of the mulattoes of the French West Indies : "Their numbers would even be bigger in our Islands, without the punishments inflicted on those who make them ; for negresses are of their nature very lascivious, and white men are hardly less so, and as they find it very easy to satisfy their passions with these creatures, one would see nothing but mulattoes, wherefrom many disorders might flow, had not the King met the danger by condemning those who are proved to be their fathers to a fine of a thousand pounds of sugar "—a meet punishment for such a sin. As for the English West Indies, here is Moreton : "It is quite usual for a Creole gentleman after dinner to send to the field for one of his favourite wenches, who is instantly hurried home and conveyed to his chamber (or if he has a wife, to some other apartment) piping hot and drowned with perspiration, in which condition he enjoys the savoury object ; after which he takes a nap for an hour or so, and she returns to labour till night : thus he takes one almost daily in rotation, and roves with as much ease and dignity as a plenipotentiary through raptures of delight." Moreton adds that, as a result of this way of life, "in one family I have seen white, mestee, quadroon and mulatto children, all brothers and sisters playing together." Nor was profligacy the only cause of union between negroes and Englishmen. Dickson reports that "many white men [in Barbados] are not ashamed to live in habits of *intimacy* with the female domestic servants " ; while the Anonymous Visitor, praising St. Christopher as the island in which, with perhaps the exception of Grenada, the free-coloured people

were best treated, adds : " There are instances here of respectable white and coloured persons intermarrying, which is a
conquest over the last and most natural of all prejudices."(3)

The mating of a black man with a white woman was
undoubtedly a much rarer occurrence, owing to the social
relations prevailing between the two stocks. But it must have
occurred more frequently than meets the eye. Labat records
some curious cases, and avers that, but for deliberate abortion,
" the case would be much less rare." Miranda has written a
pathetic page on one he observed in the United States. " On
the left bank of the said Cape-fear river is the house and estate
of the American general Howe, in which (while he enjoys a
life of dissipation elsewhere) live his unhappy family ; for
his wife is on a footing of divorcee, and a lovely daughter of
his, 18 years of age, has just had two children by one of his
black slaves. Oh Lord, what human nature, and what laws
to afflict it ! "(4)

*　　　*　　　*

In Spanish territories the case cannot have been rare either,
both because there were many poor whites and because the
number of free, often prosperous negroes, was much greater,
absolutely and relatively, than in new world territories ruled
by other nations. The Blacks lived in fact in a closer com-
munion with the Whites than did the Indians. This was due
in part to the more open or, as we now say, extravert type of
their character ; in part to the fact that they came by sea
and entered by the harbours, where many of them remained
in domestic service, or engaged in crafts looked down upon by
the paler sort. The influence of the Black on the White in
Spanish lands overseas may be observed in more ways than
one. Ulloa and Jorge Juan, for instance, mention the habit
of smoking and offering ready-lit cigars which in Cartagena,
they say, " the ladies of distinction learn from childhood, and
it cannot be doubted that they borrow it from their wet nurses,
who are their own black slaves." Nor is it likely that this was
the only habit the rich Whites learnt from their black slaves.
" Hardly born "—writes Azara of the Creoles of the Plata—
" they are handed over by their parents necessarily to black
or dusky women, who take care of them for six or more years,

and then to small mulatto boys, from whom they never see or hear anything worthy of imitation, nothing but that false idea that the object of money is to be spent, and that to be noble and generous means to squander, destroy and do no work."(5)

But there is an even more significant instance of the influence of Black on White. In their description of Cartagena Ulloa and Jorge Juan write that " a number of odd features are also to be observed with regard to condolences, funerals and ceremonies in connection with death, one of which is the greatness and lordly ostentation which everyone tries to observe in such cases, even at the expense of his own comfort. When the dead man is a person of distinction, the body is laid on a sumptuous catafalque erected in the main room of the house, surrounded by a number of burning church candles, and so it remains for twenty-four hours or more, during which time the doors of the house are never closed, so that the persons who may wish enter and leave at any time ; and in general, all the women of the low classes of the city are in the habit of going to weep for the dead man ; they arrive dressed in black, usually towards nightfall or in the course of the night, and so enter the room where the body is lying in state, come close to it, and sometimes kneeling and other times standing, and in most cases as if they were going to embrace it, they begin their wails with a weeping air, mixed with exorbitant yells ; through which they let one understand that they call the dead man by his name, and after some exclamations, without changing their tone nor abating their cries, they go on to relate all the qualities, good or ill, the dead man possessed ; not excepting from this lamentable report all the impure habits and weaknesses which they knew him to be afflicted with ; in all accuracy and with every possible detail and circumstance, so that a general confession could not have been more individual. When the women engaged in this exercise are tired [. . .] they withdraw to one of the corners of the room, where the afflicted family have put at their disposal a vessel of brandy and another of wine, and they drink of whatever they prefer ; but as soon as they leave the side of the body, other women arrive ; and so they succeed each other till there are no more from the outside. Then the ceremony is carried on by the slave domestic servants, and those who had been familiar with the household, through the whole night ; so that it is easy to imagine what confusion will be caused by such a crowd of wailing women. When the funeral is over, and it takes place amidst the same loud disorder, the mourners remain in the house for nine days ; and the victims, men and women, are supposed not to move from the room where they receive the condolences of all. Those who have relations of friendship or family with them are supposed to accompany them during those nine nights from sunset to sunrise, so that regret is sincere in all concerned."(6)

These curious ways, in which there is no doubt a Spanish element, notably in the gathering of the family and intimate circle to receive their friends, nevertheless contains so many elements utterly foreign to Spain that a negro influence must be suspected. Haenke's description of a funeral gathering among the negroes of Lima would appear to confirm this view. " The tribe gathers together when a corporal or a ' twenty-four,' or one of their wives dies. There they honour the dead body which lies with four candles burning. The sons and daughters place themselves at the foot of the bier, and at the sides the relations, addressing themselves from time to time to the dead person. The mourners jump and turn around, stopping now and then to murmur some prayers of their rites in their native language. Everyone who comes contributes half a real for the expenses of the funeral, and for the drink distributed, which generally is cane liquor. Before drinking they offer the full glass to the face of the body, and address him in a long discourse as if to offer him the drink. The body's libation being supposed, the vessel is passed to the more intimate mourners ; and so on to the last person present, keeping the most punctilious accuracy as to seniority. At last, drinking, singing, and dancing, they end the ceremony in tears."(7)

* * *

This element of turbulence and liveliness was perhaps the chief contribution of the Blacks to the life of the New World, in contrast with the Indian who supplied the quiescent and passive attitude. It is not possible to attribute exclusively to the negroes the unseemly dances and masquerades which used to make a somewhat incongruous festival of the Corpus Christi procession in Mexico ; for negro influence was less felt in Mexico than in any other kingdom of the Indies ; moreover, dances and masquerades have always been an element of Corpus Christi celebrations in Christian Europe, probably a carry over from pagan festivals in connection with mid-summer. The unseemliness of these dances had already been condemned by Fray Juan de Zumárraga, first archbishop of Mexico, in 1544. " It is a thing of great shamelessness and lack of reverence that before the Holy Sacrament masked men, dressed like women, should dare appear dancing and jumping with unseemly and lascivious movements, with much noise, cutting across the hymns of the Church, representing profane triumphs, such as that of the god of love, so indecent, and even to honest people so shameful, to look at." The archbishop condemns " that such things should be ordered to be done, at no small cost to the natives, the settlers, the workers and the poor, compelling them to pay for the festival." There may well be a charitably veiled hint of some African origins in the following words : " Though in other lands and among other people this habit so vain, profane and gentile might be tolerated, it can on no account be suffered in this new Church."(8)

Despite the archbishop's efforts, the custom was revived after his death, since in 1585, the third Mexican Church Council felt bound to prohibit " the dances, balls, shows and profane songs," though allowing " those on sacred history or other things that are holy and useful for the soul." But nothing proves the persistence of the habit and the negro influence on it better than Haenke's description of a Corpus Christi procession in Lima towards the beginning of the nine-teenth century, in which the negroes took a boisterous part, " some with their heads adorned with cocks' feathers, others with boards on their arms and sticks in their hands, simulating a kind of battle, striking each other in tune with the music on their would-be shields [. . .] others imitating kings and queens, marching under parasols with a whole array of servants and with a gravity and a measured step which provoked

laughter in everybody." And the German observer concludes : " They are not without a good sense of fun for
buffoonery, these poor people, who thus forget their slavery
and present several of the ways of their fatherland."(9)

*   *   *

All authors are agreed about the strong negro influence on
dancing in the Indies. The most eloquent on the subject is
Labat, whose fierce frowns are never dark enough to hide the
secret glimmer of pleasure in his eyes as he describes the
Calenda, the favourite dance of the negro slaves, of which he
says : " The Spaniards have learnt it from the negroes, and
dance it all over America in the same manner as the negroes."
The French slave masters had forbidden it because " the
postures and the movements of this dance are most indecent,"
but the negroes danced it all the same, and " children hardly
able to stand try to imitate their fathers and mothers whom
they see dancing it, and would pass whole days in this exercise."
Having described to his heart's content the " gestures altogether lascivious " of this dance, the French friar goes on to
say : " It is easy to see from this abridged description how
contrary to modesty this dance is. Nevertheless it is so much
to the taste of the Spanish Creoles of America, and so frequently
in use with them, that it makes up the best part of their diver-
sions, and enters even into their devotions. They dance it
in their churches, and in their processions, and their nuns never
fail to dance it on Christmas Eve on a stage raised in their
choir, opposite their railings, which are open, so that the
people may have their share of the joy which these good souls
evince upon the birth of their Saviour."(10)

French wit is too trenchant. *He who looks most sees least,*
says a Gallegan proverb. " It is true "—Labat goes on to
say with his pawky humour—" that they do not admit any
man to dance so pious a dance with them. I am even ready
to believe that they dance it with a pure intention, but how
many onlookers are there who do not consider the matter as
charitably as I do ? " The French are too conscious, too
differentiated and intellectual to live freely without sin.
Holiness or sin are their only two possibilities. Not so with

other peoples, such as the Spaniards (or the English or the Russians, i.e., the three European suburbans) whose life is too much of a unity for them ever to dwell either in the holy or in the sinful corner of it. These nuns, well, they were dancing with their whole being, and that was good enough for them. Moreover, French dancing falls from the brain to the feet and the dancer is but a geometric figure of the feminine sex ; while Spanish dancing rises from the feet towards the whole body of the dancer, who is nothing less than a whole woman, body and soul ; and it enters the feet from the earth— which adds a peculiar significance to the fact that the *Calenda* should have become so popular in the Indies in the midst of a people whose Spanish strain came from an earth so rich in dancing rhythms.(11)

*   *   *

All this, of course, shows a certain amount of absorption of negro blood. The mulatto was an abundant type particularly in the part of the Indies round the New World Mediterranean, i.e., the Gulf of Mexico, Darién, Paria and the Isles, with a fair amount of influence also towards Peru in the direction of Lima. They were often well-to-do craftsmen, and in Lima at any rate, ranked above Indians and even *mestizos*, and seem to have enjoyed an independent and, on the whole, honourable status. They were, however, considered by most friars and Viceroys as dangerous enemies of the Indians. They were a most active part of the population, even though keeping a way of living of their own, with a peculiar sense of what was seemly. This was particularly in the English and the French West Indies. " As for mongrel women "—says Moreton of Jamaica—" though the daughters of rich men, and though possessed of slaves and estates, they never think of marriage, their delicacy is such, for they are extremely proud, vain and ignorant, that they despise men of their own colour ; and though they have their amorous desires abundantly gratified by them and black men secretly, they will not avow their connections." Moreton has a poor opinion of what he calls " mongrels." " All mongrels, male and female, have a vast share of pride and vanity, baseness and ingratitude in their composition [. . .] the men, if born to estates or properties (as many are) are much of the same nature of the illiterate white Creole men. [. . .] When those spurious cubs, having no trades, squander what their infatuated parents bequeathed them, they turn out the most thieving, pilfering vagrants ; for never having practised any industry, but beggared themselves by their profligacy and dissipation, Creole fashion, they are quite ignorant ever after of the ways and means to earn their livelihoods, industriously and honestly."(12)

The general picture in the Spanish Indies was quite different, because the offspring of the mixed unions was generally absorbed into the crafts. But most mulattas lived on their beauty, seeking to rise in the scale of colour. Moreover, should the negro woman be a slave, the offspring, by a free man in Spanish lands, was free. This, of course, created a kind of premium on the mating with Whites, already favoured by social prestige, wealth and colour prejudices and advantages. Ulloa and Jorge Juan report that " these *mestizo* or mulatto women from the second to the fourth or fifth degree give themselves over to a licentious life, though they themselves do not consider it as such, for it is indifferent to them to be married with an equal or to live in concubinage [i.e., with a superior in rank or colour]. But the corruption in those countries is such that they think it more honourable to take the latter course when they can obtain advantages that they would not be able to reach through matrimony. Nor are mulatto or *mestizo* women the only ones to keep this kind of life, for it is also found among those who having already come out completely from the race of Indians or negroes, are reputed and held as Spanish ; and in proportion as the quality of each is higher, so do they endeavour to give themselves only to persons of a higher rank ; so that a person with an employment either in the political, civil or ecclesiastical sphere will usually incline to a Spanish woman, possibly without considering the injury he does to the family, or to a woman of distinguished birth ; but those who are not in such circumstances will be content with women who are not so near to being Spanish [i.e., white]."(13)

Still the standing of the mulatto rose as time went by, as a result of this readiness of the community to absorb coloured people into regularly constituted families, and also because in most towns the mulattoes were able to thrive as skilled workers. "Superior to mechanic employs, and averse to them, both from pride and indolence, the Spaniard and the blanched Creole, leave such to be pursued by their darker fellow-subjects, who are industrious in their respective callings, as shoemakers, taylors, barbers, free hired servants, keepers of dram-shops, carpenters and little retail-traders." So writes Gillespie of Buenos Aires, and he adds : " There were two blacksmiths in the city, who were very slow in the work but solid in the finish." This application made the mulatto a useful member of the community, sometimes in the country, wielding the driving whip over the slaves, more frequently in the town as a prosperous and well thought-of craftsman. We can remember that mulatto craftsman pictured by Ulloa and Jorge Juan, walking about the streets of Lima, dressed in a " rich gold or silver tissue, of such a quality that no man of higher rank could have found one better."(14)

This shows how the country had gradually assimilated her African stock, and up to a point, freed it from its initial serfdom.   There is a page in Frézier, describing the festivities of the mulattoes of Pisco, which deserves quotation because it illustrates the wealth and ease of the land, the perfect assimilation of the mulatto to the Spanish life and culture of the Indies, and the provincialism with which this otherwise intelligent Frenchman could dismiss as unworthy of him what he did not understand.   " The plenty of provisions the country affords, together with a good trade, makes the inhabitants easy ; so that they often divert themselves with public shows, such as bull-feasts, plays and masquerades.   I was there at the time when the mulattoes kept a festival in honour of Our Lady of Mount Carmel : those poor people, like all the other Creolian Spaniards, that is, the mixed races, are so much infatuated with a thousand apparitions, either true or false, that they make them the principal object of their devotion. [. . .] On Thursday the 14th of September, the mulattoes began the solemnity with a play called *El Príncipe Poderoso* or

The Powerful Prince written by a Spanish-European poet. The depraved taste of that nation leading them to mix in their shows things sacred with profane ; I observed that in this they had indulged their natural genius, beyond the bounds of good sense and decency : in short, nothing could be seen more ridiculous than the decoration of the farther part of the stage, the point of perspective thereof terminating in an altar, on which was the image of Our Lady of Mount Carmel, with lighted candles about it ; and all the actors began their prologue kneeling, with a dedication of the play to the Blessed Virgin. One would have judged by this pious invocation that the play would be to the edification of the spectators ; but I was sufficiently undeceived of that notion, when I beheld on the stage the disagreeing medley of Sigismund's piety embracing a Crucifix, to which he made his application under an adversity, and the licentiousness of buffoons in the play ; and of interludes or little farces between the acts, which consisted of gross obscenities, but a little wrapped up or disguised."

There were more shocks in store for our Frenchman on Spanish soil. " Sunday night they acted a comedy of the life of St. Alexius, written by the Spanish poet, Moreto, which I have since found in the tenth volume of the collection of Spanish plays printed in Madrid with licence in the year 1658, by the name of *Nuevo Teatro de Comedias varias de diferentes Autores*, or *The New Theatre of variety of Plays by sundry authors*." Words fail him to condemn the " depraved taste " of this comedy : " The extravagancy of those conceits, and of the persons the poet brings upon the stage, was to us Frenchmen, who happened to be present at that spectacle, a subject the more ridiculous, in regard that we were used to correct pieces [. . .] there is no man that has travelled in Spain but is acquainted with the taste of their dramatic poems, in which the subject of devotion has always some part." Frézier castigates this bad taste of the Spaniards with a dose of Boileau ; then goes on : " As for the particular faults in that piece, the distance of time and place therein is shocking. St. Alexius in the first and last act is at Rome, and during the second he is several years visiting the Holy Land ; however that variety is not looked

upon as a fault among the Spaniards." And a new dose of
Boileau is administered. Yet Frézier is bound to confess that
" in other respects, in such a little town, nothing better could
be expected as to the decorations of the theatre, which was
contracted into a small compass, after our manner ; and it
may be said, that the actors, being of the meanest of the people,
for they were all mulattoes and who did not make acting their
profession, played their parts well enough, according to the
Spanish taste." Frézier thus records how deeply Spanish
culture had penetrated into the body politic of the Indies ;
but he is also led to note certain facts which do not tally with
his prejudices. It was for long an article of faith that all
Spanish life must be oppressed by the power of the Church
and that the Inquisition must be busy everywhere " spreading
gloom, " as good Sir Clements Markham would put it. But
here is Frézier's quandary : " I observed in their interludes,
or little farces between the acts, an affectation of introducing
doctors in their robes, representing extravagancies. I do not
understand how the churchmen, who are almost the only
persons entitled doctors, have the complaisance to admit of
those sports ; for if there be any impertinent part, the man in
the cap is sure to have a share in it."(15)

*   *   *

These men, who for their enjoyment staged two Spanish
classic plays in a small provincial city down the coast of Peru,
were thoroughly absorbed into the Spanish life and culture of
the Indies. Nothing suggests that they lived under an inner
tension similar to that which made the *mestizos* so taut and so
shifty. Like the *mestizos* they were a hybrid type of men ;
but unlike the *mestizos* they had no earth, no tradition on
which to draw in order to load the activity of the white blood
with the resentment of the native. Their negro blood came
to add vigour and turbulence to the active urge of the white.
But this vigour and this turbulence were there, so to speak, in
their own right, and sought no common aim as such. The
Blacks had suffered and were still suffering daily wrongs
almost as abominable as those the Indians had undergone.
But whereas out of the wrongs done to the Indian, the White

within the *mestizo* could and did build a collective wrong done to the Indian as a whole, the Black within the mulatto had no special collective political grievance to hand over to the White within him, for the Blacks were but individuals cut off from their native soil, while the Indians were a people arrested and deflected in their development by the onrush of the Whites ; and so, while the sufferings of the Indians acquired a political significance and a collective impetus in the heart of the *mestizos*, the sufferings of the black slaves remained past and inert like a dust of nameless memories.

* * *

It was but natural that the negroes should enter into as close a relationship with the Indians as with the Whites. Though there were in many ways closer natural affinities between African and European than between either and Indian, natives of Africa and natives of America were drawn together both because they were at a stage of culture less dissimilar and because socially and economically both were exploited and oppressed peoples. There is perhaps no striking likeness between the ways of the negro and those of the Indian ; both, however, were closer to the earth and to its animic forces than were the soldierly and lettered Spaniards. Labat, recording that the negro slaves of Major Crips in St. Christopher swore to him not to hang themselves, says that " this oath consists in picking up some earth which they put on their tongue after raising their eyes and hands to the sky and striking their chests." This ceremony is almost identical with the Aztec oath as described by Sahagún. But beyond this and other parallel ways which no doubt might be discovered between two peoples still very close to nature, Indians and Blacks were very different. The Black was fond of life and went out to meet it. He was merry by nature and needed no artificial stimulant to arouse him to dance and song. The Indian was turned inwards, silent and passive and as a means of escape he sought the release of inebriation.(16)

The Anonymous Visitor has set down his impression of this contrast in a page worth quoting. " The amazing contrast between these Indians and the negroes powerfully arrested my attention. Their complexions do not differ so much as their minds and dispositions. In the first, life stagnates ; in the last, it is tremulous with irritability. The negroes cannot be silent ; they talk in spite of themselves. Every passion acts upon them with strange intensity ; their anger is sudden and furious, their mirth clamorous and excessive, their curiosity audacious, and their love the sheer demand for gratification of an ardent animal desire. Yet by their nature they are good-humoured in the highest degree, and I know nothing more delightful than to be met by a group of negro girls, and be saluted with their kind ' How d'ye, massa ? how d'ye, massa ?' their sparkling eyes and bunches of white teeth. It is said that even the slaves despise the Indians, and I think it very probable ; the latter are decidedly inferior as intelligent beings. Indeed their history and existence form a deep subject of speculation. The flexibility of temper of the rest of mankind has been for the most part denied to them ; they wither under transportation, they die under labour ; they will never willingly or generally amalgamate with the races of Europe or Africa ; if left to themselves with ample means of subsistence, they decrease in numbers every year ; if compelled to any kind of improvement, they reluctantly acquiesce, and relapse with certainty the moment the external compulsion ceases. They shrink before the approach of other nations as it were by instinct ; they are now not known in vast countries of which they were once the only inhabitants ; and it should almost seem that they have been destined by a mysterious Providence to people a third part of the globe, till in the appointed time the New World should be laid open to the Old, and the ceaseless and irresistible stream of population from the East should reach them and insensibly sweep them from off the face of the earth."(17)

*　　　*　　　*

Though too radical in his pessimistic conclusions about the Indians, these observations of the anonymous Englishman register an adequate estimate of the differences between the two coloured peoples of the New World. Such differences of course worked for rather than against sexual attraction.

Humboldt speaks in similar terms. " There hardly exists a more striking contrast than that between the impetuous vivacity of the negroes of the Congo and the apparent phlegm of the copper-coloured Indians. It is particularly this sense of contrast which leads Indian women to prefer negroes not only to the men of their own race but even to the Europeans." This natural attraction was indirectly fostered by the laws and even more so by the practices which weighed heavily on the Indians. For in actual fact the relative fate of the two subject peoples in the Spanish Indies found its level according to the character of the people concerned rather than to the laws. While in law the negroes were slaves and the Indians free, in fact there was a trend to invert the position. In later days, the accumulated effect of the Spanish laws and practices favouring manumission brought about similar results, as Humboldt points out : " This mixture of Indians and negroes is very common in these countries "—he writes while travelling in the valley of the Magdalen river.—" The women of the copper-coloured race feel a strong inclination towards the African race, and many negroes of Choco, in the province of Antioquia, and of the Simiterra, after having obtained their liberty as the fruit of their industry, settle down in the valley of the river." (18) No wonder the number of *zambos* or *zambahigos*, as the offsprings of these mixed unions were called, grew rapidly in the New World. As early as 1600 and 1608, royal *Cédulas* were addressed to the Viceroys Velasco and Montesclaros " in which they were told that it appeared that the number of *mestizos*, mulattoes and *zambahigos* was growing excessively, and they were ordered to keep a watch on the matter so that men of such mixtures and so vicious most of them, should not cause trouble and damage in the kingdom " ; a fear, as Solórzano Pereira goes on to explain, based purely on classical authorities, even if wisely qualified by a sound belief in the virtues of work. Hence it was decreed that " the *zambahigos* should not be allowed to carry arms which were allowed to the *mestizos* and Spaniards, nor to live without a master whom they were to serve, and all that was prohibited to negroes and mulattoes was to be also prohibited to them. (19)

Of all the combinations of colour in the Indies, the *zambo*

was the only one free from social prepossessions due to
White prejudice—though considerations of freedom and comfort were not altogether absent from the *zambo* women who
entered into alliances with the Whites.   The Whites looked
down upon them, as an entertaining anecdote of Humboldt's
shows.   " We stayed at an old sergeant's, a native of Murcia,
a man of a most original character.   To prove to us that he
had been educated by the Jesuits, he recited to us in Latin
the history of the creation of the world. [. . .]   He insistently asked for a remedy for gout, which made him suffer
cruelly.   ' I know '—he told us—' that a *zambo* of Valencia
[of Venezuela], who is a well known seeker, can cure me ;
but he wants to be treated with a consideration which one
cannot have for a man of his colour, and I prefer to remain in
the state in which I am.' "   Prejudice also has its heroes.   As
usual, however, the Crown did not share these shortcomings
(being, be it admitted, at a comfortable distance).   At Nirgua,
in Venezuela, Humboldt found a regular republic of *zambos*
dating from the sixteenth century.   " The whole municipal
council, the *cabildo*, is made up of coloured people, to whom
the King of Spain has granted the title of *his faithful and loyal
subjects, the Zambos of Nirgua*.   Few white families care to live
in a country ruled under a system so contrary to their claims,
so that the little town is known by derision *the republic of
Zambos and Mulattoes*."   Whereupon the wise German sen-
tentiously concludes :   " It is as imprudent to delegate
government to one caste only as to isolate this caste by depriving it of its natural rights."(20)

*   *   *

Mestizos, mulattoes and *zambos*, simple mixtures of the
three colours two by two, mixed in their turn either with
one of the two colours whence they came or with the third
colour or with other mixtures.   The outcome was a rich
palette of human blends, with an equally rich vocabulary to
describe them.   There was hardly a combination of colours,
a mixture of mixtures, without its own name ; particularly
those which marked the stages in the ladder from black to
white :   Mulatto, *Tercerón* (*Mulatto* and White), *Cuarterón*

Tercerón and White), *Quinterón* (*Cuarterón* and White).   The
cause of this wealth of names was the extreme touchiness of
the parties concerned with regard to their position in the
adder.   " Everyone gives so much importance to the rank of
caste and draws so much vanity out of it that if inadvertently
one of them is treated as belonging to a degree lower than
that to which he is entitled, he blushes and holds it as the
worst insult."   This observation of Ulloa and Jorge Juan
shows to what an extent the whole society of the Indies hung,
so to speak, from its white apex.   Some of the names given
to the middle mixtures express it most felicitously.   The
struggle between the sexes which we decorate with the name
of love, acquired in the Indies a new zest owing to colour
differences.   The dusky lady sought always to lose her heart
to swains better placed than she was on the ladder of whiteness,
and the swain as usual, *fell* in love—for language gives us
away.   The offspring was better off than mother, but had to
pay for this advantage by being worse off than father.   There
were cases, however, in which Cupid won on his own account,
paying no heed to black or white ; cases in which Six married
Half-a-dozen.   When *Tercerón* married *Mulatta*, or *Cuarterón*
married *Tercerona*, the offspring neither gained nor lost, but
remained in the same state of suspended animation.   Its
name expressed it admirably.   The children of such marriages
were known as *Tente-en-el-aire*, Hold-yourself-in-the-air.   On
the other hand, when a fairly advanced type, *Cuarterón* or
Quinterón, married a mulatto or a negro, their children were
known as *Salto-atrás*, Backward-leap.(21)
  This yearning to be white started from the very bottom of
the coloured pyramid, even though it may not have been very
general in the pure black or pure Indian.   It is reasonable to
surmise that it was a kind of longing of the white blood fallen
into the Black or Indian ocean, to rescue itself back to its
own kith and kin.   Humboldt has left several curious scenes
which illustrate this tension.   " In the missions "—he writes—
' every coloured man who is not absolutely black like an
African, or copper coloured like an Indian, holds himself a
Spaniard ; he belongs to the *gente de razón*, to the race gifted
with reason, and this reason, it must be owned, sometimes

arrogant and lazy, induces the Whites and all who believe themselves white, to consider the tilling of the earth as the task of slaves." " We were surprised to find in *la Esmeralda* many *zambos*, mulattoes and other coloured people who, out of vanity, call themselves *Spaniards*, and believe themselves to be white, because they are not as red as Indians." In his travels Humboldt came across a picturesque specimen of this kind. " We spent the night in the open, although in a plantation the owner of which was a tiger hunter. He went about almost naked and his skin was of a blackish brown, like that of a *zambo* ; which did not hinder him from considering himself a white. He called his wife and daughter, who went about as naked as he, Doña Isabela and Doña Manuela. Though he had never left the banks of the Apure, he was keenly interested in ' the news of Madrid, and those wars which never end, and all the things of over there.' He knew that the King of Spain was due to come soon to visit ' the greatness of the country of Caracas ' ; ' nevertheless,' he added pleasantly, ' as the people of the Court can eat nothing but wheat bread, they will never consent to come this side of the city of Victoria, and we shall never see them here.' I had brought along a *chiguire*, which I meant to have roasted ; but our host assured me that *nosotros cavalleros blancos*, white men such as he and I, were not made to eat that Indian game. He offered us some venison he had killed the day before with an arrow, for he had neither powder nor fire arms." In the night, spent in hammocks hanging from trees, drenched with rain and kept awake by a storm, Humboldt was congratulated by his host on his " good luck not to have had to sleep on the river shore, but to be in the estate of white people and people of a good family, ' *entre gente blanca y de trato*.' "(22)

* * *

An invaluable document which casts a ray of light into the depths of the soul of the Indies. Even there, on the edge of the Apure, in the tiger-infested forest, far from any society, from any vanity, from even a roof, the white blood inside the dusky skin longed for its kind and sought salvation . . . in Madrid, in the King of Spain. This strain runs through the whole collective soul of the Indies—a desperate effort of the white to come back to himself. The irrational value attached to whiteness is deeper than rank, wealth or social prestige. It lies rooted in the *arcana* of the blood, possibly of the spirit. But, as this example shows, the Creole, from nearly white to nearly black, sought in the name *Spaniard* a guarantee of white blood. Not till now can we gauge in all their depth the motives which for three centuries gave such an anomalous meaning to the word " *Spaniard* " in the Indies. To this day, the Mexican peons one sees working as gardeners in the suburbs of Los Angeles, California, with little or no white blood that one can see, when asked their nationality always answer " Spanish "—an answer which, coming after a century of independent rule, can have no other meaning than this age-long tradition which attaches to the word " *Spanish* " a specifically white value. The longing for whiteness must therefore be counted as one of the two chief springs in the soul of the Indies, a spring which held it together, pulling it up towards its white apex and attaching it strongly to Spain, to its people, fountain of pure white blood, to its King and Crown, fountain of honours, traditions, records of whiteness, to its Church, origin of the religion of the Whites, to the Conquerors, founders of the families of White Creoles.(23)

The other force within the soul of the Indies was the pull of the earth, the earth of the Indies, dragging down all those who lived on it in the contrary direction, working through the antagonistic principle—the mixture of blood, the attraction of opposites, which led the three peoples to blend their souls under the ægis of unruly love, and thus through the native Indian rooted Whites and Blacks to the soil of America. The sap of the American earth worked its way up the ladder of colour through the rooted Indian and the transplanted Black, through the *mestizos* and the mulattoes till it reached the grafted Spaniard. This sap of the earth worked also to hold together the soul of the Indies and to mould it into a unity. But while the longing for whiteness tended to shape the soul of the Indies into one single being, drawing much of its force and stimulus from Spain, and attached to Spain by living channels, the sap of the earth worked under the spell of local and definite forces and was therefore moulding not one but several units of collective life, later to become the Spanish-American nations. Thus every negress or Indian woman who conquered a white boy with her charms, every mulatta or *mestiza* who raised by one degree the colour of her offspring through the judicious choice of her love-partner, however crafty in her love affairs, was the innocent instrument of the spirit which worked for the unity of the Spanish empire ; while every man who *fell* in love down the ladder of colour, rakish as he might fancy himself to be, was the no less innocent instrument of the earth of America which craved its white blood and must have it to rise to the sun of whiteness and achieve the unity of its people by mixing the three colours which its sap was feeding.

NEGROES IN THE QUASIMODO PROCESSION

NEGROES DANCING BEFORE THE ALTAR OF OUR LADY

from "Types and Customs of Old Lima," by Pancho Fierro

YOUNG WORKER

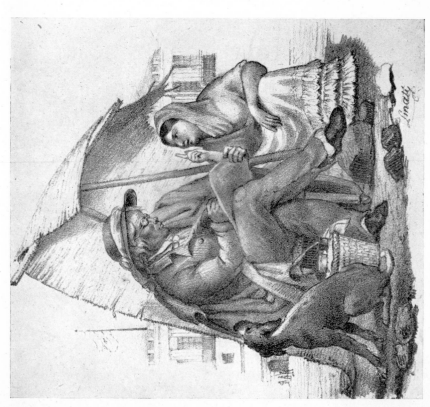

PUBLIC LETTER WRITER

PART II

INTERNAL ORIGINS OF THE SECESSION

E

Chapter IX

PERIOD OF THE AFTER-CONQUEST

THE wars of secession are the crisis between these two springs within the soul of the Indies : the longing for whiteness which tends to unify all the Indies and, through the Whites, to keep them attached to Spain ; and the strength of the earth, which calls its peoples to itself and moulds them into a oneness to fit its own genius. Such is the inner meaning of the struggle. But as it unfolds itself in History, it takes on the colour of the time and adopts the gestures, ways and passions of the men who incarnate it. When men or nations enter a fight, no matter the occasion, they fight with all their being, including memories and emotions which to our logic are irrelevant to the issue. These memories and emotions, however irrelevant, belong to the fight and have to be understood if the event is to stand clear before our eyes. The wars of secession are rooted in the history of the Indies in many topical ways. Grievances of the vice-regal period ; risings against the authority of the King or his Viceroys ; evolution of the sense of loyalty to the Crown ; foreign influences ; every action, movement, conspiracy which tended to sever the Indies from Spain, either in part or as a whole, must be included in the study of their origins. Politically speaking, this study might be reduced to that of relatively late events. But politics are the mere skin of collective life—as vital to it as our own skin is to us ; yet not the whole body, still less the soul of events. We shall never fully understand the wars of secession if we do not consider as their living roots all the dissentient, separatist risings of the past, in the *mood* of which lies the origin of the separatist mood of Bolívar and San Martín.

The setting of the events changes ; the actors also. It is a far cry from the rising of an Indian tribe to guard its gods against the Christian friars or the rebellion of a conqueror fiercely defending his hard-won conquests against the paper-laden lawyers sent from Madrid or the revolt of a Maroon negro escaped from slavery, to the stand of the brilliant intellectuals, encyclopedists and revolutionaries who in the eighteenth century rose before the world as the apostles of the freedom of the new continent.   Yet they are all living roots of the event, which through different twists and turns come to feed and support its trunk.   Relatively quiet as the Spanish Americas were, there were far too many risings and turmoils during those three centuries for a comprehensive narrative to be even attempted ; the best that can be done is to set down samples of them so as to indicate their outline and colour in the general picture.

Three periods may be discerned : after-conquest ; vice-regal epoch ; and pre-revolutionary phase ; and in each of them the movements of Whites, Indians and Blacks should be separately observed.   These distinctions are but ways of access for the mind, and no excessive importance should be attached to them.   But they help us to see more clearly events which are both too complex and too vast for a summary statement.

*   *   *

Since, from the Indian point of view, the wars of secession were a recoil from the conquest, all movements of resistance to the conquest itself should be considered as forerunners of the events which separated Spain from her kingdoms overseas. Typical of these movements, the revolt of New Galicia, i.e., the North-West stronghold of New Spain, which took place in 1541, was a vigorous reaction of the Indians of Mixton, gallantly fought in the name of their own god, Tecoroli, against the religion of the Whites.   This was the war which cost Pedro de Alvarado his life.   Had these Indians remained unpunished after the defeat in which Alvarado was killed, the whole conquest of New Spain might have been com-promised, for there were reports that " the Indians of Mechoacan were in touch with those of Tlaxcala to rebel." Herrera, who records this, rightly says that things might have led to " greater turmoils in those kingdoms " where the hold of Spain was still precarious ; despite the fact that many Indians fought on the Spanish side, notably " five thousand

Mechoacan Indians whose captain was an Indian gentleman known as Don Pedro ; " but the Viceroy Don Antonio de Mendoza reacted vigorously and took the leadership of the campaign in person, going so far as to give " permission to the Indian caciques and chiefs to buy horses to ride, and to use Castillian arms, and so they provided themselves with lances, spears, curved knives, swords, daggers, sallets, helmets and other such arms, and fifty thousand Indians thus assembled made a fine show, most gallant and handsome, not without causing some grousing among a few [Spaniards] who argued that it was unwise to arm Indians and teach them the use of Spanish weapons."(1)

Revolts of this uncompromising kind occurred also at all times among the warlike Indians of Chile, and for long they amounted to an endemic war. Cruelty on both sides was extreme, and the Spaniards tried without success every possible method from blockade to extermination, to get rid of the spirited Araucanians. Nothing but the passing of the centuries was at last to reduce the fierce fighters. Similar situations existed on every frontier, in the north with the Chichimecas, in New Granada with the Chiriguanas and other warlike tribes. These endemic wars were the backwash of the initial resistance to the conquest. They fed an obscure tradition of opposition to the intruders on the part of the original dwellers of the continent, which, though submerged during three centuries, will come to light again through the medium of the half-breeds, to add its secular impulse to other younger forces leading to the wars of secession.(2)

This obscure effort dispersed in time and space gathered some symbolic unity in the tradition of the Incas. Of the two pre-Spanish Empires, the Inca proved the richer by far in historic resilience and creativeness. The Aztecs died for good with Cuauhtemoc. The Incas did not die with Atahuallpa, despite the ruthless thoroughness he displayed in exterminating his own kith and kin. As one gathers the few pearls that can be found from a broken necklace, the Indians gathered the few pure Incas left of the legitimate royal family murdered by the bastard Atahuallpa ; and they stood by them, acknowledging them as their rulers with truly moving

loyalty.   That is why in the inner history of Indian rebellions,
a place apart should be made for those who were led by an
Inca—whether true or spurious is not material.

The first of these rebellions was led by Manco Inca, heir to
the throne after Atahuallpa's death. Weary of Pizarro's
delaying tactics, he managed to be allowed to leave the
fortress of El Cuzco, where he lived in royal confinement, and
easily aroused his kingdom against the Spaniards (1535).
Three Pizarros, Hernando, Gonzalo and Juan, with two
hundred Spaniards and a number of domestic Indians were
besieged for five months by a huge army of loyal Indians in
El Cuzco.   Francisco Pizarro, who was in Lima, believed his
brothers had perished.   Cortés-like, he sent away his ships to
Panama, to force his Spaniards to fight with their backs to
the sea ; and asked the Viceroy of New Spain for help.   More
than 700 Spaniards were put to death by the Indians, nearly
300 in their mines and farms, 470 in various ambushes against
sundry troops moving about the country unaware of the
rebellion. Lima was nearly lost. To make the picture
complete on the Spanish side, Diego de Almagro came back
from Chile towards Cuzco, and instead of going straight to
the help of the besieged Spaniards, tried to strike a bargain
with Manco Inca against the Pizarros—civil war.   Manco
Inca spurned the suggestion, gradually lost spirit and withdrew
to the inaccessible Andes with his wives, family and close
friends.(3)

This rising showed both the fidelity of the Indians to their
Incas and their dependence on leadership. Garcilaso, however, mentions two other aspects of Indian psychology : The
first is the loyalty of the Indian servants to their Spanish
masters who had overcome them in battle. These servants
acted as spies, as purveyors of food and even as soldiers against
their own people. The second is that one of the tribes, the
Cañaris, who in earlier days had been most loyal to the Incas,
having transferred their loyalty to the Spaniards, fought
bravely on the Spanish side in the siege of Cuzco. This
shifting of allegiance seems to have been a recurring feature
in Indian life, and Garcilaso points out that when Manco
Inca gave up the fight and withdrew to the fastnesses of the

Andes, he sent away his warriors " giving them orders to go to their provinces and to obey and serve the Spaniards."(4)

The Indians wept and sobbed abundantly—also a regular feature when Incas were defeated or died. " His people shed so many tears, with so many sobs and moans, that they could not breathe for them." Tears and sobs which will burst out again in later years, when a Spaniard killed Manco Inca in circumstances having nothing to do with war or state-craft. During the period of civil wars which afflicted Peru, small groups of Spaniards had gradually found their way to the residence of the self-exiled Inca in Villcapampa ; and they lived in some familiarity with Manco Inca whom they had taught to play a game of bowls. During a game a Spaniard known as Gómez Pérez, behaving with less courtesy than required towards the Inca, was pushed back by the indignant prince, who said : " Bear in mind with whom you are speaking." The Spaniard seized a ball and struck him dead. The Indians immediately attacked the Spaniards, who fled for their lives and locked themselves in their quarters. And here is Garcilaso's version of the sequel : " The Indians set fire to the house. The Spaniards, for fear of being burnt out, came out into the square, where the Indians attacked them with arrows, fiercely, with a bigger rage than any in the world, seeing their prince dead. When they had killed the Spaniards, they nearly ate them out of rage ; then they thought of burning them and throwing their ashes into the river, so that not a trace of them should remain ; but at last they decided to scatter them over the fields for birds and animals to eat, as the direst punishment they could inflict on their bodies."(5)

Manco Inca left three sons. The policy of the Crown towards these pretenders was to convert them and to keep them contented in golden idleness. This policy required much tact, as the Incas, not unnaturally, were shy of running risks by coming out into the midst of the Spaniards. After laborious negotiations, success was achieved with the eldest, Sayri Tupac, in 1558. *Mestizos* took an important share in these negotiations. One of them, Juan Sierra, was the son of Doña Beatriz (a *Coya* or Inca princess, an aunt of Sayri Tupac)

and of that Mancio Sierra who had gambled the golden sun
of the chief temple of Cuzco the very night he had received it
as his share of the booty.   Another of the negotiators, though
not a *mestizo*, was the husband of another *Coya*, Doña Angelina,
daughter of Atahuallpa.   The Inca's advisers trusted the
mestizo more than the White man.   After much arguing,
Sayri went to Lima and was received by the Viceroy who
offered him a fairly respectable bargain considering the
circumstances, including a good rent, many Indians and some
estates close to Cuzco.   He accepted it all, even though at a
banquet offered him by the Archbishop Loaysa, he gave a
striking demonstration of his feelings about it.   " He seized
the table-cover, which was of velvet with a silken fringe, and
tearing a thread of the fringe, said to the Archbishop : ' All
this cloth with its fringe was mine, and now I am given this
hair to keep myself and my household.' "(6)

Sayri became a Christian and his wife also.   He died two
years later, still young.   Of his two brothers, the elder, Titu
Cusi Yupanqui, was a bastard ; and Tupac Amaru seems to
have been either weak-minded or altogether abnormal.   Titu
Cusi kept his younger brother in seclusion, and on the death of
Sayri assumed the position of pretender and ruler of the
Villcapampa exiles.   He was a cruel but an executive man.
Two friars, Fray Marcos García in 1566 and Fray Diego Ortiz
later, ventured into the land to catechise the Indians.   Well
received at first, they were later persecuted ; and Fray Diego
terribly tortured for days and finally killed in most barbarous
circumstances.   One of the chief advisers against the work of
the friars, and later the leader of the mob of sorcerers and
others who tortured Fray Diego, was a *mestizo* born in Cuzco,
Martín Pando, who acted as the Inca's secretary.   Tito Cusi
died apparently of pneumonia, during the martyrdom of
Fray Diego ; and his brother Tupac Amaru had already, so
to speak, succeeded him when the emissaries of Don Francisco
de Toledo, the Viceroy, came to win over Tito Cusi whom they
thought still alive.   Events are not unanimously told at this
point.   Garcilaso minimises Tupac Amaru's resistance and
responsibility.   Fray Gabriel de Oviedo, who was one of the
emissaries, is not so favourable.   Others state that Tupac

Amaru's troops fought against the Spaniards, whether with or without the pretender's permission is not clear. It seems well proved, contrary to what Garcilaso suggests, that hostilities were begun by Tupac Amaru; for a nobleman, Atilano de Anaya, who came from the Viceroy with thirty loads of presents, was murdered by the Inca's men. The Viceroy sent some troops who took all the passes, and the pretender surrendered to Don Martín Oñez de Loyola (a relation of St. Ignatius) in 1571.(7)

He was sentenced to death. Friars and conquerors begged the Viceroy not to have him executed, but to send him to Spain and let the King decide the case. The Viceroy was adamant. Tupac Amaru was beheaded in the main square of Cuzco, black with a crowd of Indians who could hardly believe their eyes. The roar of the voices and laments was ominous. But the Inca, with a movement of his hand, silenced it all; and in the deadly silence, the head fell to the stroke of a Moorish sword brandished by a Cañari Indian. "I sent you to serve kings, not to kill them," said Philip II to the Viceroy. And that was all the thanks Don Francisco de Toledo received when he came back to Spain after his great government.(8)

This episode is important not only as an illustration of the strength of the Inca tradition among the Indians; but also because it shows the growing share taken by the *mestizos* in this movement of revolt against the Crown, so early in the history of the Empire. The fact is revealed by Garcilaso, a *mestizo* himself; though he shows a marked bias against the Viceroy, he dares not say one word to throw doubt on the accusation made against the *mestizos* that they had appealed to the Inca and offered to serve him or die since, being conquerors' sons, they were left poor and without means of livelihood: i.e., because they suffered as Whites, they resolved to serve as Indians. The Viceroy sentenced none to death, but exiled most of them to Chile or to other parts of the Indies, and even to Spain.(9)

From the earliest days, therefore, the chief features of the risings against the rule of Spain from the Indian side are clear: an attachment to pre-Spanish ways; the Inca tradition ; and a ferment of discontent born and bred in the disgruntled *mestizos*.

*　　*　　*

On the Spanish side trouble is caused not so much by a specific anti-Crown state of mind as by rivalry, the duel of ambitions and civil war. The civil wars of Peru which began with the breach between Francisco Pizarro and Diego de Almagro and ended with the rise of Hernández Girón are true to pattern. A disgruntled man, or a man too ambitious to wait, rebels against the man in authority. First he makes sure he can count on enough malcontents to make up an army. Then he proceeds to clothe his cause in legal form, by securing some kind of commission from a municipal council, preferably that of the chief city, which, according to custom could in exceptional cases take on a national authority. Garcilaso relates how during these civil wars the municipal council of El Cuzco elected one Alvarez Holguín as Captain General and Chief Justice of Peru ; and he goes on to say : " Those of that city were able to do so with a good title because in default of a governor appointed by His Majesty, the cabildo of El Cuzco was entitled, as the chief city of the Empire, to appoint ministers for War and for Justice, pending His Majesty's appointments." This kind of popular support becomes the " legal " basis of the revolted man's authority, who now can call himself Captain General and Chief Justice. He then seizes any cash that may be handy in the royal treasury and even levies taxes. Then he fights. If he wins, he is the chief. If he loses, he pays with his head. (10)

There is a modern name for this in Spain : " *Pronuncia-miento*." In Spanish America they call it " Revolution." In more recent times, the leader need not always be an army general ; though he is still a General : for instance, the general secretary of a trade union. But under the bunting and the noise, the bones of it all are always the same ; and this framework of all Spanish risings was evolved almost to completion during the earliest days of the conquest. Indeed, it had grown to full size during the Middle Ages. It remains true to pattern in the Indies from the earliest days of the discovery, so that insofar as Bolívar was the head of a *pronunciamiento*, his first precursor was Roldán, the man who rebelled against Cristóbal Colón in Santo Domingo. The conquest of Mexico was achieved by means of the *pronunciamiento* of Cortés against Velázquez, Governor of Cuba and representative of the Crown of Spain. For Cortés there was a difficulty : Mexico not being conquered yet, there was no commonwealth on which to found his authority. He solved the problem by setting up a city with his own soldiers as citizens and his trusted captains as aldermen. He made Veracruz a city, and Veracruz made him Captain General and Chief Justice. An important stage in the process was Cortés' resignation of the powers he held from Velázquez. He resigned, not because he shunned power, but because he wanted his power to be reborn as his own. Three centuries later we are to see many a dramatic resignation due to similar tactics.(11)

These risings always implied a certain element of disloyalty to the Crown ; a disloyalty within a wider loyalty ; a complex feeling, not unlike that of the German Barons who claimed

> *der König absolut*
> *Wenn er unseren Willen tut.*

The Spaniard's personality is so absorbing that it absorbs even that to which it gives itself—the beloved, the fatherland, the king, thus become the slaves rather than the masters of the lover, the citizen, the vassal. The feature stands out with impressive relief in all the civil wars the conquest gave rise to. From this as from many other points of view the most symbolical episode is that of Gonzalo Pizarro.

*   *   *

The trouble began with the new Orders signed by Charles V on November 20th, 1542, in Barcelona, as the outcome of Las Casas' untiring efforts on behalf of the Indians. In virtue of these Orders most of the Spanish conquerors were deprived of their Indians. Two men were appointed to carry them out. Don Francisco Tello de Sandoval was sent to New Spain as Visitor ; Blasco Núñez Vela was sent to Peru as Viceroy. Tello was a gown man ; Núñez Vela was a man of cape and sword. The former, on finding New Spain in turmoil, took a conciliatory course, allowed the citizens of New Spain to appoint *procuradores* who went to Germany, where the Emperor was at the time, and waited for their return. These *procuradores*, two *regidores* and two friars, arrived in Germany, " the two friars putting on soldiers' clothes, for in those days and in those parts monasteries and friars were suffering at the hands of the heretics." In the end, with a mixture of firmness and suppleness, Tello de Sandoval solved the difficulty, applied a substantial part of the orders and succeeded in persuading the Emperor to shelve the rest.(12)

Núñez Vela was a rigid soldier, a martinet and no diplomat. He applied the regulations in their entirety and at once. The conquerors reacted vigorously. The cities of Cuzco, Arequipa, Chuquisaca and Huamanga decided to appoint a *Procurador General* who should stand up for their rights. They claimed the right " to defend their vassals with their arms and their privileges, as the squires of Castille their liberties, which they had conquered helping their kings to win back the kingdoms from the Moors, just as they had won Peru from idolaters." They chose Gonzalo Pizarro as their *Procurador General*. Gonzalo Pizarro himself had a grievance. He thought himself entitled to the governorship general of the empire conquered by his elder brother, Francisco, to whom Charles V had granted that governorship for two lives. Francisco Pizarro had appointed his brother Gonzalo as " the second life." Gonzalo saw his opportunity. Under various pretexts, he succeeded in persuading the cities to let him recruit an armed force to back his paper claims. And though there were some qualms about it, this was done. What had been born as a movement of widespread discontent became a *pronunciamiento*.(13)

" Gonzalo Pizarro was a handsome man, with a very fine face and good health, capable of undergoing great hardship. A most elegant rider in both styles, an expert arquebuser and archer, he could draw anything on a wall with his bowshots. He was the best spear who had gone to the New World, according to all those who knew the famous men who went over. He loved good horses and had excellent ones. When he rode his little chestnut he did not trouble about squadrons of Indians any more than about swarms of flies. He was a clear, noble and clean soul, free from trickery, concealing or double-dealing ; truthful and trustful of his friends, and of those he thought his friends, which was the cause of his undoing ; that is why authors say he was of little understanding, but his understanding was very good and much bent on virtue and honour. Good-humoured, universally liked by friends and enemies, he had, in one word, all the good parts a nobleman should have. He was lord of all Peru, and governed it with so much justice and uprightness that the president praised him for it. He was a good Christian, most devout of Our Lady the Virgin Mary, Mother of God. Nothing was ever asked of him for her sake which he ever refused. When Francisco de Carvajal or any other of his ministers had made up their minds that someone should be executed, they invariably managed to see that no one got at Gonzalo Pizarro, for they knew that, no matter the case, if a reprieve was asked in the name of the Virgin Mary he would grant it."(14)

This tribute from Garcilaso, whose father was one of the captains who forsook Gonzalo Pizarro not once but twice in the hour of need, and who knew personally his model, shows the kind of man he was. Sound in his core ; yet ambitious and impatient of any authority than his own. His rebellion, thinly covered with popular backing and " republican " or at any rate " municipal " consent, came closer to a breach of loyalty than any other *pronunciamiento* in the Indies. This was partly due to the intemperate character of his first opponent, Nuñez Vela, but mostly to the original, vigorous, picturesque figure whom Gonzalo displayed by his side as his chief of staff. Francisco de Carvajal had fought under Gonzalo de Córdoba in Italy, and technically was perhaps the best field officer who ever fought in the Indies. During this, his last campaign, he was anything between 75 and 84, the age he was when he was beheaded. Fat, red-faced, a heavy drinker but a hard worker and a tireless officer ; cruel, cynical, a bad Christian and an irrepressible wit, he was a tower of strength for Gonzalo Pizarro in military affairs but also a most dangerous adviser in political matters.(15)

In its legal forms the movement was loyal to the King though openly against the King's Viceroy. Gonzalo Pizarro announced that he would go to Lima to obtain a stay in the execution of the Orders and to arrange to send *procuradores* to the King in the hope that the King would put a remedy to things—and if not, " they would all obey, breast on the ground, whatever the King should order." Yet even at the outset many prominent men (including Garcilaso's father), disliking the show of force with which Gonzalo Pizarro meant to back his enterprise, forsook him and returned to Cuzco, ultimately to join the Viceroy's party at Lima. Meanwhile the Viceroy had so far lost all sense of restraint that, with his own hand, he had slain a high official whom he unjustly suspected of conniving with Gonzalo Pizarro ; and the *oidores* had him arrested and sent to Spain to save his life from the anger of the people. Yes, of the people. " Which caused much anger in the people," says Garcilaso of the events which led up to the imprisonment of the Viceroy. And when the Viceroy had claimed his right to imprison and kill a citizen " by way of government, for he was not bound to give any explanations thereon to them ," the *oidores* answered that " there was no other government but to do what was in accordance with justice and the laws of the kingdom." And when the Viceroy was taken prisoner, the people, i.e., the people of conquerors, expressed their feelings in language which can be read in Garcilaso as he wrote it in 1610 : " The fatherland is already liberated, since the tyrant is in jail." Bolívar breathes already in these words.(16)

But why " the tyrant ? " Garcilaso explains it in the preceding line, that which leads up to this Bolivarian utterance. " A man who brought such laws deserved such a reward. Had he come over without them, he would have been worshipped." Which laws were these ? The laws safeguarding the freedom of the Indians. History is subtle and complex. These laws made Blasco Nuñez Vela a tyrant, at whose fall the conquerors were able to say : " The fatherland is liberated."(17)

But of tyrants there is no end ; and the *oidores*, left almost without a garrison, had to surrender to Gonzalo Pizarro's demands. After his first disappointments, his party—and army—had grown. He had all but besieged Lima and persuaded the *procuradores* of all the cities to meet in a kind of Peruvian Cortes, and to ask that he should be made Governor-General. After Carvajal had hanged three prominent citizens of the recalcitrant faction, the *oidores* complied with Pizarro's request. Gonzalo became Governor-General of Peru. In the hour of his triumph (October, 1544), the first thing the conqueror did was to call on the *oidores* and then on the *cabildo*, i.e., to pay formal compliments to the royal and to the municipal authorities. Presently he arranged for a deputation of two emissaries to go to Spain and have his appointment ratified by the King. One of the emissaries represented the *Audiencia* ; the other " the whole kingdom," i.e., the assembly of *procuradores* or elected representatives of all the cities of Peru.(18)

Nothing better depicts the picturesque anarchy under which the affairs of Peru (unlike those of New Spain) evolved in the sixteenth century than the fact that the ship which conveyed Gonzalo Pizarro's emissaries carried also an emissary of the Viceroy Nuñez Vela dispossessed by Gonzalo Pizarro, as well as Vaca de Castro himself, an upright man who as President had governed Peru before Nuñez Vela with signal moderation and success. (Being the best of the three, he spent five years in prison in Spain, purging sundry calumnies of which he was accused, before being reinstated and rewarded as he deserved.) Meanwhile Nuñez Vela, set free by the *oidor* who had been told off to convey him to Spain, had set up a rival government and an *Audiencia* in Quito, whither disgruntled captains and soldiers drifted now and then, gradually increasing his military power. After a chain of most complicated episodes, risings and counter-risings, Gonzalo Pizarro won a final battle over the Viceroy, who was slain on the battlefield, and whose head was exposed on the pillory of Quito till Gonzalo Pizarro ordered it to be withdrawn (January 15th, 1546).(19)

With this success, Gonzalo Pizarro became *de facto* ruler of Peru in the teeth of the royal authority. His *oidor*, Cepeda, his fieldmaster, Carvajal, and many others advised him to

break with the King and to have himself proclaimed King of
Peru. Cepeda blandly pointed out that " all kings descend
from tyranny ; all nobility comes from Cain, and all plebs
from Abel ; which anyone could see from the blason and arms
noblemen displayed about themselves ; " while Carvajal
advised Gonzalo Pizarro " to look up Adam's will to see
whether Peru had been bequeathed to Charles V or to the
kings of Castille." Carvajal went so far as to write a long
letter urging Pizarro to crown himself king ; to set up military
orders with such habits, insignia, titles and income as would
attract all the New World Spaniards ; to draw the Inca out
of his retirement, grant him honours and formal dignity, and
marry one of the Inca's sisters or daughters ; and to legislate
in favour of the Indians. He argued that all this would imply
" no tyranny against the King of Spain, for as the saying goes,
no king can be a traitor. This land "—added the cynical fieldmaster—" belongs to the Incas, its natural lords, and since no
one thinks of giving it back to them, your lordship is more
entitled to it than the King of Castille, since you won it by
your exertions with your brothers."(20)

Gonzalo Pizarro seems to have listened all too willingly to
these witches of Macbeth, yet to have walked warily on the
road to disloyalty. Thus he entered Lima in triumph, surrounded by bishops, preceded and followed by soldiers,
acclaimed by the crowd of citizens who saw in him the man
who had stood for their interests and preserved for them their
Indian vassals and their privileges, and to the tune of " much
music of voices, trumpets and musicians, for he kept many and
very good minstrels in his household ; " but he refused all royal
or excessive honours with which his hangers-on kept tempting
him. Garcilaso gives a number of reasons for this. The only
one strong enough to explain Pizarro's behaviour throughout
his chequered career would appear to be the first : " Because
the natural respect he felt towards his prince was stronger in
him than his friends' blandishments." The other chief reason,
his hope to be recognized as the Governor of Peru, was soon
shattered. On May 27th, 1546, the new ruler left Sanlúcar
for Peru. He was a gown man. The Crown, having tried a
cape-and-sword man to improve on a gown man, tried now

a gown man again to improve on a cape-and-sword man.
But mark the point : while the cape-and-sword men came as
Viceroys, the gown men came as presidents—a curious confirmation of that subconscious tendency to the monarchical
form in the men of arms and to the republican form in the
men of letters. Pedro de la Gasca was a cleric and a lawyer.
He was small and ugly but wise and shrewd as well as
courageous ; above all he had that power which comes from
complete lack of self-seeking. He drew no salary and lived
like an ascetic.(21)

He brought a letter from the King for Gonzalo Pizarro and
wrote him another. The Crown had taken a conciliatory
policy. A blind eye towards Gonzalo Pizarro's rebellion ;
a general pardon ; the Orders on the Indians cancelled ; and a
general consultation of the *procuradores* of the cities, i.e., in practice,
the *Cortes* of Peru, to find out what was best " for the service of
God, the prosperity of the land and the well-being of the
settlers." Gonzalo Pizarro put the matter to his two chief
advisers who, first privately and later at a meeting of about
eighty notables, expressed the views to be expected of their
respective professions : the man of war spoke for peace and
the man of law spoke for war. At the public meeting someone
shouted to Carvajal : " The fieldmaster is afraid ! " Whereupon Carvajal answered that his opinion was for negotiating,
but that " should it fall otherwise, I have lived long enough
and have as good a length of neck for a rope as any of your
lordships."(22)

While Gonzalo hesitated, the President flooded the country
with copies of the new orders cancelling the detested old ones
and promising a free pardon. Every day he made converts
among the numberless Spaniards who felt uneasy about having
taken arms against the King. That was the crux of the matter.
The feeling was gradually undermining Gonzalo Pizarro's
position. While in Lima, Paniagua, the President's envoy to
Pizarro, received many secret visits of men who outwardly
followed Pizarro, come to assure him of their loyalty to the
King and to his President. Little they knew that la Gasca
brought secret instructions to give the governorship to Gonzalo
Pizarro if he found such to be the general desire. By their

defection, they undid Pizarro's fortunes and drove him to rebellion.   But in their turn these men who went in the night to call on Paniagua did so because the rebellious velleities of Pizarro had shocked them as loyal subjects of the King. Throughout the land, defections took place daily and captains were forced to transfer their allegiance to the President by their own soldiers.   In vain did Gonzalo burn his ships to prevent more men from forsaking him.   He lost a powerful fleet, which Carvajal wept for, for they had been burnt in his absence and against his advice ;   and defections continued, even after Pizarro had written a letter to the President protesting that his intention " had always been and was to serve His Majesty ; " and explaining that he had been elected as their general procurator by all the cities of the empire to turn the Viceroy out.   On the advice of the *oidor* Cepeda, Pizarro called together a meeting of the " neighbours, lords of Indians," i.e., conquerors, who still remained by him, and having explained that he meant to resist the authority of the President pending the return of his emissaries to the King, he made them swear fidelity to him.   They all did it.   But Carvajal " laughed, cracked jokes and made fun about all these oaths."(23)

War it was to be.   Two battles settled it.   In the first Gonzalo Pizarro, thanks to Carvajal's shrewd tactics, won a victory over far superior numbers.   His opponent was a turbulent captain then at the service of the President, i.e., of the King, but who, in Carvajal's picturesque language, was a " weaver," one of those men who keep passing from one side to the other like a shuttlecock.   The second and last battle ended in failure for the rebels.   Cepeda had advised Pizarro to come to terms after his first victory ;   but preferring to listen to his young bloods, the conqueror decided to fight to the end.   This decision displeased many a captain and soldier who, willing to fight against another captain, were averse to standing up to the royal standard.   The President drew near with his army. Disdaining Carvajal's advice to refuse battle, live on the land and tire his enemy by constant marches, Pizarro chose a favourite spot near Cuzco, the valley of Sacsahuana, and faced the royal arms (April 9th, 1548).   He felt invincible, for he had better if not more men, numberless Indians and ample food. But as soon as the sun rose defections began. Captains and soldiers simply passed to the other side under his eyes, beginning with Garcilaso's own father and Cepeda, his *oidor*. Gonzalo watched the scene from the meadow above the river. He sat there on his chestnut horse, wearing magnificent armour, covered with a coat of yellow velvet sewn over with plates of gold, a golden helmet and visor which showed his fine, chiselled face and round, black beard. He looked on frowning, while Carvajal on his gigantic reddish-brown mule, clad in a purple burnous, his head covered with a black taffetas hat with a row of hen's feathers in x-shaped patterns round the crown, jeered, laughed and sang a Spanish song :

> Oh my mother, my hair, my hair,
> In twos and threes they fly away in the air ! . . .

Both knew they were doomed. But the young man frowned and the old man laughed. Their army melted away. Pizarro turned to one of his captains, Juan de Acosta : " What shall we do, brother John ? " " Sir, let us fight and die like Romans." " Better die like Christians ! " quietly retorted Pizarro. And he moved over and surrendered to the forces of the King.(24)

*   *   *

This episode is typical. Gonzalo Pizarro rose because his personal ambition coincided with a general grievance. He hovered on the border line of treason, so measuring his actions that the question whether he was a traitor or not is still debatable. He paid with his life and died a noble and Christian death, conscious of the fact that he had a strong case but that his judges had as strong a case against him.

But there is one point in which Gonzalo Pizarro's case differed from that of other rebellious captains. When he entered Cuzco in the hour of his triumph between his victory and his defeat " the Indians of the City in the order of their districts and nations were in the square acclaiming him, calling him Inca and other names of majesty which they used to bestow on their natural kings." Garcilaso, who reports this, adds that it was done on orders of one of Gonzalo Pizarro's captains. It was none the less spontaneous, for as the same chronicler says : " All the Indians served Gonzalo Pizarro most willingly [. . .] for they held the first Spaniards who came to be children of the Sun and brothers of their Inca kings, and so called them Incas ; and as Gonzalo Pizarro was one of them [. . .] they never lost the love and deference they felt for him as an Inca, and at his death wept tenderly for him."(25)

Let us note this point. The loyalty of the Indians to the Incas was transferable ; and it could be transferred to Spaniards great enough to deserve it.

*   *   *

There always were negroes who did not accept their slavery and ran away. They were known as *cimarrones*, which in English became maroons. Whenever nature afforded them a relatively easy retreat, they left their masters and organized outlaw, yet by no means lawless, communities. As early as 1553 a number of negroes of Venezuela rose in Nueva Segovia. They were about 250. They organized and armed themselves and they chose a king. They killed six Whites including a priest and were already distributing the white women which every one of them would have after victory. Their leader, one Miguel, had himself crowned king and a negress by whom he had a child became queen under the high-sounding name of Guiomar ; the child was sworn heir to the throne. King Miguel went so far as to appoint a bishop, who started a church and preached with more eloquence than letters. The Spaniards sent for reinforcements, beat and killed or took prisoner the rebels, despite Miguel's signal bravery and, respecting the negro women who were brought back to slavery, liquidated the incident.(26)

This was but an adventure of unprepared fighters. Seven years later the maroons were already a force to count with in several parts of the tropics. They had become so dangerous to travellers that no one dared take to the road in groups of less than twenty men. Immunity increased their numbers daily. The maroons of Darien had a king, whom Herrera calls Ballano, no doubt mistaking the name for the forest city of Vallano which was their chief abode. The Viceroy Cañete

sent a force against them ; and though the negroes asked to
negotiate, the Whites were glad to make peace—a not un-
generous one at that. It was agreed that the maroons should
remain free, but that newcomers should be returned to their
masters ; that every negro ill-treated by his master would be
entitled to his freedom on paying his purchase price ; and
that the maroons should settle as free men under the laws of
the Indies and not as outlaws in the hills.(27)

*   *   *

These risings of the three colours of men were by no means
the only incidents recorded during the first period, but they
serve our purpose as typical. They provide a number of
elements which will later reappear in the wars of secession.
On the negro side, a black solidarity, a desire for freedom from
slavery and a yearning for State-order, discernible under the
forms, odd and even grotesque as they may seem, adopted by
some of their chieftains. On the Indian side, an instinctive
reaction to defend their own destiny against the intruder,
weakened by the tendency to accept authority from the
stronger man, and strengthened by *mestizo* collaboration which
underpins the Indian grievance with Spanish stubbornness and
purpose ; as well as an Inca-tradition which tends to idealize
and sentimentalize the old native empire but is transferable to
White leaders. On the White side, personal ambition rising
to within reach of the glittering Crown, stretching avid hands
towards it, yet hardly daring to touch it ; exploiting the
grievances of the privileged aristocracy, democratically organized within its own ranks, used to living as it wanted under
forms of loyalty to the Crown ; and a tradition of municipal
sovereignty assumed in particular by the *cabildo* of the chief
city—a combination which led to dramatic conflicts between
assemblies and leaders, now condemned and doomed by the
popular assembly, now strengthened after a staged-up resignation with renewed full powers which made of the leader an
omnipotent dictator and enabled him to commandeer men,
money and materials in a so-called common, but mainly
personal, cause.

CHAPTER X

VICEREGAL PERIOD—THE WHITES

ON the Spanish side there were during this period a number of cases of disloyalty on the part both of European and of American Spaniards. "This year"—records the historian of Potosí under 1596—" by order of H.E. Don Luis de Velasco, Viceroy of Peru, four men from Spain were beheaded in Potosí as traitors to the king." No details are given. Considering the period, these men can have been little more than adventurers. That there was in Madrid a certain amount of watchfulness about possible treason is shown by the case of the Duke of Escalona. His names reveal his Jewish ancestry : Don Diego López Pacheco Cabrera y Bobadilla. Appointed Viceroy of New Spain in 1640, he entered Mexico " with great festivals of joy " on August 28th. He set about to refit the shipyards of San Juan de Ulúa, and was able to send the fleet back with a brand new escort of eight galleons and a patax on July 23rd, 1641. Shortly afterwards, however, he was deposed. Portugal had rebelled. At Court in Mexico there happened to be two noblemen with symbolic names : Don Pedro de Castilla and Don Cristóbal de Portugal. Each had presented the Viceroy with a horse. H.E. was heard to say : " That of Portugal is the better of the two." He had appointed a Portuguese gentleman as governor of San Juan. He wrote to Spain and to Portugal and had the misfortune that his letters to Portugal arrived before those to Spain. Too many coincidences. His goods were confiscated and sold by auction. Later he was exonerated and reinstated in his dignities, but was not sent back to New Spain : he was made Viceroy of Sicily.(1)

The prototype, however, of the adventurer-traitor may well be Don Diego de Peñalosa, a Creole of Lima, who significantly enough styled himself *indio español*. He was a dissolute, unscrupulous blackguard, as shown in his lamentable governorship of New Biscay. Exiled from New Spain by the Inquisition, he turned up in London, where he offered ministers and princes wonderful plans for the conquest of Havana and Panama. Upon pressure from the Spanish Ambassador, the English authorities turned him out. Nothing daunted, he tried again in Paris, where he paraded as Count, Governor and Captain-general of New Mexico and Knight of the Order of Calatrava. Peñalosa's success with Cardinal d'Estrées and other prominent figures of the Court of Louis XIV was due in part to his ability to exploit the growing animosity between Creole and European Spaniards, and to the fact that, when he assured the French that on arriving in Pánuco with a fleet of French buccaneers backed by the King of France, Creoles in their thousands would flock to his banners, his voice carried conviction.

At the time, however, La Salle was busy also in Paris with plans against the Indies. With their usual eye for strategy, the French, having entered the continent by the St. Lawrence, were considering another attack by the mouth of the Mississippi, a river La Salle had already navigated down to the sea. His schemes put those of Peñalosa in the shade. In 1687 an expedition fitted out by the French Government, under him, with four ships and 280 colonists, came to grief. La Salle missed the mouth of the river and sailed too far to the west. After many misfortunes, he was murdered by his own men. The expedition had to be rescued by Spain, the very nation against which it had been conceived. The Spanish Government, as a result, had the coast of Veracruz and Florida more closely studied, and this measure was fatal to Peñalosa's fantasies.(2)

*　　　*　　　*

Of more significance are the cases of Martín Cortés and of " the tyrant Aguirre."

Don Martín Cortés, second Marquess del Valle, eldest legitimate son of the conqueror, lived at first a courtier's life and accompanied Philip II in Flanders, at the battle of St. Quentin, and in England when the King went to marry Mary Tudor. On his return to Spain Don Martín married his own niece and left for his estates in Mexico in 1562. He was very rich, powerful and magnificent. Hence, envy all round, and true or simulated fear and suspicion of his intentions. He was young and careless. His wife gave birth to twins who were christened on June 30th, 1566, with too much pomp and luxury. During the festivities, crowns of laurel were laid on the heads of Don Martín and his wife, and even a cup of gold on Don Martín's light head, while foolish people were heard to say : " How well it suits your lordship ! " Finally the *oidores* who governed *ad interim* after the death of the Viceroy Don Luis de Velasco senior, were, or chose to be, alarmed, and arrested a number of people, including Don Martín himself. Two young friends of his, Alonso and Gil de Avila, were beheaded, even though it was said of the second that he was innocent, and of the first, a handsome youth, that women " were the strongest ammunition with which he made war." At this juncture, the new Viceroy, Falces, arrived upon the scene. He must have known Don Martín, because their respective fathers had been close friends, the old Marquess de Falces being one of the members of the private academy which used to meet in Cortés' house in Madrid towards the end of his life. Falces sent Don Martín and a number of other alleged conspirators to Spain, and tried to calm down passions. But his conciliatory policy did but add fuel to the fire. Don Martín's enemies turned against the Viceroy, and the Crown, giving too ready an ear to his accusers, superseded him and sent three lawyers in his stead. The senior lawyer died on his way to New Spain, and power was concentrated in the hands of a vain, overbearing magistrate, Muñoz by name, who let loose an epidemic of tortures and death sentences. The scandal reached such dimensions that Philip II had to withdraw this man, who returned to Spain in the same ship with the Viceroy he had superseded. The King accepted Falces' explanation and rebuked Muñoz, who " that very night died sitting on a chair with his cheek on his hand." The episode seems to have had no real political importance. The friars of Mexico did not believe in conspiracy. Don Luis de Velasco II, the future Viceroy, then in Mexico, seems to have had a share in engineering the accusation against the foolish youths who surrounded Don Martín. The city was on the whole favourable to the victims, and when the brothers Avila were beheaded the authorities feared serious trouble. But this trouble was of a local and partisan character, and the whole thing may well have been the outcome of a petty intrigue to prevent Don Martín from becoming Viceroy.(3)

*   *   *

With Lope de Aguirre we are no longer in an atmosphere of courtly intrigue, glittering with gold and emeralds, but in the wilds of the Amazon and in the as yet primitive settlements and budding cities of Venezuela ; and the chief protagonists are rough soldiers, of the most unruly, or even criminal, to be found in the conquest. By a caprice of nature, the chief actor and criminal in the story was a scion of that Basque nation, held in such high esteem in Spain and out of it. " In the city of Oñate, in the province of Guipúzcoa, was Aguirre unworthily born "—writes Oviedo y Baños—" to stain with his deeds the ancient loyalty of so noble a nation, and, though born of humble parents, he was by nature an hidalgo ; his person was ever despicable to men's eyes, for he was ugly, very small, thin, a great talker, noisy and garrulous ; in company, none more foolhardy ; alone none more cowardly ; always astir, ready for sedition and mutiny, and so in over twenty years in which he lived in Peru, though his business was the training of horses, there was no rising and no mutiny in which he did not take part." It is fair to add that he had a sly humour and could express himself well, as his letters to Philip II and to the Provincial of Santo Domingo and others show. But his mind was anarchical and undisciplined, thoroughly unable to control and co-ordinate the promptings of his heart.(4)

The adventure started as one of the many attempts to discover El Dorado, organized by the Viceroy Cañete to get rid of a number of soldiers and adventurers whom he had reduced to unemployment and boredom when he pacified Peru. The command was given to Pedro de Ursúa, a Navarrese captain who had won distinction against the wild Indians of the north. After many vicissitudes the expedition started down the valley of the Huallaga river towards the Amazon, on September 27th, 1560. Ursúa took with him his mistress, Doña Inés de Atienza, a beautiful *mestiza*, and a

Spanish woman, known as la Torralva, who belonged to Aguirre's household. The beauty of Doña Inés and the ambition of Aguirre seem to have been the two chief obstacles to good harmony. There was in the army a nobleman, young, inexperienced and weak, Don Fernando de Guzmán. He became a kind of puppet in the hands of Aguirre. Ursúa was warned that some plot was afoot. " To which he answered that he need not be watched, since there were so many Biscayans on his side who, at the first word he said in Basque, would all rush to die for him." So says Zúñiga, one of those who chronicled the events he lived through, and he adds : " And they were the first to rebel and to kill him."(5)

On January 1st, 1567, Ursúa was murdered by a band of conspirators led by Aguirre. " *Libertad, caballeros* "—they shouted—" *Viva Don Fernando de Guzmán.*" And having terrorized the camp with a number of other murders, " the tyrant Lope de Aguirre, who from then on styled himself Fieldmaster, forthwith distributed all the vessels of wine which the Governor Pedro de Ursúa had brought for the Mass, and they drank them off." After inflicting a number of other deaths with the utmost callousness, Aguirre made the whole army share in his treason, forcing them to sign a document of allegiance to Don Fernando de Guzmán, whom he later declared King of Peru, and announced that he, Lope de Aguirre, " broke his allegiance to the kingdom of Spain." Brawls, conspiracies and violent deaths without the slightest legal formality or even confession marked the progress of the desperate band down the Amazon, a voyage which repeated Orellana's prowess. Doña Inés fell first, a victim of the rivalry of two fierce Basques over her favours. Then Don Fernando was also murdered. Aguirre became the leader, more hated than respected, more dreaded than hated, of a band which dwindled daily by his summary and arbitrary executions. To his would-be conspirators he said : " Make haste to kill me, for I will overtake you ; for he who should make an afternoon meal of me I will eat him up at lunch." And his welcome to a new soldier was : " I curse you if you ever die a poor man." After many adventures he succeeded in leading his men—the *Marañones*, as he called them—to

Venezuela, where he stressed the rebellious and disloyal character of the enterprise, partly through sheer temperament and a wild hatred of all order, partly to bind his men to him with ties of common guilt. One Diego de Alarcón, who had tried to desert him, was quartered and as the wretched victim was being dragged to his death, the tyrant's crier announced : " This is the justice ordered by Lope de Aguirre, the strong *Caudillo* of the noble *Marañón* nation, on this man who tried to serve the King of Castille loyally!" And, the sentence executed, they put his head on the pillory of the Main Square where the tyrant said to it with great laughter and in fun : " There you are, friend Alarcón, how is it that the King of Castille does not come to raise you up from the dead. "(6)

In the end, as in the case of Gonzalo Pizarro, disloyalty to the King was too much for most of his followers ; and when he was finally brought to book, only one, a bloodthirsty henchman, chose to remain by his side. But what a contrast with Gonzalo Pizarro ! None of that serenity before death which shines in Gonzalo Pizarro's last scene. " What shall we do, brother John ? " The tyrant Aguirre was in a fortified house. " Noticing that only Antón Llanoso remained by his side, his courage gone from him and his voice broken, he said : ' Why don't you go also to enjoy the forgiveness of the King ? ' To which Llanoso made answer that, constant in his friendship, he wanted to keep his word and die by his side ; and the tyrant, without replying a single word, went into a room where his daughter, whom he had brought over from Peru, was in the company of another woman of Molina de Aragón, known as la Torralva, and possessed by the devil [. . .] with his harquebus pointed, ordered her to commend herself to God for he was going to kill her to free her from the shame of being known as a traitor's daughter." La Torralva seized the weapon, but Aguirre let it go, drew his dagger and slew his daughter with repeated thrusts.(7)

As he went out of the room the King's men were pouring in. " Seeing which, his spirit broken and without force to attempt anything, he leant sadly over a barbecue which was there in a corner of the room." A soldier shouted that the tyrant had surrendered. " I do not surrender to such villains as you "—

he said—" and no longer able to articulate properly owing to his dismay," he tried to obtain a respite from the fieldmaster. The officer would have granted it, but the soldiers advised him not to delay to get rid of such a dangerous man and shot him dead.(8)

*   *   *

This story would have but little permanent interest did it not present in a living form the core of unreasoned, primitive impulses which animates Spanish and Spanish-American rebellions, revolutions and *pronunciamientos*. It is meet that its hero should be a Basque ; for the Basque is in Spain the provider of natural strength straight from the soil, still un-coloured by ideas or by rationalized emotions. The Basque stands at the opposite psychological as well as geographical pole of Spain from the Andalusian, whose wealth of ideas and images, like the gorgeous colours and shapes of creeping plants, rests on a slender stem of impulse. It is piquant, by the way, that the two should be found paired off in the ballad which the popular muse struck out of Aguirre's life :

> The waters of Marañón
> Saw the dastardly delusion
> Of that treacherous Biscayan
> Worse than the worst Andalusian . . .

We have seen Andalusians, Castillians, and Extremadurians revolt. But they put method in their madness and law in their lawlessness. Aguirre did not and could not. His mind was in chaos. He revolts against the King of Spain more openly and explicitly than any other Spaniard ever did ; and even writes to King Philip a picturesque letter hardly a line of which does not deserve quotation for its vigour, and yet wholly devoid of any coherent sense. The very opening seems to spring from the soil in verbal spurts : " *Rey Felipe, natural español.* . . ." No one could have imagined a more magnificent opening to attack and repudiate a king. But lest we are tempted to read into the past modern political develop-ments, this Basque who revolts against Philip begins by proudly asserting his Spanish nature before repudiating his loyalty : " King Philip, natural Spaniard, son of invincible

Charles ; Lope de Aguirre, your most humble vassal, an old
Christian, from middle-class parents and in my prosperity an
hidalgo, a native Biscayan in this kingdom of Spain and
domiciled in the city of Oñate, passed in my youth across the
ocean sea to the parts of Peru, so as to be worth more with
my spear in my hand. . . ." And after re-stating the complaints of many conquerors that the King is ungrateful to
them, he adds : " With my companions (whose names I shall
state anon) I have forsaken your allegiance and we have
denaturalized ourselves from our lands, which is Spain . . ."
—a magnificent sentence in its mixture of plural and singular,
as befits any description of " these lands which *is* Spain."
And later, still worried in his conscience for his murder of
Ursúa, he seeks to excuse it in these words : " In 1559 the
Marquess de Cañete granted the expedition of the Amazon
to Pedro de Ursúa, a Navarrese, or rather a Frenchman."
Again a subconscious Spanish reaction.(9)

But this Spaniard who forswore Spain, did he really do so ?
He did not even know. Along with his defiance and declaration of open war he shows respect for the King whom he
always addresses as " King and lord." Thus : " We cannot
believe, Excellent King and lord, that you are in fact cruel
towards the good vassals you have in these lands. . . ." And
he goes on to complain about a small affair concerning the
fish in a lagoon near Lima. In religious affairs he is equally
chaotic. He killed friars, sometimes most cruelly, and had
no regard for Christian dogma, faith or behaviour. " God
has made heaven for those who deserve it and the earth for
those who are stronger ; " was one of his sayings. He assured
his soldiers that " they were not to refrain from anything their
appetite might order them for fear of hell, for it was enough to
believe in God to be saved." " Raising his eyes to Heaven
he would say : ' God, if you intend to do me any good, do it
right now and keep your glory for your saints.' " Yet this
man writes to Philip II : " On this day we deem ourselves the
happiest of all creatures because in these parts of the Indies we
are holding intact and without corruption our faith and the
Lord's commandments and all that the Church of Rome
preaches." In Margarita, he goes on, " we saw some Reports

come from Spain about the great machinations of the
Lutherans, which put us in great fear and terror, for here in
our company there was one, a German, by name Monteverde,
whom I had quartered." And he concludes : " Let there be
wars wherever men like, for they were made for men, but in
no time and for no adversity which may befall us, shall we
ever cease to be the obedient subjects of the commandments
of the Holy Roman Church."(10)

Chaos everywhere. And under this chaos a vigour of
natural impulse breaking away from all law and all tradition,
in which we already perceive the wind of future revolutions.
Aguirre's rebellion is not merely directed against the King of
Spain : " In this land we hold your standards in less credit
than the books of Martin Luther." It threatened all kings :
" I hold for certain that few kings can arrive in Heaven, for
I believe you would be worse than Lucifer, seeing your ambition, your thirst and hunger to be surfeited of human blood ;
but I do not marvel thereat nor pay any heed to you, for you
always call yourselves minors, and innocent men are madmen
and your government is but air. . . ." Marat is already here
and even Beaumarchais. But not yet with their full political
development, as forces conscious of a future to create as well
as of a past to be demolished ; only in their primitive human
impulses, as purely destructive and anarchical forces. This
explains even Aguirre's political ideas and vocabulary. His
policy consisted in setting off the uneducated low class of sea-
port scum he made his friends against the better class of
officers. " Then the cruel Lope de Aguirre "—says Zúñiga—
" was appointed Fieldmaster and took many soldiers for his
guard, so that he always went about well watched and safe.
And they were all Biscayans and sailors and seashoremen and
people of little honour, accursed and thoroughly bad people
when they are let loose to rob and indulge in their vices as he
let them ; and so with the cruel tyrant they became great
butchers and cruel people, for he could not stand knights and
noble people."(11)

These were the people Aguirre relied on to establish his
power ; as for his method, it consisted in the gradual destruction of the better educated class. There was no political

thought, urge, tendency in all this ; just personal ambition, without any care for to-morrow. This indigence of ideas showed itself in the tyrant's vocabulary. All the other rebels or leaders who had striven for power and glory in the political wilderness of the New World had sought to don the robes of office as soon as they had triumphed, styling themselves " Governor " or " Captain General " and " Chief Justice." Aguirre could do no such thing because he had butted with his hard head against the very foundations of law and the State. So he chose as his title : *Fuerte Caudillo de la Nación Marañona.* Thus rises over the bloody waters of the *Marañón* this name *Caudillo,* which was to be the title of so many irresponsible tyrants and dictators in the history of the Spanish New World that it gave forth the word *caudillismo* ; till a time came when even the mother country found herself so destitute of political capital as to have humbly to receive in her discarnate hand this political alms from her American daughters. *Caudillismo,* first expressed in all nakedness by the pure Basque Aguirre, springs from two roots in the Spanish character, that character of which the Basque is the hard core—dictatorship and separatism. Hence *Caudillo* and *Nación Marañona* : i.e., the pure dictator, without the slightest pollution with political theory or statesmanship ; and the pure separate nation, without the slightest foundation for its existence, either in history or in geography. Aguirre is the pure spirit of whatever is worst in Spanish public life. If the trappings of rhetoric and politics, the colour of history and geography, and the gestures of emotion and civil war are removed from so many past and present episodes and problems of Spanish and Spanish-American public life, what remains is Aguirre : the purely subjective spirit of dictatorship ruling in total anarchy over a purely invented separate nation of unruly Spaniards. The spirit of Aguirre was one of the hidden impulses under every Spanish enterprise in the New World, whether creative and magnanimous, such as that of Hernán Cortés, or selfish and destructive, such as those of many a smaller adventurer ; and it will move with its vigorous drive every one of the great leaders of the wars of secession.(12)

*   *   *

We know that, along with this individual element, a collective ferment of strife stirred in the Indies : that tendency to civil war which even slight differences of interest or of opinion suffice all too often to arouse in the Spanish soul ; and we have seen in the *Annals of Potosí* that the Basques were also powerful and active in this field. Their pride and over-bearing ways, together with the touchy character and high-handed reactions of " the other nations," gradually led to an actual civil war in the first quarter of the seventeenth century. Two individuals who came to lead the anti-Basque faction seem to be at the origin of this new phase. " This same year " —writes the annalist under 1618—" came to Potosí Don Antonio Xedels or Xeldres, born in Almagro, a man of pride and terrible in his deeds, a bitter enemy of the Basques, Castillians and Extremadurians ; and he ordered all the Basques to be exterminated, and became leader of the Creoles."(13)

So much for one of the leaders. As for the other and the causes of the trouble : " The same year "—the annalist goes on to say—" came Don Luis Valdivieso, an Andalusian, a brave young man, though turbulent and noisy, who was the occasion of a lively incident that same year. During a game of tennis, having struck Martín de Usurbi, a Basque, with his racket, Creoles and Andalusians fought against the Basques and many on both sides were wounded. The Andalusians, Creoles and Extremadurians nursed then a most remarkable rancour against the Basques. . . ." Note the grouping and compare it with those Xeldres hated, for it is not quite the same, i.e., there is no reason, no policy, under it all " . . . and if one looks at it dispassionately, not without reason were the Basques destroyed by their adversaries, for with their arrogance and intractability, they themselves caused and provoked the trouble and irritated their enemies." This, however, is not all. " In the same year, 1602, the Basques began to stand out both in arms and wealth ; 80 of them were silver-makers ; 160, merchants ; there were Basques in the city worth a million, 500, 600, and 800 thousand *pesos*, all Basques ; and out of 12 silver merchants there were, 8 were Basques ; out of 12 aldermen, 6 were Basques. In most years 2 *alcaldes* elected

YOUNG WOMAN OF TEHUANTEPEC   FRIAR SETTING OUT ON A JOURNEY

from " Costumes Civils, Militaires et Religieux du Mexique," by C. Linati (Brussels)

TRAVELLING—by carriage from Mexico to Xalapa

TRAVELLING—by mule litter from Vera Cruz to Mexico
from " Costumes Civils, Militaires et Religieux du Mexique," by C. Linati
(Brussels)

[Facing page 16

were of this nation, though it was against the Orders of the kingdom ; the *alcaldes* in charge of the inspection of the silver mines were also Basque ; out of 38 officers of the Mint, 22 were Basque ; out of 10 in the Royal Treasury, 6 were Basque ; and so everywhere in the commonwealth ; so that, wealthy and with such public offices, they were the lords of Potosí and paid no heed to the other eleven nations which inhabited there ; on the contrary they outraged and insulted them all ; that is why the Creoles, who are by nature touchy on their honour, having considered the excesses of the Basques, begged their fathers—Castillians, Andalusians, Extremadurians and of other nations—that they should on no account give their sisters in matrimony to the Basques ; for they wanted to destroy their conceit ; which being noticed by the said Basques, they grew indignant against the other nations ; both sides took to arms and so there was a civil war."(14)

So that most genuine of Spanish political plants—civil war —grew spontaneously out of the New World soil, providing another of the aspects which colour the wars of secession.   The entries in the *Annals of Potosí* register the growth of the feud— always complex, never or hardly ever defined so as to pit New World against Old World men.   " This year [1619] the partisans of the Basque, Creole, Andalusian and Extremadurian nations carried on their feud."   And the following year : " This year came to Potosí as visitor of the Royal Treasury the Accountant Alonso Martínez Pastrana, who later became the hidden leader of the *Vicuñas*."   Who were the Vicuñas ?   An army of Creole soldiers organized by the Andalusians and the Extremadurians against the Basques.   " This same month of June [1622] the Andalusians, Creoles and Extremadurians, having met in the house of Diego Sambrano [. . .] ap- pointed 12 captains for 200 soldiers they had enlisted " ; and now mark these words :   " and the Andalusians and Extre- madurians ordered the Creoles to destroy the Basques in open fight, for which the rich men promised to help them in every way."(15)

The picture is clear.   The rich Andalusians and Extrema- durians, jealous of the power and wealth of the Basques, armed the poor Creoles against them.   This word, *Creole*, begins now to spread to other New World men than mere Whites. In another entry under the same month and year, we read of the murder of a Basque captain at the hands of " Diego Reinoso, Luis López and another *mestizo*, a skilled worker, all Creoles." The land begins to win over the colour, the root over the foliage. Nor were the Creoles quite blind to the meaning of the events they were living ; as shown by the comment of the annalist : " and I surmise that this was due to the fact that the Extremadurians and Andalusians wished to keep back in safety and let the Creoles run the risk [. . .] for out of 200 soldiers, 150 were Creoles ; yet the powerful heads of Extremadurians and Andalusians conquered no more safety for that, for their own Creole soldiers took a considerable sum of silver from them for having left them in the lurch ; and the soldiers took the lives of many of them." Nevertheless, though undisciplined and difficult to handle, the *Vicuñas* were a Creole irregular army raised against the Basques by the Andalusians and Extremadurians ; they had adopted a hat made of *Vicuña* cloth, hence their name. We shall hear again of the hat and of the name, during the wars of secession.(16)

Just as we shall hear again the name of their leader Xeldres or Xelders. He had to leave Potosí for murdering a Jesuit who had dared preach, even though mildly, against his militant activities. His parting words were : " that all the Basques leave Potosí, those at any rate who do not leave it for the other life " ; and to that effect : " let you, all the nations, remain united with the Creoles, for that will make it easier to destroy these Basques " ; adding that if any man in authority, from the *corregidor* to the Viceroy, were to stand in the way, his instructions were : " Fortify yourselves in this Potosí, and never surrender."(17)

The war lasted for years, giving rise to dramatic scenes and ferocious battles. Much of the trouble came from the political power the Basques managed to secure. In 1621 the two *alcaldes* elected were Basques. " This year, Francisca de Asoz, a noble maid, while at home, saw a guilty man entering her house seeking a refuge, for he was being followed by the *alcalde* Uribarren. The maid, although at the time she was not in the company of her father, intimated to the *alcalde* that the guilty man was not to be seized in her house. The *alcalde* was indignant and administered the young lady a few fisticuffs ; and she in a rage embraced the *alcalde* and drove her teeth into his arm so that to pull her off he had to lose part of his arm. On hearing of it, Basques and Creoles arrived with their weapons at the moment the guilty man was coming out handcuffed and the girl being dragged into the street by her hair. In a fury the Creoles killed the servants of the *alcalde* with fierce strokes of their swords, and the *alcalde* himself just managed to escape."(18)

This was the spirit of the civil wars of Potosí, in which both sides gave themselves over to an orgy of cruelty, dragging their victims with ropes made with their bowels and making drums with their bellies' skins. Once this spirit of ferocity was abroad, it did not remain subordinate to its original passion ; " the wars were not limited to that against the Basques [. . .] for the eleven European nations of Potosí quartered each other, and the same applies to the Creole nation and the same to the Indians." And to be sure in the midst of the civil war, in 1624, we read : " This year during the month of March there was a bloody battle above San Martín in which the Manchegans, Extremadurians, Gallegans and Santander-men fought against the Andalusians, Creoles, Castillians and Portuguese, helped on each side by the Indians of their watch." No mention of the Biscayans. Here again a typical sight : one of the sides to a civil war starts a civil war of its own while the other side looks on or is perhaps busy at the same game. The civil war against the Basques, however, went on : the *Vicuñas* were cruel to any woman or craftsman who worked for the Basques. The authorities favoured the Basques and fiercely persecuted the *Vicuñas* and executed their leaders, usually Andalusians. These leaders rapidly succeeded each other till one surpassed them all. This was " Don Francisco Castillo, the most warlike young man in those days produced by Potosí ; and moreover very rich." He was a *caudillo* true to pattern, brave, imaginative and picturesque. He began with small means and bold guerrilla-like strokes, such as his raid against the *corregidor*, who was of course pro-Basque. " The *corregidor*, Don Felipe, was absorbed in a game of cards ; and the report of a harquebus astounded them all ; the 12 intruders rushed in and killed five men ; the *corregidor* went into another room followed by the twelve *Vicuñas* shooting at him and repeating : ' Long live the King, death to the greedy *corregidor*.' He hid under some mattresses ; he was hit by two bullets. They left him for dead ; they seized his torches and tying them to their harquebuses, they set fire to the four walls of the house ; always repeating : ' Long live the King ; to death with the bad *corregidor*.' The crowd was in turmoil ; the bells began to ring."(19)

Castillo was first a wild and dangerous chieftain ; later, through his daring and ability, a strong and dreaded general of a relatively well organized force ; with enough sense of responsibility to yield to the entreaties of a wise, brave friar in one of the many dramatic scenes of this picturesque civil war. The final assault against Potosí had been decided upon (1624) ; the city was " all prayers, clamour, bells, tears of women and cries of children. The night came, and towards midnight 80 horsemen and 120 infantrymen of the *Vicuñas* entered Potosí ; they came down by San Martín and they were already entering the street where the convent and church of Our Lady of the Mercies is situated, when the V.R.F. *Comendador* and all the Community with the Sacrament uncovered and many candles burning came out, surrounded by innumerable women and children all weeping [. . .] [The *Vicuñas*] alighted from their horses, for after all they were Christians, adored the Holy Sacrament, and as the Father *Comendador* saw their fierceness turned to meekness, he ordered a procession."(20)

Everybody took this as a good omen, and so it was, but first, " owing to abominable reports spread by the Basque nation," a royal *cedula* was received in Lima ordering the destruction of the *Vicuñas* " by blood and iron." Castillo decided to resist, turning Potosí into a fortress. This time the Basques negotiated, and peace and amity were sworn in September of that year. The pact was consolidated by a marriage between a daughter of Castillo and a son of one of the Basque leaders, Francisco de Oyanume. The story, however, does not end there ; nor would it be truly representative of Spanish and Spanish-American history if it did. Two epilogues complete it. First, the *Vicuña* soldiers, out of a job, found another leader. In the course of this war, started by rich against rich, many poor adventurers had sided with the *Vicuñas*. " The triumphant *Vicuñas* "—writes the annalist— " and in particular the scum which had taken sides with them, went about streets and squares with bull-horns ; entered the houses and demanded that these horns be filled with silver ; and if they were not so filled, they struck the householders with the horns on the face, killed people and committed other excesses." This scum chose a leader known as *el Galleguillo*. Castillo asked the Viceroy for powers against his old soldiers, still known as *Vicuñas*, and still wearing the *Vicuña* hat. The Viceroy made him Captain General and *alcalde* ; and Castillo " raised a squadron, went out in search of the rebels and wheresoever he met one he hanged him until he disposed of them all." Let us take note of this : The revolutionary *guerillero* turns Captain General and Conservative, while his soldiers blossom out into sheer anarchy. The second epilogue must be given in the words of the annalist : " The city thus remained quite quiet, as concerned the *Vicuñas* ; for as to killing each other among these nations, that is another matter, for it ever was a plague of Potosí."(21)

CHAPTER XI

VICEREGAL PERIOD—THE CASTES

DURING the sixteenth century the numbers and power of the maroons increased, both because more and more slaves escaped into the woods, particularly in the region of Panama, Portobelo and Darién, and because the maroons kidnapped tame negroes and forced them to join the outlaws. By 1571, those in Vallano, thirty leagues from Nombre de Dios, were estimated at 2,000, a figure probably referring to their fighting strength and not to their total numbers including women and children. They attacked the pack-trains and throve on their robberies, for they lived on the flank of one of the richest currents of traffic then existing in the world. They took away negresses from the stream where they were washing the clothes of the citizens of Panama. By 1573 they were reported as a serious threat to the very existence of Nombre de Dios, and considered strong enough to enter into an alliance with French corsairs, or with the English who, with their help, were establishing a clandestine base on the coast of the Isthmus and exploring the land for further inroads. Letters to the King were of no avail, even when the murder of a Dominican friar was reported. So the officials of Panama wrote that the pack-train conveying gold and silver had been robbed of 100,000 *pesos*, including 18,363 for His Majesty; a case in which the maroons had opened the way for the English and French corsairs to advance to within four leagues of the city; and the officials " asked for help for they could not meet the emergency with their own means." The King was good enough to sign a *Cédula* allowing his subjects in the Isthmus to spend 10,000 ducats of the royal treasury for the war against the maroons, but expecting some co-operation from the cities and merchants (Escorial, September 3rd, 1573). The *Audiencia* raised the tax on meat and the cities were generous, but the maroons were not impressed and carried on the struggle.(1)

They were still going strong in 1577 when two captains

of maroons, under torture, confessed they were expecting the English whom they were to help to carry on piracy against Spain on the Pacific side. On Tuesday of Holy Week, 1577, Pedro de Ortega Valencia, sent in pursuit of English corsairs in the Gulf of San Miguel, came upon a nice picnic of " some thirty Englishmen and more than eighty negroes who were cooking a quantity of pork in kettles and amusing themselves together." He fired, killed twenty-five Englishmen and many negroes, and pursued the rest to the negro settlement where Englishmen and maroons had fortified themselves. He forced them to surrender or to flee to the woods, and from an English boy on whom " pressure " was exerted, he learnt where the booty of gold and silver the English had robbed was hidden. The report to the King entreats him to send galleys to defend the coast and to garrison the Gulf of Acla on the Atlantic and that of San Miguel on the Pacific with four hundred men. Meanwhile, arguing that with this new threat to the Pacific the financial means granted by the King were inadequate, the *Audiencia*, pending the King's wish, of course, and since the matter brooked no delay, decreed that the Panama treasury should be freely called upon for this war. In August of the same year Don Cristóbal de Erasso took a maroon village of 217 large houses, burnt it and destroyed large plantations of fruit trees, killing some of the leading negroes and two Englishmen. On October, 1577, more appeals were addressed to the King, not only on behalf of Panama but also of Peru, to settle garrisons and keep galleys on the Pacific and Atlantic coasts.(2)

These maroons were by no means negroes going back to wild life. Their weapons had perforce to be somewhat primitive for lack of raw materials—iron with them was more precious than gold—but they were civilized men who had built for themselves at least two towns, one of which, that which Drake visited, had " five or six and fiftie households. In this Towne "—says the Englishman—" we saw they lived verie civilly and cleanly, for as soone as wee came thither, they washed themselves in the river, and changed their apparell which was verie fine and fitly made (as also the women do weare) somewhat after the Spanish fashion, though nothing so costly." The English visitors noted that the town was " plentifully stored with many sorts of Beasts and Fowle with plentie of Maiz and sundry fruits." The civilization of these runaways was naturally of Spanish origin. Their religion, though by no means orthodox, for they had no priests, was Christian to the extent that " they held the Crosse in great reputation." The English taught them the Lord's prayer, but unfortunately also to desecrate churches while jointly attacking Spanish cities, and they now and then gave the negroes the spectacle of obscene and dirty behaviour towards members of the clergy and images of Catholic worship.(3)

Richard Hawkins is responsible for the statement that the maroons " accustomed to roast and eate the hearts of all those Spaniards whom at any time they could lay hands upon." But though the maroons were by no means tender to their enemies—who in their turn were no lambs—the detail does not ring true, for it does not tally with the general trend of all we know of the Blacks in the Indies—at any rate till the late eighteenth-century revolutions in Haiti. The maroons helped the pirates against the Spaniards because in so doing they helped themselves ; but despite the assertions of some of these pirates, whose objectivity can hardly be taken seriously, there was no savage, unbridgeable enmity between the Spaniards and the maroons, and after one or two failures, the two chief maroon communities, that of Vallano and that of Portobelo, made peace with the Spanish authorities and were allowed to live in peace and freedom with their own men in all posts of authority, though under a Spanish Governor.(4)

Small risings of negroes were now and then reported in the regularly constituted kingdoms. " This year "—writes Vetancurt referring to 1609—" there were rumours that the negroes assembled on the day of kings [January 6th] had elected a king and granted titles of dukes and counts and others ; many were lashed and punished." The punishment was of little avail, for in 1611 " the conspiracy was discovered which the negroes had prepared, and companies of soldiers were raised and an order given suspending the procession of the Blood, and on Holy Thursday, the day when it was known the conspiracy was to break out in Mexico and in La Puebla, a special watch was set in the churches. It so happened that a herd of pigs was coming along the road and what with the noise and the fear, the voice ran that the negroes were entering the city and there was a great turmoil till it was found out that they were swine and not negroes ; they arrested many and after Easter this year of 1612 they hanged thirty three, twenty nine men and the others women, in the square, and the heads were left on the gallows till they were taken away owing to the stench."(5)

This episode shows that there was a certain feeling of insecurity abroad among the Whites, even though they did not take the trouble to arm adequately. Blacks were forbidden to possess fire-arms, but the Whites who were not so forbidden, had precious few, as shown hereafter. The negroes were never a serious menace in the Spanish New World. Gage reports how in his days " all the power of Guatemala, nay all the countrey about (having often attempted it) is not able to bring them under subjection," " them " being " some two or three hundred Black-Mores Simarrones." But it is clear from his description (once his usual tendentious aspersions are brushed aside) that these maroons and the Spanish merchants on whose pack-trains they preyed had come to a tacit agreement ; for the maroons took what they needed without injury to limb or life, while the Spaniards went about practically unarmed. " All the strength of this place "— says Gage—" may bee some twenty Muskets." Now and then single mulattoes are found helping pirates or invaders. Yet, anticipating similar suggestions to be made later by Ulloa and Jorge Juan, a committee of prominent statesmen meeting in 1677 suggested that, in Santo Domingo, " the Governor ought to endeavour to foster and encourage the staunchness and fidelity of the mulattoes whose valour, agility and utility for the country he ought to trust more than those of the Spaniards." A similar compliment was paid to the mulattoes of Puerto Rico.(6)

Due note must be taken of this. The mulattoes are to be trusted to use the country well, better in fact than the " Spaniards," i.e., the Whites. The countries in question are Santo Domingo and Puerto Rico—Antilles both, lands in which the negro had replaced the vanished Indian as the human stock next to the soil.

*   *   *

Leaving aside the campaigns which had permanently to be waged against the wild Indians on the outskirts of the Empire (chiefly the *Araucanians* in Chile and the unreduced tribes to the north of New Spain), the vice-regal period saw few Indian risings of importance ; for there was not much to such things as the mutinies which enlivened the vice-reign of the Count of Alba de Liste (1650-3) or the rising of the *mestizos* of Chuquiabo in 1661, promptly repressed by a local governor.

The case of the Topia Indians should be singled out because it illustrates the forces at work. They were hillmen of a Chichimeca tribe known as Acaxecs. They rose in 1601 owing to the violence done to them by the ministers of the law who came " to drag out of their homes free and Christian people and take them away to perform painful work such as that they generally have to do in the mines." There were 40 leagues of " small *pueblos* newly built with their churches," but also single families of unconverted " gentiles." Christians and gentiles united in a conspiracy to exterminate the Spaniards. Hostilities broke out and the Spaniards were hard pressed while help was coming to them from Durango. The Governor of the province (then known as New Biscay) arrived on the spot with a few companies of soldiers ; but simultaneously came the Bishop, all the way from Guadalaxara, a trip of 200 leagues, which the good man had undertaken lest the military had it all their own way. The Governor seized the roads, " and he began to wage war and to press them hard and destroy their crops," to force the Indians to come down from the mountain fastnesses. Whereupon the Bishop " considering on the one hand the great affliction, hardship and death which these Indians were undergoing, and on the other that, as he knew through reliable persons, the mutinies and risings were due not so much to their malice and disloyalty to the King as to the ill-treatment, vexations and cruelties which they met with at the hands of the Spaniards on their own lands and in their own houses, he decided to send them his own legates and ambassadors ", advising them to come down peacefully trusting his own paternal word ; and so that the Indians should give credit to his legates, he gave the latter a mitre and a ring. These symbols fulfilled the good Bishop's purpose beyond his expectation ; while the Indians waited for their wisdom to blossom (" for they had an old custom never to carry out what they had decided in one moon till the next moon had set in ") a company of soldiers fell upon them. Whereupon a " latinised " Indian advised his brethren " to display the Bishop's mitre and they would soon see how, out of respect for it, the Spaniards would do them no harm ; they did so and, on seeing the mitre, Captain Canelas, a Portuguese, alighted from his horse and kneeling on the ground kissed it." There was no bloodshed. The Indians were impressed and sent messengers to the Bishop who received them with joy. " And on this very day the Bishop preached to the Governor and the soldiers." He told them how the trouble arose from the intolerable tyranny and vexations of the Spaniards, and the incident ended in general peace. Not content with this the Bishop entered the territory of the warlike Tepehuanes, preached to them in Nauatl, which a native translated into the local vernacular and succeeded in converting the five chiefs and in bringing the whole tribe into the fold.(7)

This episode shows the process of absorption, vexation, alienation, absorption again, as it was apt to take place under the ebb and flow of antagonistic forces, as well as some of the complexities within such notions as " the Indians " or the " Spaniards." There were, of course, many minor cases of Indian risings in this period, some of which will be considered anon, because they occur within the framework of wider events than the mere Spanish-Indian tension.

*   *   *

The civil wars of Potosí enable us to observe the first glimmers of a Creole solidarity based on soil rather than colour. But this was not a movement conceived in some isolated brain and spread by word of mouth ; it was a living growth hardly aware of itself. Therefore, as a growth of nature, it will take complex and at times unexpected forms. The feeling of solidarity between Creole, *mestizo* and mulatto (though not with the pure Indian) manifests itself at times in activities consciously and politically anti-Spanish, subconsciously and psychologically Spanish. " In January last there arrived in England, in the port of Fristol [sic] a little ship declaring it came from the Indies, and brought nine Creoles of those parts, mulattoes, *mestizos* and others, who came to prod the corsair Francis Drake, asking him why he delayed so long to sail over there, where they were awaiting him." This detail supplied by Sarmiento de Gamboa, in 1581, shows how early the New World solidarity was taking on both an all-colour and an anti-Spanish character. But it happened that the tendency to cross the colour-line was stimulated by events which broke the solidarity within the same colour—a not infrequent case with men of Spanish stock. We know that the " familiar Indians " felt a stronger solidarity with their Spanish masters than with the " unfamiliar " Indians. Raleigh reports that the Indians fought loyally for the Spaniards against the English.

There is a picturesque episode in the history of the City of Mexico which shows the Indians taking sides hotly in the most unexpected of Spanish civil wars. In 1569, the Franciscan friars and the secular clergy of Mexico came to blows over the right to hold a procession through the city and to say Mass in the Church of Santa María la Redonda—a right asserted by the friars and denied them by the priests. The procession left the monastery " followed by a multitude of Indians and some Spaniards." This detail, supplied by Torquemada, gives the clue to the whole episode : in general the Indians were on the side of the friars and the Spaniards on the side of the priests. " The priests took up positions in the middle of the street and endeavoured to stop the procession." There was parleying and some pushing. " And as the Indians (who kept very watchful and had gathered in considerable numbers) saw that the priests were ill-treating the friars, they began to murmur among themselves [. . .] and when they saw that entreaties and words were of no avail and that lack of respect towards the humble friars was on the increase, the Indians stooped for stones and began to attack the priests (who were numerous and well prepared for every emergency) and suddenly there were so many stones that it was like a deluge. [. . .] Many Castillians drew their swords to keep the Indians off and protect the priests ; Dr. Sandi [the *alcalde*] interposed his authority, but neither the Castillians with their steel nor the *alcalde* with his authority availed anything, and the priests had to flee, for they would have been killed had they remained, the Indians being by then bloodthirsty (though by nature they are meek) and the best the *alcalde* could do was to save himself, though very wet indeed, by diving into the street canal." The friars won the battle but wisely desisted from triumphing and gave up the procession ; and, no less wisely, the Viceroy decided to turn a blind eye on the events, for the whole Indian population had been roused.(8)

*   *   *

A curious riot. The municipal authority had been roughly handled, but the loyalty to the Crown had remained intact. The friars had the highest opinion of the loyalty of the Indians towards the King of Spain. In his letter to Philip II on the alleged conspiracy of Martín Cortés, the Franciscan Provincial of Mexico gave the King to understand his scepticism of any such conspiracy " not only because this land ever since the conquest has been of its own accord the most quiet, peaceful and obedient to its king which the world ever saw, [. . .] but also because Y.M. owns in it very many loyal vassals among the Spaniards of all conditions, who would give one thousand lives, if need be, in Your royal service, if a few traitors ever appeared ; and above all because the Indians by themselves, all of whom are most faithful to Y.M., are enough and to spare to secure this land against all the Spaniards in it." This statement, often confirmed during the wars of secession, tallies with a detail supplied also by Torquemada on Monterrey's departure from Mexico (1603) where he had been Viceroy for seven years. " His going was very much regretted ; and so on leaving the city he was followed by a multitude ; and what astounded people most was that Indian men and women marched behind him weeping and lamenting aloud, a thing never seen before in this country."(9)

All this shows that the Indian was gradually growing attached to the new community in two ways : to the Crown through the friars and the royal magistrates who happened to be just and protected him ; and through the *mestizos*, in a kind of biological link which gave him access to the political and economic activities of the Whites.   Here again, therefore, we find the two forces at work whose antagonism rules the history of the Indies : attachment to the Crown and inter-colour solidarity rooted in the earth.   The wars of secession will mark the last crisis between these two forces, one of which is then finally destroyed, at any rate on the constitutional plane.   But before this final crisis, it is possible to see the work of the two antagonistic forces in a number of risings of lesser importance which took place in the Indies during the vice-regal period.

One of the most significant was that which broke out suddenly on June 8th, 1692, among the Indians of Mexico City while the Viceroy, Count Galbe, and his wife were at evening prayers in the Monastery of St. Francis.   They had to pass the night in the monastery while the mob set fire to the royal palace and the municipal building.   The causes seem to have been scarcity of maize and excess of *pulque*. Vetancurt sums up the outcome of the rising in words which provide a number of telling and useful details : " Eight were sentenced to death and many were whipped ; *pulque* was forbidden and the public crier announced that the Indians would no longer wear long cloaks nor their hair long, and that they should dress according to the use of their nation, as was prescribed ; it was ordered that they should go and live in their own quarters of the city [. . .] and this was the wisest measure, both in order to find out whether they are Christians and go to confession and to make sure that they pay tribute to H.M. ; for while they live in the back yards of the gentlemen of the city, hidden away beyond the eye of both civil and Church justice, protected by the owners of the houses, who on no account allow anyone to enter their yards, they live like Moors without a lord, as was found out, for it was discovered that more than seven hundred of them for six years and even more had not fulfilled their religious duties nor paid any tribute."(10)

This picture of the Mexico of 1692 shows how the several classes and colours tended to weave themselves into a pattern of solidarity, and how both in habitation and in dress the composite society of the Indies was absorbing the aborigines. The measures taken at the time were bound to be ineffective and the process went on of its own momentum, gathering strength from the very earth on which it took place. The New World nations were growing. In 1629 Father Bernabé Cobo wrote : " But as the noise of war abated the weather cleared up and the Spaniards began to enjoy peace and quiet, thanks to the wisdom and good government of the viceroy, Marqués de Cañete, the first to whom this kingdom rightly grants the title of father of the fatherland."(11)

* * *

As the solidarity of the new nations or kingdoms grew, conflicts were bound to occur in which the community asserted itself on the basis of the soil and across the line of colour, particularly as the risings came often from the poor, the most mixed class of all. In January, 1624, there was a riot in Mexico. The Viceroy, Marqués de Gelbes, had begun his vice-regency well. Gage asserts in his honour " that since the conquest unto those dayes of his there had never been so many theeves and malefactors hanged up as in his time." He was named : " The terrible man of justice," and the " Fire against thieves." It would appear, however, that by his ruthless persecution of all thieves, this magnate was merely getting rid of his rivals ; for under a man of straw, Don Pedro Mexía, the spirited Viceroy organized a corner in maize and wheat ; and when the people asked for the price to be fixed at the legal maximum for famine years, the Viceroy, as president of the *Audiencia*, blandly pointed out that there was no famine, for the country had plenty of maize and wheat, as he (who owned it all) knew for certain. Both rich and poor (i.e., wheat eaters and maize eaters) were robbed. Both appealed to the Archbishop, Don Juan Pérez de la Serna, who excommunicated the Viceroy's man of straw. The Viceroy countered by raising still higher the prices of wheat and maize ; and the Archbishop re-countered by fixing on all church doors a bill of *Cessatio a Divinis*, i.e., by declaring a church strike. This was in those days a dreaded decision. Mexía took refuge in the palace. The Viceroy ordered the strike bills to be torn from the church door. The Archbishop held his ground. The Viceroy gave orders for him to be arrested and sent to Spain. The Archbishop left Mexico for the neighbouring shrine of Guadalupe, leaving on his cathedral doors a decree of excommunication against the Viceroy. He was arrested at the foot of the altar of the Virgin of Gaudalupe after a priest, brought over for the purpose, had taken from his hands the Holy Sacrament ; and he was sent to San Juan de Ulúa and later to Spain.

The sequel can be seen through the picturesque prose of Gage, twisted and retwisted though it is by the conflicting demands of truth and sense on the one hand and of his bias against the Catholic Church and Spain on the other. " Some of the City of Mexico in private began to talke strangely against the Viceroy, and to stomach the banishment of the Archbishop, because he had stood out against so high a power in defence of the poore and oppressed, and these theire private grudges they soone vented in publicke with bold and arrogant speeches against *Don Pedro Mexía*, and the Viceroy, being set on and incouraged by the Priests and Prebends, who it seems had sworne blind obedience to their Arch-Prelate, and therewith thought they could dispense with their consciences in their obedience and duty to their Magistrate." An important point to note, this early appearance of the priest as a promoter of popular revolutions in the Indies. But let us read on : " Thus did those Incendiaries for a fortnight together blow the fire of sedition and rebellion, especially among the inferiour sort of people and the Criolians, or native *Spaniards*, and the *Indians* and *Mulatto's* whom they knew brooked not the severe and rigorous justice of the Viceroy, no nor any Government that was appointed over them from *Spaine*." Matters came to a head when Tiroll, the officer who had arrested the Archbishop, returned from San Juan de

Ulúa. He dared not appear in public. As he was crossing the town in a carriage with drawn curtains, the crowd guessed and began to shout : " *Judas, Judas, there goes Judas ! Death to the excommunicated blackguard !* " " The coachman lashed the mules, the Coach posted, the boyes hasted after with stones and dirt, the number increased so that before Tiroll could get through two streets only, there were risen above two hundred boys, of *Spaniards, Indians, Black-Mores* and *Mulatto's*." Here is the soil and the natural solidarity it entails kneading together the four colours. Tiroll reached the vice-regal palace. The gates were closed behind him and defended. In a flash two thousand persons were roaring their anger outside, " all of inferior rank and quality," says Gage. " They all cried out for Tiroll the Judas, sparing neither stones nor dirt which they did fling at the palace windows." They were the people of Mexico.

It was very Spanish for all that, as this English witness reveals. The Viceroy having tried to calm the crowd by alleging that Tiroll had fled by a back-door, " the rude multitude would not bee satisfied with this, being now set on by two or three priests who were joyned with them." This will be a regular feature of civil wars both in the European and in the American Spains. We can already catch a first glimpse of the *cura guerrillero*, the guerrilla priest, busy in the angry crowd in this Mexico of 1624. " Amongst them was much noted one Preist named *Salazar*, who spent much shot and bullets, and more his spirits, in running about to spie some place of advantage, which hee might soonest batter downe." Nor is this figure of the priest who has strayed out of his vocation and finds it at last when he can drop prayer books and incense to grasp powder and shot the only Spanish feature of this significant episode. Here is another which reads like a press record of events we have lived in our day : " They found, it seems, the prison doores easier to open, or else with helpe within they opened them, and let out all the malefactors, who joyned with them to assault the Palace." This freeing of the prisoners, whatever the rights or wrongs of their case, is a typical bee in the Spanish bonnet, as shown by all Spanish revolutions, not to speak of the episode of the galley-slaves in

Don Quixote. " The day drawing to an end "—goes on Gage
—" the multitude brought pitch and fire and first fired the
prison, then they set on fire part of the Palace, and burnt
downe the chief-gate."   A certain amount of looting occurred,
but Gage adds an illuminating detail : " They were soon
perswaded by the better sort of the City, to desist from spoile
or robbery."   This and other passages in Gage show that
while " the better sort " remained outwardly aloof, they were
at heart with the crowd.   Indeed when the Viceroy sounded
the royal trumpet and hoisted the royal standard, " all the
chief of the city kept within doores."   As for the crowd, they
reacted typically :   " They cried out and often repeated it :
Viva el Rey.   Muera el mal gobierno, mueran los descomulgados "—
the first popular cry of the wars of secession.   Nor is the least
Spanish feature of the episode the fact that the Viceroy had
to escape disguised as a friar and seek refuge in a monastery,
from which he dared not come out during a whole year.
These events of 1624 already, therefore, contain some of the
typical features which will appear later when the American
kingdoms break their political connection with Spain.(12)

Chapter XII

THE EIGHTEENTH CENTURY :
SPANISH AND CREOLE CRITICISM

With the eighteenth century a new tempo animated history. Till then events turned up here and there as fruits of the same historical tree, seemingly disconnected in space and time, though endowed with biological solidarity. But the eighteenth century brings a new style of a more sweeping and general nature. The medium seems less broken up into separate compartments, more uniform and universal ; and movements, trends, waves of thought and action pass through both worlds, the Old and the New, paying little heed to frontiers. The old patrimonial and feudal conception of the State as the king's estate dies down, and a more republican form takes hold of the general mind ; a change of outlook in itself a potent stimulus for the solidarity of the soil which was growing of its own in the kingdoms of the Indies. This attitude was not exclusively foreign in its origin, a kind of air of freedom blowing in to purify the confined atmosphere of a benighted and bigoted Spain. Far from it. There was a strong republican tradition in the Spanish Church, embodied with much variety of individual shades in men such as Vitoria and Mariana. Due note has been taken of the republican trend of the gown as opposed to the monarchist trend of the cape and sword. This republican feeling was of course perfectly compatible with the monarchical form of government ; it differed from the cape-and-sword concept in that the friars were more aware of the functional meaning of kingship and therefore of that of all the members of the body politic. They saw all social and political situations as trusteeships, and so attained an objective conception of collective life which was bound to make them more republican than the cape-and-sword-men, for whom all power came from, and was due to, the self of the great.

The political criticism which the eighteenth century brings to the Spanish world from France and England comes thus to meet, strengthen and at times oppose a powerful current of Spanish criticism as vigorous, if not more so. In what concerns the ethical and legal justification of the sway of Spain over the Indies, the movement of criticism had been flowing from the days of Palacios Rubios and Las Casas ; and throughout the sixteenth and seventeenth centuries, a line of outspoken and courageous Spaniards had kept this human issue under constant revision at a level of intellectual integrity far in advance of their time—and even of ours.

Nor were their writings concerned only with the theory of Spanish rule. For in the course of such a theoretical discussion they had to take stock of the failures and achievements of the ruling people ; since it was their contention that the sway of one people over another could only be justified if the conqueror opened to the conquered the gates of Christendom. Thus it was that the jurists and theologians of Spain often became the most outspoken critics of their own countrymen, and described in words burning with indignation the misdeeds of conqueror and settler, and the sufferings of the patient Indian. As time went by and the mother country, enfeebled by her inability to adapt her economic life to the windfall of the New World, gradually sank into corruption, administrative chaos and poverty, this line of criticism veered from the ethical and legal to the political ; and men of no particular holiness, for whom the salvation of the Indian was by no means a live issue, raised their voices to denounce the folly and incompetence of the Spanish State.

One of the first of these political critics was Count Gondomar, for many years Ambassador in London. Most of his letters touch on this subject. One, however, is of special importance. Written in Madrid on March 28th, 1619, to Philip III, it is a kind of bird's-eye survey of the Empire. After pointing out that the European balance of power is most delicately poised, Gondomar asserts that England is still hesitating, still seeking the Spanish marriage, but will go over to the other side " if in this equilibrium and balance the Empire falls, or even becomes embarrassed." This grim possibility is set down coldly at the beginning ; and the Ambassador goes on to say : " It will be very easy for England to put to sea one

thousand ships in different armadas and fleets, and one
hundred thousand men in them, and as for numbers of ships,
Holland can do more still." But Spain ? He points to " the
depopulation, poverty and misery of Spain to-day, which is
such that foreigners report that travelling is more painful and
uncomfortable than in any other deserted land of Europe, for
there are neither beds nor inns nor meals, owing to the many
taxes and vexations which weigh on your subjects, and this
cannot be denied, for it can be experienced travelling from
Madrid to Burgos and Victoria and from Madrid to Córdoba
and Seville, which are the roads which should be best provided
for." Spain, he adds, is too poor to keep her friends abroad
well provided, over which " weep many lords of Scotland and
of England and all the Catholics of Ireland " whose pensions
are poorly paid, when paid at all, by the needy Spanish
Treasury. Spain has the best wool in the world, yet " most
of what we put on is manufactured by England, Holland and
other foreign nations." The law ordering all exports from
Castille to sail in Castillian bottoms was imitated by a Parliament of Queen Elizabeth, but it is enforced in England and
not in Spain, so that " our ports are full of English and Dutch
ships, while in their ports there is never a Spanish ship to be
seen." Every year " more than twelve millions of gold and
silver go out of Spain, and even though ten come in, we have
to mint bad money to live, and grant it the value it has not nor
can have anywhere." Gondomar sees the economic cause of
the trouble : " In Spain more than five people out of six are
useless for trade and the support of human life, while in
England and Holland the idle do not number one in a hundred." But his eye penetrates deeper than the economic
crust of things, to the very core of the sick soul of Spain : " to
devote so much time to the interests and pleasures privy to
anyone must perforce deprive the commonwealth of the men
and time needed for it, whence our general trend to hold it
less regrettable gradually to die out in common than to seek
adequate remedies for our own ills."

Powerful though the enemies of Spain were, they did not
need to fight to conquer her. " Warfare nowadays is not
limited to sheer force, as among bulls, nor even to battles, but

seeks to diminish or increase friends and commerce." " And during a debate on peace or war with Spain in England's Council of State, a Councillor said they ought to consider that in war, though they had sacked and looted all the cities they had wished, still it had cost money and fleets, and the sacked cities were still standing ; while in peace, they in fact had Seville and Lisbon and the Indies right in London, so that were peace to continue for a few years, Spain would be ripe for them to go and take possession of her without meeting with any resistance or having to fire a shot." And Count Gondomar concludes : " This monarchy is dying out post haste."(1)

*   *   *

Later in the century the Court of Charles II was flooded with the writings of a biting and prolific critic of the Empire. Gabriel Fernández de Villalobos was born towards 1642 in Almendros, in the diocese of Cuenca, of humble extraction. He was twelve when he went to the Indies and was successively foreman in a sugar mill, soldier, sailor, Black-slave trader and smuggler. He was shipwrecked five times ; was made a prisoner in Brazil, sold as a slave in Barbados and rescued by the Dutch on condition he should settle in Curaçao to engage in clandestine trade with the Spanish Indies on their behalf. In 1675 he was in Madrid parading as a Captain from the Indies ; later, the Spanish Minister in Lisbon reported that he was a dangerous person who might try to go to France and work against Spain. He was attracted to Madrid, made Marqués de Varinas, Admiral and Knight of Santiago and allowed to dabble in foreign affairs. It was mostly during this period that he wrote over a hundred letters to the Queen mother and to the King ; and several treatises on the Indies and their misgovernment. He was imprisoned in 1695 and sent to Orán, whence, though nearly blind, he escaped in 1698. From Algiers he offered his services and ideas to Louis XIV, who does not seem to have been interested in the offer.

Varinas was an adventurer bent on hewing a career for himself, and all he says must be handled with caution ; but he knew the Indies well, and the abuses he reported, though

possibly exaggerated, rested on a foundation of fact. The
picture he draws is lamentable, even if due weight is given
to the fact that it corresponds to the lowest period of Spain
and her Empire. He lays special stress on the corruption
which had eaten up the whole body politic owing to the sale
of public offices. He points out that Spanish theologians had
always advised against the sale of offices even when, as in
Spain, the money went to the Royal Treasurer ; but that, in
the Indies, the Viceroys, in the teeth of royal orders, sold
every post in their gift, i.e., 160 in New Spain and many
more in Peru. He asserts that the pillaging of Veracruz by
Van Horn and Graeff in 1683 was due to the fact that the
governorship of the city had been sold by the Viceroy to a
man with no military qualifications ; and describes the de-
plorable effects on justice and finance which such a system
entailed. Nor does he stop in awe at the threshold of the
Council of the Indies ; for, having pointed out that the system
of settling by " composition " i.e., money payments, such
crimes as sacrileges, simonies, sham sales, usuries, rapines,
murders, crimes against God or the King, was bad in itself
wherever the money went, he adds : " Would anyone believe
that this money is distributed among the ministers on the
ground that it is a custom which the years have made in-
violable ? It is not very much in agreement with the laws of
God, but it is done." The responsibility of the Crown was,
therefore, heavily engaged in this pernicious system, particularly as, after the death of Don Juan de Austria, when
power was wielded almost absolutely by the Queen mother,
the Viceroys of Mexico and Peru had to pay heavy sums to
be appointed.(2)

The conclusion of this outspoken critic of the system (or
lack of it) in the Indies is already a prophetic vision of the
wars of secession. " How all these evils "—he puts as a
title to one of his chapters—" caused by greed in the Indies
and in the other domains of Y.M. are consuming them and
may well drag after them the whole monarchy for reasons of
State." From the sale of offices, he writes, comes contempt
of the laws. " A few steps away, the very kings are despised."
" It is a recognised maxim that kingdoms in which ill blood

is inbred by politics against justice, corrupt loyalty as well, for every law is a king, and every insult to the law is a public offence to the king." Varinas, however, is no republican in our modern sense : " For laws have no more force or will than the living will of the kings who enliven and authorize the laws." He describes how, when the local authorities prevail over the orders sent from Spain by the King, contempt for the King spreads throughout the kingdoms, and that therefore it is inevitable that " those kingdoms [of the Indies] should gradually turn away their eyes from the original power of Spain, since it seems to them that they have all they need in the Indies." And he concludes with these striking words : " The separation of the Indies from the Crown of Y.M. hangs by a hair."(3)

With the uncompromising objectivity of the Spaniard, Varinas puts forward the view that the coming end of the Empire may be due to the doubtful legal value of its origin and to the crimes perpetrated under its flag. He lays down the rule that " no kingdom tyrannically conquered by force of arms has prevailed for more than two hundred years." He then points out that " the Indians gave no cause to the King of Spain for him to despoil them," so that " there was violence and force " on the part of the Spaniards. Luther, he remarks, was born in the same year as Cortés, which shows that the Lord balanced the loss to the true faith in Europe with the gain to it in the New World. He grants, moreover, that Alexander VI gave the New World to Spain, and that the Incas and Moteczuma renounced their rights into the hands of the King of Spain. Yet, he adds, we may still doubt whether the King of Spain owns the Indies with a good conscience, since they are being ruined and lost so quickly within 193 years of their conquest. Is there a hidden cause ? Were the Indies possessed in the spirit and intention in which they were granted by the Vicar of Christ ? As for the abdication of the Incas and Moteczuma, was it free ? " Legitimate con- tracts "—he argues—" require liberty, and the contracting parties must be free in their enjoyment of all that is allowed them by natural law." Such, he asserts, was not the case with the Incas and Moteczuma ; and therefore the end of the

Spanish Empire is coming : " I conclude that six and a half years only remain until the loss of the Indies."(4)

He is writing to the King, to his King.   And he goes on to assert that God wants to punish his monarchy.   He gives his proofs : " The houses of the conquerors are all ruined. Colón, Cortés, Pizarro, Almagro, none has prospered." " The other descendants of the conquerors who remain in the Indies are the poorest, most abased and despised people in those kingdoms, so much so that when any one family is seen in the deepest destitution, everybody says : ' These people come from the conquerors', and it is always true."   The Viceroys who return with big sums of money " are seen to die poor and buried by charity."   The same applies to most of the high magistrates and churchmen who return from the Indies. All the wealth that comes from the Indies brings nothing but death and corruption to Spain.   The deaths of Moteczuma and of Atahuallpa were unjust and even though the Prince did not give his consent to them, the wrong done justifies the fear of the loss of the Empire.   Darién, though rich, has never been really mastered by Spain, and the 1500 Indians there remain free, which God permits for them to be the accomplices of the English to keep the Spaniards on the alert and bleeding to death."(5)

*   *   *

This moral attitude openly condemning the Empire on the ground that it lacked a sound ethical basis, a striking human and universal point of view never absent from the Spanish tradition, reappears time and again under the pen of our critics.   " I bequeath to my successors "—writes Macanaz in his biting " Testament of Spain " (1740)—" some valuable possessions which a Genoese acquired for me, dethroning Emperors and depriving of their liberty peoples over whom I had no better rights than they over me ; however, after consulting Ambition and Force, they approved me for it, and I now declare that I possess such vast domains by usurpation and fraud, so that all arguments and justified complaints against me on that score are met."(6)

This strain, not merely of self-criticism but of self-condemnation and sense of guilt, will grow throughout the century, as the liberal Spaniard takes in (somewhat naïvely) the heavy doses of historical punishment administered him by censors from countries whose record was no better.   It will culminate in the agonized cry of Quintana, addressing to America the poem of the guilty Spaniard :

> With blood and tears are written
> In life's eternal book the cries of grief
> Which thy afflicted lips to Heaven utter,
> Accusing my own country,
> Forbidding her to write of glory or venture
> When o'er the field lies crime.
> Is crime never to cease ?   Have we not paid
> Three centuries of bitter expiation ?
> We are no longer
> Those who before the world, the wings of daring
> Donned and across the seas flew to thy shores,
> And from thy silence dragged thee
> Bleeding and chained.
> . . . .
> Oh Virgin of the World, innocent America !(7)

Macanaz was one of this long line of embittered and pessimistic idealists.   He was a devout Catholic, the author of a Memoir in defence of the Immaculate Conception of the Virgin, as well as of many works on religious themes, including some upholding the Inquisition.   But he was a man who thought for himself, deeply imbued with a rationalistic sense of order, a typical product of the era.   Born in Hellin, in the kingdom of Murcia, of a family of small nobility, he studied in Salamanca, where he gave early proof of his reforming zeal by inducing his fellow students to give up a tradition whereby the election of the new Rector was celebrated with turbulent festivities, usually ending in brawls and deaths, replacing them by a peaceful procession.   In the War of Succession he sided with Philip V, rose rapidly in the King's confidence, became his secretary and later *Intendente* of Aragón.   This brief period of power lasted from 1710 till 1714.   Macanaz came into conflict with the Inquisition ; not through any of his ideas, which were strictly orthodox, but because he advised the King against granting the see of Toledo to the Italian Cardinal del Giudice, who was Inquisitor General, and because he wished to put the Holy Office more fully than it already was under the authority of the King.   The duel which ensued between the two men acquired more than merely personal substance on this second account.   This sealed his fate.   Weakly defended by two successive monarchs, Philip V and Ferdinand VI, Macanaz was exiled, sometimes on diplomatic missions, sometimes for reasons of health ; and even when the Roman party, Giudice and his countryman Alberoni, had left Spain which they had ruled, he remained a suspect. His exile lasted thirty-four years.   But it turned out to be the best part of his life.   He was sent as a plenipotentiary to the Congress of Breda, with instructions to keep in strict agreement with France and on the basis of the Treaty of Utrecht.   But he allowed himself to be drawn into a separate treaty with Britain by Lord Sandwich, who dangled Gibraltar and Minorca before him.   He was recalled, and for the first time in thirty-four years re-entered Spain.   He was 78.   He was arrested and sent to La Coruña, where he spent twelve years in jail.   The first act of the Queen Regent on the death of Ferdinand VI was to set him free.   He was 90.   He went straight to his native city and died.

He had written copiously and on nearly every subject concerning the government of Spain, including, of course, the Indies.   And he mentions a manuscript " against several authors who tried to blacken the Spaniards of the New World whom the visible hand of God led there to spread His Gospel and keeps there against so many enemies who in so many ways have tried to turn them out of those lands."   At first sight, this is an attitude in open contradiction with that which, one year later, he was to take in his Testament of Spain.   But a merely logical contradiction.   For, in the realm of life, there was room for both : an assertion of the relatively good cause of the Spaniards in the Indies, especially if pitted against the foreigner who attacked them with no better title or record ; and an anguished cry of rebellion and protest against the shortcomings of his own countrymen which he had experienced in his own broken life.(8)

For the Testament of Spain, particularly in what concerns the Indies, is by no means an objective statement, like Gondomar's letters, or a more or less interested criticism, like that of the disgruntled Varinas ; it is a bitter cry of a wounded heart, disappointed in its idealism. " True "—Spain is made to say—" in actual fact I own but little [of the Indies] besides the bare minimum on the coasts, together with a few islands ; and a very small portion is owned by France and England ; but the industry of these powers has enabled them to develop the inner part of their colonies by their activity and my negligence. To administer them, there are in Madrid a tribunal known as the Council of the Indies, and a Secretariat of State in my palace, both equally well organized, so that the sagacity of my Council in governing such vast domains is much admired in Europe, considering the Councillors have hardly gone beyond the borders of Spain (and many of them not even beyond the borders of their own dwellings), whose knowledge of America is not due to their own study, nor to their keenness to read ; so that their decisions are hard to understand and to foresee. [. . .] It is my wish that viceroyalties and governorships should be given to the neediest, so that powerful estates may be founded, and titles of nobility be bought and written on parchment to feed moth and swell vanity. I recommend them not to hinder as rigorously as they should, as provided for in Royal Orders, the trade of foreign nations known as contraband, and to grant tacit permits in exchange for some stipend to cover the risk should they be found out. And though by law such a trade can only be carried on by Spaniards, these shall act as men of straw for the benefit of the foreigners whose the goods are. As for the abuses committed against the Indians, I allow them to continue owing to their useful results, without fear lest the Court may ever hear of them, since even if it did, the grievances of these wretched people would find no redress ; for the very labour they spend in working the mines and in serving their despotic masters shall be their worst enemy. In the books and Customs offices of Cádiz, the sums of money shall not be registered to ensure payment of the royal dues according to their actual amount, but according to the will of their owners, this being allowed against the sacrifice of a small part thereof as a present to the officials. As for troops, fortresses and other war matters, I have already said nothing must be done, since in this way freedom will be restored to those wretched kingdoms, who weeping in their slavery will in the end arm on their own behalf to recover what belongs to them ; and I shall be delivered from this scruple which torments me in my last hour. The fancy and honour of ownership, I give the Spaniards ; but the usufruct I give to all the nations of Europe, particularly to Englishmen and Frenchmen, whom I allow to trade on their own [with the Indies] without scandal, for the benefit of my governors, and I order the coast guards to help them as much as they can."

Macanaz' conclusion is the same as that of Gondomar, but couched in bitterer terms. Beholding her coming death, Spain commits suicide : " Disillusioned as to what I am and in despair as to what I might have been (a torment which makes my ills more acute) and guessing from my weakness that my end is near, I beg all the powers of Europe to be present in person at my funeral, particularly England to whom I entrust my heart as a proof of my affection."(9)

*   *   *

When the mother country felt in such a gloomy mood, the Indies themselves could hardly be more optimistic as to the fate of the Empire of which they were then the wealthiest part. About the same year, in 1745, a book was published in Madrid in which we perceive this critical, even contemptuous attitude of the Spaniard overseas for the metropolitan Spaniard and his ways. It purports to be a Letter from the Marqués de la Villa de San Andrés, a nobleman from the Canary Islands, to a friend of his, on what he thinks about the Court of Madrid. But the editor is not the alleged author. He is a friar, " the senior brother in the province of St. Joseph in the kingdom of Peru." No printer's name is given, no licence, no approval by any civil or ecclesiastical authority. The book contains passages of so Voltairian, indeed so blasphemous a character, that one may take for certain that its publication was clandestine. The bogus friar, who parades as a bogus editor, says he printed one hundred copies for the author's friends, " for he has many in Lisbon, in Galicia, the Canary Islands, the Indies and Spain." Rather an odd list of countries. Speaking of the persons he consulted before publishing it, he mentions Dr. Don Ignacio Zevallos, " a person worthy of all trust, for his deserts, both inborn and acquired, though a graduate of the University of Mexico, a school the dollars from which are more highly esteemed than the texts. He has been my best standby ; for all Americans, whether out of jealousy or spite, look down upon European people as inferior. Such is the golden haughtiness which money is apt to breed." The book is little else than a biting satire against Peninsular Spaniards on the part of the mysterious author, who may well be a Canary-islander after all, for he turns his contempt now eastwards, now westwards. In the course of a story of how he proposed to form a company for selling Spanish wines in England, he tells how he was referred to the Secretary of State for the Indies, " of whose New World these people in Madrid consider we are a part." And he significantly comments : " Indians, Sir, on what map ? *Mestizos*, the Canary islanders, who said it ? Americans, why ? "(10)

Yet though not American, he is no metropolitan either, and looks on the things and people of Spain with that eye of the observer enough at home to see all, yet foreign enough to criticize all—an attitude which was by then beginning to be typical of the Creole. " The churches are more or less ordinary, little better than good churches for a village. St. Philip which is the one they most praise to us at home, furrowing their foreheads, raising their eyes and twisting their necks, perhaps because they mistake us for Indians, or because, without 'perhaps' they are Indians themselves, its plaster mouldings, the smallness of the church withal (as they all are) can only be admired by nuns and friars. For anyone who has seen St. Peter in Rome, St. Paul in London or the Invalides in Paris, it is sheer ignorance and simplicity to speak of the churches of Madrid." He says of himself that he made " a league and friendship with the cold weather of London, Paris, Brussels, Liège and Amsterdam." With this well-travelled outlook, he remarks on the dirty, insanitary habits of Madrid

in bitter words—a sharp contrast with the reports on the
cleanliness of the cities of the Indies from so many Spanish
and foreign visitors.   The habit of throwing household refuse
on the street from the windows is, he says, " an affront to
reason and a scandal for foreign nations."   He swears " not
a single visitor of good sense can be found to speak well of
Madrid ; very many, to be horrified at it " ; and remarks
that " for the sake of amusement not a single man comes to
Madrid while thousands go to Rome, London or Paris."
No wonder that, across the century, he picks up a quarrel with
the author of that other book on Madrid we have often quoted :
" I cannot tell, for the life of your mother-in-law, or even of
mine, how Castro dared write that *Only Madrid is a Court.*"
And he tells a story which illustrates the Creole point of
view : " An American [i.e., a Creole] priest was walking with
me when an olive-oil hawker cried his goods, which they do
with the last three letters of the word oil, *aceite*, i.e., *ite*, which
as you know is the imperative of the latin verb *eo is*.   Whereupon, my friend turned to him and said : ' We shall not fail
to please you.' "(11)
    The author, however, is a true Spaniard and proud of it.
He scorns the facile generalizations of what he calls *characterists*
on the character of the Spaniards ; and reminds his friends
of the land and sea battles which they fought against heavy
odds in the past.   He concludes that the trouble is of recent
growth, and its chief cause poverty.   " Alcalá "—he writes—
" has twenty-four canons with the corresponding clergy, with
very good incomes ; a hospice of Devoted Franciscan Women
who go out only to mass, shepherded by their friar, who
shrives them in public, and in secret I cannot tell ; two
hospitals, five parish churches, nine convents, nine monasteries,
twenty-two colleges and a University.   If Paris had all that,
one would be astounded.   What of a place with only 397
hearths ? Alcalá has no more."   " Sigüenza's inhabitants are
the bishop, the Cathedral and their dependants."   After
giving some more examples, however, he adds : " You may
have heard it said that this depopulation comes from the greed
to go to America."   He does not agree.   For, in proportion,
ten times more families go from the Canary Islands to the

Indies than from the Peninsula, and yet the islands are not depopulated. The cause, he says, is poverty, and the cause of poverty is the tyrannous way in which taxes and dues are exacted and the peasant deprived of his capital property. Many, he asserts, who used to own 50 to 400 sheep have now none and so all they can do is to emigrate to Portugal.(12)

*   *   *

In these pages of the Canarian critic can be discerned some of the chief motives which led to the estrangement between the European and the American Spains. One was this sense of disappointment and humiliation on finding that Spain was not comfortable, rich, clean, alert enough to stand as the metropolis for such cities as Mexico and Lima. We should not underestimate these motives, superficial though they may appear at first sight. The rich Creole who had visited Rome, Paris and London, could hardly bear to think of himself as the subject of a king whose Court could not compare in point of cleanliness, dignity and (as Cortés would have put it) *nobility* with the two vice-regal Courts of the Indies. Too much value should not be given to ideas passing on from books to books. Ideas did play their part, and we shall come to it presently ; but less as original springs of action than as tools for a deeper mood, such as this estrangement, fed from the sap of the earth and the blood of three centuries of private and public history.

We know that this estrangement between Creoles and Europeans was fed by rivalry over civil and Church honours and functions. Ulloa and Jorge Juan have repeatedly described the heat which these feuds were apt to cause ; and in their time, the line of cleavage was already sharp ; they add, however, a valuable detail. After pointing out that even the Jesuits, though " the most cautious, the wisest Order, the one which, by its own government and prudence, teaches prudence and government to everybody," had been unable to avoid this kind of dissension in its midst, they go on to say : " Their colleges include subjects of all nations, Spaniards, Italians, Germans, Flemings, and all live in harmony except Europeans and Creoles, which is the only point on which no dissimulation is possible, though, after a rule adopted with the utmost wisdom, the direction of the colleges is sometimes given to Creoles, sometimes to Europeans, with no other consideration than the merits of the candidate. But for lack of matter on which to found their discord, the Europeans point to the inaptness of the Creoles for certain offices, and the Creoles reply that the Europeans are brought over from Spain as slaves to serve in the colleges, a truly ridiculous assertion to make in the midst of persons of so much gravity and science." This shows that the Creoles closed their ranks not so much against the Spaniards *qua* Spaniards as against Europeans, i.e., foreign-born persons, rivals in the market of honours and power.(13)

But the odium which the European Spaniard brought upon his head was worse still when, as was nearly always the case, he filled offices given by royal appointment. This is well illustrated by another remark of Ulloa and Jorge Juan. They are suggesting that half-breeds should be recruited for the army, and they significantly add : " The recruiting should be carried out by the ordinary *alcaldes* [. . .] without any meddling whatsoever on the part of the *corregidor* [. . .] ; for if the matter is left in the hands of the *alcaldes*, who are patricians, looked upon by the plebeians, as all other noble persons, with complete submission and obedience, everything will go through without a hitch. The reverse will be the case if the *corregidors* do it, for they are outsiders, very much disliked, and considered as men who go there to make money and not to govern."(14)

This tension due to rivalry over offices grew worse with the century. In a page which seems to reflect strong Creole influence, perhaps exaggerating the facts, yet the more illuminating as to trends, Humboldt points out that " for a number of years Madrid has been appointing persons to even the humblest offices in the Customs or in the tobacco Monopoly," and that " often it was due not to a distrustful and suspicious policy, but to mere money interest that every office passed into the hands of the Europeans." This, how-ever, sounds truer of the Spain of Charles II than of that of Charles III. The papers of Macanaz early in the century

G

and those of Floridablanca at the end of it show that while Spanish statesmanship oscillated between an optimistic (Macanaz) and a pessimistic (Floridablanca) view of the Creole, in both cases what was sought was the good of the land. Macanaz urges Philip V to allow no Spaniard to go to the Indies except officials, and even of these as few as possible, for he thought the Creole as capable and deserving as the European, and "it does not seem reasonable that they should be excluded from the husbanding of their own household." And Floridablanca lays down a number of rules which in the main rest on the belief that Creole churchmen and civil servants are corrupt, but that care must be taken to reward and trust those among them who are capable and honest. (15)

The pride of the Creole was offended when he saw a European Spaniard of lesser family or qualifications given the post he himself had coveted. As a compensation, there grew in him the tendency to see Spain as a backward power, when compared not only with other European nations but with the great kingdoms of the Indies. Humboldt records an amusing detail of the competitive form this rivalry between Europeans and Creoles was taking. Found without a passport by some soldiers in Venezuela, he was arrested. "I owed my liberty to an Andalusian who became most tractable when I told him that the mountains of his country, the Sierra Nevada of Granada, were much higher than all the mountains of Caracas." The German scientist has left us also valuable evidence of the change which was taking place in this respect towards the close of the eighteenth century. "The men of the distant provinces"—he writes—"understand but with difficulty that there may exist Europeans who do not speak their language ; they consider this ignorance a sign of low birth, since around them none but the lowest class of people are ignorant of Spanish. [. . .] They think that Spain still exerts a strong preponderance over the rest of Europe. For them the Peninsula is the centre of European civilization. This does not apply to the Americans who inhabit the capital [i.e., Mexico]. Those who have read the works of French or English literature easily fall into the contrary mistake ; they hold a worse opinion of the mother

country than that which was held in France at a time when
communications were less frequent between Spain and the
rest of Europe. [. . .]   They fondly imagine that intellectual
culture makes more rapid progress in the colonies than in
the Peninsula."(16)

This led to two consequences. The first was a change in
the name the Creoles gave themselves. For nearly three
centuries, they had been " Spaniards," giving so much value
to the word that they reserved it for themselves and called
true Spaniards " Europeans." We know the reason for
this : the yearning towards whiteness. We also know that
this psychological spring was counteracted by a force which
drew the Creoles to their earth. We now find that through
this under-valuation of Spain and super-valuation of themselves, a new force was rising which was to strengthen the
magnet of the earth as against the white yearning. The
outcome of it all was that the Creoles ceased to call themselves
Spaniards and became " Americans." Humboldt has
registered the fact. " These natives prefer the name of
Americans to that of Creoles. Since the peace of Versailles,
and particularly since 1789, one often hears them say with
pride : ' I am not a *Spaniard*, I am an *American* ' ; words
which reveal the effect of a long resentment." The spell was
therefore broken which had united many Creoles to Spain
through colour-pride and made them members of the Spanish
congeries of kingdoms.(17)

The other effect of this change of attitude was also noted
by Humboldt. " They prefer foreigners of other lands to
Spaniards "—a feature which to this day has remained
ingrained in many Spanish Americans. There were in this
the seeds of many an act of *donjulianism*. *   Ulloa and Jorge
Juan noted a tendency to accept English domination in order
to escape the gradual absorption of property by the religious
Orders. " This scarcity, in which secular persons find

*Count Don Julian, towards the end of the eighteenth century, brought the
Moors over to Spain to avenge the honour of his daughter insulted by the
King of the Goths, Don Rodrigo. Hence my new word " donjulianism " to
describe a tendency so deeply rooted in the Spanish character that it has all
but determined the course of the civil war of 1936-39. Don Julian belongs
to legend more than to history ; but this makes him the more significant as a
symbol.

themselves bound to live and keep themselves on what is left over by the Orders, or on what the Orders waste, has disposed their minds against the friars to such an extent that the situation might lead some day to unpleasant events. They never fail to point it out every time one comes within a short distance of the subject, and so they did it clearly enough when the war against England began ; for even the wisest and most capable of them did not refrain from saying (and we even heard it from some secular churchmen) that on condition the English allowed them to live in the Catholic faith, it would be bliss for those countries, and the highest their inhabitants could wish, that England should take possession of them, since in that way they would be able to escape the tyranny of the religious Orders."   And later on, Humboldt will write these significant words : " They [the rich municipal aristocracy] prefer to be deprived of certain rights rather than to have to share them with all ; they would prefer even a foreign domination to the authority of Americans of an inferior caste."(18)

*   *   *

There was no lack of Spanish thought on both sides of the sea to meet this situation.   Campillo, one of the Ministers of Philip V, wrote in 1743 a *Nuevo Sistema de Gobierno para la América*, in which he advocated that land should be distributed to the natives, that inter-marrying between Creoles and Europeans should be fostered and that the civil administration should be reformed by creating *Intendencias*.   When this system of *Intendencias* was discussed in a later reign (1768) Aranda contributed a report remarkable for its statesmanlike advice in favour of the " Americans " as well as for its tacit assumption of the centralising tendency in the Empire—a French conception utterly at variance with the opinions that were attributed to him much later.   He advises the King to " employ his American vassals in the army " and adds : " I do not merely mean the Creoles and Spanish-born, but also the Indians who descend from Indians [. . .] for whether born in Europe or in America, provided it is under the same lordship, I fail to see how we can justify the neglect in which we keep the bigger part of the Spanish Empire."(19)

Many Creole and Spanish minds in the New World were thinking on similar lines. An *Informe sobre Inmunidades del Clero*, sponsored by the Bishop of Michoacán, Antonio de San Miguel, but written by his Vicar, Manuel Abad y Queipo, analyses the defects and abuses of the social system and puts forward a number of reforms. It is significant to find among the defects of the system the distance which kept apart the " Spaniards," both Creole and Peninsular, from the Indians and castes. The chief evil, for the Bishop, was what still is the evil of most capitalistic countries : the rich tenth owned most of the wealth. But the difference of colour made matters worse. The privileges which the laws of the Indies granted to the natives worked in practice against them and should be removed. The Bishop proposed the abolition of the tribute, and of the " legal infamy " implied in the existence of separate legislation for the coloured peoples ; declaring them apt for all civil offices which did not require titles of nobility ; the grant of Crown lands to the Indians ; a land law similar to that which in Asturias and Galicia gave peasants the right to till all land left fallow by its owners ; and other similar reforms. Were this not done, the Bishop bluntly declared, not even the authority of the clergy would suffice to keep the people loyal to their sovereign.(20)

Towards 1796-7, Victoriano Villava, Protector of Natives and *Fiscal* of the *Audiencia* of Charcas, published two works of capital importance : *Discurso sobre la Mita de Potosí* and *Apuntamientos para la Reforma del Reino, España e Indias*. In the first, he condemns the system both on ground of justice and of expediency. In the second, he advocates a radical change, less pomp and more efficiency, a monarchy under a national council chosen by lot from persons elected locally, and in which the American kingdoms would be represented on the same footing as the European kingdoms of the Crown ; no Viceroys, but *Audiencias* composed of an equal number of Americans and Spaniards. Though he realised the possibility that his reforms might lead to a severance of the kingdoms of the Indies from those of Europe, Villava considered the preservation of commercial relations as more valuable than political domination. At any rate, he thought the prevailing system calculated to lose Spain "America both as subject and as friend." Typical of his age, Villava achieves a synthesis of new thought, mostly foreign, and traditional Spanish thought, for he is a disciple of Solórzano Pereira. In Spain this trend of thought was to lead to even bolder conceptions. A minister of Ferdinand VI, Carvajal y Lancaster, seems to have been the first to engage on this road, putting forward a plan for semi-independent kingdoms in the Indies. Later Godoy will take up the idea in an eleventh hour effort to stem the tide towards independence.(21)

Chapter XIII

EIGHTEENTH-CENTURY PRECURSORS

MEANWHILE, along with the struggle of ideas, men of action were here and there incarnating the general discontent. There were risings due to sheer personal ambition, in which we shall be able to observe the now familiar features of Spanish rebellions and *pronunciamientos*. Such is in particular that of Antequera in Paraguay. The Viceroy of Peru had appointed one Diego de los Reyes as Governor of Paraguay. He seems to have been a mild and unsuspecting man, who soon fell a victim of local intrigues, due partly to the jealousy of other notables of Asunción, the capital, partly to a feud between these notables and the Jesuits. Complaints against the new Governor reached the *Audiencia* of Charcas and an enquiry was ordered. Antequera was at the time *Fiscal* of the *Audiencia* and Protector of Indians. Moreover, the Archbishop of Lima, then also Viceroy of Peru, had granted him the successorship of Reyes as Governor of Paraguay. By law as well as by common sense, he was thereby disqualified; yet the *Audiencia* sent him as Judge-Inspector. He deposed Reyes and took his place, starting on a career of corrupt get-rich-quick government. Reyes escaped from prison and, in Buenos Aires, found that the Viceroy had rebuked the *Audiencia* and reinstated him in his governorship. He returned to Asunción. But Antequera resolved to resist by arms. Reyes, who came unarmed, just escaped an ambush by Antequera's troops. The *cabildo* was behind Antequera, almost to a man, and advised him not to yield the governorship. The reasons for this will appear anon. The *Audiencia* of Charcas, which played throughout an ambiguous game, issued an order (1723) confirming Antequera in the governorship till the Viceroy should decide otherwise *through the Audiencia*, a detail which was put to marvellous account later by Antequera. The Viceroy firmly insisted on his decisions, confirmed Reyes, ordered Antequera to leave Paraguay and appointed another man, García Ros, in temporary command, to allow for a cooling-off period. Antequera succeeded in kidnapping Reyes and had him brought to Asunción in chains. He then made the *cabildo* send a Manifesto to the King begging H.M. to confirm him as Governor, and attacking the Jesuits, suspected of having favoured Reyes. This Manifesto advocated taking away from the Jesuits the " Reductions " or missions of Indians which they had organized, the granting of seven of them to the Indians themselves and the annexing of the remaining Indians for the service of Asunción, where they were sorely needed. Behind the Antequera-Reyes feud there was the feud between settlers wanting Indians for their own service and the Christian socialism of the Jesuits which prevented them from getting these Indians.

Now we have the key. García Ros was approaching with troops. Antequera had the backing, not of " the people," but of the privileged Whites who wished their privileges respected and if possible extended. The open sitting of the *cabildo* of Asunción, which Antequera held at this stage (1723), was in line with all the similar gatherings held in the Indies since Cortés founded Veracruz in order to hold the first. Antequera spoke and threw his baton on the floor of the house. He was begged to pick it up. The whole scene had been prearranged by him and his secret council. Ros was confronted with superior forces and an imposing array of notaries and legal papers, again in the classical style of Cortés.

He withdrew, then came back in strength. But as the bulk of his troops had been supplied by the Jesuits, Antequera had the Jesuits expelled from Asunción (1724). Antequera had put together an army of three thousand men "made up of Spaniards, Indians, *Mulattoes*, *mestizos* and Blacks," most of whom were serving on a compulsory basis backed by threats. In his address to his troops he promised them abundant booty, but particularly " that the Indians would be distributed to the officers and to the chief families of Asunción." He won the battle through a ruse and owing to the carefree incompetence of Ros ; and while the mulattoes after the battle hunted and killed the fleeing Indians in the woods, the Spaniards (i.e., the Creoles) " thought of nothing but taking prisoners, and they made many." " Who were given as slaves to those who had shown the greatest zeal in the service of the dominant party."(1)

Among Ros' papers Antequera found an Order of the new Viceroy, Castelfuerte, commanding that he should be brought to Lima as a prisoner. He decided to resist, to cover himself with a legal form by the *cabildo*, and to promise Indians —ever the same style. "The only precaution he took— which he always took in important matters, to do nothing but upon request by the *cabildo*—was to have a Request presented to him in the name of the Province, asking him to repair to the Reductions [Jesuit missions] in order to submit their inhabitants to the service of the settlers who had merited to be rewarded, and to that of the public." He led his troops against the Reductions, but the flight of the Indians at his approach put him in a predicament : he was unable to keep his promise to distribute Indians. His partisans " began to grumble. He feared that they might give him up." Threatened, as he thought, by a strong body of Indians who came to avenge their brothers, he withdrew from the Reductions and went back to Asunción.(2)

Thanks mostly to the energy of the new Viceroy and to the wisdom of a new Bishop, Antequera had to leave the city soon after his return, before the arrival of a new Governor, a Basque, Don Martín de Barúa (1725). Reyes was set free and sent away ; wrongs were righted, including that inflicted on the Jesuits, who were received back in procession. Antequera fled to Córdoba, then to la Plata, and finally arrived in Lima, a prisoner of State, in April, 1726, where for five years he lived in the royal prison with as much freedom as if he lived in his own house. Time was to show that he put this liberty to the best possible use, ingratiating himself with the city to the detriment of his enemies, and in particular of the Jesuits. Two new authorities were sent to Asunción : another Judge-Inspector and another Governor. In his turn Antequera had sent from Lima another agitator, Fernando de Mompox. This Mompox organized the rising known as the *Comuneros*, a name reminiscent of the Castillian rising against Charles V. Barúa, disgruntled, countenanced the movement though not openly. The general trend remained the same : against the Jesuits and for securing Indians to serve the settlers. The *comuneros* ruled the city and province for months. Barúa resigned, afraid of his responsibilities. The *comuneros* adopted republican forms and set up a *Junta de Justicia* whose chairman took the title of President of the Province. (Note again the tendency of the *cabildo* of the chief city to assume authority over the whole province.) Their choice for this important post, however, was, from their point of view, a mistake. Don José Luis Barreyro turned out to be a loyal royalist who, by a ruse, seized hold of Mompox and sent him to Buenos Aires. This action did not prevent Barreyro from remaining President ; but later personal squabbles did, and he was displaced by a rival, Garay, an enemy of the Jesuits. Under the civil war between the citizens lurked a civil war within the clergy. Here and there in the drama we see the black mantles of churchmen coming and going, for or against the *comuneros*. Meanwhile the Governor appointed by the Viceroy had returned to Lima and reported that Antequera was still so strong among the rebels, whom he had led from Lima, that the Viceroy's nominee had been unable to assume power. Indignant, the Viceroy had his prisoner searched and, upon incriminating papers being found on him, judged, sentenced and executed (1731). This sentence, no doubt just, was received in Lima with indignation. Everyone saw in it a vendetta of the Jesuits ; and the Viceroy, till then loved and respected for his integrity, lost favour with the public. On the day of Antequera's execution cries of *Pardon* and *Injustice* were shouted from the windows. The clerical civil war raged at the very foot of the scaffold. " A lay brother of St. Francis "—writes the French historian of these events—" climbed to the scaffold, shouted *Pardon* at the top of his voice, then came down under the scaffold, hiding a big stick under his gown. Shortly afterwards one could see a crowd of people in which two Franciscan friars were at work ; the soldiers of Callao were ordered to shoot at this crowd, which seemed to have come there to wrench the criminal from the authorities ; and the two Franciscan friars were killed." The lay brother with the big stick ran for dear life. Cool and self possessed, the Viceroy appeared on the scene on horseback followed by an escort. His presence raised the heat of the turmoil ; and, fearing the crowd might try to set the rebel free, he gave orders to shoot him dead there and then as he rode on a black-robed horse to the scaffold. He was dead when the executioner beheaded his body. Impressed by the Viceroy's courage, the crowd dared not move.(3)

This execution and that of Antequera's lieutenant, Juan de Mena, had far-reaching repercussions in Paraguay. Mena's daughter, who was in mourning for her husband, a captain of the *comuneros*, donned bright colours on hearing of her father's death, explaining that she must show no affliction for a glorious death in the service of the fatherland. This shows that the *comuneros*, whatever their motives, felt the struggle to be a patriotic endeavour of a fatherland which was their land and not Spain. They were already what ninety years later Bolívar's men will call themselves : *patriots*. The *comuneros* fought against the authorities off and on till 1735. Though begun as a movement of the rich and aristocratic settlers, the rising became in time a popular and democratic affair : " There was then "—writes Charlevoix—" little nobility in this faction, the people had gradually become masters of its deliberations and sought to establish a kind of Democratic Government under no other rules but those of caprice and insolence." Discount the description of democratic government from the pen of a Jesuit and it sounds convincing enough. The patriotic and democratic character of the movement is further illustrated by the fact that the neighbouring city of Corrientes, summoned to provide troops against the rebels, sided with them ; and that when a new Governor, Ruiloba, having failed with wise and conciliating means, took to arms, he was deserted on the battlefield by all but a handful of men, and cruelly murdered. So that nothing should fail to make this movement typical, when left alone he shouted : " Long live the King ! ", and the bullets that shot him dead vibrated in a wind which brought back the answer : " Long live the King and death to bad government ! "—the classic cry of all Spanish rebels.(4)

The movement was strongly inimical to the Jesuits, who

were expelled for the second time from Asunción with more
violence than the first.   Behind this animus were two facts :
The Jesuits armed their Indians, who thus often became
useful as auxiliary troops for the authorities against foreign
invasion or home rebellion ; and the Jesuits stood between
the Indians and the Creoles who wanted the natives as servants
in Asunción and not free in the Reductions.   As late as 1730,
Indians of lukewarm patriots were confiscated " to the profit
of the chiefs of the General Junta."   Nevertheless, within the
borders of the Indian-possessing class, the movement was
republican in feeling and drew to its ranks members of religious
Orders at loggerheads with the Jesuits, and in particular a
Franciscan, Arregui, Bishop of Buenos Aires, who at the ripe
age of eighty, butted in, ousted the loyalist Bishop Palos,
and consented to cover the Junta's doings, accepting appointment as Governor.   Finally beaten by the Governor of
Buenos Aires in 1735, the movement of the *comuneros* collapsed.
But in its relatively long period of resistance to authority,
it presented nearly every one of the features characteristic of
Spanish and Spanish-American revolutions : the ambitious
man, the parliamentarian *cabildo*, the influence of the priests,
internal civil feuds, the opening of prisons to free the inmates
and a readiness to decide issues by force of arms rather than
by compromise.   This episode is, therefore, far more than
so far recognized, one of the clearest prodromes of the wars of
secession.(5)

*   *   *

Some of these elements will also be found in the rebellion
of Francisco de León in Caracas, an episode which recalls
the wars of Potosí in more ways than one.   This time—as in
Potosí—the oppressors and the tyrants were not the Spanish
authorities, but the Basques.   In 1727 a number of enterprising Basques came to an agreement with the government
whereby their association, the *Real Compañía Guipuzcoana* of
Caracas, should enjoy the monopoly of trade and in exchange
undertake to track down and destroy contraband.   The
Company was set up in 1728 " under the protection of St.
Ignatius Loyola."   The grit and tenacity of the merchants of
San Sebastián conquered all obstacles, chief of which was

scepticism. The very success of the Company called forth reprisals from a number of foreign, notably Dutch, clandestine traders who, with the connivance of Spanish authorities, were flourishing on the coast of Venezuela, where they even had offices and factories. Intrigues backed by these agents raised the first rebellion against the Guipuzcoans. It was led by a *zambo* known as Andresote, in the valley of the river Yaracuy, and was put down by the Governor with the help of the Company.

This early incident showed that the Company was powerful and that it had enemies, both abroad and at home. Efficiency and activity were its virtues ; trade and prosperity its reward. It grew to be a kind of State within the State, and during the war with England (1739-48) it shared dangers, losses and victories at sea with the Spanish royal navy. It was already so rich that in spite of these war activities it kept its trade unimpaired, and even undertook to reopen the lines to Veracruz and the Canaries, which had been closed for some time. But like a State, it soon began to feel the troubles which afflicted the Spanish State itself. Distance weakened central authority and its far-off agents acted often on their own. The Company was, however, a source of comfort, wealth and development both in Guipúzcoa and in Venezuela. San Sebastián, the seat of its central offices, grew from little more than a fishing village to a handsome city ; Pasajes and La Guaira built ships for the Company ; Plasencia developed its arms factory ; Puerto Cabello was cleaned up and rebuilt and the valley of Aragua studded with European-looking villages. Cocoa, tobacco, cotton were developed, and prosperity was widely spread. Yet, despite all these benefits, the Company soon lost the sympathy of the country, or at any rate of its leading classes. It was accused of monopolizing power as well as trade. Grumblings began in 1735, but the general feeling did not find its leader till 1749.

Don Francisco de León, *poblador* of the town of Panaquire, was *Teniente de Justicia* of the valley of Caucagua. Of Canarian extraction, he had a house on Candelaria square, in Caracas, which means that he belonged to the rich upper class. During the troubles of 1735, he had been approached by the hotheads, who wanted to get rid of Don Nicolás de Francia, chief agent of the Company, by murdering him.   He had advised calm and legal ways.   But in 1749 he was suddenly dismissed from his post of Lieutenant of Justice in favour of a Basque creature of the Company, Don Martín de Echeverría.   Then the usual game began.   León would not give up his post, wrote to the Governor, argued and opposed passive resistance.   While the two men discussed, the inhabitants took the matter in their hands and shouted from outside that they would have no Basque as Governor.   They would take Canarians, any Spaniards, Creoles, but no Basque.   An echo of Potosí. Echeverría withdrew.   León, nevertheless, at the head of a troop of landowners and their clients, marched on to Caracas (April, 1749).   Though he had no more than 800 men, the Governor, Castellanos, had less, and appealed to the *cabildo*. The *cabildo* met, one of its members, by the way, being Don José Miguel Xelder, a scion of the family of that " Xeldres " who had wanted to exterminate the Basques of Potosí ; and it was decided to go out to meet the rebel and ask him what it was all about.   The delegates of the *cabildo* could obtain from León nothing but two declarations : that he came out of hate for the Guipuzcoans and their Company ; and that he was determined to enter the city and achieve his aims, if necessary by violence.

León was more explicit in his two letters of April 20th to the Governor.   The first reveals that the chief grievance against the Basques was not economic but military.   The Company, he explains, had boasted of having defended La Guaira against the seventeen sail of Knowles (March 3rd, 1743) while, he says, " it is patent that all those of that Company fled " ;   and that along with numerous other acts of hostility committed by the agents of the Company, this justifies their resolution to expel all the Basques from the province.   But he expressly adds that the Governor has nothing to fear.   In his second letter he describes his aim as " the total destruction of the Royal Guipuzcoan Company, and the expulsion of all the Basques, so that in the whole of the said province there remains not one single person of that race "— another echo of Potosí.   Again he reassures the Governor as to his person, but declares that he will enter the town the next day with as many men as he thinks fit.

He entered in fact the same day, at four o'clock, drums beating and flags flying, and settled his headquarters at the Bishop's palace. The next day the Governor held a kind of Parliament : the *cabildo*, the chief citizens and the chapter of the Cathedral. Backed by their authority, he went to call on the rebel. León declared himself ready to guarantee order in the city and asked that a lawyer should be appointed to present his case. Under the guidance of this gown-man, Don José Pablo de Arenas, the irate captain wrote a more sedate letter in which he began by disclaiming any intention of rebellion against the city and still less against the King ; and asked that the Governor, *cabildo* and chief citizens should certify that the Royal Guipuzcoan Company worked against the interests of the King's Treasury and that all the public officials who depended on it should be dismissed. The meeting took place and heard many complaints against the Company including, for the first time, some commercial grievances such as that the Company raised the prices of Spanish goods and lowered that of cocoa. Moreover, León asked that the Governor should officially certify that he, León, had in no way acted against the loyalty he owed to the King and that the public crier should ask the citizens of Caracas three times " who and in whose name this cause had been promoted, and when this had been done three times, that the Governor should certify what the answer of the people was, and should give me witness thereof whenever I ask for it." This was done on April 23rd, and to the question : " In whose name has the Captain Don Juan Francisco de León acted when upholding the cause of the nobility and of the people ? " the answer was : " In the name of all those of the Province." Whereupon, with this paper in his pocket, León went back at the head of his troops by the same road he had come.

An emissary had been sent to the King asking for the abolition of the Company. The Governor left Caracas disguised as a friar, and, hearing this, León came back and obtained confirmation of the promises given him that everything would be done to satisfy the province. The Governor meanwhile asked and obtained from the *cabildo* a record of the April events—for he also felt the need to erect a barrier of legal papers round his responsibility. Entrenched behind this report, he wrote to the King informing him of the rebellion. León, seeing that the Basques were not dismissed nor expelled, gathered a much bigger army (the figure is given as 9,000, but this is hardly credible) and camped under the walls of Caracas for the second time, on August 1st, 1749. The Governor formally requested all the agents of the Company in La Guaira to leave Venezuela, and, for the second time, León withdrew.

Three new men then arrive upon the stage in quick succession. The *Oídor* of Santo Domingo, Dr. Francisco Galindo, comes to investigate the position and opens an enquiry at which León is abundantly heard. Don Julián de Arriaga, the new Governor, brings 1,500 seasoned soldiers and a cavalry squadron to crush the rebellion ; but finding none and being a man of sense, he promulgates a general amnesty for all who had demanded the expulsion of the Basques, and announces his intention to foster agriculture and commerce in every way, no doubt to offer to the province economic activities outside the scope of the Company. But the Company watched, and, by pulling strings in Madrid, had Arriaga promoted to the rank of Cabinet Minister and a safe friend of its interests appointed as his successor in Caracas. The new Governor, Don Felipe Ricardos, brought 1,200 more veteran soldiers, and started at once a campaign of ruthless persecution of the Company's enemies, paying no heed to Arriaga's amnesty.

León and his son Nicolás took the leadership of the rebels. Shooting squads executed some of the Creoles and New World Spaniards who had bravely defended La Guaira against the English seven years earlier. The Governor put a price on León's head. He fled, lived two months in the woods, came back and surrendered with his son on February 5th, 1752. His house was razed to the ground and salt spread over the land, and a copper tablet nailed to a pillar recorded " his infamy." He himself was sent to Spain with his son, and after a short spell of prison, volunteered for military operations

in Africa, fought well and died later in Spain. The King
rewarded his son by restoring him his property and good name.

Some authors have made of León the precursor of Bolívar.
As a political precursor, the claim is extravagant. León was
always a respectful subject of the King, and even of the
Governor, within the elastic meaning the word respect has
with Spanish people. He dreamt of nothing resembling
secession. He was, however, a precursor of Bolívar in a
psychological sense, just as much as Gonzalo Pizarro and
Cortés. He was an ambitious man, though the inefficiency
and lack of resolution with which he served his ambition has
led some of his historians to forget the fact ; an ambitious
man who profited by a general discontent, and after a pattern
now familiar, was drawn towards power as by a magnet ;
though, feeling the need of legal cover more than is usual in
his type, he failed three times to seize his prize. He was,
moreover, chiefly the representative of the white, rich nobility,
who felt ousted out of both their economic and their political
privileges by the Basques. The Basques may well have been
overbearing and over-ambitious, indeed even oppressive.
Movements against them cannot have occurred as widely
apart as Potosí and Caracas without some common cause.
They seem to have been the object of a general aversion not
unlike that directed against the Jesuits, whose founder, St.
Ignatius, was their protector. And in both cases the cause may
well have been a mixture of qualities and defects : success,
efficiency, discipline, mutual protection and push, and a
certain amount of secrecy. Yet it cannot be doubted that the
resentment shown by León's two letters was that of a man and
a class who felt outstripped on their own ground. León and
his followers were fighting less against the power of the Basques
as such than against those Basques who prevented them from
exerting that power themselves. The rising is, withal, one more
example of the series with which we are now familiar, and
the psychological springs it reveals help us to understand many
a feature and tendency of the wars of secession.(6)

*   *   *

There were other risings in which the spirit of the new days

was more apparent.   During one of the numerous episodes in
the life of New Granada, when English men-of-war threatened
Cartagena, the Viceroy, Don Manuel Antonio Flores, settled
there, leaving civil affairs in Bogotá under a Visitor, Juan
Francisco Gutiérrez de Piñeres, who had been sent from
Spain to put in operation a new system of taxes much disliked
by the Creoles. The Visitor went ahead with his plans in
the teeth of popular opposition. On March 16th, 1780, the
little town of Socorro rebelled. A woman, a shopkeeper,
tore up the King's edict shouting as usual : *Long live the
King and death to bad government !*—The movement spread
throughout the whole country, and many persons of social
weight took a share in it.   In fact, it soon became (if it was
not so from the outset) a rising of the Whites counting, for
their battalions, on the castes ; one of those movements which
were gradually detaching the " Spaniards " of the Indies from
the Spaniards of Spain, and linking them up with their
coloured countrymen in a new alignment of loyalties.   The
rebels took on a name also classic in the annals of Spanish
risings ; like those of Paraguay fifty years earlier, they styled
themselves *comuneros*. On June 7th, 1781, the *comuneros*
presented to the authorities a document embodying their
demands. The *cabildo* of Bogotá was favourable to them.
The authorities, too weak to repress the movement, owing to
the English threat, negotiated a covenant including the with-
drawal of Piñeres. This covenant, known as the pact of
Zipaquirá, was broken by the very authorities who had signed
it as soon as the English danger had vanished and reinforcements from Cuba had arrived in New Granada. One of the
Creole leaders, José Antonio Galán, was sentenced to death ;
but by the stupid and perfidious attitude of the Spanish
authorities the seeds of more trouble were sown in a land
which by then was ready to receive them.(7)

*   *   *

The most dramatic episode, however, came from quarters
much closer to the earth than any White could be.   Towards
1780, there were in Peru a series of risings of Indians, the
chief of which was that of José Gabriel Condorcanqui, who

took the name of Tupac Amarú Inca. He was *cacique*, or local native leader officially recognized, in the city of Tungasuca, in the Province of Tinta. On November 4th, 1780, he seized the *Corregidor* Don Antonio Arriaga, had him executed on the 10th, in the main square of the village, and thus began a rebellion which soon spread over the whole land. The rebels committed fearful excesses, literally wallowing in the blood of European and Creole Spaniards, and of others who sided with them. Condorcanqui was an able if somewhat erratic leader ; he had to share his adventure with another Indian, Tomás Catari, and with a third picturesque, illiterate miner and sexton who decorated himself with a mixed name, Tupac-Catari, styled himself Inca and Viceroy, and indulged in every form of lust while the going was good. After many campaigns in which the Indians fought with magnificent courage, while the King's commanders were often hampered by the indiscipline and cupidity of their so-called loyal troops, the leaders were caught and sentenced to those dreadful executions which fear, relieved, usually dictates and were then normal occurrences not merely in distant Peru but in such centres of European civilization as Paris. There was an aftermath three years later, when Felipe Velasco led the Indians of Huarochirí to another rebellion under the name of Tupac Inga Yupanqui, spreading the rumour that Tupac Amarú was not dead. He was also caught and quartered.(8)

Such, briefly put, are the outer facts. But what matters is the inner sense. What were these men after ? These men, that is, not only the leaders but the led. The answer is clear, but it is not simple. The trends are intertwined and they are of different, and at times of contrary, spirit. One of the chief trends was a hankering back to the Inca rule. This is shown in the eagerness with which the leaders seize upon the traditional names, Inca, Tupac Amarú, Guaynacapac, Yupanqui . . . but there are other signs, such as the attempt to restore the use of quipus or knots in strings for conveying messages, and the refusal to speak Spanish. " As I arrived in his presence "—writes Father de la Borda describing his first meeting with Tupac-Catari—" I met a most ridiculous

Indian, about thirty, dressed in uniform, with a black velvet jacket, a stick and a considerable suite, whom I greeted in Castillian, and he rebuked me, ordering me to speak no other language but Aymará, under pain of death, according to a law he had laid down." Indians had also been forbidden to take off their hats in church ; and when Father la Borda begged permission to bury the hundreds of men, women and children murdered by Catari's men, it was refused him and the bodies were scattered over the fields.(9)

Condorcanqui rose boldly as the heir of the spoliated Inca emperors. His proclamation is the work of a man either not altogether normal or who uses words according to sound rather than sense. No translation can adequately render the Gilbert-and-Sullivan character of its high-falutin, first paragraph : " Don José I, by the grace of God Inca of Peru, Santa Fe, Quito, Chile, Buenos Aires and Continent, of the Seas of the South, Duke of the Superlative, Lord of the Caesars and of the Amazon, with Dominions in the Great Partiti, Commissioner and Distributor of the Divine Piety through the Peerless Treasury. . . ." Shorn of its fancies, this preamble is *mestizo* enough ; for nothing but the Spanish Conquest could have enabled any genuine Inca to call Santa Fe, Buenos Aires and the Continent his own, and still less to give them such names. Thus, even when asserting its pure Inca nature, the grafted Empire showed signs of its mixed nature in this strange document.(10)

The second paragraph is remarkable both because it unmistakably asserts Condorcanqui's claim to the Crown of Peru and because it provides an excellent summary of native grievances : " Whereas it is agreed by my Council in prolix meetings on repeated occasions, now secret, now public, that the kings of Castille have held in usurpation the Crown and dominion of my people for nearly three centuries ; oppressing my vassals with their insufferable taxes, tributes, lances, deductions, customs, *alcabalas*, registers, tithes—Viceroys, *Audiencias, Corregidores* and other ministers all equal in their tyranny, selling justice for coin through their scriveners to the highest bidder ; including church dignities without fear of God ; injuring the natives as if they were beasts ; taking the

life of those who do not know how to rob ; all of which is
worthy of the most severe reprobation ; therefore and because
the just complaints of the people have reached Heaven. . . ."
Now therefore—what ? The conclusion of the paper is final.
He is to be recognized as King-Inca (again a *mestizo* title) by
all the cities of Peru. But the conclusion in the facts will
turn out to be somewhat more complex. Two points must
be brought to light before this famous rising is understood.
What was its attitude towards the Crown of Spain ? What
was its attitude towards the several castes and colours ?(11)

The first enquiry might well seem idle after a study of
Condorcanqui's proclamation. But there are other documents
equally authentic. On July 1st, 1781, Condorcanqui signed
a circular informing all " the neighbours, Spaniards, Creoles
and natives " of the facts which had driven him to rebel. It
evinces a surprisingly different spirit. The story starts with
one, Dr. D. Ventura de Santelices y Venero, one-time Governor
of Potosí, who " on the request of D. Blas Tupac-Amarú
Inga, my relation," " reported to H.M. the lord Don Carlos
III " on the grievances of the natives. But when the King,
Condorcanqui goes on to say, " with the Catholic desire to
remedy these evils," promoted Santelices to be a minister of
the Council of the Indies, this upright magistrate was poisoned
by the vested interests on his arrival in Spain. Whereupon,
Condorcanqui goes on to explain, his relation Don Blas Tupac
Amarú went in person to Spain to report on " the above-said
iniquities to the King our lord " ; and " the King our lord
was pleased to appoint him perpetual captain and Defender
of Natives for the town of Potosí, with a good salary on the
city's Treasury ; giving him full powers to wipe out and
depose the bad government of *Corregidores*, tax gatherers,
foreign usurers, the heavy *Mita* of Potosí, and other grievous
tributes and services which weighed on the natives." But
again, Don Blas was poisoned. And then comes that strange
paragraph which stamps Condorcanqui either as a mere
impostor or as a man not altogether in his senses : " I made
a third report to H.M. whose royal integrity, offended and
even indignant, imparted to me his ample commission aiming
at the total ruin and final extermination of *Corregidores*, tax

gatherers, *Chapetones* [European Spaniards] and other oppressions with which were loaded the poor natives and Creoles of this kingdom ; with special provision that if there were to be set up any opposition on the part of the *Corregidores*, with the help of the Creole settlers, or if the natives did not vigorously back me in my activities on their behalf, all of them were to be hanged, decapitated and destroyed." Whereupon the " Inca " announced that the King had granted him " the Viceroyalty of Lima, raised armies, bid all ' Creoles and natives ' enlist from the age of seven " and announced that " battles and marches forward will continue by dint of war alive and by blood and fire [. . .] in order to punish the pertinacious rebellion and to destroy bad government, so that the King Don Carlos III may live for many years."(12)

This and other proclamations to the same effect from the " Inca " and from his son and deputy, Andrés, show that Condorcanqui soon found his first stand—open rebellion as the Inca dispossessed by the King of Spain—too weak or even too dangerous ; and that, to carry the Indians with him he had to respect and honour the King of Spain. The explanation for this can be found in Ulloa and Jorge Juan. Observing in the eighteenth century exactly the same feature the friars had noted in the preceding periods, the two Spanish seamen insist on the touching loyalty of the natives to the King of Spain. In the course of their narrative of the persecution of a *cacique* by an infamous priest, they write : " but nothing afflicted the *cacique* more than that the priest should have falsely accused him of attempting a rebellion, smirching him with the infamous blot of disloyalty, and he rightly argued : ' Why should I offend my lord the King, when his royal kindness favours us so much, and it is the priest who vexes us, and why should I be so vile as to dishonour my fidelity so that the priest should triumph over me ? ' " And Ulloa and Jorge Juan conclude with this remarkable statement : " If one considers their loyalty, no nations in the world speak of their King with more respect and veneration. They never utter the King's name without putting the word ' lord ' before, and taking off their hats, a ceremony no one, neither priest nor *Corregidor* has taught them, nor can they have observed it in Spaniards, since it is not in use among the Whites. They always say ' the Lord King ' and sometimes, according to the matter, add ' the Lord our King,' deeming it irreverent to mention the sovereign otherwise."(13)

Feelings, however, are not inert stone-blocks ; they are as mobile as the very word *emotion* suggests. This loyalty of the Indians, staunch and sincere as it was, could be swayed by deeper emotions ; and some of the actors in the events of those days have left on record that there were Indians who were apt to change their allegiance, often with the tide of victory and defeat. Thus the Indians, once faithful subjects of the Incas, had become no less faithful subjects of the King. A rebellion against the King of Spain could not prosper among the Indians unless, as Condorcanqui soon found, it began as a rebellion *for* the King against bad government ; and the trend to disloyalty had to be kept carefully concealed till military victory could win over the Indians, persuading them to transfer their loyalty to their new masters.(14)

*　　*　　*

The second point to probe in this rebellion is the attitude which its leaders, father and son, took towards the several human colours and classes. Two facts are clear : they rise *against* the Spaniards of Spain ; and they rise *for* the Indians. Moreover, they are, if not the first, the most consistent in referring to the European Spaniards as " foreigners." In all their proclamations the persons to be destroyed are the " *Corregidores*, *chapetones* and tax gatherers." In a paper evidently drafted by, or under the power of, Andrés Tupac Amarú, seven men who call themselves " Spanish Creoles," i.e., white Americans, write these revealing words : " the foreign *chapetones* who used to come across the seas eating bran like pigs treated us worse than beasts, whether we were Creoles or natives, and they ate us alive with usuries and robberies, and for this reason the order has been given for them to be expelled or wiped out."(15)

This paper suggests the line taken by the two Condorcanquis. Out with the Europeans ; attract the Creoles ; death even to them if they do not join—what ? What was already a

national separatist movement, and not merely an Indian
rising.   The oft-repeated name of Charles III as the protector
and source of whatever power " Tupac Amarú " assumed
was an imposture to win over timid or loyal subjects.   But the
two features stand out clearly from the texts : the rising was
national and not racial, and it was separatist.   True, on the
whole, the Creoles fought with the government against the
Indians.   Humboldt says why : " The American Spaniards
felt, like the Spaniards born in Europe, that the struggle was
one between the copper-coloured race and the white race,
barbarism against civilization. [. . .] A movement towards independence became a cruel war between the castes ;
the Whites remained victorious."   There was more to it,
however.   By then, many Creoles were already brooding over
their dependent status ; but how could they back a movement
which, led by a *mestizo*, and resting on the Indians, would, if
victorious, challenge their own privileges ?(16)

Yet, the two Tupac Amarús did all they could to win them
over, and repeatedly made it clear that they fought for the
country of " Creoles and natives."   Condorcanqui constantly
refers to his solicitude for Creoles and natives ; to the many
vexations " which weigh on the poor natives and Creoles of
this kingdom " ; and both lament the fact that the Creoles
should fight against them " allowing themselves to be deceived
by their adversaries," and implore them to realize where their
true interests lie.   Tupac Amarú, junior, in particular often
addresses them as *paisanos*, countrymen ; and Condorcanqui
writes of " the charity which I feel towards my Creole compatriots."   In another paper which Andrés made the Creoles
sign he makes them say : " Creole countrymen of the city of
la Paz : As the love we feel within Creoles, countrymen and
compatriots [allows of nothing else] we announce to you the
success and plans of the Marquess [Condorcanqui] which is
no other than to abolish all taxes, customs and other tributes
suffered till now, which are not liked by our monarch Charles
III, from whom the said Marquess holds a special commission
to wipe out these abuses, which he has begun to do in favour
of the Creoles."   As for the European Spaniards they were
to be sent to " their country "—a logical outcome of the

growing consciousness of the Peruvian fatherland—" so that you should know my love, I should not like any poor Creole to die ; and as for the little Whites [*Blanquillos*] who are in that city, if European they may go to their country, and to that end I shall give every facility and do them no harm ; and if Creoles they are allowed to come out with their weapons and so declare themselves loyal." Thus Miguel Tupac Amarú, Inga, on October 6th, 1781, to the Creoles of la Paz ; and still more clearly this document, which must be given in full, since it is an excellent summary of all the trends observed in the rising : " From this royal chapter of Collana, October 11th, 1781.—My dearest nephews, descendants of the King Inga : I know not what reason you have not to come out and obey the commands of Charles III, who has given me orders to abolish bad government caused by those thieves, the *chapetones*, customs officers, *Corregidores* and other accomplices, all of whom herein mentioned may return to their country, for I shall give them an open road, and should they resist, I shall feel bound to punish their iniquities ; and should they not come out within six days, all shall be in danger, Creoles as well as *chapetones*, owing to the great activity and means I possess. I inform you that all those who have come out of that city are already beside me and have suffered no harm. I implore my most revered priests to come out as soon as possible. May God our Lord guide you for many years. I the Inga."(17)

*   *   *

The *mestizo* spirit of this rebellion is striking. Where did it come from ? The answer is that the life of the Indies was bound to be *mestizo* in any case, no matter who happened to incarnate it. Nevertheless, there is in this case a curious fact worth recording. Referring to Condorcanqui, Humboldt writes: " He was the son of the *Cacique* of Tongasuca, [. . .] or rather of his wife, for it seems certain that his father was a friar." This explains all. The grievance came from the Indian woman ; the civil-war spirit from the Spanish friar. Carlism before Don Carlos.(18)

PART III

EXTERNAL ORIGINS OF THE SECESSION

CHAPTER XIV

THE FOUR PHILOSOPHERS

No better proof could be given of the ancillary part which ideas played in the emancipation of the New World than the contrast between what Montesquieu and Rousseau stood for and the influence each exerted on the Creoles. Everything predestined Montesquieu for the leadership of Creole America. He was a liberal-conservative aristocrat, intelligent, constructive, fond of English institutions though by no means a blind importer of them, conscious of the fact that general ideas must be modified and qualified by time and place ; aware of the importance of time as the only ripener of political institutions, and above all convinced of the value of liberty rather than equality, in fact, a believer in liberty because, among other things, it helps to create a healthy inequality. It was Montesquieu who taught the world at large the value of a public-spirited aristocracy, as he had observed it by studying—with foreign eyes—the aristocracy of England. All this might have sufficed to make Montesquieu the born leader of Creole thought. But on top of that, his attitude towards slavery was elastic enough to allow the system prevailing in the Indies ample room in his political philosophy. He is clear enough in his condemnation of slavery in general, though able to argue the pros and cons of other institutions such as taxes on the tacit assumption of slavery. And on negro slavery, he is ironical to the point of ambiguity. Raynal wrote that " Montesquieu could not bring himself to deal seriously with the question of slavery." Slavery was then considered in France as indispensable to the prosperity of the Islands ; more deeply rooted and unshakable than any institution ever was anywhere ; and in 1716 French slave owners had been empowered to pursue their slaves when they fled from them even in France, which led to Paris becoming a slave market, where " there is no bourgeois, no worker who does not own a Black slave." A French author went so far as to advocate slavery for Europe. This explains why Montesquieu who, unlike Voltaire or Rousseau, was no tilter at windmills, attacked the subject in the curious way he did, so oblique that it led Members of Parliament in England and scientists in France to take his ironic arguments in earnest and use them to defend slavery. Any enlightened reformist slave-owner of the Indies, who looked on Spain as old fashioned, who desired to live in the century, and took his social pre-eminence and his slaves for granted, could just quote Montesquieu, ironize, feel superior and be happy working for better days on the lines advocated by the eminent Frenchman.(1)

* * *

And yet Montesquieu was not the leader of Creole America ; few Creoles quote him and few can have studied him, even though his books, and particularly *L'Esprit des Lois*, are often found in their libraries. The leader of Creole America was Rousseau. Now with Rousseau we are in the realm of incoherence. To find in European history a man as chaotic as Rousseau one must go as far back as Colón himself. The two are linked by a number of parallel features : the same ambulatory mania, less an urge seeking the new than a flight from the uneasy self ; the same prophetic attitude ; the same tendency to make the Lord say what they wish to hear. Both are discoverers of new worlds, and both find their new worlds first in their own ardent, chaotic and arbitrary imagination ; but both through sheer spiritual power and genius bring forth their new world and actually put it before mankind. Moreover, just as a few words from Esdras had sufficed to inflame Colón into believing in a new continent, so a few words from Colón sufficed to inflame Rousseau into believing in the natural goodness of man. The discoverer's extravagant impressions on the idyllic life of the Guanahani Indians— even though soon belied by gruesome events in Haiti—were propagated by Peter Martyr all over Europe. Vives took them up. Having praised the humane way in which the Indians, if sued for peace, treated their enemies, the Spanish philosopher adds : " These rude and barbarous peoples, beyond letters, beyond all worship and piety, are taught true and healthy ideas by straight and pure nature." Vives, a friend of Thomas More and an author Bacon knew well, may have been one of the channels through which these ideas passed on to the *Utopia* and the *Nova Atlantis*. The land of *Utopia* is discovered through a Portuguese who had navigated with Americo Vespucci, and *Nova Atlantis* begins with the words : *Navigavimus e Peruvia.*(2)

In all these dreams of a life regulated according to simplicity and reason, the New World is ever present, even if more or less mixed with reminiscences of classic dreams ; but a new world of simple men, shunning jewels, gold and pearls ; the very opposite of the life Spaniards, European or American, were actually living in the Indies ; a new world, therefore, discovered afresh by the mind, inspired in the idealized simple, naked native first imagined, rather than observed, by Colón. Las Casas had also been led by his evangelic zeal to idealize the Indians, giving a new lease of life to the myth even after Colón and Peter Martyr had found out those natives they had discovered. And this re-idealization held the field in world culture because it suited the designs of the three sea powers aligned against Spain. England, France and Holland saw to it that Las Casas was widely read.(3)

Hence the ideal savage. It was a creation of the Renaissance in which memories of Hesiod and Ovid met with narratives about the Indies, forming an ideal of a perfect society and outlining a philosophy of man which foreshadowed that of Rousseau. Erasmus, Vives' friend, is one of the leaders of this movement. He puts forward a thought which will be fundamental in Rousseau : that man is good by nature : ' I call nature an inherent docility and propensity to honest things "—he writes in one of his colloquies ; thus, undersigning with his glowing name the notion of the good savage he may have found in Vives, who found it in the *Hispani nautae* of his letter to the Bishop of Lincoln. It was from the Spaniards too, particularly Gómara, that Montaigne drew it for his famous comment on the cannibals : " It seems to me that what we see by experience in these nations goes beyond not only the pictures with which poetry has embellished the Golden Age [. . .] but also the conception and desire even of philosophy ; neither Plato nor Lycurgus was able to imagine a naïveté as pure and as simple as we see by experience : *Hos natura modos primum dedit.*"(4)

Through Montaigne certainly and possibly also through French books of voyages to the Indies, the notion of the ideal savage and that of the natural goodness of man reached Rousseau. He found in these conceptions far more than a stone for building his political philosophy ; he found a plank of salvation. For Rousseau was a Calvinist unable to square his puritan tendencies with his love of wine and women ; a sensuous, rather heavily incarnated man, who, time and again, had to yield to the demands of his flesh ; selfish, cowardly, lazy ; but an imaginative, creative mind who longed for mental harmony. As he himself wrote with his usual terseness : " Conscience is the voice of the soul ; the passions are the voice of the body. Are we to wonder that these two languages contradict each other, and then, which are we to follow ? " The discord could only be solved by making the unruly Rousseau obey the rules, i.e., cease to be unruly—which he was too weak to do ; or by building up a system of political and moral life in which the unruly ways of Rousseau should be promulgated as *the* rules.(5)

Rousseau was thus bound to become the apostle of anarchy. " Foresight ! . . . That is the true cause of all our miseries." " The truly free man wishes only what he can do, and does what he likes." " All our wisdom consists of servile prejudices ; all our usages are but bondage, hindrance and constraint. Civilized man is born, lives and dies in slavery." " The state of reflection is a state contrary to nature, and the man who meditates is a depraved animal." " Expect from me no long moral precepts ; [. . .] I have but one to give you : be a man." That, in practice, means : " I am Rousseau. When I live as Rousseau, I am a moral man, since the only moral precept for Rousseau is to be Rousseau."(6)

The concept of the ideal savage was a godsend for such a man. He worked it out most carefully, of course, like all his doctrines, out of his head. " A savage is a man, and a European is a man. The half-baked philosopher at once concludes that the one is no better than the other ; but the philosopher [i.e., Rousseau] says : In Europe, government, laws, customs, everything binds men to deceive each other constantly ; all make vice a duty for them ; they must be

AN ENGLISHMAN FROM BARBADOS SELLS HIS MISTRESS—
From " Histoire Philosophique et Politique des Etablissements et du Commerce
des Européens dans les Deux Indes," by Raynal, 1780

A WILD " CANADIAN " FAMILY SHOWS GOODWILL TOWARD THE FRENCH—from " Histoire Philosophique et Politique des Etablisse ments et du Commerce des Européens dans les Deux Indes," by Raynal, 1780

[*Facing page* 22

bad in order to be wise. [. . .] Among savages, self-interest speaks just as loudly, but it does not say the same things. Love of the community and regard for common defence are the only bonds which unite them ; this word, *property*, which costs so many crimes to our honest people, is among them almost devoid of sense ; no difference over interests divides them ; nothing induces them to deceive each other ; public esteem is the only good everyone is after, and they all deserve it. It may be quite possible that a savage commits an evil action, but not that he makes a habit of it, for it would avail him nothing. [. . .] I say it with regret : a good man is a man who need deceive no one, and such a man is the savage."(7)

Such a savage was a pure creation of Rousseau's brain, whereby he endeavours to justify himself in his own eyes. An inveterate liar, but a liar who suffered when he lied, he was ever ready to unload the burden of his sin on to society. Hence : " A good man is the man who need deceive no one," because Rousseau had no will-power to resist the temptation to deceive. Nor was he in any doubt whatever as to the fact that this ideal savage was but Jean Jacques Rousseau disguised as an Indian. " A man had to depict himself in order to show us primitive men "—he writes in his *Rousseau Juge de Jean Jacques*.—" But where is this man of nature who truly lives a human life ? [. . .] It would be idle to try to find him among us. [. . .] Had you not depicted me your Jean Jacques, I should have thought that the man of nature did not exist."(8)

The artificial nature of this creation has been exposed, unwittingly, of course, but most aptly, by Rousseau himself, in his play, *La Découverte du Nouveau Monde*. It purports to be a tragedy. It is a short kind of ballet-comedy, conceived and written in a style unbelievably conventional and old-fashioned. In this play, in which Rousseau attempted to put on the stage that most dramatic and momentous of historical events, the meeting of Colón and his Spaniards with the still virgin New World and its dwellers still unpolluted by civilization, everybody, Spaniards as well as Indians, speaks and thinks like Racine, and the clash of destiny is

H

reduced to the dimensions of a petty love affair in the style of
Versailles.

Seule en ces bois sacrés, eh, qu'y faisoit Carime ?—asks *Le Cacique*.
Thus begins the play. Anger is *courroux ;* feminine beauty is
appas or *charmes*. Everybody says *vous* to everybody, and love
is *feux*. The naked *cacique* speaks thus of his wife :

> *Digizé m'appartient par des noeuds éternels ;*
> *En partageant mes feux elle a rempli mon throne.*

And so the inventor of the ideal savage unwittingly makes
him don a wig *à la Louis XIV*. Every now and then a character
is good enough to utter Rousseau's political opinions. Thus
the Indian beauty says to the Spanish captain :

> *Vos arts sur nos vertus vous donnent la victoire.*

The Spaniards, of course, enter like lambs into the role of tigers
assigned to them by the author, and make no bones about it,
for the play is short and they have no time :

> *Répandons dans ces lieux la terreur, le ravage ;*

yet the play forces Rousseau to give up this time-honoured clue,
although it fits his own views on civilization as to the manner
born ; and in the end the Spanish captain behaves with the
required generosity and the Indian *cacique*, of course, better
still ; which makes the Spaniard quote Rousseau at once :

> *Vante-nous désormais ton éclat prétendu,*
> *Europe ! en ce climat sauvage,*
> *On éprouve autant de courage,*
> *On y trouve plus de vertu.*

So that the orchestra is at liberty to strike a ballet to which
" *Une Espagnole* " sings this delightful comment on discovery
in general and its uses :

> *Voguons,*
> *Parcourons*
> *Les ondes ;*
> *Découvrir*
> *De nouveaux mondes*
> *C'est offrir*
> *De nouveaux mirtes a l'amour.*(9)

*   *   *

This chaos which was Rousseau, this conventional naturist who made the Indians of Guanahani wear a flowing wig *à la Louis XIV* held views which, unlike Montesquieu's, were in sharp contradiction with the ways of the Spanish Creoles, and with most of the traditional lines of policy of the Spanish Empire. Indeed, he begins by condemning the discovery lock, stock and barrel and far more thoroughly than any man ever did before or after. " The crusades, commerce, the discovery of the Indies, navigation, sea voyages and other causes I do not wish to state, have maintained and developed disorder. Everything that makes communications between nations easier, brings to some not the virtues but the crimes of the others, and changes in all of them the ways which befit their own climate and the constitution of their government." His works seem at times a repertory of noes to all the ayes of the Spanish Indies. The poor kings and viceroys who strove so hard to " reduce " the Indians from their far-flung wildernesses into the " polity " of cities, are told : " Men are not meant to be heaped up in ant-heaps, but to live wide apart, scattered over the earth they must till. The more they swarm together, the more they corrupt each other." The conquerors and viceroys whose pride it was to " ennoble " their cities with handsome buildings are thus rebuked : " For every palace I see erected in the capital, I fancy I see a whole country reduced to ruins. The walls of towns are built out of the rubble of the houses of the countryside." To the Empire glittering with the gold and the silver, the tin and the copper of the mines, Rousseau bluntly says : " The mineral kingdom has nothing attractive or lovable ; its riches, locked up in the entrails of the earth seem to have been put out of reach of men's eyes so as not to tempt their greed." The keen culture which rejoiced in letters, poetry, the theatre and the play of wit in the easy-going and enjoyable society of the rich capitals of Mexico and Peru is condemned in a sharp sentence : " Morals have degenerated among all the peoples of the world as they grew more inclined to scholarship and letters." And a society founded on so rich a gamut of inequalities was met with the most uncompromising assertion of equality ever penned : " In a well constituted State all

citizens are equals to such an extent that no one can be preferred to anyone else for being the best scholar, nor even the
most skilful, but at most, for being the most virtuous ; and
even this last distinction is often dangerous, for it fosters sly
and hypocritical men." On slavery, his conclusions are no
less terse and final : " From whatever angle we consider
things, the right to slavery is of no value, not only because it
is illicit but because it is absurd and means nothing." And he
plainly says that " a slave made in warfare or a conquered
people are bound to nothing more towards their masters than
to obey them while forced to." As for Spain, here was
Rousseau's condemnation : " Nothing is more downtrodden
or miserable than conquering peoples ; [. . .] their very
successes do but increase their misery."(10)

It would be difficult to find a set of doctrines less calculated
to fit the views and interests of either Spaniards or Creoles.
Yet Rousseau took both Spain and the Indies by storm. For
the success of a thinker is often due to the effect of his views
less on our ideas and interests than on our yearnings, desires,
emotions and instinctive trends. The first cause of Rousseau's
success was, and still is, precisely that he is chaotic ; so that
his books supplied, not only answers for all questions and
solutions for all problems, but neat formulas which bridged
over insoluble and self-contradictory propositions in words
and phrases the very perfection of which satisfied the mind to
the point of making it forget the ditches and abysses they
covered. What for instance more delightful than Rousseau's
definition of the problem of society : " To find a form of
association which will defend and protect the person and the
goods of every member with all the might of the community,
and in which, everyone uniting with the others, will nevertheless obey no one but himself and will remain as free as
heretofore." This ideal shines so persistently on the horizon
of men that no better definition could be found of most people's
ideas on " collective security."(11)

It is, of course, sheer nonsense ; but of the kind which
conquers and fascinates generations of men. It flatters both
the bourgeois sense of security and the bohemian sense of
anarchy. It was mostly as an anarchist, as the true inventor

of anarchy, that Rousseau appealed to the Spaniards of both
worlds. He was, however, rich also in texts which Bolívar
and San Martín will ponder on ; and which could be invoked
to justify dictatorship, and even slavery and intellectual
intolerance. " Despotism befits hot countries." " The more
the State grows the more the power of the Government must
be tightened up. [. . .] It follows that, in general,
democratic government is good for small States, aristocratic
government for middle-sized States, and the monarchy for
big States." Better still, Rousseau it was who wrote these
words, over which we may imagine Bolívar poring in his later,
disenchanted days : "Here is, in my old-age ideas, the great
problem of politics : *To find a form of government which will put
the law above the man.* [. . .] If unhappily this is impossible,
and I honestly confess that I believe it to be so, my advice is
to go to the other extreme and suddenly put man as much
above the laws as is possible, and therefore to set up arbitrary
despotism, the more arbitrary the better." As for intolerance,
Rousseau could not have been clearer : " There is therefore
a purely civil profession of faith the articles of which the
sovereign is entitled to define. [. . .] Though unable to
bind anybody to believe in them, he is entitled to banish from
the State whosoever does not. [. . .] Were anyone, after
having publicly acknowledged these dogmas, to behave as
if he did not believe in them, let him be punished by death ;
he has committed the worst of all crimes : he has lied in the
face of the law."(12)

These texts bring a much needed sense of shading and
complexity to the problem of Rousseau's influence on the
Spanish world. There is a revealing light shed on his deep
sympathy with the Spanish character, on the impatience of
all law typical of both, in the following words whereby the
rebel of Geneva applauds the sceptics who, in Spain and the
Indies, refused to believe in the legal profession : " And when a
residue of humanity led the Spaniards to forbid legal men to
enter America, what sort of an idea must they have had of the
legal profession ? Does it not look as if they had wished to
cancel by this one act all the evils they had brought down upon
the unhappy Indians ? " Rousseau seems to have entertained

a high opinion of Spain. In praise of Manuel Ignacio Altuna, his young Basque friend, he will say " one of those rare men whom only Spain produces and of whom she produces too few for her glory." This young man may have been the model he had in mind when he wrote : " Since the less cultivated people are usually the wiser, those who travel less travel best [. . .] less occupied by the objects of our vain curiosity, they bestow all their attention on what is truly useful. The only people I know who travel in this way are the Spaniards. While a Frenchman runs to the artists of a country, while the Englishman will have its antiquities drawn, and the German will take his album to all its scientists, the Spaniard silently studies the government, the customs, the police, and he is the only one of the four who, back home, brings to his country some observation useful for it." These words reveal Rousseau's usual lack of information and the gusto with which he generalized on scanty knowledge. The true reason of his liking for Spain was that in the Spaniard he guessed the volcanic, spontaneous, anarchical nature he himself was. He writes somewhat unexpectedly (if anything can be unexpected in Rousseau) : " Bullfights have contributed not a little to maintaining a certain vigour in the Spanish nation," a typical statement, for it has no other foundation than his own opinion. He hailed the expulsion of the Jesuits from Spain with words of extravagant praise : " Rousseau tells me "—writes Aranda to Floridablanca—" that if Spain keeps on this way she will lay down the law for all nations, and though he is not a doctor of the Church, one must hold him as a good authority on the heart of man and I prize his judgment very highly." Finally, asked which was the nation he held in highest opinion, Rousseau answered : " The Spaniards. Because they have a faith."(13)

*   *   *

Many of them suffered badly enough from the *maladie du siècle* to develop an unlimited faith in him. They did but follow the vagaries of their age. We owe much to the eighteenth century ; but if we were to sum up its folly in a few words, what better than this : it took its ideas on education

from a man who left his five children in a foundling hospital.
A truly dramatic symbol of that divorce between thinking and
doing, between ideas and life, which is the besetting sin of the
" century of the lights." The best minds of the age saw
through Rousseau. Feijóo refuted the *Discours si le réta-
blissement des Sciences et des Arts a contribué à épurer les moeurs ;*
and he did so less than two years after its publication. But the
works of Rousseau were eagerly read all over Spain and the
Indies ; and it is worth noting that one of the chief instruments
for their propagation in the Spanish world was the *Journal
de Trévoux*, a periodical published by the French Jesuits,
which, both in its original and in its Spanish edition, circulated
widely in Spain and in the Indies.(14)

Rousseau's works were prohibited in most European nations
and he himself hardly knew where to live, exiled as he was by
Government after Government. The Spanish Inquisition
was by no means prompt to grow uneasy about him. Not
till 1756 did it condemn one of his works, the *Discours sur
l'Inégalité parmi les hommes*. In 1762, the *Emile* was burnt by
the hangman in Paris by order of the *Parlement* and Rousseau
compelled to flee from pillar to post. The Council of Geneva
thundered its condemnation in no uncertain terms : " These
books are impious, scandalous, temerarious, full of blasphemies
and of calumnies against religion. Under the guise of doubts,
the author has put together in them everything likely to sap,
shake and destroy the main foundations of revealed Christian
religion. They attack all Governments." Rousseau had to
leave Geneva. In Neufchatel, where he had taken refuge, he
was excommunicated by the Protestant parish in which he had
settled, and stoned by the crowd as a heretic. He fled to the
Island of St. Pierre in the lake of Bienne. But although he
offered to turn his stay there into perpetual captivity, the
Senate of Berne expelled him again. He had to leave
Switzerland altogether and in the end took refuge in
England.(15)

Burnt in Paris and in Geneva, prohibited in Holland, the
Emile was widely read in Spain, where it found ready disciples
and admirers. Needless to say both Church and State took
defensive action, and in 1764 the works of Rousseau were

prohibited in all the Spanish dominions. This was, of course,
excellent propaganda. " Do not smile, my honoured countryman "—wrote François Grasset to Rousseau in 1765—" when
you learn that I have seen your *Emile*, in the form of a volume
in-quarto, burnt in Madrid in the main church of the
Dominicans, one Sunday after Mass, in the presence of a
great number of idiots and *ex-cathedra ;* which precisely
induced many Spanish magnates and the Ambassadors of
the foreign Courts to procure copies at any price and to make
them come by post."   On the very year of the prohibition of
his works in Spain, Rousseau received from Keith, the ex-
Governor of Neufchatel, then in Berlin, a letter in which the
Scotchman informed him that a Spanish friend, whom he
believed to be an officer of the Inquisition, was enthusiastic
over *Emile*. " Strength was required to break the barriers of
bigotry in Spain : *Emile* has done it." Rousseau's popularity
in Spain—a popularity, of course, in the restricted sense of the
day, among those who read—is proved by the frequent
mention of his name in the press, and by the flattering terms
in which he is often mentioned : " The 13th of January, 1766 "
—wrote the *Mercurio Histórico y Político*, referring to the date on
which Rousseau had arrived in London—" is a very great
day for England. Were M. Rousseau to die in London, after
many years of life, he would no doubt find his place beside
that of the kings of England, in Westminster." And here is
an interesting confession from the same newspaper : " The
famous Rousseau is at present in the vicinity of Paris. [. . .]
There are persons who speak too ill of this philosopher, yet there
is no lack either of people who esteem him over-much." (16)

The editor of the paper in which these words were printed,
and probably their author, was a Spanish disciple of Rousseau
who won a famous place in literature, more perhaps as an
object than as a subject of it, for José Clavijo y Fajardo was
to become the hero of Goethe's play *Clavigo*. A true measure
of the liberalism of the Spanish Court till the French terror
made it recede can be gathered from the fact that this man,
who never hid his infatuation for Rousseau, was Keeper of
the Royal Archives and head of the Royal Theatre. His
translation of Buffon won him a high post in the Cabinet of

Natural History of Madrid.   Clavijo was a fervent admirer
and an assiduous disciple of Rousseau, but by no means servile.
In the pages of *El Pensador*, which he began to publish in
1762, with considerable popularity in Spain and in the Indies,
he spread many of Rousseau's ideas, along with one, at least,
which was as dear to him as it was repellent to his master—
feminism.   Rousseau on women is final :   " Women are
specially made to please men."   " Every woman who shows
herself dishonours herself.   There is no good behaviour for
women except in a retired and domestic life."   " I own that
politics is hardly the competence of women."   Such are by
no means the views of Rousseau's Spanish disciple.   In his
Carta Instructiva a una Señorita recién casada, he advises her to
adorn her mind with as much care as her body, so as to be a
good companion for her husband ;   and his Thought XXXI
is cast in the form of a letter supposed to be addressed to him
by one of his readers, in which it is pointed out that since
women have been good queens, why should they not be
entrusted with embassies and ministries ?   Evidently shy at
his own boldness, he put forward his views with a smile of
irony and incredulity—perhaps the more shy for the fact that
the idea ran so contrary to Rousseau's views.(17)

There is much of Rousseau in the following *Thought*, consisting mostly of a Dialogue between " a gentleman fairly
well known in Madrid and a Canadian, his servant, by name
Sam."   This Canadian is, of course, a red Indian.   He
complains of a change in his master's attitude towards him
since their arrival in Spain, and when his master counter-
complains that Sam, contrary to instructions, had left the
house unguarded, Sam argued that the house was not likely
to run away.   His master points out the danger of thieves.
" Thieves ? " asks the Canadian.   " What animals are those ?
In my country there are none."   And we are treated to a
tirade in the true style of Rousseau on the virtue of savages.
Not so, however, when the enlightened savage objects to the
majority vote in the Courts and Municipal Councils of Spain,
for, since the many are ignorant and few see the light, " why "
—asks the Canadian—" should the vote of many possibly
blind people be preferred to that of one perhaps well

educated ? " This was a heresy against Rousseau : " The
vote of the great number always binds those of the others."
But Clavijo returns to the doctrines of the priest of nature
when he makes Sam urge mothers to nurse their children and
develops other favourite doctrines of Rousseau, till the
Spaniard, not without some irony, concludes : " I see what
you mean. You are merely telling me in so many words
that I am a barbarian."(18)

*   *   *

Two sets of facts contributed at this time to spread the
ideas of Rousseau in the Spanish world : one was the creation
of the " Economic Societies of Friends of the Country " ;
the other the rise to power of a number of Spanish noblemen
imbued with the ideas of the century. The first owed their
origin to Altuna, Rousseau's first Spanish friend. They were
started in the Basque provinces in 1764, and soon imitated
in Madrid, Seville, Cádiz and other cities. All their leaders
were familiar with Rousseau's doctrines. The Royal Seminary
of Vergara, an educational establishment which formed the
next generation of Basque noblemen, was likewise in the
hands of disciples of Rousseau and translators of his works.
On the other hand, Aranda, all-powerful from 1766 till 1773
as President of the Council, and from 1773 to 1787 still very
influential as Ambassador in Paris ; the Duke of Huéscar,
later Duke of Alba, Spanish Ambassador in Paris from 1746
to 1749, and other prominent figures at the Court of Charles III
were all friends, disciples and advocates of Rousseau. His
philosophy permeates the intellectual life of Spain, from
politics and economics to literature. Cadalso, the first of the
romantics, sought to be a Young in his *Noches Lúgubres* and a
Montesquieu in his *Cartas Marruecas*, but he is above all a
Rousseau in his undisciplined individualism ; and from him
on the influence of Rousseau remains predominant in Spanish
literature till it bursts out in the naïve verses of Quintana to
America :

Virgin of the world, innocent America !(19)

*   *   *

By then, of course, the innocence of America was a thing

of the past. Rousseau entered the Indies mostly by way of
Spain. The periodicals which discussed his name and views
in Spain carried them to the New World. The leaders of
Spanish thought widely read in America, such as Campomanes,
were imbued with Rousseau's ideas. Many young Creoles
travelled about Europe and brought back the latest produc-
tions of French literature, including, of course, Rousseau.
The first New World book devoted to his doctrines was a
refutation of his Discourse on the Sciences and the Arts,
written by a Cuban Dominican friar, Cristóbal Mariano
Coriche, under the title of *Oración Vindicativa del Honor de las
Letras*, published in La Puebla (New Spain) in 1763. It was
through Feijóo that Coriche had just heard of Rousseau.
But Rousseau throve on refutations. There is abundant
evidence that he was widely read in the Indies before he was
put on the Index, and even more so after. The *Sociedades
Económicas* which, after the model of Spain, were set up in
several capitals contributed to spread his views ; and his
works were found in the libraries of all intellectual leaders.
Nothing but dead texts which everybody forgot, and the
Inquisition which by then could be squared, stood in the
way. From the Court in Madrid and its Viceroys in the
Indies down, the whole official world was in tune with the
spirit of the century. Baquijano, one of the intellectual and
social leaders of Creole Lima, denounced to the Inquisition
for lending French books to his friends, calmly continued to
do so. In the viceroyalty of Río de la Plata, the chief works of
the epoch, the Encyclopædia, Rousseau, Voltaire, Raynal,
Bayle are found time and again in the libraries of prominent
citizens without any trouble accruing to them, though many
were priests. Azara, landing in Buenos Aires, found Buffon's
books translated into Spanish, and as there were only the first
twelve volumes available, someone lent him the rest in French.
Rivadavia's library lacked nothing worth having and contained much not worth having of the free-thinking literature
of the age. Voltaire was even found in the hands of artisans,
for instance a baker called Guzmán. In 1789, a *loa*, a kind
of curtain-raiser, was staged in Buenos Aires. The censor,
while allowing it to be represented, reported that it showed

the influence of *Emile* and " much of the impiety and libertinage of the philosophers of these days, given over to caprice and corruption ; and one can see how the spirit of Rusó overflows in it." Which shows that the censor knew his " Rusó " as well as the censored. In 1790, no less a person than Baquijano gave the imprimatur to a pamphlet (of very bad verse on the death of Charles III) arguing that " there was nothing in it contrary to the royal prerogatives of the monarch." Not a word about the faith.(20)

All these influences, though with different shades of feeling and meaning, had one feature in common : they shook the faith, the traditional faith. Rousseau's views, his uncompromising equalitarianism and his bold assertion of the value of the human person, could be traced back to a Christian source. He was, nevertheless, deeply anti-Christian, because he was proud as well as vain, and in Christian humility he felt a spirit inimical to his own doctrines. " Christianity preaches nothing but servitude and dependence. Its spirit is too favourable to tyranny not to profit always from it. True Christians are made to be slaves ; they know it and are not moved by it ; this short life has too little value in their eyes." So he writes in his *Contrat Social*. And again, aiming straight at the Pope : " One has seen how this so-called kingdom of the other world has become under a visible chief the most violent despotism in this one." So Rousseau. And Voltaire : " *Ecrasez l'Infame*."(21)

*   *   *

The brilliant wit who was for most of the century the intellectual king of Europe, took an early interest in New World affairs. As a business man, which he was all his life, he owned shares in a ship which the King of Spain chartered to transport troops against the Jesuits of Paraguay, in 1756 ; and it is plain from his letters that from that moment on until at least 1767 he kept a correspondent in Buenos Aires. His universal spirit made him cover with his imagination the New World as well as the Old ; and so Candide travels over Paraguay and El Dorado. He is far closer to realities than the solitary and self-fed Rousseau.

The entertaining scenes of Candide in Paraguay have a real enough air ; there is also a grim reality about his sketch on Candide and Cocambo arriving in Surinam : " They found a negro lying on the ground [. . .] the poor man had no left leg and no right hand. ' Now, my friend,' said Candide in Dutch, ' what are you doing there in that horrid state in which I see you.' ' I am waiting for my master, M. Vandenderdur, the famous merchant,' answered the negro. ' Is it M. Vandenderdur,' said Candide, ' who treated you so ? ' ' Yes, sir,' said the negro, ' this is the custom. [. . .] When we work in the sugar mill, and our finger gets caught in the stone, they cut our hand off ; when we try to run away, they cut our leg off. I found myself in both cases. Such is the price at which you eat sugar in Europe.' " Here are both accuracy and that burning spirit of justice which was perhaps the only, but a fine, warmth in Voltaire's otherwise cold light.(22)

Yet, on the whole, his treatment of America is, like most of his work, intellectual ventriloquism. In Voltaire, everybody is Voltaire. His *Oreillons* are a tribe of cannibals, no relation whatever to the *Orejones* of the Spaniards (i.e., the Incas, an aristocratic and anti-cannibalistic class of Indians, whose ears were monstrously lengthened by artificial means), mere puppets of Voltaire's show disguised as Red Indians. His El Dorado is yet another Utopia, more abstract, dialectical and glittering than that of More, which it calls to mind at times, as for instance in the contempt in which the inhabitants of El Dorado hold gold and precious stones. This abstract quality of Voltaire's New World reaches its climax in his play *Alzire*. It is as clearly built as a theorem of geometry, and its purpose is to prove that the conversion of the natives can be effective and complete only through the exercise of the Christian virtues on the part of the conquerors. The very names of the characters illustrate Voltaire's ignorance of the New World. His Indians have fancy names, not of Peruvian but of Spanish origin (*Zamore, Alzire, Montèze*), or vaguely suggesting Arab origins (*Emire*) or Greek (*Céphane*). We are inevitably treated to Racinian verse, images and even feelings, which sound fantastic on the lips of Incas and even of Spaniards.

Alzire, the Peruvian princess, says of Zamore, her Peruvian lover :

> *Sa foi me fut promise, il eut pour moi des charmes,*
> *Il m'aima : son trépas me coûte encor des larmes.*

And the Indians are throughout described as *Américains*. We are also treated to a display of the good savage :

> *L'Américain, farouche en sa simplicité,*
> *Nous égale en courage, et nous passe en bonté,*

says Alvarez, the good ex-viceroy.   And Alzire :

> *Qui peut se déguiser pourrait trahir sa foi :*
> *C'est un art de l'Europe : il n'est pas fait pour moi.*

While Zamore proudly asserts :

> *Le ciel, au lieu de fer, nous donne des vertus.*

But the clear mind of Voltaire succeeds in painting a varied and balanced picture, even with this obviously defective material.   Thus Alzire's father argues that there are Europeans sent to the New World by Heaven

> *Moins pour nous conquérir qu'à fin de nous instruire ;*
> *Qui nous ont apporté des nouvelles vertus,*
> *Des secrets immortels et des arts inconnus ;*
> *La science de l'homme, un grand exemple à suivre ;*
> *Enfin, l'art d'être heureux, de penser et de vivre.*

This last line shows enough the abstract character of the play. The good ex-Viceroy has a son, Gusman, who succeeds him as Viceroy, proud, overbearing and cruel ; but he loves Alzire. Zamore, Alzire's Indian lover, is caught fighting against the Spaniards and sentenced to death. The old ex-Viceroy comes to his prison cell to urge him to embrace Christianity and save his life. Zamore asks Alzire's advice, who answers that she is already a Christian because her heart ratified her words when she accepted the Christian faith :

> *Mais renoncer au Dieu que l'on croit dans son coeur*
> *C'est le crime d'un lâche et non pas une erreur,*
> *C'est trahir à la fois, sous un masque hypocrite,*
> *Et le Dieu qu'on préfère, et le Dieu que l'on quitte.*

So that not even to save his life will Zamore accept the Cross. But what could not be bought by life is freely given by the beauty of a Christian deed. After many (admirably contrived) situations, Gusman, stabbed to death by Zamore, forgives him and grants him his freedom, his estates and his beloved :

> *Des dieux que nous servons connais la différence :*
> *Les tiens t'ont commandé le meurtre et la vengeance ;*
> *Et le mien, quand ton bras vient de m'assassiner,*
> *M'ordonne de te plaindre et de te pardonner.*

Voltaire, therefore, though unaware of it, is in the line of the Spanish Christian authors who had pleaded against conquering by the sword and for conquering by the Gospel, and when Alvarez says to his son

> *Nous égorgeons ce peuple au lieu de le gagner,*

he echoes generations of Spanish friars and magistrates. But his play is not meant to depict Spaniards as they were. He is rather satirizing, by showing what should be. He has no doubt that he brings a new and liberating gospel to both the New World and the Old, with that mixture of moral greatness and courage with intellectual arrogance so typical of him and his time.(23)

These features were more likely to help than to hinder his fame among the wealthy intelligent Creoles, generous like him, ardent in their humanitarian feelings like him, and, even more than he, theoretical and abstract in their dreams and ideas. Voltaire's attitude towards fanaticism was not unlike theirs, that of a clean, aristocratic mind, who frowns at sloth and dirt, and at lack of taste. Arguing with strange aesthetic narrowmindedness, with Horace Walpole on the art of the theatre, in favour, of course, of the three rules and no clowns in serious plays, he writes: " All enlightened Europe thinks so to-day ; and the Spaniards are beginning to get rid at the same time of bad taste and of the Inquisition ; for *le bon esprit* proscribes both equally." He was not an enemy of religion, but only of fanaticism. " Religion is nearly everywhere nowadays substituted for fanaticism. The fires of the Inquisition

are being put out in Spain and in Portugal," he writes
to the Prince de Ligne in 1769. The Christian deism freed
from all dogmas, friars, superstitions, inquisitors and censor-
ships, which Voltaire stood for was precisely the kind of
structure which suited the Creoles. His wit, his felicitous
formulas, his speed, that chief quality of Voltairian style, were
in keeping with the keen mental alertness of the two Athens
of the New World, Lima and Mexico, and of so many other
capitals of the Spanish Indies—Habana, Caracas, Santa Fe,
Santiago, Buenos Aires—marts of ideas not necessarily in
touch with the depths of the country where the money came
from which fed the lamps of culture.(24)

*   *   *

The contrast between Creole life and Creole thought strikes
the mind even more with Raynal than with Rousseau or
Voltaire. The *Histoire Philosophique et Politique des Etablisse-*
ments et du Commerce des Européens dans les Deux Indes, by
Guillaume Thomas Raynal, attained an instant success both
in Europe and in America. It is now considered to be a
hotch-potch of documents, information and declamations
contributed by a number of friends of the enterprising Abbé.
So far as the Spanish part of it is concerned, we know the
names of some of these contributors from no less a person
than Miranda. " He confessed to me "—writes Miranda after
a visit to Raynal—" that Heredia had given him the news
referring to Spanish America ; and the Marqués de La Torre
of Habana." True, he mentions Aranda also, but not, as has
generally been written, as the provider of documents on the
Indies, but only of chocolate. " He gave me chocolate of that
which Aranda sent him from Spain " . . . " the best chocolate
perhaps I have drunk in my life."(25)

One of Raynal's contributors was Diderot, and though
Raynal himself needed no encouragement against religion, the
collaboration of Diderot made the book an ardently anti-
religious work. It is a passionate, inaccurate, picturesque
and rhetorical accusation against the nations of Europe for
their crimes in the other continents and against the other
races. Typical of its spirit, four illustrations adorn its first

four volumes : the first shows a Portuguese captain pointing to a heap of cannon ball and saying to an eastern potentate : " That is the coin in which the King of Portugal pays tribute " ; the second depicts the Spanish conquerors seizing hold of Moteczuma ; in the third an Englishman is seen selling his beautiful black mistress, who, naked, weeps, an iron ring round her neck and another one round her ankle, and a chain between the two. That covered the Portuguese, the Spaniards and the English ; Orientals, West-Indians and negroes also. What about the French ? They are the subject of the fourth picture. Some Frenchmen are shown landing presumably after a shipwreck, imploring help from an idyllic Canadian (of course native) family, over the caption : " Charity of a savage family of Canada towards the French." This patriotic little trick does not, however, blind Raynal to the crimes of France ; for both he and his chief inspirer, Diderot, whatever their shortcomings, are imbued with the universal spirit of their nation. Both advocate that view of rationalistic progress on this earth which was to be, and still is, the main myth under political opinions after the unity of Christendom had been shattered by the Reformation and by the discovery of America. He advocates a return to the earth and to agriculture rather than the development of commerce. His ideal is an unrestricted liberalism in international as well as in national affairs, and he praises the English constitution which, he says, " ought to serve as a model for all peoples." He is far from sharing Rousseau's naïveté about the good savage, whose noble qualities, however, he praises in a style which betrays his lack of direct knowledge of the subject. But above all, he is an outspoken denouncer of slavery and an uncompromising champion of human liberty.(26)

His success was prodigious. His book raised him to a level equal to that of the Montesquieu-Voltaire-Rousseau trinity, a promotion which his creative gifts by no means warranted. It was printed in 1770 and began to be well known in 1772. Raynal denied authorship at first. The French Government prohibited the work " considering that H.M. has found that it contained bold proposals, dangerous, temerarious and contrary to good morals and the principles of religion." This increased its success, and a second edition (1774) was soon necessary. The Government tried in vain to have it forgotten. The Church put it on the Index and persecution began. Voltaire stepped in to protect Raynal. In the shifting and shallow atmosphere of the eighteenth century one hardly knows what is what. The library of a canon was being sold after his death. Raynal's book was announced. General astonishment, which becomes tenser as the Archbishop of Cambrai, present at the auction, bids ever higher. The hammer falls. The Archbishop throws the book into the fire. Smiles and sighs of relief mingled their ambiguity with the lights and shadows of the scene. A third edition, swollen with additions, is issued in Geneva in 1780. Raynal this time signs it and has his own portrait engraved on the first page. He braves the Government and sets foot in Paris. On May 25th the book was condemned by the Parliament of Paris as " impious, blasphemous, seditious, tending to rouse the peoples against the sovereign authority and to upset the fundamental principles of civil order." Raynal had to flee abroad and the book was burnt by the hangman in Paris on May 29th, 1780.(27)

In Spain the considerable errors of the *Histoire Philosophique*, along with its fierce anti-religious bias, made it an object of detestation and fear to the authorities. Gálvez, the efficient and intelligent Minister of the Indies, " took a fit of temper as soon as anyone spoke about it." Bourgoing adds : " I have heard him utter imprecations against Frenchmen who taking advantage of a temporary permit to stay on the coast of Cumaná, had smuggled in a few copies of this *infernal work*." Nevertheless, Raynal soon became a kind of prophet for that world of Creole intellectual aristocracy which was beginning by then to seethe with political and philosophic activity. It was read both in its original French and in the Spanish translation of the Duke of Almodóvar, and found in every private library from Mexico to Buenos Aires and Santiago. Raynal was particularly liked by the Creoles, of whom he painted a most flattering portrait : " History reproaches them with none of those cowardices, those treasons, those low deeds which sully the annals of all other peoples. It would be hard

to find a shameful crime ever committed by a Creole."
Humboldt writes about Raynal and the Creoles in a letter to
his brother in terms which must be noted. Praising Cumaná,
the very place where Raynal had been smuggled by Frenchmen, he belauds its out-of-the-world atmosphere : " Among
the inhabitants of this country which hail from Europe, I
wish to deal particularly with the settlers up country. They
have preserved all the simplicity of the Spanish fifteenth-
century way of living ; and with them I often find features
of humanity and principles of true philosophy which one would
seek in vain among nations considered as more cultivated.
For these reasons, it would be difficult for me to leave this
region and to visit richer and more populated colonies. True
one finds there more means to instruct oneself ; but one also
meets often men who, with their mouths full of beautiful
philosophical maxims, nevertheless belie the first principles
of philosophy by their behaviour ; ill-treating their slaves
with a Raynal in their hands, and speaking enthusiastically
of the cause of liberty while selling the children of their negro
slaves a few months after birth."(28)

* * *

Yet another contradiction with which man abounds. But
man is one and if searched deep enough, his contradictions
lead to his unity. Raynal, Voltaire, Rousseau, Montesquieu,
each in his peculiar way was for the Creole a far-off intellectual
star in an abstract heaven. It was this abstraction, this
luminous and distant perfection which the Creole found most
precious in them. Their un-Spanishness was, in this respect,
a further advantage. It added distance. This flight to an
intellectual heaven was for the Creole a spiritual need, a
compensation for the weight of the earth which was attaching
him to the castes, and breaking his connection with the other
heaven, that of Spanish whiteness, which had been till then
his spiritual home. He is a shallow critic who reproaches
these Creoles of the eighteenth century for their inconsistency
in preaching liberty surrounded with slaves, and equality
hedged in with privileges. The more unreal, the more

abstract, the more general, the more distant the philosophy and " philanthropy " of the century, the more precious was it to them as a spiritual heaven over that many-coloured earth which was claiming its rights over them and making them its own.

CHAPTER XV

THE THREE BROTHERHOODS

THE JEWS—THE FREEMASONS—THE JESUITS

I.—THE JEWS

THE Jews played an important part in the disruption of the Spanish Empire. Their expulsion in 1492 had been a disaster for Spain in more ways than one. First as to numbers, for they made up a considerable part of the population ; then as to quality, for they were for the most part highly able and developed, particularly in the arts and crafts ; but even more so because the Jews, who were passionately attached to Spain, never forgave her the loss of the soil in which they had taken root more than in any other soil of the world, and they became her bitterest enemies. The psychological tension which developed was curious in the extreme. Indeed, extreme is the word for it, for no nation had ever been more generous to the Jews, had given them more power, treated them better, than Spain ; so that, under Ferdinand and Isabel, most pro-Jewish of Princes, the Jews were cast from the height of power into the abyss of exile. The Jews became the enemies of Spain precisely because they felt so deeply Spanish. A strange fate ! They left behind a deeply judaized Spain ; and they went abroad no less deeply hispanified. They felt themselves to be, on account of that fact, the aristocrats of all Jewry. Nothing is more striking than the insistence on this point on the part of the historian of the Jews, Graetz, who belonged to that German branch of Jewry which the Sephardim or Spanish Jews despised as ignoble rabble. The Sephardic Jews, writes this fierce hispanophobe, " had lost everything except their Spanish *grandezza*, their distinguished manner [. . .] they far surpassed the Jews of all other countries in culture, in manners, and also in internal worth, as was shown by their external bearing and language. Their love for their country was too great to allow them to hate the unnatural mother who had cast them out.   Hence, wherever they went they founded Spanish or Portuguese colonies.   They carried the Spanish tongue, Spanish dignity and distinction to Africa, Syria and Palestine, Italy and Flanders ; [. . .] they cherished and cultivated this Spanish manner so lovingly, that it has maintained itself to this day in full vigour among their descendants. Far from being absorbed in the majority of the Jewish populations in countries which had hospitably received them, they, as a privileged race, looked down upon them with contempt, and not infrequently dictated laws to them.   This arose from the fact that the Spanish and Portuguese Jews spoke the languages of their native countries (which by the discoveries and conquests of the sixteenth century had become the languages of the world) with purity, took part in literature, and thereby, even when conferring with Christians could do so on equal terms with manliness and without fear or servility."(1)

Fear and servility were the lot of the Jew everywhere else, while in Spain he moved on equal terms in the highest spheres of State, Church and society.   In the Middle Ages, the Low Countries were practically closed to them.   They were considered as " *animaux brutaux* " and payed taxes at the city gates ;   they had to wear a yellow square sewn on their garments.   The Jews expelled from Spain were not allowed to enter Antwerp unless they allowed themselves to be baptized first—on which condition they could also have remained in their native country.   England had not admitted them back on her own soil since she had expelled them in 1290 ;   and the laborious negotiations to that effect undertaken under Cromwell by some Jews of the Netherlands actually failed despite Cromwell's good will ;   the recognition of their right to enter being admitted only by a curious quibble, at the back door of English law, so to speak.   Germany was then as ever the home of Jewish persecutions.   Poland, Venice, the Papal States enslaved them.   Sweden allowed them to reside only in two small towns, and " even there so enslaved that they must have died out."   Only in Italy and in some parts of France were the Jews allowed to practise their religion ;

but in neither country did they reach the splendid position which they had conquered in Spain on the eve of their expulsion.(2)

Hence the peculiar tension which developed between the Jews and Spain after their exile. For the worst possible treatment that Spain ever inflicted on the Jews was precisely to exile them from the country which had treated them best. Graetz provides abundant confirmation also of the high culture the Spanish Jews had acquired in Spain and to which they owed the eminence they enjoyed in the midst of all other Jews wherever they went. " The *Marranos* who had fled from Spain and Portugal "—he writes—" manufactured for the warlike Turks new armour and fire-arms, cannon and gun-powder and taught the Turks how to use them." And again : " Jewish physicians were held in high esteem in Turkey ; they were for the most part clever pupils of the school of Salamanca, and on account of their skill, higher education, secrecy and discretion were preferred to Christian and even to Mahom-metan doctors. These Jewish physicians, mostly of Spanish descent, acquired great influence with grand sultans, vizirs and pashas."(3)

But the picture would not be complete if the Jews from Spain were shown parading nothing but Spanish qualities. They took with them Spanish defects as well, defects moreover which, in the light of both Spanish and Jewish history, it is only fair to surmise, the Spaniards had taken from them at least as much as given them. They took that intolerance and that " Inquisition " which their brethren had done so much to set up in Spain even against their own kith and kin, and which abroad was to show itself in so many persecutions of Jews by Jews on religious but also on social and economic grounds. The case of Espinosa (as Spinoza called himself), excommunicated by the Portuguese Rabbis in Amsterdam, is well known. Graetz describes another case in which the newly arrived Spanish Jews forced the Mostarabian Jews of Egypt to alter their liturgy in an orthodox sense, with a bigotry against which the author would have thundered had the bigots been Christians, but which he smoothes over and excuses as best he can. " Terrible sufferings had hardened the heart of the Sephardic Jews, and they were but too ready to exercise the utmost severity in religious matters, and slavishly to follow the letter." (4)

It was this spirit of orthodoxy and the sense of frustration at losing the promised land Spain was for them which turned the Jews into enemies of the Spanish Empire. Their very fidelity to the Spanish language was not exclusively sentimental. Graetz has shown how much prestige they derived from it. Here is another sidelight : " All the Jews of the Levant "—writes a sixteenth century Spanish traveller in the Mediterranean—" speak Castillian, and in Tripoli I asked a rabbi why this was so, and he answered it was not because of the quality of the language, but because of its secrecy ; for the Turks know Hebrew, Chaldean, Italian and Greek, but do not understand Spanish." This secrecy, the dissimulation of men who knew themselves watched, their mobility, their capacity for striking root in all lands and yet remaining in touch across all frontiers, and their superiority over all their brethren and over many Christians as well, made of the Spanish Jews the most dangerous, pertinacious and intelligent enemies of the Spanish Empire. (5)

Their activities were directed against Spain in the two chief fields of Spain's own life : the religious and the imperial. The Jews were assiduous agents in the dissemination of the Reformation ; less out of any genuine interest in the Reformation as such than because it implied a schism and a division in the rival faith. The sixteenth century was for the Jews, as for the Christians, an era of religious earnestness ; and it is hard to see why the Jews should be expected to feel less attached to the faith of Moses than the Christians to that of Christ. Exiled or persecuted, they disguised themselves as Christians, but remained true to their faith as well as to their race. The Reformation was a godsend for them. They worked for the Reformation because in so doing they weakened the Christian fortress within the walls of which they had suffered so much.

The Portuguese *conversos* of Antwerp provided a powerful stimulus to Lutheranism at the outset. Although Luther himself did not return the compliment and was as anti-Semite

as the average German, the *conversos* fostered the Reformation
by all the means in their power. By July, 1521, they had
set up a fund to print Luther's works in Spanish. Charles V,
always cautious and often liberal towards the Jews, remained
passive ; but Aleander, the Papal Nuncio in the Low Countries,
had 400 heretical books burnt in Antwerp, and declared that
the whole thing could be stamped out if " the Emperor burned
half-a-dozen Lutherans and confiscated their goods." Charles,
however, persevered in his leniency and allowed Jewish exiles
from Spain to remain in the Low Countries for thirty days
(plenty of time for money and skill to gain more time again).
Antwerp became a centre of immigration. Thus began to be
woven the threads of a spider's web centred in the Low
Countries and connecting the enemies of Spain with London,
Paris, Venice, Salonika and Constantinople. A young Portuguese Jew revealed the intrigue to Charles V's confessor in
1532. The leader of this international net of Jews was
Diego Méndez, a Portuguese Jew of Antwerp who traded in
spices. Méndez lent money to the King of Portugal and
even to the Emperor ; and was not an easy man to fell.
The widow of his elder brother, Gracia Méndez, a Spanish-
Jewish woman of much beauty and character, after many
tribulations and persecutions, most of them due to her own
younger sister who denounced her as a secret Jewess to the
authorities of all the countries in which she had invested her
fabulous wealth, settled in Italy ; her nephew, Joâo Miques,
was a great favourite with Charles V's sister, Mary, Governor
General of the Netherlands. After many adventures, some
romantic, other financial, he publicly " returned " to Judaism,
styled himself Don Joseph Nassi and married Gracia Méndez'
daughter, Reyna. He rapidly rose to a position of great
wealth and power in the Court of Solyman, and still more
under Selim II, who made him Duke of Naxos and Lord of
twelve islands in the Aegean Sea. Miques-Nassi-Naxos became one of the chief agents of anti-Spanish power in the
East. William of Orange wrote asking him to persuade the
Sultan to declare war on Spain ; and the Emperor Ferdinand
tried to influence him in the opposite direction. He served
the Jewish cause, but being an ambitious man, he served him-

self better still ; and he died when he was trying to secure for himself the Crown of King of Cyprus (1579).(6)

Next to the Méndez family, the family of Pérez, also Peninsular Jews, exerted the most powerful influence. Lutherans at first, the Portuguese Jews of Antwerp had turned to Calvinism, a fact which won for them not a little popularity in the Low Countries. By then (1560) their leader was Marco Pérez, of a family of Spanish Jews probably connected with the famous Antonio Pérez, Secretary of Philip II. Rich and powerful, in 1566 he became head of the Calvinist Consistory of Antwerp. He stood at the centre of a ring of political intelligence and influence, and at the origin of the 80-year war between the Low Countries and Spain. Under his direction 30,000 copies of Calvin's *Institution de la Religion Chrétienne* were smuggled into Spain, along with many Protestant tracts, hidden inside barrels. He also fostered the printing of Bibles, catechisms and other Calvinist books in Spanish. He sent Calvinist preachers to Spain. He corresponded with William Cecil, and was in close touch with Thomas Gresham, Cecil's agent in Antwerp. He was an accomplished linguist and Latin scholar, and became the chief financier of the revolt of the Low Countries against Spain. He seems to have lent a hand in the disorders of 1566, and boasted of having hindered a wholesale massacre of priests on Palm Sunday, 1566.(7)

His power, as in general that of the Jews of Flanders, might have been crushed at any time by either Charles V or Philip II. It was not, partly because Charles V was a man of conciliatory ways ; partly because both father and son needed the financial ability and push of the shrewd, businesslike Jews. But these Jews, while collaborating with the Spanish monarchs when it suited them, worked persistently as the political enemies of Spain both in Europe and in the Indies. Branches of the Pérez family turn up in the kingdoms beyond the seas. Manuel Baptista Pérez was a powerful and rich citizen of Lima, " esteemed by churchmen, both regular and secular, who dedicated literary festivals to him, and even in the royal University where he was granted the first seats." This potentate, outwardly a Catholic, proved to be so ardent a

Jew that after trying to commit suicide when found out by
the Inquisition, he died unreconciled at the stake, with
" demonstrations of anger which he made with his eyes
against those of his house who had made avowals." Another
member of the family, Luis, lived in Mexico, when in 1642
he was expelled as a secret Jew. Links between the Pérez of
Flanders and those of the Indies are by no means rare.
Agustin Boazio, a Genoese who had left Mexico for fear of
the Inquisition and had settled in Antwerp as an outwardly
Catholic merchant, remained in touch with Calvinist circles
in Mexico.(8)

These facts show that the number of Jews in the Indies
must always have been high. In a letter written on November
26th, 1606, the Bishop of Puerto Rico complained of the
flood of heretical books constantly brought to the country,
and he added : " In the chief harbour of this island, ships
are constantly coming for shelter, Portuguese as well as from
the Canary Islands under register [. . .] and in those of the
Portuguese come merchants, mostly Hebrews ; they are nearly
all scouts who come to find out all about the land and its
strength." The Crown was aware of the danger, and Jews
were forbidden access to the Indies. But " Jew " in those
days was a confessional, not a racial term ; and it was enough
for a Spanish Jew to profess the Catholic faith to have the
Indies opened to him. That these conversions were not always,
indeed not usually, to be trusted was known. A Royal *Cédula* of
August 22nd, 1534 reminds officials of the Casa de Contratación
that " it is forbidden for reconciled persons, or sons or grand-
sons of persons burnt at the stake, or newly converted from
Moors or Jews, to go to our Indies." But what no one, not
even the Inquisition, suspected at the time was the staunch
fidelity of the vast majority, almost the whole of the *conversos*,
to the Jewish faith—a fact known to-day thanks to the Jewish
historians. There were, of course, frequent warnings given by
experience. Luis de Carvajal, who rose to be Governor of
the New Kingdom of León, in New Spain, turned out to be a
practising Jew. His nephew, of the same name, was not merely
a secret Jew but a secret rabbi, and so staunch in his faith
that he went on professing it after being found out, and

forgiven, by the Holy Office ; found out for a second time, he was burnt at the stake, though not alive, as custom and the law required in such a case. The union with Portugal opened the Indies to many Portuguese merchants, most of whom were found to be Jews, and some of them conspirators in contact with the Dutch. Under Queen Elizabeth, the *Marranos* or Crypto-Jews of London began to play a part in Anglo-Spanish affairs. " Dr. Hector Nuñes, one of the most active merchants in the City "—writes Dr. Cecil Roth— " seems to have organized an elaborate information service in Spain and Portugal. He enjoyed the complete confidence of Burleigh and of Walsingham, and actually brought the latter the earliest news of the arrival of the Great Armada in Lisbon. His brother-in-law, Bernaldo Luis, did extensive espionage work for Burleigh in Spain, where he was arrested in 1588." Francis Añes did spying for Drake in the Azores. The Jews in Spain helped Drake in his beard-singeing expeditions. In the following century, Simon de Cáceres, co-operated in the conquest of Jamaica, " gave sound advice concerning trade with Barbados, and [. . .] suggested raising a Jewish force under the English flag for the conquest of Chile." The pilot who took Penn and Venables to Jamaica, Campoe Sabbatha, is believed to have been a *Marrano*, and another *Marrano*, Acosta, ran the commissariat and negotiated the capitulation.(9)

All this help given England was the outcome of the passionate tension of the love-hate of Spanish Jews for Spain. For England granted no equality to the Jews, who were not admitted as such into the country till the days of Cromwell— and only surreptitiously ; and could not be members of the armed forces till the nineteenth century. Even after the French Revolution " scions of Jewish families " in order to " percolate into the commanding ranks of the regular army had to be necessarily camouflaged as Christians," and no Jew was admitted at Oxford University till the end of the eighteenth century. To this love-hate towards Spain the Jews seem to have added at one time another passion typical of their lineage : a messianic dream which made of the New World a kind of Promised Land. Antonio de Montesinos, otherwise Aaron Levi, had been travelling in the Indies. On his return, towards 1644, he reported, on the faith of a *mestizo*, that there were Jews of the tribe of Reuben who lived in the Indies, no less persecuted by the Indians than the Indians by the Spaniards. Montesinos went back to Brazil, where he died, repeating this story on his deathbed. This yarn raised a wave of messianism ; an Amsterdam leader, Manasseh ben Israel, published a book, *Israel's Hope*, in which the return of these ' lost tribes ' was hailed as the coming triumph of the People of God ; and the burning of a young Portuguese-Dutch Jew at Lisbon provided the human emotion of martyrdom.(10)

But the chief peril of Jewry for the Spanish Empire did not come from enthusiastic orthodoxy. It came from cold business and calculating politics, which was the tone of the eighteenth century. The wealthy Jews of the day found in the philosophic, agnostic, " philanthropic " atmosphere of the century a welcome climate, since it tended to free them from their social thraldom and to blur the edges of the Christian dogma which had oppressed them. This attitude need not imply an absolute sense of freedom for all men, nor even for all Jews. The rich " Portuguese " (i.e., Sephardim) Jews of Bordeaux, contemptuous of their poorer German brethren, succeeded in expelling numbers of Jews who, in 1760, had come to their city from Alsace, Lorraine and Avignon. Voltaire having attacked the Jews somewhat harshly, the Portuguese Jew Isaac Pinto wrote to him granting the truth of Voltaire's strictures as to the German and Polish Jews, but denying that the Portuguese Jews deserved them. Pinto reveals the aristocratic attitude of the Sephardim to the point of naïveté. They " do not wear a beard and they do not display any singularity in their dress ; those among them who are well off carry their refinement and elegance, and the luxury in these matters, as far as the nations of Europe, from which they differ in nothing but their worship " ; and he recalls that many Sephardim had fulfilled important functions of State including Baron de Belmonte, whom the King of Spain employed as Minister-Resident in Holland. These aristocratic Jews were all Encyclopædists. Pinto in a letter to his Paris agent Pereira declares himself Voltaire's greatest admirer : " I should think

I had something to reproach myself for "—he adds—" if there were anybody in Europe who had read, and studied more than I his works which I consider as an Encyclopædic Library." Pinto was settled in the Netherlands, where he was most powerful and active, as were his co-religionists in other capitals. The results of all this Spanish Jewish activity on behalf of the philosophical and philanthropic ideas of the century can be observed at the other end : On November 3rd, 1777, the Bishop of Cuba wrote to the Inquisitor General : " Every day new books arrive here vomited by Amsterdam, Leyden, London and other like mouths. . . . "(11)

2.—THE FREEMASONS

The fermentation of the Indies with universal and abstract ideas of " philanthropy," as the phrase went in those days, was also favoured by the spread of Freemasonry both in the Old and in the New Spanish world. There is a certain connection between Jewry and Freemasonry, as appears in a number of forms, symbols and names ; even though in Germany Freemasons have often been anti-Semitic to the point of excluding Jews from their Lodges. Some Roman Catholic authors of the orthodox Catholic school tend to exaggerate this connection and to see a Jew behind every Freemason—which is, to say the least, extravagant. Yet, the presence of symbols, to-day known as masonic, in one or two buildings of Avila, erected in the sixteenth century by a prominent Jew, Mosen Rubi de Bracamonte, as well as other features of those buildings, have led a prominent Spanish Freemason to declare them a work of the Brotherhood. Nor is the coincidence less strange that a descendant of this Mosen Rubi (who was well acquainted in Flanders), the Duke of Medina de Ríoseco, should have been one of the most prominent associates of Don Carlos in his conspiracy against Philip II with a number of Flemish accomplices.(12)

All this, however, is conjectural and, as far as Freemasonry goes, so to speak, prehistorical. Freemasonry in Spain begins when, in 1726, the Grand Lodge of England gave a licence for a Lodge to be set up at Gibraltar. The first Lodge in

Madrid was founded in the following year, and its membership soon reached 200. In 1734, there were four Lodges in Madrid. The leading one was *Las Tres Flores de Lis*, a kingly and aristocratic name ; but the others were housed in inns and taverns and probably sought humbler layers. In 1748 the Spanish Ambassador in Vienna informed the Court of the discovery of a document in a Vienna Lodge, revealing the existence of a Lodge in Cádiz with 800 adepts. This was easily to be explained, Cádiz being then an important centre of English commercial activity, owing to the trade of the Indies. At least one Lodge was also known to exist in Barcelona in 1753, while in 1750 the Freemasons of Spain circulated a " Credo and Articles " printed in Portugal. Ferdinand VI prohibited Freemasonry by a *Pragmática* of July 2nd, 1751. But with the advent of Charles III, Freemasonry in Spain saw better days. Naples was Freemason to the very top, and members of the royal family were either in sympathy with, or even actually in, the Craft. Freemasonry under Dutch or English leadership was nationalized in 1767 under Prince Caramanico, Viceroy of Sicily, as Grand Master. When Charles III came to Spain his heir's tutor, Prince San Nicandro, was a Freemason. Wall, the Irishman in the service of Spain, was an adept and fostered the Craft, led by his favourable feelings towards England. Freemasonry was still mainly foreign in inspiration : a historian of Spanish Freemasonry writes that " foreigners organized it in 1728, inspired it in 1744 and gave it its organ, laws and liturgies making it subservient to the English Grand Orient." Its adepts at first were also foreigners, apart from the aristocratic circles of the cosmopolitan Court. The only notable case of a Freemason persecuted by the Inquisition was that of a French buckle-maker, Tournon, brought to Spain by the Government to train Spanish workers and who after a year's imprisonment was sent back to France. But Aranda was also a Freemason and he did not view with kindly eyes the fact that the Craft should work for the benefit of England, of which he was no friend. He organized a *Gran Oriente* of his own of which he became Grand Master (June 24th, 1780). It was an aristocratic society, comprising the leading spirits of the day, such as the

Duke of Alba, Campomanes, Conde de Montijo, Jovellanos and the great architect Ventura Rodríguez. This group of leaders was strong enough to induce the King to forbid the Inquisition to meddle with any cases other than apostasy or heresy (1768). Another movement of humbler station was developing independently both of the pro-English and pro-French branches of Freemasonry. This popular movement, revolutionary in a social and not merely intellectual way, had been sown in Spain by the famous adventurer Cagliostro, who had founded lodges in Andalusia and Catalonia.(13)

Cagliostro came into contact with Spain early in life, if he was not himself a Spanish Jew, which is likely. That Althotas whom he declares to be his first mentor, and who was " perhaps Spanish perhaps Greek and spoke many languages and had papers in Arabic and was versed in alchemy," sounds like one of the numberless Sephardim who dabbled in Cabala and occultism. In his travels over Europe, he met everywhere with a mysterious leader of Freemasonry, a " Spaniard Tomás Ximenes," obviously a Sephardi ; and his own Egyptian rite of Freemasonry is a close cousin of the Masonic brotherhood of Elus-Coëns founded in 1754 by a Spanish Jew of Bordeaux, Martínez Paschalis or Pascual. Cagliostro was in touch with all this masonic activity wherever he went, and added much of his own flamboyant and inventive genius to it. He created an Egyptian rite, and seems to have acquired some destructive and revolutionary impetus from his dramatic visit to the mysterious centre of Masonic Revolution he himself describes hidden away near Frankfurt am Main. One of the leaders of this centre was Ximenes, with ample funds in the Banks of Amsterdam, Rotterdam, London, Genoa and Venice, and its chief aim was to upset the French Monarchy and fight against Rome. Plain, ordinary Freemasons seem to have disowned this variety of their Craft which they describe as the *Illuminati*. The oath of its adepts contains this statement : " Avoid Spain, avoid Naples, avoid all cursed lands." It is curious to find in the diplomas of Cagliostro's Egyptian rite the letters L.P.D. Though the designer of the diplomas, he declared himself before the Inquisition (of Rome) unable to interpret them. They stand for *Lilium pedibus destrue*, a

PANIARDS MAKE THEMSELVES MASTERS OF MOTECZUMA
*N MEXICO ITSELF—from " Histoire Philosophique et Politique des Etab-
:sements et du Commerce des Européens dans les Deux Indes," by Raynal,* 1780

[*Facing page* 256

TRIBUTE MONEY FOR THE KING OF PORTUGAL
from " Histoire Philosophique et Politique des Etablissements et du Commer
des Européens dans les Deux Indes," by Raynal, 1780

[*Facing page*

singular motto if one remembers that the first leading Masonic
Lodge of Madrid was *Las Tres Flores de Lis*. In his second
trip to Spain, where he travelled under the assumed name of
Don Tiscio, Cagliostro founded Lodges in Barcelona, Cádiz,
Valencia, Sevilla and Madrid, all in a spirit contrary to those
of Aranda. His movement gave rise to the republican
conspiracy of San Blas, discovered just after his departure
from Madrid. The leader of this conspiracy was one Juan
Picornell, from Majorca, together with an Aragonese José
Lax, Sebastián Andrés, Manuel Cortés and others. They
met in a Lodge, " La España," in Bastero Street. The conspirators were denounced by two workers who knew of it
through a Freemason ; most of them were sentenced to death
(1796) but were reprieved, it seems, under pressure from the
French Embassy. Picornell was exiled to Panama ; Lax and
Andrés to Puerto Cabello ; Cortés to Portobelo. And so
the Spanish Government sent to the Indies the seeds of
rebellion, for some of these men were to be among the most
active precursors of Bolívar.(14)

In the New World Freemasonry was gradually spreading,
as shown by the *Centinela contra Francmasones*, by the Franciscan
José Torrubia in 1752. " Our Catholic Monarch "—he
writes—" has also prohibited it. I know that many Spaniards,
unaware of this, have been at fault owing to the intercourse
they necessarily hold with Freemasons while travelling about
the world in the foreign colonies of East India frequented by
our Philippine countrymen as in those of West India, Jamaica,
New Orleans, Guarico, Martinique, Providence, Virginia,
etc., in which this invention is well established. In the
Windward Islands it was most vigorous these late years, with
its main Lodge in the city of St. John, capital of Antigua
Island, the Grand Master of which was the famous William
Matthews, Commander-in-Chief of all the islands, and a
Creole born in one of them, St. Christopher. Everywhere
great insidious schemes are being laid against our Spanish
voyagers, for Freemasons deem it more valuable to add to
their number one of our nation than five of any other." The
Council of the Holy Office had followed up Ferdinand VI's
prohibition of Freemasonry in Spain by addressing to the

I

officials in the Indies a letter (August 21st, 1751), requesting them to send lists of the " military and political persons living in those kingdoms " who might have spontaneously confessed themselves Freemasons, and of those they might have denounced as such, and promising secrecy and clemency if they adjured Freemasonry " pending a day when those who refused to follow this advice will be deprived of the benefit of this secret graciousness and dealt with in a legal and public way under the Holy Office." The Inquisitors of Lima made answer " that in the whole Kingdome there is not the slightest sign [of Freemasonry], and news of its having spread in Europe is known only through a few papers, and Mercuries received here during the last two or three years."(15)

The Inquisitors were not accurate. A few days before the receipt of the letter from the Council of the Holy Office some small prints describing Masonic ceremonies had been confiscated in the house of a Lima tradesman, and sent to Spain. Soon after, the first persecution of Freemasonry was initiated by the Holy Office of Lima. The guilty parties were a French surgeon, Diego de la Granja (Jacques de Lagrange) and the Governor of Valdivia, Ambrosio Saez de Bustamante. La Granja, according to one of the witnesses, held that there were forty Freemasons in Lima, and he " named one who lives opposite the Gate of the Jews, by name Don Esteban Urrutia, a merchant." This would appear to establish a link between Jews and Freemasons, natural enough if one bears in mind the general trend of the " Portuguese " Jews of Lima to secure freedom for their secret faith. It is at least curious that the said Frenchman is described by the witness as *narigón*, long-nosed. " And as the said witness spoke of the erroneous maxims on which the Jews lived, she told the said Diego that in this city a Jewess had been burnt for refusing to be converted to the Catholic faith ; whereupon the said Diego asked her ' which lady was that ? ' ' Doña Mariana de Castro,' answered the witness ; and then Diego de la Granja said : ' a good lady, who knew how to give her life rather than forsake her faith.' " La Granja lived in the house of a Don Joseph Zamur or Zamar which strengthened the Jewish flavour of the whole incident. La Granja was sent to Spain by the Viceroy ; and no proceedings seem to have been taken against the 40 Freemasons said to exist in Lima.. As for Saez de Bustamante, the proceedings were cut short by order of the Court of Madrid, and his *residencia* led to no censure.(16)

*　　*　　*

A foreign element was also prominent in the early history of Freemasonry in New Spain. In 1762 Captain de la Piscina, in command at Bahía del Espíritu Santo, sent the Viceroy a book he had found in the hands of some wild Indians who had destroyed and looted an English ship. It was in English and entitled : *The Constitutions of the Most Ancient and Honourable Fraternity of Free and Accepted Masons.* The Viceroy referred it to the Holy Office, which passed it to their *calificador*, Canon Vallejo, of Mexico Cathedral, in case it dealt with the " New Sect of Freemasons." Vallejo found it did, but thought it idle to refute the doctrine contained therein, since the book had to be considered as altogether forbidden, owing to the two Papal bulls (April 28th, 1738, and June 17th, 1751) condemning the Craft.(17)

In 1785 the Inquisition of Mexico opened its first proceedings against Freemasonry. The accused was one Felipe Fabris, sculptor and painter, well known in New Spain as the author of a portrait of Revillagigedo, the second Viceroy of this name. Fabris was a Venetian who, ever since his arrival in New Spain, had been a suspect in the eyes of the Holy Office owing to a report from the ship's chaplain, who had seen Masonic insignia in his possession and informed that Fabris just before landing in Veracruz had thrown his diploma of master mason overboard. His imprisonment was something of a sensation. His examination and that of a host of witnesses revealed a number of unsavoury details. Fabris had made a competent fortune painting and selling obscene miniatures on powder or snuff boxes and on watches. He had forsaken his wife and child and wandered about with a mistress ; he had tried to enlist apprentices to the Craft, appealing to their sense of liberty—a liberty which he was apt to understand in a sense not unrelated to his miniatures. He was exiled to Spain.(18)

Revillagigedo was a great Viceroy, one of the greatest New Spain ever had. But he seems to have brought over to Mexico a host of Frenchmen not always very judiciously selected. Most of them were Freemasons and revolutionists, which after all was their right and, considering the times, perhaps even their duty. But they were not all discreet, some were even foolish and not a few but poor samples of humanity. They used to meet in the house of a French watchmaker, J. E. Laroche, where they read the Gazettes from Holland, gossiped over the news from France and read the prohibited books of the Encyclopædists. Revillagigedo sheltered them from the Inquisition effectively enough during his term of office, but after he withdrew to his country house near Xalapa, the Holy Office began to stir, less, it would appear, through zeal for the purity of the faith than at the instigation of interested parties prompted by personal motives. Most of these Frenchmen were artisans of luxury trades who, on account of their work, enjoyed a certain familiarity with the great, whose wigs they combed, whose beards they shaved, whose watches they set in order, whose meals they cooked, whose gorgeous suits they kept spick and span. One of these Frenchmen, a barber, Burdales, accused of Freemasonry, boasted that the Viceroy-Archbishop was a Freemason, and that the Freemasons of New Spain planned to make him Grand Master, while he had promised them a hall in the palace, money and protection. The chances are that this foolish man spoke the truth ; for this Viceroy-Archbishop, Don Alonso de Haro y Peralta, born in Cuenca (Spain) of an illustrious Castillian family, was a scholarly aristocrat, an accomplished linguist well versed in Hebrew, Chaldean, Greek, Latin, Italian and French, with a long residence in Rome behind him, and a smiling eighteenth-century culture throughout his life. That he was a Freemason is, to say the least, not unlikely, and the mild way in which the Holy Office treated Burdales would appear to add weight to the view.(19)

Burdales shared with Fabris that lubricity which seems to have followed the " philosophy " of the eighteenth century, as Faust's dog followed Faust. He was caught caressing a girl of four ; he was accused of advocating regicide. A similar

combination of sexual and political tendencies are to be
observed in a number of other Frenchmen who were prosecuted
as Freemasons by the Holy Office of Mexico, but particularly
in the most famous of all, Jean Laussel, Revillagigedo's cook,
whose prosecution was instigated by the Viceroy Branciforte
(Godoy's brother-in-law) less for the sake of religion than to
annoy and vex his predecessor. Laussel who, someone said
at the proceedings, was liked by Revillagigedo, though a bad
cook, because he was a Frenchman, seems to have been very
much of a fool and quite a bit of a knave. Like a number of
those French barbers and tailors, he appears to have understood freedom mostly from a bedroom point of view, and he
praised Stockholm because " there you could have as many
wives as you liked " ; he also found Spaniards very backward,
particularly in the sexual arts. He was imprisoned in 1794
on a charge of Freemasonry and finally sentenced to appear
in public with a rope round his neck, " wearing the insignia
of a blasphemous heretic and a Freemason," to be exiled from
Mexico and Madrid and to spend three years in a prison in
Africa.(20)

*   *   *

All this was bound to create a certain fear of foreign immigration in the Indies. A Royal Order of July 13th, 1750, requests
the authorities in the Indies to keep a special watch on the
foreigners who by royal permission worked in factories and
workshops ; and enjoins the *Casa de Contratación* to check the
influx of heretical foreigners who arrived in the Indies as
sailors and managed to remain there. On the other hand, the
very authorities who, in the Indies or even in Spain, had to
apply these and similar regulations were growing more and
more averse to the restrictive and exclusive spirit which
endeavoured to close the Spanish Empire to the intellectual
and commercial intercourse of the century. Most of them
were sceptics ; many were Freemasons. This period of easy-
going liberalism, covering practically the whole reign of
Charles III, will enable the spirit of the century—both, of
course, the good and the bad of it—to permeate the Indies
and to set them alive with new hopes and ideas. Freemasonry,
introduced by Frenchmen rather than by Englishmen, was

apt to bring in a strong anti-Church and anti-Crown passion which the storms of the French Revolution were to render more violent.   Meanwhile, it worked along the line of evolution of the Indies themselves, and so most of the prominent men of the wars of secession will turn out to be Freemasons.(21)

CHAPTER XVI

THE THREE BROTHERHOODS (*Continued*)

3.—THE JESUITS

A MASONIC impulse was one of the forces which led to the expulsion of the Jesuits from Spain and Portugal. This milestone of eighteenth-century Western history is seldom told without bias one way or another. Those who would paint the Jesuits as martyrs of an evangelic religion must first explain away the papal bulls *Immensa Pastorum Principis* and *Ex Debito Pastorales Officii* denouncing the abuses the Order was apt to commit or allow its members to commit in matters of trade and tax-evasion. Those who sing the praises of the enlightened despots who expelled them should ponder over the repulsive cruelty Pombal evinced towards his Jesuits and over the disastrous effects the expulsion had in the Spanish and Portuguese empires.(1)

In the Indies, the constructive and civilizing work of the Jesuits was immense. From New Spain to Chile, they covered the continent with colleges ranging from High School to University standard and soon there was hardly a city of any importance in Spanish America, or the Philippines, in which they were not powerfully contributing to educate the leaders of the country. Too much stress is often put on the tendency of the Jesuits to concentrate on the rich. True though this is, it was not so narrowly applied in the Indies as to neglect the other classes. Humboldt praises their Missions, though he denounces their warlike raids to " conquer souls " ; and Ulloa and Jorge Juan absolve them of all the " disorders " of which they accuse other monastic institutions, and declare that " one does not see in them the lack of religion, the scandals and the loose behaviour so common in the others." The Jesuits paid the utmost attention to the mental, moral and artistic education of their flock in their Missions of the Río de la Plata, fostered printing, architecture, painting, sculpture, gilding and music and, a modern Argentine author avers, banished illiteracy in their jurisdiction. The artists and craftsmen were nearly always Indians. Pending negotiations with the mother country for setting up printing works, the natives copied MSS with that perfection which Indians are apt to bring to all minute and patient arts. When the Royal Licence came they manufactured presses and type. One of their first books was a *Vocabulario de la Lengua Guaraní*. In 1705 this press published *La Diferencia entre lo Temporal y lo Eterno*, by Father Nieremberg, with illustrations by an Indian engraver which have been compared to Dürer's.(2)

St. Ignatius wrote to Father Rivadeneira on March 3rd, 1556, that Jesuit missionaries were in demand for " a city of Castillians known as Paragay, in the Río de la Plata." Missions were founded there in 1608-11 by Father Diego de Torres on the explicit understanding that the Indians would not be required to perform any personal service, which the King granted by Royal *Cédula* of October 21st, 1611, over and above the exemption of any tribute during the first ten years of their Christian life which he had already granted to all Indian neophytes. The Jesuits rapidly organized their " reductions " or villages of peaceful Indians along the rivers Paraná and Uruguay ; about 48 missionaries founded about as many *pueblos* in about as many years, between 1610 and 1652. By the middle of the seventeenth century, 175 Whites, 110 of them priests, governed all these Missions as well as eight colleges and one University. The Indian population varied from 40,000 to 114,000 which it reached in 1702. The Jesuits were of all nations : Spaniards, Portuguese and Englishmen were the founders ; there were some Italians and Flemings, and, from the beginning of the eighteenth century, a German contingent, whose influence contributed powerfully to making these Missions a centre of culture for the whole region.

The Jesuits seem to have succeeded in creating and maintaining a prosperous, humane and peaceful community from 1610 till 1768, the continuity of which makes of it, in a sense, a historical entity of its own. It is sometimes claimed that their Missions in Paraguay differed in nothing from other Missions of other Orders in other territories of the Spanish

New World, and that they lived just as subject as the others
to the Laws of the Indies. There was, we are told, no " Jesuit
Empire," no communism, no monastic discipline beyond the
commonsense prohibitions of alcoholic drinks and of private
and public vice. " The Indians "—writes a modern English
historian—" had as much liberty as is at present enjoyed by
the citizens of any civilized country." There was much
self government in the Spanish style, of course, with native
alcaldes and other officials. The administration of justice,
however, was in the hands of the missionaries themselves.
Arts and crafts flourished to such an extent that the other
regions of the Plata came to Paraguay for artistic furniture
and other comforts and luxuries of life.(3)

* * *

This picture, though by no means altogether inaccurate,
is somewhat idealized. Serious charges can be levelled against
the Jesuit regime in Paraguay both from the point of view of
Spain and from that of the Indians. The French director of
the Asiento Company, during the brief period before the
Treaty of Utrecht when France carried on the slave trade for
the Spanish Government, wrote from Buenos Aires four letters
to the Chancellor M. de Pontchartrain which throw a much
less favourable light on the subject. He was no idealist, no
sentimentalist. Speaking of his own business, he coldly
registers the following fact, which illustrates the psychological
background of slavery better than volumes : " They have
brought over in two ships about 800 Blacks, both infirm and
sound ; as we were in winter and there was a danger that we
might lose many if we kept them, I resolved to sell them all at
once, the sound ones at 250 *pesos* a piece, and the infirm at
150. This sale has been most advantageous for the Company ;
for more than half of these Blacks have died in the hands of
those who bought them from us."

Now this man points out that the Jesuits treated their
Indians with justice but with the utmost severity ; punishments consisting in flogging, from which not even the Indians
entrusted with military or civil powers by the Jesuits were
exempt ; that one single man ruled absolutely over 10,000

families, his sleeve being kissed with gratitude by every Indian he had flogged ; that the Indians had no right to keep for themselves a single hen, a single egg, for everything must be delivered to the common stores ; and that the distribution was fair and equal but strictly limited to food and clothing. As the land was rich in animal and vegetable wealth as well as in mines (a point on which this witness is not as sound as on the rest) the fathers drew immense benefit from their territories to the deprivation of their frugal flock. They firmly refused to teach their Indians Spanish and kept their preserve carefully closed to strangers.

The King of Spain, he writes, was defrauded in three ways : the Jesuits reported less than half of their Indians, thus reducing the amount of tax per capita they had to pay to the Crown ; they bribed the Governor of Buenos Aires to keep him off ; and they reported three times as many Indians as they provided when they were required to send a detachment for public works, so as to get higher payment for the labour of their wards. The witness estimates that, were the King to exact two million *pesos* yearly from the Jesuits, they would be well advised to accept. Their military establishment, he argues, though ostensibly kept to guard against the Portuguese, was directed to ensure the autonomy of the Jesuit rule.

This Frenchman is perhaps biased against the Jesuits ; but he is well informed and there is no ground for doubting that in the main his picture is correct. In the aggregate, we find a highly successful form of enlightened despotism (after all, the ideal of some of the chief enemies of the Jesuits in the eighteenth century) in which the Indians were well treated, though like children, and the interests of the Spanish State altogether disregarded.(4)

This very success was one of the causes of the downfall of the Jesuits ; but the chief reasons were of far wider import. The campaign against them was the forerunner of a war against the Catholic Church on the part of the " philosophers " and Encyclopædists. Hostilities would never have broken out but for the philosophers, for the Company is not warlike and the Jesuits had even tried to collaborate in the famous Encyclopædia, writing the article on Theology. The leaders of this European movement were Voltaire and D'Alembert. Their aims were not the same. Voltaire wanted to purify God from dogmas, religions, priests, churches and fanaticism. He was a pure deist, a Newtonian. D'Alembert did not believe in God at all. He was a rationalist and a materialist. But they were allies for the time being and held each other in high esteem. In a letter on the abolition of the Jesuits in France, D'Alembert writes to Voltaire these revealing words : " *Ecrasez l'inf* . . . you keep repeating to me : eh, mon Dieu ! Let her rush to it herself ; she goes thither quicker than you think. Do you know what Astruc says ? *It is not the Jansenists who kill the Jesuits, but the Encyclopaedia, mordieu, the Encyclopaedia.* There might be something in it. [. . .] As for me, seeing as I do at present everything rose-coloured, I can see the Jansenists dying next year of a natural death, having this year killed the Jesuits by violence ; tolerance established, the Protestants called back, the priests married, confession abolished and the infamous one crushed without anybody noticing it." Throughout this text " the infamous one " is treated as feminine. A clear proof that for both Voltaire and D'Alembert it meant *la religion catholique*.(5)

Such was the programme and such were the men—first-rate minds both of them—who fought for it. Galling as it may be for its faithful, it is evident that by then the Catholic Church stood not merely as the only, but as the chief, obstacle to intellectual progress. The authors of the Encyclopædia found that they had to submit their texts to theological censors. Their scientific minds found the claim not only irksome but extravagant. The current of the human mind was flowing away from the dogmatic Church which claimed the exclusive right to regulate it ; and while it is questionable whether the direction in which it was moving was itself right, it was at any rate relatively right when it demanded its freedom of error as part of its movement towards truth. The Jesuits were not attacked because they were the citadel of mental reaction, which they were not ; but because they were its scouts, the most get-at-able of the powerful army of the Church. In their ultimate aims, therefore, these philosophers, D'Alembert, Voltaire, Choiseul, Aranda, Roda, whatever we may think of their methods, were justified. Something had to be done and they chose their adversary well.

But if their aims were in line with the progressive requirements of the time, their methods were not always popular and revolutionary. None of these men felt it beneath him to recruit Court intriguers, royal mistresses or confessors in the campaign for freedom of thought and tolerance. " Be sure "—writes Voltaire to D'Alembert—" that Madame de Pompadour and M. l'abbé de Bernis are far from declaring against the Encyclopaedia. I assure you that both of them think as true philosophers, and that they will act with authority when time requires and when they can without compromising themselves." The " philosophy " of the King's mistress consisted, of course, in holding fast to her royal prey ; and when two successive confessors, both Jesuits, refused absolution to the King while the irregular union lasted, and the Pope declined to sanction the situation by means of a papal bull which the nice lady had tried to smile out of him, this philosophic deity became a staunch enemy of the Jesuits.(6)

And of course there would be no lack of support in an absolute monarchy. The Jesuits were traditional upholders of the universal monarchy of the Pope as against the national monarchies of mere temporal kings. Hence the scanty favour they found in Philip II, a nationalist king, in contrast with the friendship which united Charles V, a European and universalist emperor, with St. Francis Borgia, the third General of the Order. On November 16th, 1613, Gondomar wrote to Philip III that James I's attitude towards the Catholics had taken a turn for the worse on the arrival in London of " a book written by Father Suárez which made him very angry, and he spoke aloud disparagingly about the fathers of the Company and about all Catholics, complaining also of Your Majesty for having allowed such a book to be printed in Spain, considering the doctrine of this book so contrary to his authority." Father Suárez' book was *Defensio fidei catholicae* ; and the doctrine is indirectly explained by Gondomar in another letter of the same date. " When this king had ordered the Irish representatives who were here detained by his orders to return freely to Ireland, he received

Father Suárez' book, and holding the chief of these Irish representatives as a scholarly man, a man who had been imprisoned in the Tower of this city for the reasons I have reported to Your Majesty, he commanded him to explain how the opinion of Father Suárez was to be understood when he says that subjects and vassals are entitled to kill their King, when he is a tyrant, deposed and excommunicated by the Pope. The representative saw the passage in the book and answered that such things are matters of faith, and therefore he was not in a position to explain them, since he believed and held all that is held and believed by the Holy Roman Church, whereupon this King conceived such anger that he ordered him back to the Tower and it is even believed that he will have the man put to death."

The doctrine, therefore, which angered James I was that which in those days another Spanish Jesuit, Father Mariana, was also to put forward in his *De Rege*. James I could not tolerate it. Gondomar wrote to Philip III on December 1st of the same year (1613) that at twelve o'clock on that very day two sacks of copies of Suárez' book had been burnt in St. Paul's Churchyard after a sermon in which its errors were exposed. The Jesuit doctrine condemned to the stake by James I in 1613, reborn in Cromwell, was to behead Charles I in 1649.

Absolute kings of the seventeenth century and enlightened despots of the eighteenth were natural enemies of such a revolutionary doctrine. True, the Jesuits opposed royal absolutism from the opposite side to that on which Cromwell attacked it. The Jesuits stood on a universal ground, the Cromwellians on a nationalist ground. All were absolutists. But the Jesuits fought for the absolute monarchy of the Pope, minister of God on earth, the only head of the only universal republic. The absolutism of Cromwell was that of the people, the English people defined and isolated in a world of strangers. Cromwell was already an absolutist democrat. The fact Cromwell precedes the idea Rousseau. But, though from different quarters of the roads of the spirit, Cromwell, Rousseau and the Jesuits were, for the absolute monarchies, equally dangerous. The Jesuit doctrine of a universal monarchy will arm Ravaillac, the murderer of Henry IV, in 1610 ; the doctrine of Cromwell and Rousseau will behead Charles I and Louis XVI.   Both, in an obscure blend, inspire perhaps the attempt of Damiens against Louis XV in 1757.   For the kings, threatened in their person, erstwhile so sacred, all was one and the same.(7)

A number of strangely ill-assorted forces were thus converging against the Company.   The Jansenists, or Catholic nationalists, attacked them as ultramontane, or instruments of papal authority.   In those days there were many priests and prelates of this Jansenist turn of mind in France, Spain, Portugal, Naples and even the Roman Curia.   The philosophers attacked them as the more exposed scouts of the Catholic Church.   The general trend of thought of the century towards free-thinking and political liberty saw, in them, the stronghold of reaction, of authority and of absolute monarchy.   Finally, they brought upon the Order the odium of success, wealth, discipline, efficiency and secrecy, with a complex of fear and envy which this powerful combination was bound to call forth.

*   *   *

The first storm broke out in Portugal.   Pombal, who rose to power under their shadow, found them too much in his way when he became Prime Minister of Joseph I.   Five Jesuits were spiritual directors of several members of the royal family.   He exiled two Jesuits who opposed his economic ideas.   The handsome behaviour of the Order during the disastrous earthquake of 1755, in which Pombal himself showed a fine mettle, forced him to yield to the King's wish and recall the exiles ; yet soon he succeeded in exiling Father Malagrida, a Jesuit who, more than any other, had distinguished himself during the earthquake.   Pombal was an exponent of enlightened despotism.   His ambition was to develop Portugal, reform roads, factories, harbours, schools.   He lined his pockets as well and had shares in the company he had formed (1754-5) to monopolize trade with Brazil and China.   He was no philosopher, no liberal.   But he was a Jansenist and his aim in religious matters was a Portuguese Church, as Catholic, but also as free from Rome, as the Anglican Church.   For the time being, therefore, he trod the same road as the

philosophers : war against the Jesuits. He seems, moreover, to
have had in mind a change of dynasty by marrying the Princess
of Beira to the Duke of Cumberland, who apparently had hopes
of becoming King of Portugal till the Jesuits shattered the
whole scheme.

Pombal was well served by events in the New World.
The Governor of Río de Janeiro, Gómez de Andrada,
persuaded that the Jesuits wrapped their reductions in mystery
to conceal gold deposits, induced Portugal to negotiate with
Spain the exchange of the seven reductions of Uruguay for
the colony of Sacramento. Spain, knowing no such gold
deposits existed, accepted the exchange. The 30,000 Indians
of the Reductions would be transferred to the territory ceded
to Spain (1750). The Indians resisted. The Jesuits tried to
win them over. Portugal accused the Jesuits of inciting the
Indians to resist. At any rate, the Jesuits can hardly have been
convincing if and when they advised the Indians to submit. The
war against the Jesuits took then a sharper tone in Portugal.
The confessors of the royal family were dismissed and replaced
by Franciscans (1757) ; pamphlets published by Pombal
slandered the Company ; a bull wrenched from the Pope gave
the Cardinal-Patriarch, Saldanha, full powers as a Visitor over
all Jesuit establishments, and, on the strength of these powers,
he suspended the Jesuits from preaching in his whole patri-
archate (June 7th, 1758). The King fell ill and rumours
were spread that the Jesuits had tried to kill him. On
December 9th, Pombal, under the King's signet, published
a manifesto announcing that H.M. had been the victim of an
attempt on his life. On December 13th a number of members
of the premier family of Portugal, that of Aveiro and Tavora,
were thrown into dungeons and the seven Jesuit houses were
surrounded by troops, closed, with the Jesuits as prisoners,
and searched for arms. Under torture, the old Duke of
Aveiro declared that he and the Jesuits had tried to kill the
King. He retracted his confession as soon as the screws were
loosened, but the Court—a *Junta de Inconfidencia* especially
appointed by Pombal under his own chairmanship, and with
arbitrary procedure—refused to listen. In the teeth of the
opposition of the best magistrates of the country, Pombal

signed a death sentence in his own handwriting on Aveiro, Tavora, their wives, sons-in-law and servants ; they were beheaded, strangled or burnt on January 13th, 1759.(8)

Finally, on September 3rd, 1759, the expulsion of the Jesuits took place. Shiploads of them put to sea from Portugal, Brazil, and the Portuguese East Indies, and went begging hospitality here and there. On board, the poor Jesuits were treated like beasts ; on shore, like criminals. It was true persecution and martyrdom. The fate of Malagrida was one of the paradoxes of history. Together with four other Jesuits he had been sentenced to be quartered alive as an instigator of the attempt on the King (July 31st, 1759). He was not executed then. After ten years in an atrocious captivity, he was accused of heresy by the Portuguese Inquisition, just after Pombal had appointed his own brother Inquisitor General ; he was sentenced and burnt alive. "The extreme of ridicule and of absurdity"— comments Voltaire—" met the extreme of horror. The guilty man was only condemned as a prophet and only burnt for being mad and not for having tried to kill the King."(9)

*   *   *

This comment sheds much light on Voltaire's motives in his war against the Jesuits. He considered " prophecy " as an irrelevant and somewhat innocent occupation ; and hated the Jesuits as instruments of that fanaticism which can arm the zealot and cause death on issues beyond the ken of man. He sincerely thought Malagrida guilty of the attempt on the King of Portugal. As for D'Alembert, in a letter which adds nothing to his reputation, he writes to Voltaire : " Who would have said ten years ago to the Jesuits that these good fathers, who are so fond of burning others would see their turn come, and that it would be Portugal, the most fanatical and ignorant country in Europe, which would throw the first Jesuit to the fire." It is difficult to escape the conclusion that D'Alembert felt, if he did not dare think, that the burning alive of a Jesuit was a sign of progress. Rather humiliating for France that Portugal should go ahead and leave her behind. And yet a number of small affairs had kept French public opinion alive as to the power of the Jesuits. An attempt on

the life of Louis XV (January 5th, 1757) was attributed to the
Jesuits by the Jansenists ; though Voltaire, being less intimate
an enemy of the Company, spurned the slanderous suggestion.
The time was ripe for a general assault, and after several
minor skirmishes which missed fire, a sensational affair was
launched against them. An enterprising Jesuit, Father
Lavalette, manager of large estates in Martinique and
Dominica, owner, for the Company, of thousands of Black
slaves, merchant, banker and speculator, with wide relations
in Holland and secret agents in the New World, lost heavily
when, war being declared between France and England, the
English corsairs captured his cargoes without taking the
trouble to wait for the outbreak of hostilities.   He was bank-
rupt. After many delays, legal and ecclesiastic, he was
expelled from the Company and took residence in England.
But the storm broke over the Company itself, and the converging endeavours of the Jansenists, the philosophers, the
King's mistress and the King's Prime Minister, Choiseul,
found in this affair a ready instrument for their plans.(10)

Lavalette's creditors were forgotten and never paid, even
after the Company's property had been confiscated.   The
Company was requested to deliver its Constitutions to the
Paris *Parlement* : fear of the secretive ways of the Jesuits.   A
battle was going on at Court between the Marquise de
Pompadour on the one hand and the Queen and the Dauphin
on the other.   The King asked the *Parlement* to postpone
judgment for a year.   But during that year, the *Parlement*,
strongly Jansenist and somewhat " philosopher," took several
measures against the Jesuits, such as forbidding Frenchmen
to join the Company, and Jesuits to teach theology.   An
assembly of 51 prelates of the French Church, called by the
King, gave an award favourable to the Jesuits (November
30th, 1761).   In March, 1762, Martinique was lost to the
English.   The Prime Minister thought it wise to put the
nation off the scent by a fresh attack on the Jesuits.   On
April 1st their colleges were closed.   A general assembly of
the French clergy presented a petition to the King (May 23rd,
1762) in favour of the Jesuits.   On August 6th, 1762, the
Paris *Parlement* declared that the Company was " inadmissible

by its nature in every well organized State, as contrary to natural law " ; and because it was " not an Order which truly aims at an evangelic perfection, but rather a political body " seeking " first absolute independence and later the usurpation of all authority." After accusing its members of an impressive list of vices and crimes, the *Parlement* declared the Order dissolved, its property confiscated and its members forbidden to wear the frock and to hold any office without taking a special oath of fidelity to the State.(11)

* * *

In Spain the philosophers, notably Voltaire, had two power-ful admirers and disciples : Aranda and the Duke of Huéscar, later Duke of Alba. " I hasten to impart news to you which cannot but be agreeable to you "—D'Alembert wrote to Voltaire on May 14th, 1773.—" The Duke of Alba, one of the greatest lords of Spain, a man of much intelligence and who was ambassador in France under the name of Duke of Huéscar, has just sent me twenty *louis* for your statue. The letter he has written to me on the subject is full of the most agreeable things about you. ' Doomed,' he writes to me, ' to cultivate my reason in secret, I shall seize with delight this opportunity to bestow a public proof of my gratitude and admiration on the great man who was the first to show me the way.' " As for Aranda, we know from a letter written him by Voltaire that he supplied the lusty patriarch of Ferney with excellent Spanish wines, silk and china, to the old man's delight. Huéscar and Aranda were the leaders of the movement which culminated in the expulsion of the Jesuits.(12)

But, as in the case of France, the movement, though led by a free-thinking impulse which was a spiritual necessity of the times, took on curiously tortuous forms, and its leaders did not disdain to borrow weapons from their adversaries, including that superstition it was their aim to destroy. That the moral character of the Spanish Jesuits was high and their influence on national standards on the whole favourable, cannot be doubted, since we have it on the authority of no less a censor of the Catholic Church than Blanco White. Yet they were expelled not by the people but by the upper classes, whose sons they educated. This fact surely reveals

some inner failing of a grave character. Then, as now, the
chief enemies of the Jesuits came out of their own colleges.
The only man in the conspiracy who did not belong to the
nobility was Roda, a lawyer who, for lack of parchments, had
been refused a fellowship in one of the major colleges of
Salamanca. It was said of him that, on his spectacles, there
were painted on one eye a Jesuit and on the other a fellow
of Salamanca. He took power determined to destroy both
the Jesuits and the major colleges of Spain. He became
Minister of Justice under Charles III, and introduced a plan
of educational reform well inspired and progressive on its
intellectual side, lamentable from a wider point of view, for
it destroyed the six colleges (four in Salamanca, one in
Valladolid and one in Seville) which, purged of their abuses
and defects, might have maintained a valuable tradition of
scholarship and mental manners in the country.(13)

This attitude was typical of the day : intellectualist, progressive, abstract and contemptuous of traditional values
which, under their dusty overgrowth, were biologically sound.
With Charles III, a well-meaning, good-hearted but not
intelligent monarch, this generation of men found their
opportunity. The King had lost touch with the country he
was to rule owing to a long residence abroad as Prince of
Parma and later King of Naples. The Jesuits, powerful in
the previous reign, lost their grip on the Court at the same time
as Ensenada, the Minister of Ferdinand VI, fell from power ;
and as Charles III veered from a pro-English to a pro-French
policy, and the intimacy between the Bourbon Courts developed into the Family Pact, the influence of the " philosophic " Court of France was felt in Spain and its methods
imitated. The King had a confessor, Father Eleta, known as
Father Osma from the city in which he had been born. There
had been a Bishop of Osma in the previous century, Palafox,
famous for his quarrels with the Jesuits, as Bishop of Puebla de
los Angeles in New Spain. Roda conceived the idea of
attracting the powerful confessor to his views by asking Rome
to canonize Palafox, and the spell worked. Better still, it
revealed that the King himself could be held by similar means.
While still a young Infante, as the third son of Philip V, King

Charles had visited a saintly lay brother in Seville, Brother Sebastian, who took a fancy to him and predicted he would be King. At the time, the prophecy was so far removed from probability that, when it came true, the King was persuaded that the lay brother had holy powers, and wanted him canonized. Roda was delighted. The more the merrier. The Jesuits would oppose the canonization of Palafox and trouble could thus be expected for them in Spain. The King's most precious treasure was a MS prayer-book given him by Brother Sebastian. He carried it in his pocket and laid it under his pillow at night. The Vatican claimed it as a piece of evidence. Every precaution was taken to convey it to Rome and back and everything prepared so that the King should be deprived of it for only the shortest possible time. While his amulet was away, Charles neither slept, nor ate, nor spoke, nor even hunted ; he hardly breathed. And when he found that his heavy sacrifice had availed nothing, and that Rome procrastinated, his anger knew no bounds and the Jesuits were made the object of it.(14)

The Esquilache Riot came to clinch the matter. Esquilache (Squilacci) had been brought over from Naples by Charles as Minister of Finance. He was grasping, coarse and tactless, but well-meaning and progressive. He cleansed and improved the city, turned on hard the screw of taxation, and organized a monopoly of oil, bread and other staple foods which raised their price ; he improved street-lighting in Madrid, where he installed 5,000 lamps, in order to check crime and vice at night ; and with the same end in view prohibited wide-brimmed hats and flowing cloaks. The cloak is indispensable to the Spaniard, as two proverbs show : " Under a bad cloak there may hide a good drinker " ; and " Under my cloak I kill the King." The Spaniard's cloak is the Englishman's castle. Madrid rose in revolt, on Easter Sunday, March 23rd, 1766, in a fury against the foreign Minister. *Viva el Rey, muera Esquilache* was the cry. Windows were broken and passers-by were made to unfold again the folded brims of their hats ; but none was injured save some Flemish guards who barred the way to Esquilache's house to the crowd. The King in person came out on the balcony and made a verbal covenant

with the people, promising to dismiss Esquilache and appoint
a Spaniard, to cancel the Edict on hats and cloaks, to reduce
the price of bread, oil and soap, to abolish all monopolies and
to pardon the insurgents. A friar, crucifix in hand, read
aloud the articles of the covenant, and the King beckoned
" yes."

Then the unexpected happened. When all was calm, the
King with his family and his Italian Minister left for Aranjuez
in the still of night. Suspecting treachery, the crowd rose
again next day. For 48 hours, a curiously well-controlled
populace roared, shot volleys and blank musketry, barked
furiously, hardly biting at all, and made much noise with little
destruction. A coach-maker was sent to Aranjuez to demand
the King's return. He brought back a written answer stating
that the King had been bled twice, that Don Miguel Musquiz,
a Spaniard, had been appointed Finance Minister, that the
people were to disarm and go home and that nothing but
obedience on the part of his subjects would induce the King
to return to his capital. All went back to normal and the
expenses and damage caused, mostly to public houses, were
handsomely met. By whom ? Who led this curious tumult ?
Who frightened the King into leaving his capital when all had
been calm again ? Who in fact started the whole affair ?
The answers seem to-day fairly clear. The Riot was a political
bomb cleverly laid by the group of " philosophers " led by
the Duke of Alba. " The calmness of the principal nobles at
the moment when a general massacre was dreaded," the
comings and goings, behind the crowd, of mysterious persons
with a distinguished mien and self-possessed air ; the ample
funds and food the vociferous crowd never lacked ; finally,
the Duke of Alba's own deathbed confessions prove that the
Riot was organized in order to frighten the King into expelling
the Jesuits. Rumours that Jesuits had been seen exciting the
crowd, in particular one well-known Jesuit, Father Isidro
López, circulated soon, and cries asking for the return of
Ensenada were heard at the appropriate moment from the
multitude.(15)

The King was frightened. The disorders of Madrid had
been echoed by similar scenes in Zaragoza, Cuenca, Palencia,

Guipúzcoa, and it was assiduously put to him that the hidden
hand of the Jesuits was behind it all.   A secret enquiry set up
by Roda led to no results, though it produced a crop of
sentences of more than doubtful legal value ; and it should be
noted as a sign of the impartiality with which Providence
shares out foibles " right " and " left " that a distinguished
American priest, Hermoso, just escaped torture *tanquam in
cadavere* which the prosecutor (of course of the philosophic
party) demanded for him.   The most important political
result of the whole affair was that Aranda became president
of the Council of Castille and *de facto* dictator of Spain.   He
was ruthless and expeditive.   Campomanes was entrusted
with the " secret enquiry " on the events, and his first report
explained that the rising had been due to " the evil ideas over
the authority of the King spread by churchmen, and to the
fanaticism which these churchmen had for many centuries
instilled in the people and in simple folk."   A " Special
Court " or " Extraordinary Council " set up by Aranda, also
under Campomanes, pointed straight at " the hand of a
religious body which never ceases to inspire general aversion
against the Government," and added that " it would be
advisable to enlighten the people [. . .] and to disarm that
dangerous body which everywhere tries to subjugate the
throne and believes everything legitimate which allows it to
reach its ends."   On January 29th, 1767, the Extraordinary
Council presented its *Consulta*, in which after summing up all
the grievances against the Jesuits, their expulsion was recommended " because the whole body is corrupted and all the
fathers are terrible enemies of the peace of the Monarchy."(16)

This report shows why absolute monarchies like France or
Spain worked hand in hand with revolutionary philosophers
against the Jesuits.   Suárez, Mariana, Ravaillac and all that
these names called forth must have weighed heavily on the
mind of Charles III.   He was told, moreover, that the Jesuits
had engineered the riot of the preceding year ; and that, as a
number of (faked) letters " intercepted " and shown to him
" proved," they had plotted to exterminate the royal family.
One of these letters, supposed to have been written by Father
Ricci, General of the Order, attributed to him the boast of

having put together documents proving that Charles III was the son of Queen Isabel Farnese by Alberoni. At any rate, Charles made up his mind and Aranda was empowered to act on February 27th, 1767. He worked in the utmost secrecy, children unable to understand, being employed to copy documents. The same date was chosen for the whole of Spain—April 2nd, though it was anticipated to March 28th in Madrid. The order was circulated under three seals. On the second envelope, the following words were written : " This packet is not to be opened till April 2nd, 1767, under pain of death." The order intimated full royal powers to arrest all the Jesuits and convey them as prisoners, in every case within twenty-four hours, to a port designated, where ships would wait ; they were to be allowed to take away absolutely nothing but prayer books and linen for the crossing. Pain of death was threatened to the authorities concerned if one single Jesuit remained behind " even sick or dying."(17)

On April 2nd all residences of Jesuits were surrounded by troops and the *Pragmática* was published in which the King declared that " for reasons which he reserves to himself and following the impulses of his royal benignity, and making use of the supreme economic power which the Almighty had granted him for the protection of his vassals," he expelled the Jesuits ; and he prohibited his subjects to write for or against his decision under pain of *lesa-Majestad*. A most typical decision of enlightened despotism. Progress by compulsion and no arguments allowed. " We have killed the son "— wrote Roda to Choiseul—" all that remains for us to do, is to do as much with the mother, our Holy Roman Church." In the Indies it was left to the discretion of the local authorities how and when to carry out the expulsion, but everything was done with similar precautions and silence. In New Spain it took place on June 25th. In several cities, notably San Luis Potosí, Guanaxuato and Valladolid, the people rose in arms against the authorities and compelled them to receive the Jesuits back in their colleges. Armed forces had to be sent by the Viceroy, and more than 90 persons were executed before the Jesuits could be gathered in Veracruz and shipped to Genoa. In Buenos Aires and several other places the authorities had evidently feared similar events and did not carry out the order till they were sure of enough military backing. In Madrid the inhabitants of the capital were ignorant of the event till the following morning when the Jesuits and their escort were already far away on the road. It seems certain that more disorders might have taken place both in Spain and in the Indies had the Jesuits themselves decided to stand up to the law. But they obeyed everywhere.(18)

*   *   *

The expulsion did not end the matter. The three Bourbon-Courts—Spain, France and Naples—insisted on wrenching a bull from the Pope abolishing the order. Naples, Parma, Malta, all under Spanish influence, were made to expel the Jesuits. The driving impulse came from Madrid, chiefly from Aranda and Roda. The troops of the King of Naples (a son of Charles III) invaded the pontifical States, and French troops occupied Avignon, then a papal city. An incident which took place in Madrid, the year after the expulsion, did much damage to the Jesuits. On St. Charles Day the King appeared on the balcony of the royal palace, as was the custom, to hear a popular request which he would grant. The crowd asked for the return of the Jesuits. The King was alarmed and annoyed, and the Archbishop of Toledo was banished on suspicion of having instigated the scene. Increasing pressure was put on Clement XIII ; but the aged Pope died on November 2nd, 1769 ; the Conclave was besieged by the three Bourbon Crowns, all three in the hands of " philosopher " ministers. The Crown of Spain was the most militant of the three. Cardinal Solís, Archbishop of Seville, had instructions to exact from the future Pope a written promise to abolish the Company of Jesus. He obtained a statement, clear enough as a hint, from Cardinal Ganganelli, and so this Franciscan became Clement XIV. (19)

The new Pope tried to hedge and evade the consequences of his pact ; Maria Theresa, the King of Poland and even Frederick II wrote to him in favour of the Jesuits. The ministers of the House of Bourbon insisted on their pound of flesh. In 1770, the Pope renewed his promise in a letter to

Charles III in which he asked for a respite. The fall of
Choiseul and of Madame de Pompadour, and the rise of
another royal mistress at Versailles were believed in Spain to
work in favour of the Jesuits—for of such strange threads is
religious history also woven. But Charles III kept full
pressure on both Paris and Rome. In the autumn of 1772,
Don José Moñino, later known as Count Floridablanca was
sent as Ambassador to Rome. " A good *regalist* [or, as the
French said, Jansenist], prudent, well-mannered and a good
mixer," said Charles III of him. He brought instructions to
exact from the Pope the fulfilment of his promise. He tackled
the Pope with the utmost energy and went so far as to threaten
the total extinction of all religious Orders unless the Jesuits
were abolished forthwith. He himself describes his action
thus : " Trying to impress on the Pope the terror which was
absolutely suitable, though along with friendly and respectful
monitions." The Pope yielded to the pressure, and the
Brief *Dominus et redemptor noster* abolishing the Jesuits was
actually drafted by Floridablanca and printed in a secret
press in the Spanish Embassy. The Company was dissolved
on July 21st and the news imparted to the Jesuits during the
night of August 26th, 1773.(20)

*　　　*　　　*

The expulsion of the Jesuits was unfortunate for Spain.
True the Order had, and has, the usual share of human
defects ; but, as in the case of the Jews and of the Moriscos,
these defects were more than compensated for by qualities of
hard work, efficiency and culture which a country more
wisely governed would not have thrown away. A number of
first-rate minds were lost to the nation, including, paradoxically
enough, Father Nuix, the writer of a spirited refutation of
Raynal and upholder of the Spanish rule in the Indies. Worse
still, a number of educational institutions were dissolved which
the nation could ill afford.

The loss was even greater in the Indies. Irreparable
damage was caused to the Missions of Paraguay, which were
all but sacked and destroyed by get-rich-quick, unscrupulous
officials, with much hardship to the Indians. The loss in

educational institutions was even greater than in the case of
Spain.   Yet all these evil consequences of a hasty and harsh
measure were as nothing compared with two other results.
The first was that yet another spiritual link, and possibly the
most important one, was snapped between the Indies and
Spain ; for the White, rich and conservative classes which
were the chief standby of Spanish rule in the Indies were
profoundly religious.   The air of the century had shaken the
faith of some of their sons.   But these persons who in the
Indies thought with the French philosophers had thereby
lost all political touch with Spain even though they read and
admired Spanish thinkers of their own persuasion and were
enthusiastic about Aranda, Roda and the rest.   With
philosophic ideas there inevitably came separatist trends.
The solid mass of the white Creoles, however, remained
attached to Spain because it remained attached to the Catholic
faith, to the traditional way of doing things.   Suddenly, from
this Spain of the sceptre and the Cross, from the very King of
Spain heir to Ferdinand and Isabel came that most tangible
proof of Voltaire's philosophy : "Out with the Jesuits."
On that day, the King of Spain with his own hands cut the
most solid link between his Crown and his subjects overseas.

The second result was that Europe was sown over with
Spanish-American Jesuits, between 5,000 and 8,000 of them,
burning with indignation against the mother country and
ready to scrutinize the basis of the right which a distant
monarch in Madrid could claim to drive them out of their
homes.   In his travels Miranda will procure a list of them,
knowing their value for his cause ; and Pitt in his conversations
with Miranda will attach the utmost price to this list of Jesuits.
An ex-Jesuit, Mercano y Arismendi, was to co-operate in
British plans against Buenos Aires in 1781 and 1782.   In
1790, some of these ex-Jesuits whom Miranda had seen and
prepared in Italy were brought over to London.   The
American Minister in London wrote, in 1798, that he had
seen some of them who had remained by then many years in
England, he says, "in the service of and paid by the English
Government, whom they supply with documents on the
conditions and situation of South America."(21)

The most famous of these Jesuits was Pablo Vizcardo, the author of the first clear statement advocating the independence of the New World in a *Lettre aux Espagnols-Américains par Un de leurs Compatriotes* published in Philadelphia in 1799 and broadcast all over the continent by Miranda. One of Miranda's correspondents, a Frenchman, wrote to him, on December 19th, 1798, that this letter was but " an abbreviated rehash of all that has been written by Raynal." The criticism is not altogether unfair. Vizcardo shows his animus as a Jesuit in phrases such as this : " The expulsion and ruin of the Jesuits had to all appearances no other cause than the fame of their riches "—a statement clearly untrue. But his argument in favour of independence is powerfully put. " The several regions of Europe "—he writes—" which the Crown of Spain was made to give up, such as the Kingdom of Portugal, within the area of Spain herself, and the famous republic of the United Provinces which shook off her iron yoke, teach us that a continent incomparably greater than Spain, richer, more powerful, more populated, should not be dependent on that Kingdom which is so remote, and still less when it happens to be reduced to the hardest servitude."(22)

All this was true. But human nature being what it is, Vizcardo would have been most unlikely to discover such truths had he and the Company of Jesus to which he belonged not been expelled from his fatherland by the King and Government of Spain. It is, therefore, a curious coincidence of History that, as a result of the well-meant but mistaken endeavours of a group of Spanish enlightened despots, the Jesuits were driven to co-operate with the other two international brotherhoods, the Freemasons and the Jews, in the destruction of the Spanish Empire.

Chapter XVII

THE THREE REVOLUTIONS

1.—THE AMERICAN REVOLUTION

In his *Lettre aux Espagnols-Américains*, Vizcardo wrote this significant paragraph : "The valour with which the English colonies of America have fought for liberty, which they now gloriously enjoy, fills our own indolence with shame. We have yielded to them the palm with which they, the first to do so, have crowned the New World with an independent sovereignty. Add to it the intent with which the Courts of Spain and France have backed the cause of the English Americans. Let all that be a stimulus for our honour provoked by so many insults during three hundred years." A fairly good summary of the impact of the American Revolution on the Indies. This intervention of the two Bourbon Courts in favour of the American rebels strikes us to-day as odd, especially on the part of Spain, a nation more concerned than England herself in preserving the New World from the winds of revolution and indiscipline.

Things looked otherwise in those days, for power politics still held the field unhindered by any ideology. England had two traditions about Spain. One was that which Lord Lansdowne formulated in the House of Lords during the debate on the Nootka Sound Convention. It amounted to a friendly agreement with Spain to draw from Spanish America as much profit as possible without questioning Spanish rights there. Lansdowne made this policy date from the Treaty of 1523 between Charles V and Henry VIII. He reminded the House that " the navigation in the Spanish-American Seas was expressly stipulated by the 15th article of the Treaty of 1670." Then he went on : " Perhaps there was wisdom in more respects than one, in suffering the great stake contained in the Spanish-American possessions to lie to a certain degree dormant and unimproved in the hands of Spain." Lansdowne praised the wisdom of British ambassadors of the end of the previous century, such as Godolphin, who, back in London, had urged the city merchants to trade with South America through Spain and not direct ; and the ministers such as Bolingbroke, Walpole, the Duke of Bedford, and even Chatham and Lord North, who had borne in mind the advantages this wise and moderate policy brought to England.

The roots of this tradition of calculated restraint had already been observed in the seventeenth century by Varinas, who thought that one of the reasons why Spain had kept her American Empire intact was that it was in the best interest of her three rivals to keep her there. England, France and Holland knew that " if that Empire were to fall into the hands of one of these three powers, the other two would lose the advantages they then enjoyed ; that is why they remained neutral and content with the robberies they made and the fruits of their fraudulent or licit trade with galleons and fleets." The eighteenth century was gradually to destroy this balance to the benefit of Britain. Holland had been weakened in her struggle with England, while France could no longer decently harbour plots of expansion at the cost of the other Bourbon power. England's policy towards Spain became more turbulent and boisterous. The South Sea Company had been set up to enjoy a monopoly of trade with Spanish America so as to wipe out the national debt with its profits. Eldorados of wealth rose in the eyes of a keen public. Shares soared. Yet the rights actually granted by the Treaty of Utrecht did not warrant such " general frenzy." They were the right to supply the Indies with negro slaves for thirty years and the right to keep a ship off Cartagena loaded with British goods. But the public were misled by " mysterious reports " of " imaginary advantages." " The sanguine cupidity which marked this speculation "— it can be read in Coxe's Memoirs of Sir Robert Walpole—" was not confined to the South Sea scheme : the whole nation became stock-jobbers and projectors." When the bubble was pricked there was great despondency, and Walpole was called back to power to set things right.(1)

One thing, however, not even he could redress. Till the Treaty of Utrecht, Anglo-Spanish trade in the New World had been ruled by the Treaty of 1670, under Article 9 of which sailing and trading between the New World dominions of the two contracting parties was forbidden save under a licence. This treaty had been interpreted by Spain in the most liberal fashion, and for thirty years, as Coxe puts it, " a strict friend-ship and union subsisted between the two Crowns, both in Europe and in America, and a flourishing, although an illicit trade, was, by the connivance and indulgence of Spain, carried on between the English and the Spanish plantations." But with the turn of the century Spain, governed by a Bourbon, watched more strictly over her rights, while the South Sea Company claimed the monopoly of whatever English trade there was, and took as much interest in chasing smugglers as the Spanish coast guards. The two brief wars of 1718 and 1727 did not fundamentally alter the position, as governed by the Treaty of Utrecht and the Right of Asiento, but English (including American) smugglers found it harder to flourish than in the good old days. They found this the more irksome from the fact that they had grown to consider Spanish indulgence as a matter of right. Temper against Spain rose rapidly ; a campaign of " atrocities " was started in London, and despite the efforts of Walpole and his Ambassador in Madrid, Keene, it led to war. " On reviewing the conduct of England "—writes Coxe—" we shall not hesitate to confess that it was inconsistent, unjust, haughty and violent." And he adds : " The British nation listened only to one side of the question, gave implicit credit to all the exaggerated accounts of the cruelties committed by the Spaniards without due evidence, and without noticing the violation of express treaties by the British traders." One Captain Jenkins was produced to show that a Spanish coastguard captain had torn his ear off and told him to go show it to his King. " This ridiculous story " gave its name to the *Jenkins' Ear War*. The Spanish Government published a Manifesto which, writes Coxe, " fully justified the conduct of Spain and proved to impartial Europe that, though in the refusal to pay the £95,000 she appeared to be the aggressor, the English were the real aggressors," and " had violated the spirit of the Treaty." Why then the war ? " The possessions of Spain in the West Indies were considered as likely to fall an easy prey to the

British adventurers ; the merchants anticipated the monopoly of the commerce and the possession of the mines of Peru and Potosí." And Burke was to sum it up in the following words : " Sir Robert Walpole was forced into the war in 1739, by the people, who were inflamed to this measure by the most leading politicians, by the first orators, and the great poets of the time. For that war Pope sung his dying notes. For that war Johnson, in more energetic strains, employed the voice of his early genius. [. . .] The crowd readily followed the politicians, in the cry for a war which threatened little bloodshed and which promised victories that were attended with something more solid than glory. A war with Spain was a war of plunder."

All this effervescence favoured the other tradition of England with regard to Spain, that of Westward Ho ! England had often carried on a spirited anti-Spanish policy during the century. She had occupied Gibraltar and Minorca, just as Spain would have occupied Dover and the Isle of Wight had she had the power and had the Channel led to so many places as the Straits do. The plan was to cut the Empire through at the Isthmus of Darién. Vernon would attack on the Atlantic, Anson on the Pacific. They both preyed upon the ports and ships of the Indies ; a footing was secured in Belize ; the Falkland Islands were occupied, lost, secured again by negotiation and again evacuated ; the people of England followed these Western adventures with eagerness, and with an eye on both glory and gold. Vernon's victory at Portobelo was sung in ballad after ballad :

> Of this victory rare
> You secur'd the best share,
> For the Spanish King's dollars and pelf,
> You most gallantly gave
> To your mariners brave
> And with glory rewarded yourself.

But of course Vernon's glory was well lined with Spanish gold. Another Admiral whom Spanish treasure had enriched, Charles Wager, was then at the Admiralty. He strongly urged the conquest of Cuba, to secure for England a better position than other nations once the Indies were open to all for trade on equal terms. But he was chary about plans insistently presented to him for expelling the Spaniards from the New World by helping the Indians and the Creole Spaniards to rebel. His reasons are worth quoting. " One of the reasons for my being backward in proposing this "— he writes to Vernon on June 21st, 1741—" is that I am always afraid of our English conduct, and the behaviour of soldiers when they come into a country of plenty, who being under little or no order or discipline, would be for robbing and abusing the Indians that should come over to them, and perhaps abusing their women, which might provoke the Indians to leave them and reconcile themselves to the Spaniards, as I am told the Darien Indians have done." Nevertheless he sent to Vernon the promoter of the scheme, one Captain Lee, with the hope that something might turn up ; for after Portobelo, as he writes to Vernon, " people here have set their hearts so much upon conquests in the West Indies, that we had not only taken Carthagena for you, but was gone down to La Vera Cruz, which has no strength, they say, but the Castle, and so stopped the two sources from whence the Treasure is brought [. . .] and then nothing could hinder our troops from marching to Mexico, which they say is the richest town in the world."

When the elder Pitt took office (1756) this general activity against Spain in the New World found a determined and pertinacious leader. England was then at war with France in what is now known as the Seven Years' War. But Pitt brought to office the tradition of expansion to the West which came down to him from Hawkins, Drake, Raleigh and Cromwell. His warlike tendencies are satirized in a poem written in 1746, describing the consequences of his longed-for arrival to power :

> Then shall for war
> The Dutch declare.
> Then we the Russ
> Shall meet and buss.
> Then, then shall France
> Fall in a trance.

Then, then shall Spain
Yield to thy strain.
None from that hour
Shall envy power
In high degree
Of Majesty
When Pitt a Minister shall be.

There is no doubt that England was then in a boisterous
mood, and that the nation looked to Pitt, as another poet
put it, with

New hopes reviving, to new conquests led.

France sought the help of the Spanish navy in the war.   Spain
would have remained neutral.   But while France pulled hard,
England, lured by the gold of the Indies, became more and
more pressing.   Pitt began by trying to win Spain over to an
alliance against France, offering her Gibraltar and the with-
drawal of all Englishmen from the territories occupied in
Belize ;   but the offer was rigidly subordinated to the return
of Spanish Minorca to England, the island having recently
been taken by the French from the English and offered by
them to Spain.   That Pitt's offer could be made at all shows
the spirit in which power politics was understood in those
days.   With the accession of Charles III, the policy of Spain
became more definitely anti-English, and the Family Pact
(1761) pledged France and Spain to consider every power as
their enemy who became the enemy of the other, and to
examine all proposals of peace in common.   Pitt decided to
declare war on Spain, but the Cabinet did not back him and
he resigned.   Spain was asked for explanations about her
warlike measures.   Wall, the Irishman who then governed
her, pointed out that her dominions were constantly under
an English threat.   "You have set the Spanish power at
defiance ;   you have insulted our coasts ;   you have violated
our neutrality ;   you have incroached upon the Spanish
dominion in America by cutting logwood and forming new
settlements in the Bay of Honduras.   You have extorted
from the subjects of Spain the right they enjoyed of fishing
in the banks of Newfoundland.   I have given my royal

J

master hopes that some atonement would be made for these repeated grievances ; and I am commanded to require how, when and where, such reparations may be expected."(2)

So spoke Wall to the British Ambassador while the treasure ships he was expecting were still at sea. Once they were safe in Cádiz, he owned the existence of the treaty with France. On December 10th, 1761, the British Ambassador withdrew and the war desired by Pitt began. Havana fell after a fierce struggle of two months and eight days (August, 1762) ; Manila fell also (September), and, to quote Coxe, " after several hours of plunder and disorder, which could not be restrained [. . .] the town and its inhabitants were saved from ruin by the leniency of the conqueror who accepted as a ransom two millions of dollars, and an assignment of the same sum on the Spanish Treasury." Twelve ships had been lost in Havana by the Spaniards and several more in Manila ; but the victory which they won over the Portuguese colony of Sacramento compensated them for these losses, for they secured twenty-six English ships richly laden, besides stores valued at four million sterling ; and it frustrated "an attack planned against Buenos Aires by individuals in England and Portugal who were stimulated by the hope of plunder." Aranda waged an inconclusive campaign in Portugal against the Anglo-Portuguese commanded by Burgoyne. No one seemed interested in prolonging the war, and by the Treaty of Paris a number of territorial arrangements were concluded whereby England unwittingly laid the foundations of the Dominion of Canada and of the Republic of the United States by securing from France and Spain all the territories east of the Mississippi as well as the whole of Canada.(3)

*   *   *

That history moves in ways of its own which statesmen, who think they shape it, seldom see, is aptly shown by the after-effects of this treaty. Britain acquired Nova Scotia, Canada and Florida. The outcome was that the thirteen colonies lost all fear from either French or Indian attack, and, therefore, acquired a spirit of independence from the mother country and felt their weight in the joint councils accordingly increased.

This circumstance brought to a head the standing dispute between England and her American colonists.

The dispute had arisen out of a desire on the part of Britain to raise funds to meet the war against France. As early as 1754 Governor Shirley had spoken to Franklin in Boston about raising money in the colonies by Act of Parliament. Franklin gave him an answer in writing, calling Shirley's attention to the dissatisfaction the measure would cause, and pointing out " that there was no reason to doubt the willingness of the colonists to contribute for their own defence ; [. . .] that natives of America would be as likely to consult wisely and faithfully for the safety of their native country as the Governors sent from Britain, whose object is generally to make fortunes, and then return home ; [. . .] that compelling the colonies to pay money for their own defence, without their consent, would show a suspicion of their loyalty, or of their regard for their country, or of their common sense ; [. . .] that the colonists have always been indirectly taxed by the Mother Country (besides paying the taxes laid on by their own Assemblies) in as much as they are obliged to purchase the manufactures of Britain, charged with innumerable heavy taxes ; some of which manufactures they could make, and others could purchase cheaper at other markets ; that the colonists are besides taxed by the Mother Country by being obliged to carry great part of their produce to Britain, and accept a lower price than they might at other markets ; [. . .] that an adequate Representation in Parliament would probably be acceptable to the colonists, and would best unite the views and interests of the whole Empire."(4)

This wise paper seems to have cooled the ardour of the tax-hunters. But opinion in England was divided and many were the Englishmen who held that England's wars were fought in the interest of the American colonists. The dispute gave rise at times to curious avowals. Reckoning the sums spent in or for America, an English pamphleteer refers to " the expences of the two large wars : the FORMER of those wars was undertaken for the protection of American Commerce, or rather American *Smuggling*, to the Spanish colonies." *When wives quarrel aloud, truths fly about*, says a Spanish proverb.(5)

In 1764, another Governor, Sir Francis Bernard, sent to England his *Principles of Law and Polity*, taking up the idea of taxing by Act of Parliament, within a scheme of reform of the American government, aimed at rendering the Governors of the colonies independent of the peoples they governed (i.e., the position they had in the Spanish American territories). " The rule that a British subject shall not be bound by laws, or liable to taxes, but what he has consented to by his Representatives, must be confined to the inhabitants of Great Britain only, and is not strictly true, even there." So wrote Sir Francis. His plan was to cancel the Charters, group the colonies into wider regions, and govern them by authority, in a vice-regal style (he went so far as to set up a nobility for life), on funds raised in America but by authority of the London Parliament. He did not, however, think of feeding the English Exchequer with American money. But the English Exchequer was then so exhausted and so needy that the idea of taxing from London and for London ultimately won.(6)

The change was not brusque. The Sugar Act of 1764, legalized by Act of Parliament in 1767, was explicitly defined as a trade and revenue law. Another Act of Parliament denied legal tender to colonial bills of credit, so as to check the excess of the issue of paper money in America. But the first purely fiscal measure, the Stamp Act, brought trouble to a head. Discontent was already rampant owing to the efforts of the British Government to suppress contraband with Spain in pursuance of its new policy since the Treaty of Paris. The Stamp Act was passed in 1765. By November 1st, when it should begin to operate, it had raised fierce opposition. The local Assemblies protested ; nine colonies met in Congress in New York ; and the boycott of British goods was set on foot. Boston took the lead. The house of Thomas Hutchinson, the Chief Justice, was wrecked by the crowd. Equally violent demonstrations in New York and other cities forced the State distributors to resign. Meanwhile, home politics being in a chaotic state, the Granville Cabinet resigned, and the new ministry repealed the Stamp Act while affirming Britain's right to legislate for the colonies by means of a special Declaratory Act (1766). This contentious principle

was applied the following year in the Townsend Trade and
Revenue Act imposing on the colonies duties on glass, lead,
paint, paper and tea, out of which the salaries of the Governors
and judges were to be paid.   This was, of course, Bernard's
idea, and went further than the merely fiscal import generally
attributed to the measure.   In fact it aimed at rendering the
authorities independent of the local budgets.   Boston protested through its Assembly ;   there were riots and movements
of troops, and a collision between the troops and the people
of Boston (1770).   Other Assemblies protested also.   London
set aside the protests and, reviving a Statute of Henry VIII on
treason, began to collect evidence to deport American leaders
to England for trial.   Large majorities in Parliament backed
the King and his anti-American tories ;   but Adams was
probably right when, in 1774, he wrote :   " We distinguish
between the Ministry, the House of Commons, the Officers of
the Army, Navy, Excise, Customs, etc., who are dependent
on the Ministry, and tempted, if not obliged to echo their
voices ;   and the Body of the People.   We are assured by
thousands of Letters from persons of good intelligence, that
the Body of the People are friends of America [. . .] tha
London and Bristol have declared themselves [. . .] in
favour of our cause [. . .] that many of the most virtuous
and independent of the Nobility and Gentry are for us."
Private interests, however, came to envenom a conflict which
pride made acute.   The East India Company was losing
money since the Americans refused to drink taxed tea.   Huge
unsold stores were heaping up in their harbours.   The Company was not the only loser, for, by its contract with the
Government, it had to pay to the Treasury £400,000 every
time its dividends reached 12 per cent.   The Company
suggested abolishing the duty, but, since all the other
Townsend duties had already been cancelled, this one had to
remain in order to save the face of the London Government.
It was decided instead to allow the Company to send the tea
direct to America.(7)

Everywhere but in Boston the people were adamant.   In
Boston the situation was not so clear.   The leaders feared the
close connection there was between the merchants and

Government circles through private interests and family ties, while a considerable number of persons otherwise attached to the Government by salaries or pensions were "determined to drink tea, both as evidence of their servility to the Administration and their contempt and hatred of the People"; finally, there were the numerous weak "who would gratify their appetites" in any case. The leaders resolved that they could not afford to let the tea land, as had been done in other ports surer of their populations; and during the night of December 16th, 1773, the cargo, 340 chests, was thrown into the sea. Parliament closed the port of Boston, abolished the elected Council of Massachusetts and enacted that guilty persons would be removed to England for trial. General Gage was appointed Governor to enforce the new laws. The colony countered by organizing a Congress, which, while doing much by its mere existence to foster union between the colonists themselves, was conservative in outlook and hardly separatist. Nevertheless, by its adoption of the principle of boycott of imports and exports from and to Britain and its efficient organization thereof under the name of *Association* (a name valuable in itself) this First Continental Congress planted the seeds of the American Revolution.

War was inevitable. Hostilities began in Massachusetts in April, 1775. The Second Continental Congress met while soldiers fought. It appointed General Washington Commander-in-Chief and dealt with a number of matters of a collective character, such as communications, while the old-time Governors and Assemblies crumbled down and each colony organized its own Republican Government as it pleased. Military events were both modest in their dimensions (the rebel army numbered about 9,000 troops) and chaotic. But the political evolution of the colonies was clear and the Americans had good leaders: in ideas, Thomas Paine, Benjamin Franklin; in administration and politics, Jefferson, John Adams; men capable and straight. On May 15th, 1776, Congress recommended " to adopt such Government as shall in the opinion of the representatives of the people, best conduce to the happiness of their constituents in particular and of Americans in general." On June 7th, R. M. Lee of

Virginia moved before Congress " that these United Colonies are and of right ought to be free and independent States." Taken together, these two resolutions outlined the name of the new nation : United States of America. A committee composed of John Adams, Benjamin Franklin, Thomas Jefferson, Robert Livingston and Roger Sherman drafted the Declaration of Independence which, though dated July 4th, 1776, the day it was voted, did not deserve its name till the 19th, when the State of New York adhered to it by a separate vote.

It was an act of faith. The colonies were independent only in heart—and even that not unanimously. On the military, political, economic and financial planes they were in their infancy and constitutionally they were loose and unorganized. " They have "—said an English critic in 1776—" lost at one stroke their whole trade in corn and rice with Spain, Portugal and the Mediterranean ; which at a moderate computation, brought annually £1,500,000 to North America. They have lost the supplying our own West-India Islands, as well as those of other nations, with provisions ; a branch of commerce estimated little short of a million annually. They have lost their fishery, an article too great for computation ; and they have lost the exportation to Great Britain of commodities which would not have answered in any other market, had the sea remained open to their navigation." If, in the end, the colonies won, they owed it to bungling and bad generalship on the part of the English, to luck, to their own grit and sense that the spirit of the time was with them, and also in no small measure to the help of France and Spain. Towards the end of 1776 overtures were made to France, Spain, Russia and Austria by the Americans. France and Spain were then considering action within the framework of their Spanish-American and Portuguese policies.(8)

*   *   *

The Treaty of Paris had not helped to make the Family Pact very popular in Spain ; and neither Grimaldi, Wall's successor in Spain, nor d'Aiguillon, Choiseul's successor in France, was enthusiastic about it. The partition of Poland, deeply resented in Spain, to the extent of inducing Charles III to propose an armed intervention on behalf of Poland, which d'Aiguillon firmly opposed, made matters worse between the two Bourbon Courts. Even the constant troubles with England and Portugal, leading as they often did to the very edge of war, only kept the Family Pact alive as business rather than as pleasure. Pombal pursued a policy of expansion southwards from Brazil, egged on by England. Aranda's chief idea was the annexation of Portugal. It is typical of the time and of the man that in this—in itself a natural biological and political tendency to achieve a national unity so far frustrated through the separatism of the Western Spaniards known as Portuguese—Aranda saw nothing more than a step towards decisive power over European trade and the acquisition of more wealth, industry and culture for the country. The idea of countering hostilities in Brazil by a lightning attack on Portugal before England could react was in the air. The Government in Madrid developed Aranda's idea into a definite plan which was put by Aranda before Vergennes in October, 1775. This plan started from the assumption that England and Portugal had hostile intentions towards Spain and that the question of turning England's difficulties in North America by declaring war on Spain had been considered in London. Hence the need of a preventive war. Grimaldi suggested that a Spanish army, reinforced with 20-30,000 Frenchmen, should take Portugal ; while Spanish forces would co-operate with the French in handing Brazil over to France. This would ensure peace for France and Spain against English aggression in Europe and a compensation for France for the loss of Canada.(9)

Vergennes demurred. He denied the premisses. England was too busy with her rebellious colonies. Better let her sink into civil war (with her American brothers) than wake her up to her error by an outside attack. France sought no increase of territory. All this sounded too idealistic for Aranda to believe. His report was that France had neither money nor ships (Grimaldi added " nor ministers ") ; that, moreover, she did not want Spain to become stronger, least of all by incorporating Portugal, for what suited France was to keep Spain, though strong enough to be a helpful ally, weak enough to remain dependent on France. He advised shelving the plan but not forgetting it. Aranda was right. " Nothing would less suit the interests of Y.M. in itself and in its consequences "—wrote Vergennes to Louis XVI, on October 17th, 1776, speaking of Spain's possible annexation of Portugal. Vergennes' denial of the danger of war from England was in its turn denied by the official representations made in Madrid by the French Ambassador, who the previous year had warned Spain of the growing military strength of England in the New World, due to the rise of the colonies. Vergennes was not interested in Portugal or Brazil, but he was in the American (English) colonists. England was the enemy of France. Her power rested on trade and the sea. The American colonists strove against it. They were therefore the natural allies of France. For him the Spanish plan was dangerous since it might lead to an understanding between England and her rebellious colonies. Aranda saw that the anti-English urge remained concealed under Vergennes' explanations, and he endeavoured by all the means in his power—which was exceptionally great in Paris—to foster the naval forces and war preparations of the French. To this effect he even took part in sittings of the Council of Ministers. In England he saw a power the more dangerous as her decisions were liable to be changed at any time by the passions of a public opinion allowed to meddle with the affairs of State to a degree unseemly in the eyes of an aristocrat such as he was, born to rule.(10)

It is important to emphasize this point. Aranda, the chief instigator of the militant anti-English policy of the Bourbons at the time, was an absolutist. He had nothing in common with the American colonists, not even his anti-Catholic attitude, which was sceptical and " philosophic," so that he would have laughed at the bigoted puritans of Boston if he had thought them worthy of his attention at all. He conceived a plan for landing in Ireland to declare it independent and so forestall England's aggressive plots against Spain. Grimaldi answered that the French did not see the danger of war from England and thought that the time had not come for attacking her. This was true, but Grimaldi, as events were to show, can hardly have been sincere in regretting it. On April 1st, 1776, Portuguese troops attacked the Spanish frontier in Río Grande. Aranda pointed out that, just as Pitt had said that he had conquered America in Germany, it would be easier to conquer Minorca and Gibraltar in Portugal. The American colonies declared their independence on July 3rd. Vergennes thought his time had come and decided to declare war on England. The French Cabinet met on July 7th, 1776, and agreed that war was inevitable, but Vergennes obtained from Spain that operations against Portugal should be confined to the New World. On August 31st he proposed to the Cabinet that France should side with the rebels and that Spain's expedition against Portugal could now proceed. Grimaldi, however, despite a majority in his own Cabinet for operations in European Portugal, manœuvred so as to shatter Aranda's plans : he made it clear to Vergennes that Spain's object was to annex Portugal ; and as Grimaldi expected, Vergennes withdrew his support. An expedition was sent to Sacramento under Don Pedro Ceballos ; the Portuguese were forced to surrender and after the fall of Pombal on the death of King Joseph, the two Iberian kingdoms came to terms and to a closer union, cemented by the fact that the new Queen of Portugal was a niece of Charles III (1777). This treaty was the work of Floridablanca, a new man, for Grimaldi had fallen after his ambiguous part in these events, on the attack of Aranda and his " Aragonese " Party.(11)

*　　*　　*

As for the North American situation, considered on its merits, the Spanish leaders were also at variance. Aranda saw the consequences of the Declaration of Independence with his usual cold realism. He did not fail to notice both that the new-born power assumed the name of *America* as a matter of course, and the subconscious trend this fact implied. He may have found the idea in Choiseul, whose agent, Kalb, wrote to him in 1768 : " I believe not only that this country will emancipate itself from the Crown of England, but that in the course of time it will invade all the dominions that the

European powers possess in America, on the main land as
well as in the islands." In England similar views were soon
to appear. " There can be no doubt "—wrote a London
pamphleteer in 1783—" but the views of ambition, and a
desire to extend their dominions, will [. . .] prevail in the
confederated colonies. The mines of gold and silver in
South America, will be an object of irresistible temptation.
Assisted by the power of France, or even without it, they will
be able in no great space of time, to reduce the Brazils, Mexico,
Chili and Peru and to acquire universal dominion over all
America." Aranda's broodings were apt to follow similar
lines. He saw that freedom of commerce would develop the
new nation into a formidable power. But in his view Spain
was in a dilemma : she had to choose between England and the
United States. Though the United States, independent or
not, would always be a hindrance to Spain, they would need
the immediate future to settle down in their vast territories;
while England was a country with which Spain could never
come to terms. Therefore, he concluded, let Spain enter into
a defensive alliance with the United States. This would ensure
the integrity of the Spanish New World.(12)

Floridablanca, the Prime Minister, was not convinced.
Let England weaken herself without our having to pay for it
—he argued. He pointed out that Vergennes, with an eye on
Catherine the Great and her ambitions on Constantinople,
preferred to wait and not to risk his forces so far away from
Europe ; and saw, better than Aranda, that Spain was giving
the peoples of the New World an example against her own
interests—as England did not fail to point out. Floridablanca,
moreover, was not as keen as Aranda on the destruction of the
power of England, for he feared that, as a consequence, France
would become unmanageable and reduce Europe to slavery.
Nevertheless, Spain backed the American rebels from the
beginning. The Government sent agents to Jamaica and
Florida to keep abreast of events, and secret orders enabled
port-captains to allow rebel ships to shelter in Spanish harbours.
In 1776, Aranda received four million *reales de vellón* with
orders to arrange that, through Vergennes, they should reach
the rebels with the " required dissimulation and secrecy."

Throughout that year and the next Spain and France sent money and supplies of all kinds, mostly through Beaumarchais, but some of it also direct, from La Coruña. France had gone further, for she had received the representatives of the new Republic, Franklin, Silas Deane and Arthur Lee, and prepared a treaty of commerce and a defensive alliance.(13)

On October 16th, 1777, General Burgoyne surrendered in Saratoga to General Gates. It is difficult for us to realise what this news meant then. Till then the war had been seen in Europe, in the words of an English pamphleteer of 1776, as " the insolence " of " the leaders of the infatuated colonists, ambitious demagogues " who had " led forward an ignorant populace, step by step till their retreat from ruin is difficult, if not impossible." Suddenly this ignorant populace beat one of the best armies in the Old World, one of the richest in military history. The event should have struck France, and even more so Spain, as ominous. France, however, saw in it but the immediate fact : the possibility of " calling in the New World to restore the balance of the old," as was later to be said on the other side ; and the Treaties with the United States were signed on February 6th, 1778 ; in virtue of these treaties France would fight on till the independence of the United States was recognized. This Treaty led to war between France and Great Britain, and hostilities began in June. It also led to a definite estrangement between France and Spain. The Spanish Government suspected its own Ambassador, Aranda, of having been the chief instigator of the war. Floridablanca still wanted to avoid mixing Spain in it and he started negotiations to mediate between Great Britain on the one hand and France and the colonists on the other. His proposals were a 25-year truce during which the colonies would be *de facto* independent, and a permanent peace to be negotiated in conference between the four parties. No one liked them. Paine wrote of them that they were " so exceedingly favourable to their [Britain's] interests that had they been accepted, they would have become inconvenient, if not inadmissible to America." In London they were suspected as dilatory manœuvres to arm for the coming war, a view which Godoy seems to have shared. The British Government

refused to have anything to do with them; whereupon
Floridablanca sent an ultimatum to London (April 3rd, 1779)
demanding that plenipotentiaries on both sides be sent to
Madrid and meanwhile the rebels be treated as "independent
in fact." On April 12th he signed a Treaty with France
renewing the Family Pact. On June 22nd Spain entered the
war.(14)

Military and naval operations were long and complicated,
but have now but an academic and technical value. The
chief Spanish bases were New Orleans and Habana; the
chief commanders, a brother of Gálvez, who governed
Louisiana, and his father, who governed Guatemala, as well
as Cagigal, who became commander-in-chief in Habana, and
whose aide-de-camp was to be the precursor of Spanish-
American independence: Miranda. On May 8th, 1782, the
Bahamas surrendered to Miranda. The British lost the war
against the rebels and, after the surrender of Cornwallis in
Yorktown (1781), had to withdraw to the Antilles, and to
give up the Floridas to Gálvez' army. But their fleets showed
incomparable skill and daring against the often superior
forces of France and Spain. Both sides were soon weary of
the war and the Treaty was negotiated in Versailles and
signed on September 3rd, 1783. The chief obstacle to the
agreement was Gibraltar. A long siege had been successfully
resisted by the British garrison, thus raising the sentimental
value of the Rock. Franklin strongly backed Spain's
demand, arguing that Gibraltar was as Spanish as Portsmouth
was British. But the British Cabinet, though at times tempted
by offers of exchanges now with Oran, now with Puerto Rico,
was encouraged in its resistance by Vergennes' attitude,
outwardly favourable, secretly opposed to a decision which
might, and probably would, have removed for good and all
the old distrust between England and Spain. He was very
able, far abler than Aranda, for he offered French islands to
the English in exchange for Gibraltar, and managed to get
the offer turned down by Aranda himself, on the ground that
the Spanish Indies would be reduced to slavery if the English
occupied the French Antilles as well as their own. Suddenly
Aranda, on his own responsibility, took the decision to let

Gibraltar go ; and wrote to the Ministry in Madrid : " The most astonishing step for which an Ambassador had ever taken responsibility, unique in the annals of diplomacy."(15)

*   *   *

This decision can only be explained as part of the confusion of the pre-revolutionary period in which it was taken. Aranda matters little in himself ; much as an incarnation of the period. An absolutist dyed in the wool, he had to rely for his chief support on a republican rebel such as Franklin, who embodied all that he detested. He was afraid of the rising power of the people, which took upon itself to meddle in politics, and was much incensed at Vergennes' offer of French islands to England. And yet he was signing a treaty which recognized the right of the subjects of the King of England to revolt against their King and to get away with it. " It is by this treaty "—writes Schoell, in 1833, referring to the Treaty of 1778 between France and the colonists—" that a school was opened to the young French nobility in which it learned republican sentiments and from which it brought back to France that spirit of independence and of innovation which brought about the French Revolution. Thus it was that by protecting men whom all established governments ought to have considered as rebels, the French Ministry taught the nation that it is permissible to shake off obedience to one's sovereign when one believes one has a grievance against him."(16)

These words describe how the attitude of France and Spain struck the minds of the time. They apply with even greater force to the Spanish Indies than to France. The situation was complex, for since the King of Spain fought against England, he was indirectly bound to appear before his New World subjects as in league with the rebellious American subjects of the King of England. The Spanish Government was active in keeping the Indies informed of the parlous state of England, going so far as to order the authorities in the Indies to publish the news that a rebellion had taken place in London (July 23rd, 1780). Rebellions are apt to be contagious. In La Paz, in Oropesa, ominous riots broke out in 1780, ostensibly due to ill-humour over excise affairs, yet inspired by the winds which blew from the north. The rising of Condorcanqui came to add fuel to the fire. In Oruro the *mestizos* broke into revolutionary song :

> In Cuzco they draw the sword
> To fight for a righteous thing :
> To shake off the foreign king
> And to crown their native Lord.

In Mendoza, a portrait of Charles III was burnt in the public square. English agents seem to have been working behind the stage. At any rate, it is significant that the revolutionary movements connected with the Tupac-Amarú-Condorcanqui rising lasted till 1783, i.e., till the Peace of Versailles.(17)

These movements, however, cut both ways. More often than not they were directed by the castes against the Whites ; but even when seeking to attract the American Whites, so as to unite the American born against the European Spaniards, they were looked upon with distrust and fear by the rich Whites. Fear both as rich and as Whites. The wealthy Whites were fairly well informed of the evolution of events in the north, because they read the *Gacetas* and other periodicals ; and because they were in commercial relations with the northern ports. The situation was roughly similar, even though in depth there was an abyss between the two worlds. But few of the generous, intelligent Creoles of the south were then in a position to fathom this abyss. The century was formal and intellectual ; and all they saw was that New World colonies were in rebellion against an Old World king in the north, and that a similar process could and should follow in the south.

The rich Creoles went back to their Raynal. They read this prophetic page of their favourite author : " If ever a happy revolution takes place in the world it will come from America. After having been devastated, this New World must flourish in its turn and possibly rule over the Old. It will be the refuge of our peoples downtrodden under politics or turned out by war. Its wild inhabitants will be civilized and the oppressed foreigners will there become free. But all these changes must be prepared by fermentations, quakings, misfortunes even ; and it will be necessary that a painstaking education prepares their minds to suffer and to act." The Creoles read all this, as well as the ringing Jeffersonian phrases of the Declaration of Independence : " We hold these truths to be self-evident : that all men are created equal, and that they are endowed by their Creator with certain inalienable rights ; that among these are life, liberty and the pursuit of happiness : that to secure these rights, governments are instituted among men, deriving their just powers from the consent of the governed " ; and finally : " that whenever any form of government becomes destructive of these ends, it is the right of the people to alter or to abolish it, and to institute a new government."(18)

These thoughts blew in from a different quarter of the mind from that which had till then wafted new ideas into the Spanish New World across the sea of caravels and galleons. Not Rousseau, but Locke was their inspirer. Yet there was a deep harmony between the two ; for Locke also was a believer in the perfect freedom, equality and order of the state of nature, and in reason being the law of nature and therefore bound to lead to a good society if left to itself. Locke also based the State on consent and even on a kind of contract, an idea which leads to the pre-eminence of the legislative over the executive power, and to the rule of the majority. But Locke was no anarchist. He believed in the sanctity of the right to property, and, with his insistence on the principle that " the supreme power cannot take from any man any part of his property without his own consent," he laid the foundations of the American revolution. Indeed, he took care to define the possibility of political revolution in his chapter on " The Dissolution of Government." Locke's ideas and the speculations which inspired the English revolution of 1688 were embodied in the eloquent pages of Jefferson's Declaration of Independence, in which the Spanish Creoles found echoes of their familiar Rousseau.(19)

And not only did they read these phrases which raised deep echoes and splendid visions in their hearts, but they saw, actually saw, the King of England defeated by the rebels with the help of the King of Spain ; and a government set up in the United Colonies become the Republic of the United States. True there were some of them who feared lest the phrases about all men being equal were taken literally by darkies and mongrels ; but for most of them the idea was too remote to bite into their decision. Why ? Was not Virginia full of negro slaves, and who were the men who governed the United States ? Men such as they, rich Creoles—slave owners all. And so Miranda was to write on October 10th, 1792 : " When I realised on receiving the capitulations of Sipaquirá (June 8th, 1781) how simple and inexperienced the [Spanish] Americans were and on the other hand how astute and perfidious the Spanish agents had proved, I thought it best to suffer for a time in patience till the Anglo-American colonies achieved their independence, which was bound to be in the future the infallible preliminary of ours."(20)

CHAPTER XVIII

THE THREE REVOLUTIONS (*Continued*)

THE FRENCH—THE NEGRO—CONCLUSION

2.—THE FRENCH REVOLUTION

THE French Revolution was at first received everywhere with unclouded satisfaction. Nearly every European of any standing was "philosophic" and "philanthropic." Aristocrats, merchants, bishops and cardinals, all breathed the air of the century. They all hailed the Revolution as the achievement of their hopes. But as the temper of the Revolutionists became more and more insolent to the monarch and threatening for his fate, and when finally the French sacrificed the royal family only to wallow in their own blood, many an erstwhile "philosopher" turned his eyes back to the old faiths and ways, and in every European nation measures were taken to stem the flood of revolutionary ideas.

In Spain the helm was in the hands of Floridablanca, the man who, as ambassador in Rome, had wrenched from the trembling hands of Clement XIV the Brief abolishing the Jesuits. He was thoroughly frightened, and took steps to meet the danger. He had always been a philosopher, in the wake of Aranda, Roda and others, fostering the evolution, which was preparing the revolution of the next generation, mostly through the universities. Most of the universities had chairs of History of Natural Law and Law of Nations, the first of which had been set up in Madrid in 1776. Montesquieu and Rousseau were read and the students of law were being formed in the new ideas. Even the Seminaries, or schools for priests, were addicted to the new philosophy. The sudden thunderclap from Paris came to upset this serene progress of thought. An *Index of the books that are prohibited or must be expurgated in all the kingdom and dominions of the Catholic King of the Spains D. Carlos IV* was published in 1790. The leniency till then shown in the circulation of foreigners and of printed matter both in Spain and in the Indies was drastically checked. Book censors were stationed at the frontiers, and foreigners forbidden to receive letters from France. Matters went so far that, on August 6th, 1790, the sale of certain waistcoats on which the word *Liberté* was embroidered was forbidden. Periodicals were gradually hounded out of existence, and the excellent digest *Espíritu de los Mejores Diarios* ceased to appear in 1791. On July 20th of the same year Floridablanca ordered all foreigners to swear fidelity to the Catholic religion and to the sovereignty of the King, and to renounce any rights they might have as foreigners including the protection of their own ambassadors and consuls. " By this measure "—wrote his successor Godoy—" born of the extreme panic which the French Revolution had raised in the soul of Floridablanca, he aimed at securing himself against the machinations of Jacobin propaganda by the 13,330 Frenchmen then domiciled in Spain and the 4,435 who travelled to and fro in the country." The order was so outrageous that it had to be considerably whittled down within a month.(1)

On September 24th, 1789, a Royal Order informed the authorities in the Indies that one Léger-Cottin, a member for Nantes in the French Assembly, planned to smuggle into the Spanish dominions overseas " a seditious manifesto to incite the inhabitants there by all the means persuasive seduction can give forth, to shake off the Spanish yoke, following the example given them by France." On January 5th, 1790, further restrictive orders were sent overseas, the King having heard that papers were being smuggled with " views of much falsity and maliciousness, aiming at upsetting the quietness and fidelity of my vassals." On December 9th, 1791, a French Dictionary of Physics was prohibited in the Indies. It had been printed in Paris, deliberately it seems, to introduce revolutionary ideas disguised as facts of science. " Towards the end of the existence of the Holy Office in America, almost every prosecution arose from reading prohibited books," says the Chilean historian of the Inquisition. But the political and civil, rather than the religious aspect of things was the chief concern behind this activity. A Frenchman, Pedro de

Flor Condamine, was prosecuted for heretical " propositions "
in 1791, and imprisoned in Lima. The Council in Madrid
ordered the proceedings to be suspended in 1793. One of
the books most fiercely searched for was Raynal's. Licences
for reading books on the Index were granted with relative
ease ; but " Raynal is forbidden even for those who have
licences," so that even in cases where other books were winked
at, Raynal's were confiscated. But the activities of the
revolutionists of all kinds, converging from so many quarters,
were too much for the Government and its Viceroys, and the
Indies were flooded with written and verbal effluvia of the
Revolution.(2)

*   *   *

At the beginning of 1792 Floridablanca fell and Aranda
succeeded him. This raised extravagant hopes in the French
revolutionists, particularly Condorcet who saw in Aranda a
new " Hercules cleaning the Augean stables and destroying
that vile scum who under the name of priests and nobles are
a plague on the State." True he was, as Godoy says, " lenient,
not to say favourable, [. . .] towards the French Revolution." Nevertheless in July and August, orders were sent out
to the customs to confiscate and send to the Minister of State
" all printed papers or MSS which deal with the Revolution
and new Constitution " of France " as well as fans, boxes,
ribbons and other manœuvres [probably meaning manu-
factures] which might allude to the same subjects." But
these precautions were lost, for the inspectors at the customs
let everything pass. Moreover, the seditious papers often came
disguised, so that " it was no rare occurrence that the bindings
of a St. Basil or St. Augustine covered volumes of the
Encyclopædia."(3)

Aranda, however, had been called to office as a mere
stop-gap, and before the end of the year he was displaced by
Godoy, a young guardsman, selected to govern Spain for
reasons better known to the Queen than to the King. This
shady origin of his rise and not a few mistakes committed
during his time of office have led to a somewhat unbalanced
estimate of his merits. Godoy continued the system he found
and which he himself describes : " doors and windows and

breathing openings I found them all walled up for fear of
the lights to which were attributed the horrible events of
France." But he was by no means a benighted enemy
of culture ; far from it. Under his administration every
encouragement was given to all the branches of learning which
did not touch on politics. He founded the *Instituto Pestaloz-
ziano*, and entrusted it to two men, Alea and Blanco White,
neither of whom could be considered a reactionary. The
fact was that by then the country was so deeply won to the
new doctrines that not even the government could consistently
oppose their influence. " One day the introduction of the
French constitution was forbidden (July 28th, 1793) and the
next year a defence of Louis XVI was withdrawn from circulation, or the frontier was barred to the book of Hervás y
Panduro," a Jesuit, who had written on the moral causes of
the Revolution. The Inquisition itself was a nest of
Voltairianism ; moreover, the civil authority had drastically
restricted its powers. Men with friends at Court—Samaniego
is a case in point—could, if threatened by the Inquisition,
settle matters without much difficulty and with no expense.
Had the French Revolution remained within the bounds of
either the English Revolution of 1688 or the American Revolution, an attitude of benevolent neutrality towards it might
have won the day.(4)

Two facts came to alter the situation. The first was the
change of attitude the French adopted towards Spain, since a
break with their own King meant a break with the other
member of the Family Pact. This led to a number of schemes
of aggression against the Spanish Indies, which, though
coloured as emancipation and liberty, were yet imperialistic
in nature. The second fact was the growing danger to the
royal family and finally the execution of Louis XVI, which
led to war. On taking office, Godoy found that Aranda had
already consented to a treaty declaring Spain's neutrality
between France and the nations arrayed against her revolution. The new Prime Minister tried to buy with it the life
and safety of the French royal family, sending a proposal of
friendly mediation along with the draft treaty, and writing
to the Spanish Ambassador in London to seek Pitt's help to

the same end. Godoy failed both in London and in Paris. The Convention rejected the Spanish offer on December 28th, 1792. The offer was presented again on January 27th, 1793, after the vote on the King's death sentence had been taken, but not yet counted. The letter from the Spanish envoy was not even read. The King fell on the scaffold. Even then Aranda insisted on neutrality, but Godoy chose war. He did not have to declare it. The Convention itself was bent on war as a crusade of liberty against all kings, and war was declared March 7th, 1793.(5)

As for the Indies, Revillagigedo reported in 1792 from Mexico that the French revolutionists were sending " six emissaries for propaganda with a number of seductive papers " to foster ideas of independence in New Spain. This was part of the plan conceived by Admiral Kersaint. Miranda, then in England, went over to France on hearing this (March, 1792) and he put the liberation " of the peoples who inhabit South America " among the conditions of his acceptance of service on the side of the French Revolution. " Their cause " —he added—" must be effectively protected by France, as being that of liberty, and I must be granted permission (as opportunity affords) to devote myself mainly to their happiness, securing liberty and independence for the country [an aim] which I have set myself of my own accord and for which the United States of America as well as England have promised their support at the first favourable opportunity." He found, he was to write himself later, that the French Government were thinking of a continental war, and that, in such a case, the plan was to revolutionize Spain, through Catalonia and Biscay, as well as the American colonies. But he adds : " I fought with success against the first part of the scheme ; and I also obtained that the plan regarding the colonies should be adjourned for a better opportunity, leaving its leadership to me, since the intention was our emancipation and independence."(6)

Why this postponement ? The last sentence of Miranda's " Sketch " suggests the answer. Miranda was no admirer of France nor of French character. In fact he may be described as a francophobe. He distrusted the French as much as he

admired the English. He felt the imperialistic tendencies
behind the plan. Sixteen thousand men were to be sent
to Saint Domingue (to-day Haiti) turning it into a base
against the islands and the Main Land ; and with the co-operation of England, the United States, Holland, Prussia, Sweden
and Denmark. England was to receive Cuba, the United
States Puerto Rico, France Santo Domingo, Holland Trinidad
and others small islands. This had little to do with
independence, even though other plans and decisions of the
revolutionists may have been more sincere. In 1794, the
citizen Flassau pointed out that France could not oppose the
emancipation of the Spanish colonies after having fostered
that of the English colonies, and when their commerce was
so valuable, and that France could, by protecting them,
hope for " the riches of Peru and Mexico." Miranda was
too cool-headed not to realize all this. His fear of French
imperialism disguised as revolutionary idealism was so deep-
rooted that as late as March 19th, 1799, he wrote to Pitt :
" If unhappily France conceived such a scheme [to conquer
the Spanish colonies] and the Spanish colonists are discouraged
by a refusal [of help] on the part of England, it seems likely
that France may succeed in seducing these simple peoples by
caressing them first with false promises of liberty and happiness,
only to devour them later together with those of the United
States."(7)

That is why he insisted on being appointed commander of
the expedition. On December 19th, 1792, the French
Minister of War communicated to him that he had been
appointed Commander-in-Chief in Saint Domingue, and
that an army of 25,000 and a fleet were there at his disposal to
bring about revolution and the independence of Spanish
America. Even so he was by no means keen, and his answer
to Brissot is full of ifs and buts. " The plan outlined in your
letter is really great and magnificent, but I do not know
whether its execution would be certain or even probable."
And all his discretion is unable to conceal the true reason of
his reluctance : French meddling, which he does not want.
" With all that concerns the Spanish-American continent or
its islands I am quite at home and can form a correct opinion.

But as for the French islands and their actual state, I know hardly anything, and therefore I am unable to form an exact opinion about them. As they are to be the base for all our operations under your plan, since the French colonies are to provide the active course to set in motion the people of the adjacent continent, we must be absolutely sure that this movement will actually take place." The argument could not be clearer. He also writes : " My appointment and my departure for Saint Domingue would be the alarm signal for the Courts of Madrid and London, and we should soon see the results in Cádiz and Portsmouth. All this activity would put new obstacles in the way of an enterprise too great, too beautiful and too interesting to have spoiled at the outset for lack of foresight."(8)

At this juncture, Miranda seems to have acted with a delicately balanced judgment. He carefully brushed aside all direct attacks on Spain and refused an appointment as Commander-in-Chief of a revolutionary army against Spain ; yet when, in a similar position at the head of one of the armies of the north, he took Antwerp (November 29th, 1792), he wrote a few days later : " Our troops crossed the conquered citadel and planted the tree of Liberty in its centre on the very spot where the infamous monument of the tyranny of the Duke of Alba had been erected." Moreover, he reports, the inscriptions (of Spanish victories) which " degraded its bastions " were struck out and the names of Dumouriez, Petion, Mirabeau, Rousseau and Helvetius substituted. His position, insofar as he was his own master in all this and not the protagonist of a popular army, seems to have been : let us fight tyrannous Spaniards but not Spain ; and let us at any rate not pass from being Spanish colonies to being French dependencies. He seems to have been very much of the opinion of the French secret agent, Darbault, who was shrewd enough to observe : " The question has often been put to me whether I did not believe it possible for us to excite and cause a revolution in the Spanish possessions of America, to which I always made answer that Madrid was the spot wherefrom such a commotion should start." Writing to Pitt in later days, Miranda definitely attributed to himself the adjournment of the French scheme, providing at the same time a second reason for his reserve : his fear and dislike of the Jacobin tendencies of the French Revolution. He is speaking of himself in the third person and has just mentioned that he had been appointed Commander-in-Chief and Governor of the Islands. " But he did his best to have the scheme adjourned to another time, believing the occasion not favourable, and fearing that the anarchical principles which fermented already might be of sinister omen for the enterprise—which probably saved then the Colonies from the fatal influence of this system, and the New World perhaps from its total ruin."(9)

The European campaign against the French Revolution afforded the soldiers of the Republic spectacular and unexpected victories. England suffered the loss of many ships and the King was stoned in the streets of London by the infuriated citizens. Spain was perhaps the theatre of war in which the French arms were least happy—though the surrender of Figueras in 1794 was a heavy blow for the Spanish Government, the more unexpected because the city was amply supplied and defended by no less than two hundred field guns. The " sun of Thermidor " rose over France (July 27th, 1794) with a new light ; the Revolution settled down and Europe began to settle down to it. The King of Prussia signed a peace treaty with the Republic on April 5th, 1795. Many German princes urged the Emperor to make peace also. Spain was sounded. Peace was thought necessary because the Government was ill at ease fighting on the side of England, while report upon report reached Madrid that England was dealing with South American rebels, sending seditious propaganda, alarming news, plans of insurrection, promises of help. Nevertheless the Spanish Government asked two conditions : the French were to evacuate the Spanish territories they had invaded and to deliver the two children of Louis XVI to the King of Spain. The French disliked these conditions and new preparations for war were made, though the two royal orphans began to be treated less harshly by their gaolers, and Spain by the French press. The French Revolutionists were, as good nationalists, far less revolutionary than they imagined. They were in fact so antiquated that when, during the unsuccessful campaign of 1794 in Navarra the French troops occupied Roncesvalles for a few days, the two members of the Convention attached to the army, Baudit and Garraud, wrote a bombastic report on this victory which " avenged an old time insult "—the defeat of Charlemagne's rearguard by the Spaniards and the death of Roland. The Republic had shown itself as imperialistic as Louis XIV and tried to retain beyond the Pyrenees as many places as it had done beyond other European borders. In the end Godoy had to yield to France the Spanish part of the Island of Santo Domingo, and peace was signed on July 22nd, 1795.(10)

*   *   *

There is a sentence of Thomas Paine, testifying for Miranda before a French Revolutionary Court, which brings together the North American Revolution incarnated in the speaker, the French Revolution and the emancipation of Spanish America : " the destiny of the French Revolution was intimately related to the favourite object of his [Miranda's] heart, namely, the deliverance of Spanish America—a design for which he was hunted by the Court of Spain during the greatest part of his life." How far this was the fact with regard to Miranda's persecution by the Court of Spain we shall presently discuss. But the French Revolution had a considerable effect in Spanish America. By then the four philosophers, particularly Rousseau and Raynal, were widely read among the well-to-do Creoles. The events of France came to add a new ardour to their generous ideas by crowning them with success—a second success after that of the American Revolution. Events followed in the Indies the same vacillating course as in Spain. Fear and the use of force, which it prompts, were countered by the very universality of the movement, which affected even the Government and its officials. Men of wealth and culture, such as Manuel Enderica, of Mexico, were sentenced to ten years' exile for owning a number of famous French books ; but as he had been a subscriber of the *Espíritu de los Mejores Diarios*, it is evident that the inspiration for his literary ideas had come from that same Madrid

which, now frightened, punished him.   Unanúe, the scientist
of Lima, founded his paper *Mercurio Peruano* in 1792, and
no one troubled him for it.   *El Papel Periódico* appeared in
Santa Fe from 1791.   Mariano Moreno published *La Gaceta
de Buenos Aires*.   In humbler spheres, foreigners, mostly
French cooks and other luxury workers, brought over by the
French Viceroy Croix (1766-71), by Revillagigedo and by
Gálvez, found themselves in trouble when another Viceroy,
Branciforte, Godoy's brother-in-law, came to govern New
Spain in the war days of 1794.   Those of them who read
" Vulter " and " Rusó " were exiled or sent to African prisons.
" I am grateful in my soul "—wrote, on December 16th,
1790, a Potosí merchant to a friend in Buenos Aires—" for
the news of the revolutions of France which by this post you
have been good enough to send me, and I hope you will
continue the same favour considering how much we prize
news of similar novelties in these parts."   This state of mind,
curiosity, hope, enthusiasm even, was then widespread in
the Indies as well as in Spain.   Belgrano, the Argentine
patriot, has left a telling note on it :   " As in the days of 1789 "
—he writes—" I was in Spain and the Revolution of France
brought about a change in ideas, particularly among the
men of letters with whom I held intercourse, the ideas of
liberty, equality, security, property, took hold of me, and
I could see only tyrants in all those who prevented man,
anywhere, from enjoying the rights which God and nature had
granted him."(11)

These lines aptly sum up the attitude of the progressive
and intelligent Creole of the day.   What he wanted was
liberty from arbitrary laws coming from above, from
irresponsible kings and capricious ministers ;   equality upwards
with the fine lords and ladies of the Court who lived under
the protection of time-honoured privileges ;   but mark the
sequence :   where nowadays our ear would expect " fraternity,"
we hear " security," " property " ;   words which define the
class which then felt strong enough to make itself vocal against
oppression :   the well-to-do middle class which wanted to
live as it liked without having to fear for life and property
from a State ruled by absolutist principles.   And the end

of the speech and the foundation of it all was God and natural rights.

*   *   *

So when the French Revolution ran riot and the King was executed, enthusiasm in Spanish America cooled off. Curiosity remained and was fairly well satisfied, despite official prohibitions, by Gazettes and private correspondence, not to speak of medals, coins and clay figures. Though sympathy for the French Revolution, even at its fiercest, was never altogether absent, it seems that the war against revolutionary France was popular in the Indies, for, as in Spain, voluntary gifts were forthcoming. In the viceroyalty of Río de la Plata, a sum of 372,360 *pesos* was subscribed as well as yearly gifts of 31,168. The news from France could but stimulate the tendency to meddle in the affairs of the Indies on the part of Frenchmen settled there and desirous of improving the world according to their lights. Cases of French conspiracies had been known before the Revolution. The first plot for the independence of Chile had been initiated by two Frenchmen, Gramuset and Berney, in 1781. Frenchmen will be prominent in many other risings. But the coolness which Miranda felt towards them seems to have been general in the Indies, and it weakened them as revolutionary agents. This is often to be found in the documents of the time. Here are two passages from Miranda's agent, Caro : " Some people from la Guayra told me to-day [February 27th, 1799] that the Englishmen of North America frequent the harbour and are as well received as the French are hated." And again, this time with a piquant illustration on the tension with the Basques : " It is also good to know that the French who had smuggled themselves throughout our continent are not well received nor liked in the country ; the Government protect them, but the Creoles detest them, for they say, as I do, that the Frenchman does not deserve the bread he eats nor is grateful for it nor takes it with any gesture of gratitude, but on the contrary, that he believes, as do all Basques, that all is due to him as a matter of privilege &c."

Matters could hardly be improved for the French in the eyes of the Creoles by the effect which the news from France was having on the negro slaves all over the Spanish Indies.

There are signs that Frenchmen, numerous in Spanish America after 1700, were often the active agents in this revolutionary fermentation of the negroes. Posters and bills of *Viva la Libertad* and seditious songs were rampant ; and persecution against negroes and Frenchmen became the order of the day. In 1739, 50 years before the Revolution, a case is already recorded of a Frenchman, by name Mallet, who was busy inciting the Indians to rebel in New Biscay, a province of New Spain. The Governor reports that he sentenced him to a death no less gruesome than by tearing his heart out through the back. With the French Revolution, the activity of these reformist Frenchmen greatly increased, and this time they turned their attention to the more susceptible and turbulent negroes. With the French alliance of 1796, ships with French and negro crews often arrived in Spanish-American ports, bringing revolutionary emotions, ideas, pictures, stories and dreams which set new dreams and stories in motion. The Creoles were led to reflect. Some drew back into the good old ways. Others went forward and accepted the risk.(12)

3.—THE NEGRO REVOLUTION

That the risk was not small was soon shown in Haiti, the French part of the Island of Santo Domingo. " The Negroes " —wrote Girolamo Benzoni in 1572—" have multiplied in Santo Domingo to such an extent, that in 1545, when I was on the Main Land I saw many Spaniards who doubted not but that this Island would become the property of those Guinea Moors." This was sound prophecy. Santo Domingo, the first big island discovered by Colón and for some time the seat of the chief administration of the New World, had gradually lost its standing, as new empires were discovered and conquered on the Main Land. Neglected and depopulated, its Western end in particular had become a base for negro runaways and buccaneers ; and the French had little by little established a customary right over it, recognized in 1697 by the Treaty of Ryswick, which gave them about one-third of the island. French colonists developed this territory, growing indigo, tobacco and sugar, on the basis of slavery ;

the Spanish part of the island, very much neglected at first, prospered later by supplying cattle to the French, cultivating cocoa and indulging in privateering and contraband against England whenever there was a war on. Soon, however, a certain tension arose between the French and the Spanish sides of the Island owing to the tendency of the negro slaves to escape from French to Spanish territory, where they were sure of much better treatment and of better opportunities for emancipation. An easier disposition to intermarrying over the colour bar may also have influenced this current. Spanish Santo Domingo had at one time 110,000 free men out of a population of 125,000 males. In 1754 St. Domingue, or Haiti, i.e., French Santo Domingo, had 14,000 Whites, 4,000 free mulattoes and 172,000 negro slaves. The exorbitant privilege implied in this situation led to a rapid demoralization of the Whites. In 1760 a commission was sent from France to enquire into the causes of the high rate of violent death, mainly by poison, in the colony. It was found to be due to love affairs of an irregular character. The trouble was old and the provisions of the *Code Noir* (1685) were not likely to remedy it. If a White debauched a slave, the woman and her children were sold for the benefit of a hospital and could not be rebought. Even free men, if coloured, were bound to serve in the *Marechaussée* and to forced labour for public use (*corvées*) ; while they could hold no public office nor carry on a liberal profession. The treatment meeted to the Blacks was of the utmost cruelty.(13)

As rich Creoles used to spend years in Paris surrounded with negro slaves, these negroes picked up new notions on their status from the ideas of the century, and back in Haiti, spread them among their brethren. Now and then troubles occurred, quickly put down. With the events of 1789 matters came to a head and three successive social earthquakes shook the French part of the Island : the revolution of the Whites ; that of the mulattoes ; and that of the Blacks.

Haiti was governed by a Governor General practically absolute and by an *Intendant* equally absolute in his department, finance. A Colonial Assembly, composed of the Governor General, the *Intendant*, the Presidents of the Provincial Councils and a number of high officials debated points of taxation. This Government irked the colonists who, jealous of the independence from England conquered by the Americans, sought to attain a similar degree of home rule. Of course they thought no more of the liberty of the Blacks than Washington and his contemporaries did. When the National Assembly met in France great enthusiasm prevailed among the Whites in Haiti, particularly among the white merchants of the cities. But the mulattoes did not fail to perceive the ultimate meaning of such doctrines as that of the rights of man, at any rate for themselves, if not for the negroes. As for the negroes, they could not lift their heads to look on and listen without feeling the whip or the cowskin. In Paris itself, the rich Haitian Creoles had formed a club known as the *Massiac*, the name of the host in whose house they met, while the revolutionists, sincerely desirous to free the slaves or at any rate to better their lot, had formed a society—*Les Amis des Noirs*. The gentlemen of the *Massiac* stood no nonsense from the *Amis des Noirs* and asked for complete independence for Haiti in the name of the rights of the (white) man. The mulattoes presented a petition to the National Assembly of 1789 and obtained a solemn promise of equality, which that distinguished body granted them with as much fervour as ignorance of the fact that they could no more create equality than they could create a grain of matter. The Whites of St. Domingue set up Assemblies of their own, one for each province ; Assemblies of free men, as befitted the sons of the French revolutionists ; but admitting none but Whites, as befitted good slave-owners. A mulatto named Lacombe, who thought otherwise and said so to the Assembly of the Northern Province, was found to be wrong by that Assembly and hanged accordingly. The General Assembly of St. Domingue met at last at St. Marc on March 25th, 1790, and finding the ideas of the Paris Assembly on the rights of the mulattoes somewhat hazy (those of the Blacks were not in the picture) decided to act as an independent body (May, 1790). The rich planters were the backbone of the independent or " patriotic " party. They displayed a red cockade. The smaller fry of Whites sided with the Government and took the white cockade and the name of *aristocrats* which the rich reds gave them with derision.

While the Whites fought it out the mulattoes rebelled on their own, led by one Ogé, a son of a planter, who, in Paris, where he had been educated, had frequented the *Amis des Noirs*. Ogé was unsuccessful, took refuge in Santo Domingo, was delivered to the Governor of St. Domingue despite the vehement protest of the Spanish *oídor* Dr. Faura, and, in violation of the promise made by the French Governor to his Spanish colleague, was broken on the wheel in the presence of the whole provincial Assembly. The White revolution then took a sudden turn of unheard-of violence, a disastrous eye-opener to the mulatto and negro onlookers. Matters were brought to a head by a decision of the Paris Revolutionists admitting coloured persons, sons of free men, to the primary and colonial Assemblies. The mulattoes exulted and the Whites were indignant. The Island was plunged in chaos. A mulatto, Jean François, and a negro slave, Boukman, gathered a force of negro slaves and marched against the city of Cap François, under a banner of liberty consisting of the body of a white infant stuck to a spearhead. The mulattoes of the city asked the Whites to provide them with arms to defend it against the negroes ; the Whites massacred the lot of them, defeated the negroes and massacred them wholesale with every refinement of cruelty. This raised the mass of the negroes of the Island against the Whites. On their banners they wrote *Vive le Roi et l'ancien Régime !* ; and their leader wore on his proud chest the Order of St. Louis. It seems that a certain amount of backing had come from the royalists of Santo Domingo. One of the negro chiefs, Jeannot, went in his sadistic cruelty to such extremes that Jean François had him put to death. The rich white " patriots " appealed to the English Governor of Jamaica who sent some help. An occasional alliance between Whites and mulattoes did not prosper because the Whites would not grant political equality to coloured men however slight their hue. Thus the mulattoes were thrown over to the negroes and together they beat the Whites at Croix des Bouquets (March 21st, 1792) forcing them to take refuge in Port au Prince.

LIMA, WITH THE BRIDGE OVER THE RIMAC—from "Travels in South America," by A. Caldecleugh, 1825

ST. SALVADOR—from an eighteenth-century print

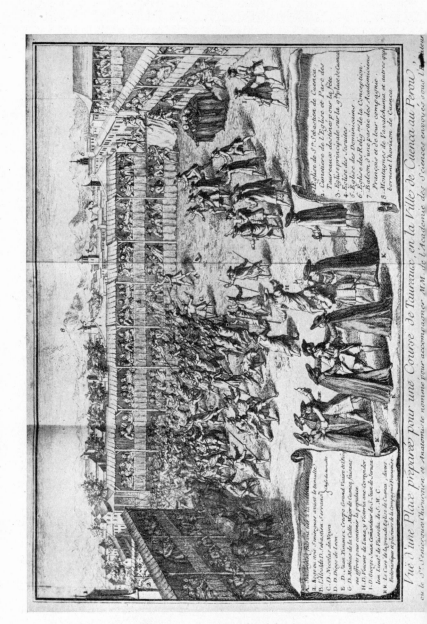

THE MAIN SQUARE OF CUENCA, UPPER PERU, READY
FOR A BULL-FIGHT—from an eighteenth-century print

By its edict of April 4th, 1792, the French National Assembly insisted on equal rights for all free men, while confirming the legal status of slavery. It also sent a force of 6,000 men. This threw the mulattoes back over to the White party. Feuds between the revolutionary committees and a local Governor led to further scenes of bloodshed. Under the threat of an attack from England in 1793, the commune issued a proclamation abolishing slavery. More slave-hunting ensued and many Spaniards of Santo Domingo made profit out of it by selling negro slaves in Cuba and Puerto Rico. The coloured leaders went over to the revolutionary government on hearing of the execution of Louis XVI, left for Santo Domingo and received commissions in the Spanish Army ; notably Toussaint, later to become so famous as the leader of the Black Republic. The English landed and took some towns, including Port au Prince (June 14th, 1794) with a large booty. Toussaint betrayed his Spanish friends and passed over to the French, thinking this step in the better interest of his negro brethren. The move was not elegant but was shrewd. By the peace of Basle, Santo Domingo was ceded to the French. The English lingered on the Island. Toussaint, the only man with enough prestige over the negroes to raise armies to resist the invaders, became in practice the chief military authority of the Island and was recognized as such by the French Government in 1797.(14)

*   *   *

These events were portentous. They called forth deep echoes in the New World, from the Southern States of North America to the rich kingdoms of the Indies. St. Domingue had lost most of its Whites in a succession of bloody social upheavals. Whites and mulattoes had been compelled to give pride of place to the Blacks. In the first island ruled by the Whites in America, a Black general was rising to absolute power, soon to become the first independent sovereign in the New World outside the Republic of the United States. The import of these facts was sinking into the men of all colours who inhabited the New World, then seething with new ideas, dreams and conspiracies.

This was particularly the case in the tropical zone where

K

Blacks were numerous. " Despite the isolation in which most of the metropoles try to keep their colonies "—writes Humboldt—" agitations do none the less pass to and fro between them. The elements of strife are everywhere the same ; and, as by instinct, an agreement sets in between the men of the same colour separated by a difference in language and living on opposite sides of the sea. This American Mediterranean formed by the coasts of Venezuela, New Granada, Mexico, the United States and the Antilles, counts on its shores nearly one million and a half free and slave Blacks ; they are so unequally distributed that there are but very few to the south and almost none to the west. They are mostly concentrated on the northern and eastern coasts. These are, so to speak, the African part of this inner basin. It is natural that the troubles which from 1792 have taken place in St. Domingue should have spread to the coasts of Venezuela. As long as Spain quietly owned these beautiful colonies, the small risings of slaves were easily repressed ; but as soon as a struggle of a different kind, aiming at independence, began, the Blacks, owing to their threatening attitude, caused fears now to one, now to the other, of the parties in the struggle, and the gradual or sudden abolition of slavery was proclaimed in the different regions of Spanish America less for reasons of justice and humanity than to enlist the help of an intrepid race of men used to privations and fighting for their own interests." (15)

These words illustrate the incidence of the events of St. Domingue on those of the Indies. Most of the leaders of the evolution of thought which led to the wars of secession were slave owners. They were beginning to adumbrate that the movement they were leading was likely to bring about untold consequences in their home life—consequences which some of them did not have the moral strength to face, perhaps to imagine. Upon his second arrival in London, on January 12th, 1798, Miranda wrote to his English friend Turnbull : " I confess to you that just as much as I desire the liberty and independence of the New World, I fear the anarchy of a revolutionary system. God forbid that these beautiful countries become, as did St. Domingue, a theatre of blood and of crime under the pretext of establishing liberty.   Let them rather remain if necessary one century more under the barbarous and imbecile oppression of Spain."(16)

CONCLUSION

The waves of influence of the three revolutions were converging on the soul of the Indies and stirring it to its depths. Of the three, the American was the most fertile because the least mixed with fear.   The misgivings of the Creoles were laid at rest by the spectacle of men such as Washington and Jefferson, living like patriarchs in comfortable wealth among their slaves.   It pleased them to know that Jefferson, the enlightened, well-off lawyer at Monticello was the author of those ringing phrases of the Declaration of Independence and yet lived none the worse.   On the other hand the French Revolution frightened some of them.   True, its principles differed in nothing from those of the American Revolution. But its practice did.   Those Frenchmen seemed to be more thorough, less disposed to let phrases remain phrases, more apt to " *croire que c'est arrivé.*"   The nineteenth century, under a kind of literary dictatorship from France, came to think that everything had begun with the French Revolution, and there- fore presented the emancipation of Spanish America as an annex of the Grande Révolution :

> *On est bête à Nanterre*
> *C'est la faute à Voltaire,*
> *Et sot à Palaiseau*
> *C'est la faute à Rousseau.*

The present trend may go too far in the opposite direction. Miranda, at any rate, was dead against French ideas and said so time and again.   In the note which he delivered to Pitt on March 20th, 1798, he foresaw that the coming French invasion of Spain would produce " an anarchical convulsion " there ; and that a similar fate awaited Spanish America.   He added : " It seems unavoidable that in the interval from one system to the other, the anarchical and subversive principles of the French system should steal in, if prompt and effective measures are not taken to prevent it ; and it is in order to prevent a catastrophe, as fatal to the New as to the Old World, that the undersigned is sent to H.B.M.'s Ministers and those of the United States by his countrymen." He repeats the statement in a note to John Adams, April 28th, 1798, in which he declares his fears lest " the abominable system of France is introduced in my country." And again to Alexander Hamilton (April 6th, 1798) : " The only danger I can see is the introduction of French principles, which would poison Liberty in its cradle and would ultimately put an end to yours also." Finally, in another note to Pitt (March 19th, 1799) he goes further still. He feels emboldened because H.M. Ministers have declared in Parliament that Switzerland was " the only nation besides England which had had the courage to resist the destructive principles of France " ; and recalls that " the chief object of the [Spanish] colonies was to stand against these same principles by forming a stable government on principles diametrically opposed to the French system." It is evident that Miranda represented the views of those he himself described to Pitt as " wise and educated persons who flattered themselves with the prospect of seeing on the American continent a system of order and morality capable of balancing the maxims of disorganization spread by France." Bearing in mind the " incalculable damage brought about by French anarchy to liberty in all the world," he writes tersely in a note on December 31st, 1799 : " Two great examples lie before our eyes : the American Revolution and the French Revolution. Let us discreetly imitate the first ; let us most carefully avoid the disastrous effects of the second."(17)

Miranda is no exception. He was the exponent of at least a sector, probably the most important, among the leaders of Spanish American emancipation. Nevertheless, the influence of French ideas on these leaders was deep and widespread ; and even after the death of Louis XVI and the Terror, Voltaire and Rousseau were held as apostles of a new era throughout the White Spanish New World. The stir they caused was apt to be intellectual. That which came from the United States was more political. It led more directly to action. The Black Revolution acted everywhere as a brake, counselling caution and moderation ; yet, insofar as it showed a change in the making, an example by facts, it stimulated the mood of action in the bolder and less saturnine men, whose revolutionary sense lay rather in the depths of character than in the smooth surface of the mind.

PART IV

BEGGARS FOR INDEPENDENCE

CHAPTER XIX

A HAIL OF PRECURSORS

EVERYTHING during the eighteenth century worked to increase the tension between Spain and the other kingdoms of her Empire. It was therefore natural that the period should see a development of that donjulianism which was too deep a Spanish feature not to have passed over to the American continent along with the rest of the Spanish character. The century is studded with adventurers, patriots, intriguers and negotiators, who, some from the lowest, others from the highest motives, some to enrich themselves, others to free their country from the shackles of Spain, if need be, at the cost of their lives, sought the help of England or of France. As France during most of the century was linked with Spain by the Family Pact, it was rather on England that this hail of precursors was apt to fall. We have seen how, despite a statesmanlike tradition of moderation towards Spain, England, under popular pressure, had engaged in frequent campaigns against Spain. These campaigns provided a favourable atmosphere for Spanish donjulianists and for plans of conquest which Englishmen and others put on paper with or without their help. The first of the series dates from 1743, when a delegation of conspirators from New Spain put proposals of independence before General Oglethorpe, who commanded the British troops in the West Indies. Upon the report of an officer he sent to Mexico, Oglethorpe wrote to London recommending the matter ; but the Duke of Newcastle, then in office, was not convinced.(1)

Ideas kept pouring in from English amateur conquerors. Adventurers of all kinds offered themselves, with an eye on personal advancement. One of the earliest was the Marquis d'Aubarède, who, on June 29th, 1766, went to London to present a scheme of emancipation of Spanish America. He styled himself a Knight of St. Louis, and a cousin of the Marquis de Crillon, a French general then in the service of Spain. Disgruntled, as he himself explains, because the King of Spain had not granted him the Governorship of Louisiana, he came into touch with the deputies of New Spain, who had come to Madrid " to complain of the grievances they had sustained for so long," and who, also disgruntled, " concerted with him the means to fix for ever an exclusive commerce with England." His plan, as explained by Aubarède himself, was " to surrender into the hands of H.B.M. the city of Vera Cruz, and the Island of St. John de Ulúa ; to receive neither directly nor indirectly, only [*sic*] the merchandizes brought by English vessels to the port of Vera Cruz, which is the key to Mexico ; to lend to England immediately after the revolution, the sum of one hundred million of Piasters, making about twenty million sterling at 3 per cent., which the religious communities alone bind themselves to furnish ; their cellars are stored with gold and silver which remains unemployed, and for that reason the furnishing so immense a sum neither detriments the circulation of cash, nor the commerce of the country ; if England is involved in a war on account of Mexico, they oblige themselves *to cause a diversion in Peru and Chili*, by means of their friends there."

H.B.M.'s Government on their part would bind themselves " to support the revolution, to protect the imperial republic of Mexico and not to extend beyond the territories of Vera Cruz." Furthermore, Aubarède proposed that to avoid clashes between the English in Vera Cruz and the Spanish Americans in Mexico, on account of religion, a kingdom should be carved out for him as " a political and religious barrier with the counties of Orizaba, Xalapa and Cordoba which he would people with Roman Catholics and later a good number of Protestants." Aubarède was given enough attention by the Foreign Office for him to take himself seriously, a pension of 500 guineas being paid—and at times unpaid—to him. But after years of procrastination the scheme was allowed to die a natural death.(2)

This was the plan which Aubarède presented. But whom did he represent ? Who offered the monopoly of trade, the " key to Mexico," and £20 million to Great Britain ? Rough and ready words such as " patriots," phrases such as " the will of the nation " will not do. Here is the way Aubarède presents the case to the British Government : " All the world knows that Mexico was conquered by Ferdinand Cortés and his followers who began and *ended this heroic undertaking at their sole costs*, without the *King* of Spain *contributing anything* thereto, nevertheless, by the political system of the Court of Madrid, the heirs of these brave adventurers are deprived of all the employs in that same country, which they think themselves authorized by just title to regard as their patrimonies ; the military offices, the magistracy, and offices of revenue, the ecclesiastical dignities, all are refused to those Spaniards born in Mexico, although there are many related to the principal families of Spain, that the greater part of them, far from having degenerated, have more genius, more activity, and more courage than the European Spaniards, and at the same time possess all the countries of that vast Empire.

" Their number is *about three millions of souls*, and the natives of the country, which are accounted *between four* and *five millions*, are their vassals, and absolutely dependent on them ; they are, however, perfectly united in their implacable hatred against the European Spaniards, who embark annually in great number for Vera Cruz and from thence spread themselves everywhere to tyrannise ; each according to his employ, enrich themselves soon, and then make room for other vultures equally rapacious and cruel. In short, after more than two centuries of suffering, after the most repeated and fruitless remonstrances, some zealous patriots have formed a resolution to deliver their country from so shameful a slavery, in consequence thereof *a republican plan was proposed*, debated and approved."(3)

This document shows that the donjulianists who were buying British help with slices of their own country—and what slices !—were the white wealthy Creoles, who considered their coloured countrymen as " their vassals," and wished to extend their economic and financial power to the political sphere. This was a natural ambition with them ; and the attitude of the Spanish Government in this respect justified their resentment. But it is a far cry from this state of affairs to the romantic views about liberty and democracy with which these events are usually decorated. The men who

were offering Veracruz to England were not seeking the
liberty of the Mexican nation as a whole ; they were endeav-
ouring to assert their aristocratic privileges over their vassals,
unhindered by the irksome control of Spain.

*   *   *

The next case of donjulianism that occurs in the century
is that of Don Antonio de Prado. He was an adventurer
who presented himself now as an officer of the Spanish army,
now as M. de la Tour, teacher of languages. He seems to
have been a Frenchman by name Duprex. He travelled, he
said, on behalf of an association of Creoles and natives, with
the aim of setting up a government of European pattern over
Chile, Tucuman, Peru and Patagonia. Towards 1782-3, he
put his scheme before some English personalities, asking for
6,000 men to land in Río de la Plata and Callao. His ambition
seems to have been chiefly personal. He arrived too late.
War with Spain was at an end, and he received but scanty
attention.

Leaving for later treatment Miranda's own doings, already
substantial at this period, the next episode is that of Don
Francisco de Mendiola. " In the name of the city and of
the Kingdom of Mexico whose representatives we are "—
said the credentials he exhibited in London—" we beg to
implore your powerful protection, oppressed and vexed as
we are by the Court of Madrid which daily makes us feel by
all kinds of burdens the tyrannical despotism which annihilates
the constitution of the liberty owed to us and reduces us to
the status of actual Guinea slaves." These words suffice to
show the spirit of the proposal. They were signed by names
such as Count of Torre Cossío, Count of Santiago, Marqués of
Guardiola, who stood for " a great number of persons
prominent in the viceroyalty of New Spain and above all
interpreters of the popular will." Their haughty reference
to being treated as " actual Guinea slaves " betrays their
social outlook. It was Aubarède's case all over again. Dated
Mexico December 10th, 1785, the plan stated that the conspirators had all the funds required for the purpose, and the
means to raise 40,000 men. They requested England to sell

them arms and ammunition in Jamaica, and engaged themselves to pay two million *pesos*. The conspiracy seems to
have been foiled by the watchfulness of Spanish diplomacy.(4)

*   *   *

The Kingdom of New Granada was not lagging behind that
of New Spain in donjulianism.   In March, 1783, two members
of the party of independence, Don Vicente de Aguiar and
Don Dionisio de Contreras, left Bogotá for London.   According
to a local tradition, " Aguiar " was no other than Berbeo, one
of the leaders of the *comuneros* of Socorro.   In Curaçao they
learnt the news of the peace between England and Spain, and
so they returned, downcast.   But though they had not gone
to England, England came to them, or so they thought, in
the person of a mysterious emissary who called himself a
delegate of the British Government.   His name was Don
Luis Vidall or Vidalle ;   his nationality hazy, believed to be
Italian ;   his English and Spanish both perfect.   These
features, particularly his name, suggest the Spanish Jew.
Miranda had dealings with a Hamburg banker of the same
name.   Vidall had negotiated in London under the protection of General Dalling, ex-Governor of Jamaica, whose
dealings with Miranda would repay study.   This gentleman
seems to have been backed by the Jesuits, as, by the way,
Aubarède had been.   The proposals put before Vidall by
the Granadinos were that the British Government should
provide 222,800 *pesos* as well as arms and ammunition enough
to equip the numerous effectives available ;   in exchange, the
" patriots " would hand over to England the provinces of
Maracaibo, Santa Marta and Cartagena.   The document in
which these proposals were embodied reveals an incredible
naivety on the part of the Granadinos who had drafted it.
They recalled " the secret help which the Royal House of
Bourbon had once, while at peace [with England], given to
the North American subjects of Great Britain who without
any adequate motive had risen in arms against the mother
country," and they agreed to cede Maracaibo, Santa Marta
and Cartagena, " reserving only our religion, and the same
privileges to which an English subject is entitled, and both

religions, the Catholic and the Protestant shall have equal privileges without any discrimination."(5)

These texts are enough to show that the movement was naive in the extreme, aristocratic and by no means sympathetic to the revolution of the "Bostonians." No better comment could be found on it, as on similar movements of rich don-julianists from New Spain, than this extract from a letter sent to Miranda on February 24th, 1782, by a number of aristocrats of Caracas, including Bolívar's father. They complain that Gálvez, the Minister of the Indies, " treats all Americans, no matter their pedigree, rank or condition, as if they were vile slaves ; and hàs just sent an order to all Governors prohibiting any American gentleman to leave for abroad without a licence from the King, which must be asked for at Madrid through him : so that you may see us here reduced to a humiliating prison and treated worse than many negro slaves whose masters trust them better." The three noblemen go on to state that " therefore they have no other way out than to rise against such an infamous and unbearable oppression " ; and implore Miranda to lead the rising, for they have watched the events of Peru and Santa Fe but " do not like the result and fear similar consequences (having moreover at home the experience of the León rise)." In short, they say to Miranda : Let us rise against Spain but under you, and let us see that no one but us rises and that our position is not endangered by the rabble.(6)

*   *   *

A place in this gallery of eighteenth-century Creoles must be made for one who does not fit into any category, yet touches all at some point. Don Pablo Olavide was born in Lima in 1725 and educated at the University there. He was twenty when he was appointed *oídor* of the *Audiencia* of Lima—hardly a good case to quote by those who claimed that Creoles were denied access to high State offices. He was twenty-one when he distinguished himself for his courage and generosity when Lima was all but wiped out by the earthquake of 1746. He set about to rebuild the city, but having at his expense built a church and a theatre, he offended the feelings of the devout, in other words, of the envious, who, jealous of his rapid success, accused him of maladministration. Called to Madrid, he was exonerated ; married a rich widow and became for a while Aranda's private secretary in the Paris embassy. He adopted French ways and ideas, even to the point of spoiling his Spanish style with gallicisms, and, back in Spain, lived as a wealthy man of the world with literary and artistic tastes, gathering the cream of the liberal and rich society of the capital in his two handsome houses of Madrid and Leganés. He carried out some public duties with devotion and efficiency, but his heart was rather in letters and ideas, and he opened a theatre in his own house, in which he staged French plays, some of which he translated, with no particular talent. He favoured the expulsion of the Jesuits. In 1769 he was appointed *Asistente* of Seville, a post in which he showed the positive, efficient yet dictatorial and centralistic tendencies of the century, building river quays, cleaning the city and depriving the University of all its local traditions and liberties.

A Prussian businessman and economist, who styled himself Don Juan Gaspar Thürriegel, was then promoting a scheme to " colonize " the wild districts of Sierra Morena with German farmers. On a favourable report of Campomanes (February 26th, 1767), the plan was adopted, and Olavide selected as superintendent. (A curious case of the way History weaves events : Thürriegel, as part of these financial dealings with the Crown, received four Commissions of Infantry Captains, one of which he sold for 85,000 *reales* to Miranda, who later was to seek Olavide's co-operation in his schemes for independence.) As superintendent of the colony, Olavide was a success. We know it from Miranda. In La Carolina, settled in an inn of which he says " nowhere have I found a better inn, nor greater abundance of food, fruit and other comforts," the young captain sings the praises of " this good patriot " Olavide, who in less than ten years had transformed a wilderness, and a nest of brigands, into " the most agreeable and comfortable spot on the road from Cádiz to Madrid." Not content with this, he adds, " Sr. Olavide has set up works and manufactures so that he meets the need for crockery of

all the townships, and it is as good as the best in Seville ; and
the cloth and needle works are fairly good. No better order
and economy are possible than one sees in this enterprise."(7)

Trouble came from unexpected quarters. The colonists
were mostly German and German Swiss, all Catholics.
Presumably they had come to Spain secure, at any rate, on
the score of faith. Some were disappointed. Olavide can
hardly have been a keen observer of the tenets of the Church.
A Swiss Catholic, Yauch, presented a *Memorial* (March 14th,
1769) complaining of religious indifference, and, presumably
to add weight to this grievance, of maladministration as well.
The Bishop of Jaen confirmed this, if only in part. Visitors
were sent, one of them the Irishman, Wall ; they reported
that some Protestants had been smuggled in ; that there was a
scarcity of priests ; and that there were no religious houses
of either friars or nuns ; a condition Aranda had laid
down when drafting the book of charges for Thürriegel.
Some Capuchins were then brought over from Freiburg.
Their Prior, Father Romuald, was a good Swiss friar with
more holiness than sense of humour. Shocked at Olavide's
flippant conversation on religious matters, he denounced him
to the Inquisition as a heretic (September 17th, 1775).
Aranda was no longer in office. Olavide was summoned to
Madrid and Roda asked the Inquisitor General to be lenient.
This Inquisitor, Beltrán, was a man of the century, on the
whole liberal and well disposed ; but he seems to have been
frightened by the progress of the " philosophic " views in high
circles into sentencing Olavide for the sins of his betters,
Aranda and the rest. For the Inquisition, it was a light
sentence : the accused was to recant in a private *Autillo* or
small *auto de fe* in the presence of a number of grandees,
officials and churchmen. The ceremony (November 24th,
1778), though private and discreet, was solemn enough ; for
Olavide was in his heart a sincere Catholic, and he swooned
on hearing himself accused of having lost his faith. He was
exiled to forty leagues from the King's residence, from America,
from La Carolina and from Seville ; bound to eight years'
residence in a monastery to learn Christian doctrine, and
ordered to fast every Friday ; shorn of all his posts and honours

and of the right to wear a sword, gold, silver, silk or rich cloth, and of riding a horse ; and his goods were confiscated.(8)

He had many enemies who gloated at his fall, but many friends also, powerful enough to enable him to escape to France after a short stay in the monastery of Sahagún (1778-80). Received in France as a martyr, even the bishop of his diocese helped him to escape to Geneva when there was a fear that he might be extradited. The Revolution enabled him to return to France ; he was made an adopted citizen of the French Republic. But as he was living quietly in Meung, he was suddenly cast into prison (April 16th, 1794) by the local Committee of Safety. Inquisition for Inquisition, Olavide preferred the Spanish-Catholic to the French-Revolutionary. He returned to the faith of his early days and wrote it all in a book, *The Gospel in Triumph*, or *History of a Disenchanted Philosopher* (1798), which reopened the gates of Spain for him. Refusing offers of public honour and service, he withdrew to Andalusia where he died in 1804. This disenchantment of his later days explains the coldness with which he received Miranda's proposals for a plan of emancipation, hereafter to be discussed.(9)

*   *   *

There is a striking contrast between Olavide and Nariño. Both were born in the class of rich privileged Whites ; but while Olavide was mostly a man of the world, taking letters, ideas and politics in his stride, Nariño was a man of action intent on putting into practice an ideal which he had conceived. He was born in Bogotá on April 9th, 1765, the son of the *Contador Fiscal*, a royal post ; and, after the usual studies, he married at twenty and became *alcalde* at thirty. The Viceroy, Gil Lemus, granted him *ad interim* the much coveted post of Tithe Treasurer, and another Viceroy, Ezpeleta, confirmed the appointment in the teeth of the opposition of the *cabildo*. So this future fighter for the liberties of his country owed his career to the protection of a Viceroy, imposing his will on the locally elected body.(10)

And not only his career, but his power and his fortune as well ; for it was customary for the Tithe Treasurer to speculate freely with the sums entrusted to him, and Nariño made a handsome fortune for himself and was rich when, in 1791, he withdrew from the post. He was, therefore, a man happy in the use, and prosperous in the abuse, of the privileges of his class. What turned him into a revolutionist ? A mistake he made and the harsh treatment he met at the hands of the authorities when he was found out. He loved books and bought enough to set up one of the finest libraries in the country ; and his house in Santa Fe, as Olavide's in Madrid, became a literary and " philosophic " centre. One day, posters against the Spanish Government were seen on the walls of Santa Fe ; and at the same time the authorities knew that copies of a Spanish translation of the Declaration of the Rights of Man were circulating in the city. A number of distinguished persons were implicated, and Nariño, who owned a private printing press, was found to have been the translator of the dangerous pamphlet. Typical of the epoch, the French original had been supplied him by a Captain Ramírez, of the Viceroy's bodyguard. He explained that he had printed but a few copies and that, hearing of the official enquiry, had burnt them all.(11)

The Courts sent most of the accused to Spain. In Cádiz Nariño escaped, went to Madrid under an assumed name and pulled Masonic strings, for he was a Freemason, and so was Godoy, the Prime Minister. He escaped to France, and in Paris had dealings with José Caro, a Cuban who worked with Miranda for emancipation. Through Teresa Cabarrús, the Franco-Spanish beauty who had made the name of Madame Tallien famous, he put before Tallien a plan whereby France was to liberate Spanish America. Tallien referred him to London and thither he repaired in 1796. Miranda was already there, begging help. The prestige of Spanish America can hardly have risen with this constant stream of Don-Julians all seeking English help. Under the name of Don Palacio Ortiz, Nariño tried in vain to see Pitt, but remained long enough to be convinced that England would not share in the adventure at less cost than the annexation of New Granada. Lord Liverpool was ready to put a frigate of forty guns at his disposal, on such terms. He returned to

Santa Fe *via* La Guaira, was caught and bought his life by
reporting his fellow conspirators and abettors—the one stain
on an otherwise attractive character. The Viceroy,
Mendinueta, who thought he did not possess the military
means to quell any untoward events, strongly advised Madrid
to grant a general amnesty, but the Government in Madrid
preferred to wait, and Nariño remained in prison, where he
ripened into an uncompromising separatist.(12)

*   *   *

As a curious aspect of donjulianism in reverse, so to speak,
the collaboration of Spanish revolutionists in the South
American rising of 1797 deserves a special place in this gallery.
On June 4th three of the revolutionaries exiled to America for
their republican rebellion in Madrid, Picornell, Cortés and
Andrés, while in La Guaira, entered into touch with the
revolutionists of Venezuela. By then the army and the
civil service were honeycombed with Freemasons. The three
Spanish prisoners escaped from prison. Picornell went to
Guadalupe where he printed a pamphlet on the *Rights of
Man and the Citizen*, and a revolutionary song, *The American
Carmagnole*. These Spaniards were fellow-conspirators in a
plot known as the Conspiracy of Gual and España, from
the names of two of its leaders. Gual was " the son of D.
Mateo Gual, who commanded at La Guaira when Admiral
Knowles attacked that place in 1743." He was a captain
of veterans in Caracas ; while España was a local magistrate
in Macuto. The conspiracy had been encouraged by the
first English Governor of Trinidad, Lieutenant-Colonel
Picton, who had printed and circulated a dispatch sent him
by the Foreign Secretary promising full help and respect for
the independence of the Spanish emancipated colonies.
There were rich merchants in it as well as *mestizos* and barbers.
The proclamation the conspirators had prepared reveals a
number of points about their attitude : first of all their aim is
to *restore its liberty to the American people*. *Viva el pueblo americano*
was to be the rallying cry. Patriotism was continental, of
course within the Spanish speaking continent. The paper
begins with : " In the name of the Holy Trinity and of Jesus,

Mary and Joseph," and it respects the privileges and the income of churches and religious orders, religious persons who respect the movement, and sacred images ; it declares that " commerce must be as free as air," opens ports and bays to all nations and calls all " provinces " to an assembly which must declare for independence. Export of gold and silver is forbidden ; members of the armed forces who oppose the rebellion are to be severely punished ; others to be given a safe-conduct to Spain or admitted in the rebel forces—again an important proviso, for European Spaniards are not excluded. In an article (32) strongly reminiscent of Rousseau under its Christian surface, complete equality is declared between Whites, Indians, half-castes and Blacks who must live " in perfect harmony, considering each other as brothers in Jesus Christ, equals in God and trying to vie with each other in nothing but merit and virtue, the two only real and true distinctions between man and man, and the only ones henceforth to exist between the members of our republic." The tribute paid by Indians and negro slavery were therefore abolished.(13)

It is plain that this was the first radical and equalitarian conspiracy in Spanish America ; and there are strong reasons for the view that it owed these features to the influence of the Spanish republicans who had brought to the continent, *via* Spain, French revolutionary, democratic and Masonic views. The conspiracy failed because, among other reasons, it was denounced to the authorities, and a number of conspirators, including España, were executed. But it would probably have failed in any case because its equalitarian character was still premature and out of touch with the realities of the New World. The nobility and the rich sided with the authorities and some of the very men who, fifteen years earlier, had signed the letter to Miranda, imploring him to come and lead the movement for emancipation, were the first to offer their services to the Captain-General and to arm militias at their own expense to quell the rebellion of Gual.(14)

Chapter XX

MIRANDA

1.—MIRANDA STILL A SPANIARD

THE greatest of all the precursors of Bolívar, the most attractive and forcible incarnation of Spanish-American donjulianism, was Miranda. A typical Creole. His mother belonged to a family rooted in Caracas for generations. His father, Sebastian Miranda, had come to Caracas from the Canaries. He was a rich shopkeeper. He had stood beside Bolívar's father when the Pact between Governor Castellanos and the rebel León had been read to the public. León was a Canary Islander like him, and a born enemy of the Basques. Bolívar was a scion—if somewhat remote—of the Basque nation. That particular Bolívar who stood by Sebastian Miranda's side was a Ponte by his mother, and a close friend of the Tovars. A Ponte and a Tovar were to be thorns in the father's side. A Bolívar was to be the master of the son's fate.

In Miranda converge all the lines, movements and trends which were at work in the eighteenth century. Through his father he felt the grievances of the Spanish settler ; through his mother, those of the American, more or less " grafted," Creole ; in the United States he breathed one revolution, in France he lived and fought for another ; and he felt keenly the dangers of the third ; he read the four philosophers and met one of them in his own house ; he visited Spanish exiled Jews and brought them messages, frequented Masonic institutions wherever he went (if he was not himself a Freemason) and collected and handed over to Pitt lists of exiled Jesuits whom he had trained as agents of secession. He was, in fine, by his romantic life, a novel in itself, a magnetic figure for Spanish America, and by his generalship during the French Revolution, a leader in whom, before Bolívar rose above the political horizon, the whole Spanish New World saw its Washington.

*   *   *

His father, Don Sebastian Miranda, lived well on the earnings of " the decent exercise and trade of a shop of Castillian cloth," but was also a captain of a company of White Islanders, which in fact he kept at his expense " so that the said company came to all royal services and musters with greater splendour, show and skill in the handling of the weapons and in their movements than any other." Yet the rich Creoles looked down upon the shopkeeper gentleman, and as sneers and jeers did not suffice, he had to give up his shop, says the Royal *Cédula* on the case, owing to " the hint made to him by his chiefs to that effect, unless he was ready to give up my royal service and the sixth company of fusiliers." This company belonged to a new battalion of militiamen in which Miranda's father had been given a commission to shelter him from the social ostracism of his uppish fellow officers. But the opposition to the upstart Spaniard was not disarmed, and ultimately drove him to resign. Even then he was dragged before the *alcalde* for " illegally " wearing the uniform and stick of a captain ; till the unfortunate shopkeeper-gentleman decided to prosecute the commander of the battalion, Don Juan Nicolás de Ponte, and a captain Tovar, chief promoters of his vexations, and to appeal to the King. The King backed him in every way, granted him the use of the uniform and of the stick, laid it down that he was to be treated as an equal by all officers, under pain of severe punishment, and last but not least declared : " I impose perpetual silence on any investigation of his quality and origin."

This last decision of the King of Spain can hardly have been due to an unqualified faith in the noble house of Miranda ; and the gratitude with which it was received by Don Sebastian himself, and brandished under the nose of his persecutors, shows that the linen shopkeeper of Caracas knew how matters stood just as well as the King. The episode is important for, taken in connection with the epoch and the man, Francisco Miranda, who at the time all this happened was twenty, it should have bred in him pro-Spanish, democratic, equalitarian, anti-Creole feelings. But the fact is that Miranda became the very reverse of all that : an aristocratic,

almost snobbish, pro-Creole, anti-Spanish separatist. And
that is what remains to be explained.(1)

*   *   *

He became a separatist by a slow evolution which repays
study.   But he was always an aristocrat and nearly always a
snob.   Born in 1750, of a father sneered at by the Whites and
of a mother who, passing as White, can hardly have failed
to bring to her son streamlets of the other two colours,
inequality was deeply embedded in his blood and experience.
But strength both of mind and of will had been granted him
in generous measure.   He was therefore to accept inequality
and to turn it to his advantage.   At an age late enough for
the impress of experience to be clear-cut and defined, yet
early enough to indent deeply into the soul, the young Miranda
had been humiliated in his father.   His chief impulse for the
rest of his life was to restore the balance by rising as high as
possible in the human scale of society.   He needed social
inequality, for he must rise.

Which in its turn leads to retouching the first judgment
as to his snobbery.   Miranda sought ever to prove himself a
man of noble descent, and he paraded his uniform of Spanish
Colonel—to which he was entitled—and his title of Count—to
which he was not—even at the Court of Catherine the Great.
But in those days a man who felt himself above the common
had to seek his peers among noblemen, whether born or made.
To seek aristocratic company in a world ruled by aristocrats
was less snobbish than to seek aristocratic company in a world
in which aristocrats are a curiosity.   Miranda's snobbery was
therefore in a sense one of the ways in which he showed his
instinct of his own individual value.(2)

Nothing proves that his father was " the scion of a distinguished Spanish family."   The chances are that his claims
to the noble branch of a family as widespread as Miranda are
formal and nebulous—for otherwise his enemies would not
have hounded him out of the army nor would he have worked
in a shop, nor acquiesced in that silence imposed by the
Crown on all search as to his pedigree.   Yet the young man's
first care upon arriving in Spain was to call on the Royal king-

at-arms and enquire about his family.   On November 28th, 1772, the king-at-arms informed all and sundry that the Miranda family was very old and had as a coat of arms " a red field and on it five half bodies of maidens " which, considering the lifelong record of Miranda in the field of maidens, would appear to show that wit and hazard can meet. Though the king-at-arms provided no real proof that Miranda belonged to the ancient family thus described, the precursor of the Spanish-American Revolution treasured the paper among his credentials.(3)

*   *   *

He was educated in the Royal Seminary and followed a course of arts in the University.   In 1771, " wishing to serve H.M. with my person in the Kingdoms of Spain as my inclination and talents may provide," he left for Spain.   In December, 1772, he purchased a commission as captain in the Princess Regiment and took part in the campaign of Morocco and Algiers in 1774-5.   His first stay in Spain shaped his image of the mother country.   His impressions were excellent and on his way from Cádiz to Madrid he found much to admire in the roads, in the cultivation of the fields, the beauty of the cities and local industries. Owing to a breakdown of a conveyance, he had to stay in a small *pueblo* in Sierra Morena.   " In this *pueblo* "—he writes— " I met the Military Governor Don Miguel de Florez, cavalry captain, a son of Quito and a man of much education, who showed me his library of books, Latin, French, English and Spanish, all very well selected."   His admiration for what he sees in La Granja, Escorial, Segovia, the Royal Palace of Madrid, is unbounded ; and he praises everything liberally, particularly mechanical contrivances, which always draw his eye.

In these first pages of his diary one is struck by the ripe and independent judgment of the young man of twenty-one.   His mind is alert, his curiosity all-embracing yet discriminating, his judgment sound. Next to his mental powers must be noticed his sincere religious faith, shown not merely in his observances but also in his tacit acceptance of ex-votos and miracles and in spontaneous utterances of devotional feeling. Thus, in a list of pictures seen : " and another one of the Holy Virgin with her most Holy Son dead in her arms. . . ." Years later, in 1778, after describing the sordid behaviour of a priest and his sexton in Almaraz, he comments : " This is the way to render despicable and contemptible the most serious and sacred things of religion." Finally, there is in these first pages a robust, at times naive Spanish patriotism. Thus of La Granja : " This is without comparison the most famous residence of the King of Spain (and even of any King in Europe) for the magnificence of its gardens, fountains and statues." And of a regiment of cavalry he says : " They put their best attention in the choice of horses for which reason if is the best of the Kingdom and possibly of the whole of Europe."

His diary of the Melilla operations three years later shows the young officer in a more critical mood. He notes the frequent bursts of bad iron guns and that " the fortification is built with little regard for the generally accepted system in modern Europe " ; but with satisfaction " the signal success of the newly received artillery," and the speed and competence of H.M.'s gunmaster. Back in Spain he profits by a stay in Málaga to visit Gibraltar, " where for two months "—he wrote later to the King—" I examined comparatively their excellent school for practical military affairs, with much benefit." Note this " comparatively." It is typical of his attitude of mind, bent on comparing Spain with other nations, measuring, forming an opinion, reflecting—the attitude he will keep all his life. This explains, among other things to be discussed later, a note of criticism which steals into his observations, together with a clear fall in his religious fervour under his still untarnished Spanish patriotism.

He records the comfort, cleanliness, beauty of the villages and cities which he crosses, but notes the excessive number of friars and the poor quality of other than theological books in a library. He belauds the library and picture gallery of a Canon of Toledo, though he finds the city flooded with friars. His criticism as well as his praise is patriotic. He is still a Spaniard. We saw how he described Olavide as a good patriot for his work in Sierra Morena ; and referring to Don Alvaro de Bazan, he calls him " our famous Admiral, this Spanish hero, the greatest Admiral of his century." Finally, when praising the horses of Córdoba as " the most perfect animals nature has formed in the species," he concludes with significant warmth : " What a pity that the breeding is not more protected of these perfect and useful animals, a special ornament of our Spain."

As time goes on his temper becomes worse. In 1778, travelling again at the head of a company, he writes : " The peasants are well dressed and their houses show an abundance which proves the good state of their lands and that they draw the profit of the harvest for themselves ; there are many of them who possess up to 20 pairs of oxen." But adds " the road is fairly pleasant and with but small cost might be made as good as those of France. Negligence and bad taste are to be seen everywhere in this unhappy kingdom." He begins to feel the impatience of a young idealist shocked by so much sloth, bad taste, the ill behaviour of the friars, dirt. Yet it is the irritation of one who speaks ill of the family ; rather like the criticism a young, go-ahead, somewhat petulant son would level at his old-fashioned parents. He repeatedly contrasts the bad taste he sees with " the good taste of our ancestors," and describes " a christening in which I saw all in a block the sloth of my nation." The following is even more telling : " I was told that the Marqués de Ustáriz, my countryman, the *Intendente* of Badajoz was nearby ; I rode to see him and found an affable person, well cultivated, and keen to work for the good of his country ; certainly fit for his duties." Four years later three of his " countrymen " were to protest to him against the fact that Caracas was governed by a Spaniard ; here was a Caracas man governing Spaniards and none was the worse for it. But, moreover, Miranda calls Ustáriz *mi paisano*, which means *countryman* in the sense which would apply, not to two Englishmen but to two Yorkshiremen ; while " his country " means Spain. In 1778 Miranda still felt a Spaniard.(4)

Very much of a Spaniard, including a royal share of courage, indiscipline, ability, impatience—and contempt for financial details. He showed his courage on several occasions.

In a minority of one, in a Council of War of Spanish officers
on board an English frigate conveying reinforcements to
Spanish troops besieged in Melilla (December 9th, 1774), he
advocated the bolder course, and proposed a raid to destroy
the enemy's artillery there. He was a brave officer throughout.
But he was not disciplined. His chiefs had to arrest him for
wearing fancy uniform. He showed his ability at every step,
and this led him to impatience : he writes to the Inspector
General of the Militia : "You cannot conceive how deeply
dissatisfied I feel for the lack of opportunities to put to some
use the ideas which, by continuous study and some travelling,
I have formed about my profession." As for his contempt
for finance, it landed him in a serious affair. Miranda
reported that 10,000 *reales* belonging to the funds of the
regiment, which he had in his house, had been stolen ; with
details which render the story most unlikely, the more so as
the money was due to a merchant for clothes supplied to the
soldiers and a complaint had been received about its remaining
unpaid. Miranda was careless but honourable ; and eventually brought money over from Caracas and paid the debt.
The most likely explanation is that he had lost the money
either gambling or in an unlucky investment.(5)

This story (1779) and accusations of ill treatment of his
soldiers, from which, granted the rough standards of the day,
he cleared himself passing well, did him much harm with the
military authorities. They certainly embittered him towards
Spain, though he found staunch protectors in the higher ranks
of the army, particularly General Cagigal. He aimed high.
Already in Melilla (1775) he had proposed himself for a reward :
" humbly begs Y.M. to deign to grant him one of the military
orders, not excluding that of St. James " ; he had sought to
be transferred to the Navy (1776) ; he had solicited a post in
the expedition which, under Ceballos, was being sent to Buenos
Aires. In all these papers he emphasized his " keen desire to
be of use to his King and country " and " to develop the ideas
which he has acquired on the military craft through his study
and industry." He succeeded in clearing himself from both
his disciplinary and his financial problems, and left Spain in
the spring of 1780 with a force commanded by Cagigal, whose

aide de camp he became. Ultimately this force was sent to help the American rebels against England. Miranda took part in the operations led by Bernardo de Gálvez against Florida, notably the siege of Pensácola, and after the surrender of the garrison was promoted a Lieutenant Colonel (August 23rd, 1781).(6)

Cagigal sent Miranda to Jamaica, under cover of an exchange of prisoners, to enquire into its military strength. On his way back, Miranda brought over three ships loaded with slaves and goods ; for which he was accused of contraband. While the matter was being investigated, Miranda took part in an attack on New Providence, organized by Cagigal with the help of South Carolina patriots ; and actually negotiated the surrender of the city and of all the Bahamas to Spain (May 8th, 1782). But in August he was arrested and on December 23rd, 1783, sentenced to the loss of his commission, a fine and ten years' imprisonment in Oran. Cagigal was also compromised. Though both were exonerated in 1799, the chances are that both were guilty, if only of those violations of the trade laws which were constantly being committed in the Indies and were dangerous only for men with more enemies than friends. Moreover, by then Miranda was acting in a way which to say the least was odd. Gálvez, the Minister of the Indies, accused him of having granted an article in the agreement with the Governor of Jamaica (clause 7) which had nothing to do with exchanging prisoners and had always been denied to the English. It provided that no ships with less than 40 men and 8 guns could be granted patents as corsairs. This cannot be denied, and in his numerous papers Miranda, who rejected all other charges, never did this one. That he was "a passionate friend of the English" was true at the time. The captain of a ship in which he lived in 1782, after two days' acquaintance, described him as "an Englishman in his heart" ; and his own agent, when imparting the fact to him, far from protesting against the accusation, confirms it, since he adds : "Be careful, Miranda ; you must have more prudence." The same agent wrote to him : "The people [he means that of Havana] speak ill of you because they are ignorant and say that you are a spy and so forth, and the military do the same because they are a wretched lot."

That he had dealings with Governor Dalling in Jamaica is doubtful. He probably did not. But what is most likely is that the English, very much alert in matters of spying, suspected what his secret instructions were and turned the tables on him. Moreover, they probably drew him on. Miranda, who, though shrewd, was naive, may have come out into the open. He was already working against Spain in South America. The letter mentioned above, sent him by Bolívar's father and others on February 24th, 1782, shows that the correspondence of these precursors of emancipation with Miranda had lasted for some time. It refers to " letters we sent you in July, 1781 " on " the lamentable state of this province." Miranda himself had recorded that 1781 was the year in which he was appealed to by his countrymen. In a draft manifesto he wrote on October 10th, 1792, he says : " Called by you to the help of the mother-country (i.e., Spanish America) in 1781. [. . .] I thought it better to bear up for some time and patiently to await the independence of the Anglo-American colonies which was doomed to be the infallible preliminary of ours." This document explains why Miranda decided that he would spend his time more profitably travelling in the brand new United States than meditating in a Spanish gaol.(7)

*   *   *

He left for the United States " to complete his education," as he himself repeatedly says. From the very first, when as a young captain he tried in vain to obtain from O'Reilly, the Inspector General of the Militia, leave to visit Germany and other European countries, and again when writing to Cagigal in April, 1783, he comes back always to this eagerness for self education. Ten years later, however, in a draft manifesto to his countrymen, this time the Spanish-Americans, he says the purpose of his travel had been to work for their independence, asserting in fact that " it was then that in 1784, in New York, the present plan for the independence and the freedom of the Spanish-American continent was laid down with the co-operation of England." Yet again when he arrived in

England, admirably received by the Spanish Ambassador, he writes to him thanking him for " the kindness wherewith you favour me as a Spaniard [. . .] which courtesy, as a Spaniard and as a grateful man, I shall not forget." Cagigal had given him letters for Washington and for Rendon, the Spanish Minister in Philadelphia, who received him cordially in his own house. And so Miranda, a fugitive from Spanish law, lived with the representative of the King of Spain to whom he owed his rapid social success in Philadelphia, as he himself generously states. It is clear, therefore, that, at this time, Miranda lived in a state of swaying loyalties. The contradictions in his words and deeds are due, not to lack of faith, but to the fluid state of his mind over Spain and her domains. Was he a Spaniard ? An American ? Both ? He hardly knew. And he was sincere when, on April 16th, 1783, he wrote to Cagigal : " Only in the hard case if the right any vassal has to be heard and judged by a competent tribunal were denied to me, would I look differently on the interests of that Fatherland and that Sovereign for whom I have so often staked my work, my fortune and my life."(8)

Meanwhile, as he proudly wrote to Charles III on April 10th, 1785, he visited the United States and the scenes of " the most brilliant actions of the last war, and conversed at leisure with the heroes and wise men who carried out that immortal enterprise," the independence of the United States of America. Not all he saw was to his liking, and mention has been made of the shortcomings he noted down. But in general Miranda was struck by the commonsense, the simplicity, the charm, the order, the zest in work of the young republic ; and he often contrasts it all with life in the Indies in terms most flattering to the United States, if at times unexpected. We forget that the kaleidoscope of nations is apt to change its pattern with time. " Foreigners complain that people here are somewhat boorish and not very hospitable "—he writes in Philadelphia—" I have only found a certain reserve and shyness at the beginning (particularly in women) which is typical of the American system " ; and he contrasts it with the habit of seeing people which " widens ideas and fosters in us [i.e., Spanish Americans] a free and liberal way." While on the way from Boston to

New Hampshire he says that the land is poor but that " such
are the industry and spirit which liberty inspires in these
peoples that out of but a small part of it they grow enough to
keep their large families, pay heavy taxes and live in comfort
and good taste one thousand times happier than the owners
of the rich mines and fertile lands of Mexico, Peru, Buenos
Aires, Caracas and the whole American-Spanish Continent."
He enjoys freedom of travelling, as might be expected of such
a wanderer. " At ten we arrived in West-Point and went
straight to the Inn without anyone troubling to find out who
the newcomers were—one of the most pleasant conditions to
be enjoyed in a free country : how many formalities would
have been necessary in France, Germany, etc. . . ." Nor
did he fail to note feminine beauty. Thus in Rhode Island :
" I say it with all ingenuity : neither a more generous and
friendly simplicity nor daintier and more beautiful complexions
have I seen anywhere." And again as a result of his quiet
observation of the women during a long silent service at the
Friends' house : " I spent the time observing the dresses and
figures of the women present : and I can say sincerely that
more simplicity, cleanliness and taste as to the former, more
natural and simple beauty as to the latter, cannot be imagined.
I am certain that neither the palette of Rubens nor the flesh-
tints of the Titian could ever imitate what nature here offers
in the skin and most beautiful complexion of these simple
Quaker girls without a grain of powder or of make-up on
them." But how far, how far he was from realizing the abyss
which this little fact—that he had spent that half hour of
Quaker meditation looking at the girls—revealed between the
destinies of the two Americas !(9)

He was still very much of a Spaniard. Every time he
brings in Spain, whether for good or ill, he says " my " or
" our " as a matter of course. " Our inimitable Cervantes,"
" our Rendón " ; " he told me he had friends in nearly every
country of Europe but Spain, and that was why he had been
glad to meet me". After painting a most unfavourable
picture of the French Consul General in Philadelphia, he adds :
" These are the main actors on the Gallic stage, if we exclude
the Spanish Minister who, owing to the accursed co-ordination

of policy [between France and Spain] and to our ignorance (though there is no man who does not hate it in his heart) has to play a subordinate part." And a secret patriotic Spanish satisfaction can be felt in his remarks on a social success as host achieved by the Spanish Minister, " our Rendón," and on the fact that his garden was the best in Philadelphia.(10)

There are two curious passages in which he reveals the strength of his Spanish feelings. One, mixed with his inveterate francophobia, the other one with his indignation against the Spanish Government. In the first he records how he observed that the French were intriguing against Spain and spreading ill-feeling over " the shameful behaviour of Spain during the last war " ; but, he says, through his own activities he rescued the Spanish Minister from " this most dangerous situation " and " I turned a contemptuous attitude on these envious Gallic politicians". The second must be quoted for its picturesque mixture of feelings. " We arrived at midday [. . .] after lunch I went to call on a Catalan settled here, Gabriel Sistaré, who had called as soon as he knew I had arrived. He is a man of about 55, perfectly loutish and ignorant even for a Catalan. . . . Thirteen years ago he put in at this harbour with his ship in a very bad state, on his way from Havana to Cádiz ; he sent the sugar cargo to Spain and kept the money. The outcome was he bought one of the best houses, took a mistress (though he has a wife in Spain) and begat seven children as savage as their father and as filthy as their mother. . . . Seems otherwise a kind man, though a beast on all four sides. His house and furniture though very good, denounce his lack of breeding and his low level of thinking. . . . I asked him if he knew of any other countryman settled in this continent ; and he answered he only knew one, Joseph Antonio Linarez, from Galicia, married in this same State . . . and here are in fine the specimens of the Spanish nation on the one hand, and on the other M. and R.n [Rendón ?] for these peoples to form an opinion of our character, ways and manners, and long live the accursed Government ! "(11)

*   *   *

His mind was moving into an opposition still loyal to Spain

FRANCISCO MIRANDA

MOTECZUMA

—a wide Spain embracing the Spanish Indies—yet more and
more inimical to " the Government," the system, the prevailing
powers. These direct and immediate utterances must be
given priority over writings of a later date, in which he or his
friends assert that he was already in favour of independence
but thought it wiser not to break yet. His mind was ever
attentive to the political ways and institutions of the countries
he visited. He watched those of the United States closely
and with a keen critical mind. He discerned the American
tendency to hero-worship probably before anyone else. He
disliked Washington, whose military deeds he found debatable.
Washington's glory seemed to him out of proportion and
unjust to other American statesmen—" a usurpation as
capricious as unjust." He calls him " the Idol." And while
in general he finds much to praise in the simple, straightforward and objective character of most of what he sees, he
records his dissent in terms invaluable to understand his
political thinking. " I have attended several sittings of the
Legislative Assembly "—he writes in Boston—" and had an
opportunity to see the defects and drawbacks under which
this democracy labours, having fully laid its law-giving powers
into the hands of *ignorance*. . . . One broke into reciting
songs he had learnt by heart in the midst of a debate he had
not grasped ; another one, having spoken for two hours, at
the end of the debate asked what the motion he was to vote
on was about . . . and so most of them. So that the most
absurd and unjust decisions were proposed, debated and
approved by these assemblies throughout the continent ; and
as their Constitution grants all power to proprietors, the chief
men are not the wisest, and senators and assemblymen are
often persons without principles or education—one was a
taylor four years ago, another one an innkeeper, a third one
a caulker, a fourth one a smith and so forth. . . ." Miranda
is not arguing undemocratically, but with an eye on the facts.
He did not object to these men as tailors, caulkers, smiths ; but
because, being tailors, caulkers, smiths, they had not, in that
state of evolution, the maturity required for government. " It
is strange "—he writes in Newport—" to see the state of
plainness and even of want in which these people live, in such

L

small and unhappy homes, without decoration or even comfort, and yet the high ideas they harbour in their minds ! The first of them was a member of the assembly, and the other one a senator of New York, and yet their houses and furniture are those of poor people, the former, however, has a few books, including Bayle's curious collection of English poets." The matter worked in his mind, probably on a background of Montesquieu or Rousseau, to judge by his conversation with Sam Adams. Miranda put to Adams two objections, to neither of which " after chewing them " Adams found an answer. " The first was how a democracy, the basis of which should be virtue, found no room for it, while all dignities and powers were given to property that is precisely to the poison of such a republic. The other one was the contradiction I observed between admitting that one of the rights of man is that of worshipping the Supreme Being as he pleases [. . .] and yet excluding from legislative and elective functions all those who did not swear to belong to the Christian religion."(12)

*   *   *

It is not clear, in view of all this, why Miranda was such a convinced admirer of the English Constitution. Perhaps he saw in it the nearest approach to that principle he had read in Montesquieu that virtue should be the basis of a republic, since it was also in Montesquieu that he might have read that such was precisely the function of the English aristocracy. Speaking of one D. Joaquín de Quintana he says " he is one of the very few of my nation who had penetrated the marvellous *arcana* of the British Constitution." And in South Carolina : " I attended the sittings of the Court of Justice many times ; and I cannot say how much pleasure and satisfaction I felt seeing the operation of the admirable system of the British Constitution. Oh my word, what a contrast with the legislative system of Spain ! " One can perceive how wide was the sense in which he interpreted the term " constitution," and the trend of his sympathy towards England, dating back to his visit to Gibraltar in his youth, and rooted in his admiration for the efficient ways of the English. Describing some military works in South Carolina he sums up : " The whole built with

that good taste, solidity, intelligence and simplicity which are
typical of English works " ;   and again, on his way to New
York : " This fort as well as the other redoubts, lines, etc., one
sees here built by the British, evince the good taste, solidity
and judgment which this wise and ingenious nation shows in
all it does."   His eagerness to visit England may be imagined.
He left Boston for London on December 15th, 1784.(13)

*   *   *

During the crossing he read Hume " with outstanding
benefit and pleasure," and Robertson's Charles V, not the
best reading to keep him in touch with Spanish realities.   He
was rapidly slipping out of the religious faith of his youth and
tradition, probably out of religion altogether, as shown by a
repeated remark on those who were afraid of the storm,
" particularly those who seem to be more religious".   His
landing (February 1st, 1785) was not auspicious ; he found
the guards put on board the ship grasping and dishonest.
But he was struck with admiration at the commercial activity
he saw.   " I positively believe that in this one river there is
more navigation and trade than in all the other rivers of the
world put together."   He settled at the Royal Hotel in Pall
Mall and spent several months " very busy admiring the
opulence, culture and magnificence and in particular the
debates in Parliament, which are actually a superb school of
Politics and Legislation for a man wishing to learn".   He was
intent on his travels and in order to be able to move about in
peace, despite his irregular situation towards the law, he
skilfully negotiated with the Spanish authorities on the basis of
a dilatory procedure.   Through the Ambassador, who received
him cordially, he sent to Floridablanca a petition addressed
to the King with a summary of his life and activities, complaining of his accusers, and asking to be relieved of his honours
and grades in the Spanish Army.   It was not, however, a
break at all, and his letter is drafted in respectful terms.   The
dilatory answer of Floridablanca seemed to him " satisfactory "
for his purpose, which was to travel in peace.   He accepted
letters of recommendation from the Spanish Ambassador for
his colleague in Berlin.   His companion at first was to be

Colonel Smith " whom he had frequented in New York."
Colonel Smith was the military attaché of the American
Legation. Miranda left his linen and bills in the hands of
the Spanish Vice-Consul ; but his papers went to Mr. James
Penman, " my good friend." (14)

2.—TRAVELS IN NORTHERN EUROPE
AND NEGOTIATIONS IN ENGLAND

Miranda's travels in Northern Europe, recorded in his
diary, are one of the most valuable treasures of European
history. His letters of introduction, his personal charm and
conversation attested by everyone who came into touch with
him, and his activities enabled him to move throughout
Europe at the highest levels of society, with direct access to
the royal Courts. He displayed the title of Count ; and his
diary reveals the pleasure he derived from the attention of
Kings, and how keenly he observed traces of jealousy in other
less fortunate courtiers—and even how mortified he felt
when he had to take second place at Court. He was ashamed
of it himself. The King of Poland offered seats to two persons,
" leaving the rest of us standing, no doubt in order that the
Ambassador should not complain and should have something
pleasant to report. . . . I own the incident mortified me for
a moment, till I realised the position. . . . What a miserable
life is that of the courtier, made unhappy instantly by the
slightest gesture or indifference of another man ! " He was
particularly well received in Russia where Catherine was all
smiles to him. Miranda was in his early thirties and was an
effective and vigorous woman-killer. Catherine was—or
rather had been—as effective a man-hunter as ever sat on a
throne, but by then was fifty-seven. She liked Miranda
and made him feel it repeatedly. Her retainers more than
once spoke to Miranda about her " motherly affection " and
she addressed him endearing requests to stay in Russia. He
himself goes out of his way to record that " Her Majesty
beckoned me to a bit of talk and made me *touch* and notice
that the gown she was wearing, though it looked very rich,

was extremely light, almost as light as a gauze. . . . She said
I seemed to be somewhat moody, etc."(15)

The Empress was so pleased with him that she invited him
to remain permanently in Russia with a pension of 1,000
golden Louis yearly ; but he refused, explaining his reasons
under the strictest secrecy—obviously his ambition to become
the leader of the Spanish-American Revolution. Miranda
had been received at Court through Russian friends. He
does not seem to have applied to the Spanish Minister, and
Ségur, the French Minister, refused to introduce him, believing
him guilty of the accusations standing against him in Madrid
and Cuba. The Spanish Minister sent him a stiff overbearing letter about his right to use the titles of Colonel and
Count, which Miranda answered in insolent terms. The
Minister was, of course, wrong in form, but he was right in
substance and excusable in that a subject of the King of
Spain, who admitted the position twice, as a Colonel and as a
Count, for both titles implied his recognition of the King's
sovereignty, should come and go without the slightest reference
to his sovereign's accredited representative. Miranda seems to
have been unaware of the incoherence of his attitude.(16)

By then he was rapidly drifting to an open break. He
had so far adjourned it, mostly to travel in peace. But the
motherly affection of Catherine was easing his mind. He had
touched her tender heart with the dangers of the Inquisition !
The Spanish Inquisition has carried many a strange load, but
none more strange than that of moving the heart of a German
Tzarina, risen to power over the body of her murdered husband,
the effective wielder over the whole Russian nation of powers
of life and death no Inquisitor ever dreamt of ; and of moving
such a heart over the purely hypothetical dangers of a Spanish-
American traveller whom the Inquisition had so far left
severely alone. True the Spanish Government were suspicious
of Miranda and watched him closely ; but even if Colonel
Smith's gossip reports are given the value they do not deserve,
the man after Miranda was Aranda, whom no one, not even
Catherine, Voltaire's friend, could mistake for an Inquisitor.
And as shown in these pages, Miranda had seen enough in
Europe to realize, as he himself writes beholding a dead

criminal hanging from the gallows at the gates of Cambridge, that " beans are boiled everywhere."(17)

These travels were a school for him. They are revealing for us. No man was ever more sincere and outspoken. His private life is duly noted down, including the " sacrifices to Venus " which he almost daily performs, the sums the modest priestesses demand and often even the details of the ceremony. But it would be a mistake to think Miranda was callous. Everywhere he went he visited the prisons—a strange foreboding for a man who was to languish and die in one of them—and criticizes them from a sympathetic and intelligent standpoint. Yet though he studied society, the poor, the destitute, as well as the forms of government and the centres of culture, he did so from the Court. Not only did he use his magnificent countship, but he passed himself off more than once as a Mexican nobleman. He felt definitely upper class. He accepted a little servant girl whom Count Ranzau sent him to sleep with ; he bought a negro slave and accepted another one as a present ; he had a white bondman and he beat his servants, when in wrath, with the flat of his sabre. Wherever he went the Court was opened to him ; and after his stay in Russia, the Russian Legations were, for him, everywhere a refuge and a home ; he enjoyed the right to wear the Russian uniform.(18)

This was most useful to him. His answer to the Spanish Minister had betrayed his inner attitude as that of a *de facto* separatist. And the Government in Madrid, while slow in dealing with his case, had every reason to suspect his activities. He thanked Catherine on his return to London for, he said, " the Court of Spain had been so openly adverse that it would have been impossible for me to move one step without taking advantage of Y.M.'s protection." The Spanish Ambassador, he goes on to say, received him with friendship, but had secret instructions against him ; he had had himself put down as a member of the Russian Embassy ; and he winds up : " Happy those who under an enlightened, wise and philosophic sovereign can shelter from fanaticism and from the Inquisition and can let their days flow cultivating letters and in the exercise of virtue." Let us not smile at this.

Neither Miranda nor Catherine was conscious of the humour hidden in their words—words which were then used in a different context from ours. The friendship of the northern Semiramis was a tower of strength and self-confidence for the still young officer, uncertain of his future. His letter to Floridablanca still shows him fluctuating between a regular career in Spain and a rebellious life. The general tone of it shows no keenness to break with Spain. If the Spanish Government in a fit of shrewdness had offered him a rise or a brilliant post in the Army or a governorship in the Indies, he might have accepted. " True "—he says—" most advantageous proposals have been made to me in Europe and even in North America, yet it is equally certain that I have contracted no obligations towards anybody nor have I ever entertained the remotest idea which might not suit the strictest principles of honour and of my birth." This he writes to Floridablanca on July 25th, 1789, and he adds : " If I had the good fortune of being half an hour chair to chair with Y.E., I should put matters before you with the utmost obviousness, but I shall leave the matter in the hands of H.E. D. Bernardo del Campo [the Ambassador] who has known me for long enough and who knows my invariable principles." This man could still be saved for Spain. But the answer was curt : " But as this gentleman is at present implicated in a law suit and must defend himself and purify his behaviour, H.M. can on no account decide yet to make use of him." Miranda decided to break ; and he wrote to Charles IV that he had thus been put " to the hardship of having to sacrifice all my fortune and interests and what is more the sweet company of my parents and family to choose a fatherland which may at least treat me with justice and ensure my civil peace."(19)

*   *   *

He had already entered into negotiations with Pitt, and, by the way, as Count of Miranda. England and Spain were then growling at each other over a clash in Nootka Sound, on the Pacific coast of North America. The story is worth telling as an example of Anglo-Spanish relations in those days. Humboldt gives a good summary of the Spanish activities on this coast. Interest in these regions arose early in the hope of finding a passage through to the East Indies in a north-westerly direction. The first ascertained voyage dates from 1543. It was led by a pilot named Pérez, and led to the discovery of White (or Orford) Cape in the 43° latitude. Francisco Gali, in 1582, discovered the north-western coast up to the 57°30', four years after Drake had reached the 48°. In 1596, Vizcaíno studied these coasts " with greater care and intelligence than any pilot before him," though, prevented by the ill-health of his crews, he was not able to sail beyond the 42°-43°. For about 170 years the quest was left in abeyance. Then, no longer, says Humboldt, out of pure scientific curiosity, but also for fear of rivals, Spain started a second period of exploration between 1774 and 1792. Pérez (a second one) left San Blas harbour on January 24th, 1774, to explore the north-west coast up to 60°. He was the first European to enter Nootka Bay (August 9th, 1774). He called it San Lorenzo. In 1782 Cook re-christened it King George Sound. He found silver spoons stolen from the Spanish ship by the natives. But before him, in 1775, Quadra led an expedition " which has advanced in a signal way the discovery of the north-western coast." In 1776, on orders from Madrid, the Viceroy of New Spain prepared a third expedition which, owing to delays in the building of the ships in Guayaquil, did not leave San Blas till February 11th, 1779. Meanwhile Cook had explored the coast. The Spaniards, again under Quadra, made a number of geographical and geological discoveries. On orders from Spain explorations were held up during the war which led to the independence of the United States. In 1788 (March to December) two Spanish ships explored not only the coast but also the Russian establishments thereon, which Cook's third voyage had brought to light. In 1789 the Spanish commander of this expedition, Martínez, was ordered to study the stretch of coast 50°-55° which Cook had left uncharted, and to settle in Nootka, in view of its growing fame in Europe as a fur market. He arrived in Nootka Bay on May 5th, 1789. One of his companions, Moziño, collected

a number of scientific and sociological data about the country
and its inhabitants which Humboldt deemed of the utmost
interest. Two months later the *Argonaut*, an English ship
commanded by James Colnet, appeared on the scene. He
imparted to Martínez that he had orders to settle in Nootka,
to build two ships there and to prevent any other European
nation from taking a share in the fur trade. The King
George Sound Company had been founded in London in
1785. Martínez retorted that Pérez had been there in 1543.
There was no agreement between the Spaniard and the
Englishman and so Martínez seized Colnet and sent him to
San Blas to explain the matter to the Viceroy.

High-handed though it was, this action seemed the only
solution for an incident which the English captain had
definitely put on the plane of force. At the time it was a
plane on which England had better chances to win than
Spain. The story was retold by Lord Lansdowne when the
convention imposed on Spain by the British Government
was brought for ratification before the House of Lords. Here
are his words : " Some young gentlemen at China, attached
to geography and a little commercial advantage, fit out a
vessel called the Sea-Otter, for the North-West coast of
America : some Bengal adventurer fits out two other ships
with fine names, under Portuguese papers and colours :
some speculative merchants, men of letters perhaps, equip
two other ships and the whole falls under the command of a
young gentleman of the name Mears, who is instructed and
instructs his followers, in terms becoming the form and pomp
of office, to violate a system regarding Spanish-America,
which it has been the policy of Europe, and in particular of
England, to adhere to for ages." The manifest of the enterprise was couched in the following terms : " Russian, English
and Spanish vessels shall be treated with equal civility in the
first instance ; but in case of any attempt to turn our
adventurers out of their way force shall be repelled by force ;
the parties to be seized, their ships brought in and condemned
as prizes and their crews as pirates. In planting a factory
we declare that we look to a solid establishment, and not to
one to be abandoned at pleasure." Lansdowne concludes :

" We thus find occurrences arising out of the enterprise of a few individuals, begun without any due warrant for it or any proper subordination to the public at large, formed the ostensible pretext of a dissension with Spain. England armed in a manner regardless of expense and summoned Spain to submit in a manner alike unprecedented and insulting."(20)

*   *   *

It was during this curious incident that Miranda turned up. Pitt thought the enterprising Creole might be of some use as a pawn in this game and perhaps in bigger games. Miranda came to him through Pownall, an ex-Governor in the North-American colonies, and one of the group of men, including Turnbull, who were weaving the net in which England was trying to catch the incautious South-American fish. There is a Spanish proverb Miranda seems to have forgotten : Fish die through the mouth. He had an interview with Pitt. It took place in Hollwood on February 14th, 1790, and lasted two and three quarter hours. Miranda went a good length for a man who two months later, on April 23rd, was to extol his " honest behaviour and patience " in a letter to Charles IV, in which he speaks also of " the strict and honourable loyalty I have always professed." He gave Pitt proposals hereafter to be discussed, memoranda on all the Spanish colonies, and their economic, financial, military and naval establishments ; the situation of the Spanish navy during the preceding war ; a list of the names, country of origin and residence of the South-American Jesuits exiled in Italy ; a plan for a free government in Spanish America ; a chart of Havana and its fortifications, as well as secret plans for its defence and reports on the Cuzco and Bogotá revolts with military details bearing on both cases.

Not a bad haul for Mr. Pitt. What Miranda does not seem to have suspected is that England was infinitely better organized than he was ; that he was being used as an English agent by the Foreign Office, and had been, probably since his early days when, as a very green officer, he visited Gibraltar and became acquainted with a Mr. Turnbull who was to finance him throughout nearly all his life. In 1790, despite his travels, he was still very green, as his Proposal shows. On behalf of South America, he offered trade, treasure " for to pay " not only " the service that she may receive " but " even an essential part of the national debt of England " ; he also suggested that South America " being united by a solemn compact with England, establishing a free and similar government and combining a plan of commerce reciprocally advantageous, these two nations might form the most respectable & preponderant Political Union in the World." In exchange for which he asked for 12,000 to 15,000 men and 15 sail of the line.(21)

Pitt was interested, introduced Miranda to Grenville (May) and received him several times. He used to study South America on large maps spread on the floor of his room at Downing Street, over which he crawled on all fours. There came a stage in the proceedings when his Spanish ancestry pulled at Miranda's heart, and he felt uncomfortable. As early as April 16th, Pownall had written to him regretting that any papers had been delivered to the Prime Minister—a clear hint that Miranda was not to expect them back. On March 18th, Turnbull wrote : " Although your present negotiation should have the desired effects which I have no doubt that it will, yet it will not probably for some time produce any money." Miranda was of course unaware of what was going on. At the time Pitt introduced him to Grenville, both Ministers were parleying with Bernardo del Campo, the Spanish Ambassador, over the Nootka Sound ; while preparing for an attack in strength against the Indies with British Honduras as a base, to intimidate Spain into surrendering. Floridablanca, distrustful of obtaining French help against England, compromised (October, 1790) ; and, of course, Miranda was dropped. He was disappointed and embittered. In conversation with Barteuer, a Russian Attaché, he said : " Pitt is a monster who seems to have no other guide than Macchiavelli's *Prince*. I am sold for a Treaty of Commerce with Spain."(22)

The note he sent Pitt on January 28th, 1791, voices three emotions : his new patriotism : " My own country (South America) " ; note his definition, South America ; nothing less. His lack of funds : he requests " a competent annual support," but promises to repay it as soon as he recovers his " property in South America." His uneasy feelings about Spain : " services must not be requested from me against Spain, with any other motive, being a point of delicacy with me ; tho' authorised by the right of nations, and the example of many great and virtuous men in modern, and ancient times." The worst point was that of money. Pitt promised but did not pay ; and Miranda wrote letter upon letter. His trust in Pitt began to fail him. He, the free-thinking man, seeking the help of England to free his country from Catholic bigotry, the Inquisition and all that, had to hear Pitt meet his requests for a regular support with the argument " that the Roman Catholic religion was an obstacle for holding employment here." He spoke of Catherine's offers. Pitt promised to send him £1,000 on arrears and gave him his word of honour he would not be disappointed any further. He sent him £500 and the balance in fine words. Miranda then wrote asking for an annual loan of £1,200, but did not go to Russia.(23)

Then came trouble. Pitt wrote (November 12th, 1791), " I must inform you that I cannot entertain the smallest idea of recommending you for a pension to the amount you mention," and denied ever having promised £1,000. Miranda asked to have his papers back, " without any copy, translation or other trace left ". He explained that the papers were more precious than money and pointed out that the information he had handed over was worth more than £2,000. Six months later he wrote : " Having patiently waited for six months an answer to my letter of September 18th, 1791, or at least the return of my papers which I had the honour to entrust to you. . . ." Pitt's secretary, he added, had returned four papers out of ten, explaining the others could not be found. We know which they were, for on the list of ten papers to be found in Miranda's files, four are marked with a cross in pencil. They are the only four which had no interest whatever from the point of view of military and naval intelligence. Of course the Prime Minister's office could not be expected to let papers go astray without discrimination.

" Sir ! "—writes Miranda to Pitt—" papers delivered in his own hand to the Prime Minister of Great Britain, considered by him as of the greatest national importance, . . . mislaid ! Allow me to put off any reflections which such singular circumstances might foster." But meanwhile the impecunious conspirator accepted £800 offered on condition that he would sign a paper stating the money had been paid him by Mr. Pitt. A golden ox was put on his tongue. He protested his disinterestedness, promised again to refund every penny but took the money and was compromised.

On March 20th, 1792, he left for France.(24)

*　　　*　　　*

He was anxious lest the French attempted to invade Spanish America. How he parried that move has already been told ; and his adventures as a French General, striking as they are, fall outside the scope of this work. At the close of his French cycle, when France and Spain entered into an alliance, Miranda turned his eyes to England again. He sent Turnbull to Pitt (January, 1797) explaining why he had served France and how he could no longer serve " a system so abominable " and how the war with Spain gave a new life to his own 1790 proposals. He waited eight months, sending constant letters and messengers to London. Tired of waiting, he crossed over, with a faked Russian passport (Catherine was dead), green spectacles and a wig. But the Customs Officer found a double bottom in his trunk with papers which revealed his real name. " Are you General Miranda ? "—" Perhaps "—he answered. He was most courteously treated, and having lost time on the way " because I slept between the harbour and London owing to thieves being about who had robbed other passengers two days before", he found that Pitt had been expecting him. He had crossed on January 12th, 1798, and saw Pitt at Hollwood on the 16th. He was received in a jovial and friendly way, and has left a detailed record of this interview, even to the points in the proposals, reading which, Pitt nodded assent or expressed satisfaction.(25)

Neither of the two partners was in the same position as in 1790-1. Pitt had goaded Spain into an alliance with France, which Spain did not particularly relish, by making her life as a neutral quite impossible. Archbishop Moscoso, a Creole Churchman, who as Bishop of Cuzco had done signal service during the rebellion of Condorcanqui, in his report to the Royal Council said : " It is not at France the English are aiming when they provoke a new break with her ; in this fight into which they want to draw us, they aim at the wealth of America which the Peace of Basle has saved from their hands." In the same month (August, 1796) in which the alliance was signed, Nicholas Vansittart had a scheme ready for the conquest of the Spanish Indies. The war was carried on by England with more spirit than success. Cádiz and Tenerife were attacked in vain, Tenerife costing Nelson his arm ; the mighty expedition against the Philippines was discomfited by storms ; Puerto Rico victoriously threw off its assailants. Minorca was lost by Spain, and Trinidad, then an experiment in foreign immigration, also. On April 8th, 1797, Dundas, War Secretary, wrote to Lieutenant-Colonel Picton, Governor of Trinidad, a letter promising help from England to any Spanish Americans who might revolt and assuring them that the intention of H.B.M. was " merely to enable them to maintain their commercial Independence, without any desire, on the part of the King of England, to acquire any Right of Sovereignty over them, or to interfere in their Civil, Political, or Religious Rights ; unless they themselves should, in any degree, solicit His Protection." This document was widely circulated in the mainland by Governor Picton.(26)

As for Miranda, he claimed to speak in the name of a *Junta* of Republicans of Mexico, Peru, Chile, La Plata, Venezuela and Nueva Granada, which had drafted his instructions in Paris on December 22nd, 1797. This *Junta* was to all appearances a loosely knit affair meeting now in Madrid, now in Paris. Miranda's papers mention as members, beside himself and Olavide, José del Pozo y Sucre and Manuel José de Salas. But Olavide would have nothing to do with it and never attended its meetings. Of the other two, Adams says they were Jesuits, but del Pozo, at any rate, may well have been an officer of Engineers. Moreover, it is quite likely that this *Junta* never existed outside Miranda's papers and

that it was merely called out of the void by the fertile Creole
in order to give himself more weight as a negotiator with Pitt.
Adams did not think much of it all. He thought the Jesuits
" corrupted by British mercenary policy," and as for Olavide,
he says : " I personally knew Olavide, his history, his character
[. . .] He was an old man, had been in Spain a great
man [. . .] a head stuffed with learning and curiosity
insatiable. Touched with the contagious heresy of the Holy
Church of philosophy of which Voltaire was the sovereign
Pontiff [. . .], he was obliged to fly to France, as an
asylum from the persecutions from the Court and the
Inquisition in Spain. In Paris he was tormented with ennui.
He went daily to the mesmeric experiments [. . .] You
will see with what eagerness Miranda and his associates
courted Olavide to join them, you will see the total neglect
and contempt of them shown by Olavide. I was confident he
had too much sense to have any connection with them. They
never could get him to meet them or to answer their invi-
tations." And he concludes with a series of questions, to
this day unanswered. " But who were the *Junta* in Spain ?
Who were the *Junta* in South America ? Whom did Miranda
and his two Jesuits represent ? Where were their full
powers ? "(27)

The *Junta* may have been ghostly, but the instructions were
real and probably drafted by Miranda himself—a not
unusual case with instructions. Civil and financial affairs
were delegated to Miranda and Olavide, military leadership
was entrusted to Miranda. The paper refers constantly to
" South America." The term should not be understood as
meaning the southern half of the continent, but the territory
south and west of the United States, as shown by clause 9, in
which the Mississippi is held to be " the best frontier between
the two great nations which occupy the American continent."
About the Islands, the " South Americans " declare they wish
to keep Cuba only, for they hold Havana as indispensable for
their security. The others, and they mention Puerto Rico,
Trinidad and Margarita, are in their opinion of no interest,
and they declare themselves ready " to co-operate in having
them occupied by their allies, England and the United States."

This is of the utmost interest, and should be interpreted as one of the typical *mestizo* features of Miranda's moves. There was no union between the several Indies other than their common Spanishness ; the Antilles were black at the root and Miranda felt no need to free them. Moreover, there was a certain recklessness in him, the hurry and inconsiderateness of a spendthrift ; for one of the Islands this Venezuelan was lightheartedly giving away was Trinidad, a limb of his own country ; so that at this juncture Miranda was very much like an Englishman who, towards 1685, to get rid of " the tyranny of the Scotch," should offer the French or the Dutch not only the Channel Islands but the Isle of Wight.(28)

*   *   *

As for his political ideas, Miranda was revolutionary *ma non troppo*. No man was more anxious to preserve South America against the excesses of the French Revolution ; and this theme was uppermost in his interview with Pitt. When Pitt told him England would see the American Spaniards remain for another century " under the oppressive government of the King of Spain rather than submerged by the calamities of the abominable system of France," Miranda went one better, pointing out that such was precisely his aim in seeking for his country independence and alliance with England and the United States " in order unanimously to fight if need be the monstrous and abominable principles of the so-called French liberty." He entertained a curiously optimistic opinion about the political culture of South America. In his will, drafted in 1805, he describes his travels as due to his desire " to find out the best form and plan of government to ensure a wise and prudent liberty in the Spanish American colonies ; which are in my opinion the best placed countries and the peoples best fitted for it, of all those I know." This optimism sprang from two causes : the first that Miranda did not know his own country at all. He had left it as a young man in his teens and had never returned ; his ignorance of South America may be gauged by the fact that, as late as 1787-8, he had no idea who Mutis was. The second was that for him, as for most of his fellow-conspirators, the country meant a fairly

restricted class of well-to-do Creoles. In his interview with
General Abercrombie, he records that the General feared that
once South America were free, the coloured people might
rise in arms and take over the country as they had done in
St. Domingue ; " but I pointed out to him how much fewer
the number of these people were in our provinces, where the
great majority were Indians and white people, of pure habits
and in just that point of civilization which later might wish
to establish his republic ; that moreover we were taking with
us a foreign force which in conjunction with the rational and
instructive part of the inhabitants, should remedy everything
while the new government was organized and entered into a
regular and safe stride." (29)

No mention of *mestizos*. This is a typical feature of *mestizo*
psychology, especially in a man whose share of Indian blood
was probably but slight. The draft of the preamble to the
treaty of alliance which he put forward to check the unlimited
power of France, reads as follows : " We the Free and Independent Powers of the Atlantic and America, We the King of
Great Britain, the United States of America and the Sovereign
States of the Spanish people of America. . . ." Note how
even in this document the word *Spanish* survives with a curious,
so to speak, life after death, to describe that part of the Indies
which refused to sink into the earth of the new continent.
The Constitution which he presented to Pitt was a masterpiece
of *mestizo* thought : " a House of Commons, another one of
noblemen, and a hereditary Inca." The idea of superimposing
the Yupanqui and the Tupac Amarú tradition on a tradition
dating from Magna Charta could only spring from a mixed-
blood. Pitt, who had his own views over and beyond the
innocent Miranda, must have smiled at this point, even though
he had to hide it : " He read it all attentively, and on arriving
at the article about the hereditary Inca he gave his assent
lowering his head."(30)

As soon as he recovered from his smile, the Prime Minister
put him off " for the time being." Miranda began another
spell of waiting, for which his impetuous nature was ill-suited.
By February, 1798, while he was busy putting his plans before
the American Minister, King, and writing to Hamilton, in the

belief that his idea had been taken in earnest by Pitt, Grenville told King that the Government had decided to retain Miranda in England but that it would not promote the independence of Spanish America unless Spain passed under the sway of France. Pitt was keeping Miranda as a tool for his policy, while the idealistic and unrealistic Creole filled reams of paper with military and political plans, sent his agent Caro on an adventurous and fruitless mission to Trinidad, and flooded Spanish America with copies of Vizcardo's Letter. His weak point was his impecuniousness. Turnbull financed him, but always hoping to be refunded by either Miranda or the Government. "His Lordship"—Grenville's secretary wrote to Turnbull on February 19th, 1799—"cannot hold out the smallest expectation that H.M.'s Government will defray M. de Miranda's expenses in this country." The forlorn Creole was enmeshed in the conflicting policies of England, France and the United States ; now encouraged, now discouraged by events ; and throughout the year 1798 he hoped against hope, kept at arm's length by Pitt. By January, 1799, he sought to leave for Trinidad. In September, 1798, he wrote in his diary : " Finding myself bored in this country, and in fact kept here under the most frivolous pretexts and wiles. . . ." He tried through his Russian friend Woronzow to obtain a passport. He was granted one for the United States, but not for Trinidad. And even then, when he had already bought his passage in " the American frigate *Washington*," word came from the Duke of Portland " that H.M.'s Council does not deem it advisable that General Miranda should be given a passport to leave England." Pitt did not want to throw away such a tool, and a man so willing and so incorrigibly gullible. A few weeks later, on January 30th, 1799, Miranda communicated to Dundas his papers on the Gual conspiracy. The Government informed him that H.M.'s Ministers " have determined that for the present you should not leave England ; but that [. . .] you should have a sufficient allowance to enable you to live in an easy and comfortable manner during the time it is judged expedient that you should remain in it." Miranda smelt a rat in this offer which, in his answer to the Under-Secretary of State, he

rightly contrasted with that of Grenville's secretary a few
months earlier ; and he insists that, money or no money, he
is to be asked nothing against Spain (" and I add now, nor
against France ") and that he is to work only for the independence of South America.(31)

He was right in suspecting that the change meant something.
It was a preliminary to a slick piece of military diplomacy.
On December 12th Penman wrote to him introducing " my
worthy friend Captain Rutherfurd of the Royal Engineers,"
who was " desirous of receiving some information which I
apprehend you can give him ".   Note " Royal Engineers."
" I confess "—writes Miranda out of bitter experience—" that
after all that is gone by, I have, against my nature, a certain
reluctance in speaking with officers or officials of this country."
Rutherfurd came.   " His intention is to inform himself about
the continent of South America from the military point of
view."   He persuaded Miranda that there was a plan to
attack Spain in South America, and therefore, he gave him
information " with more pleasure."   The Captain came again
and again, showed Miranda his notes to make sure they were
correct and " owned that he sent them to General Abercromby,
who is in Scotland with Mr. Dundas, and that it is all done with
the approval of H.M.'s Ministers.   I added : and for the
independence and liberty of my country, or else the whole
thing would be an infamy?—to which he definitely assented."
He was uneasy but weak.   How weak he little knew yet.
Evidently Rutherfurd thought Miranda's mine of news worth
Abercrombie's trouble.   And so the General came all the way
from Scotland.

He went straight to see Miranda.   " He shook my hand
with much friendship and suggested a talk, assuring me the
end was the absolute independence of the colonies, the inhabitants to be left in liberty to give themselves any government
they wish, with no trade monopoly [for England] nor anything
which might offend my liberal and patriotic feelings, etc. . . .
on which basis I showed him on the map what the military
operation should have to be in my opinion, possible in all
safety for 4,000 men of regular troops with four to six men of
war—against the province of Caracas ; with which he

completely agreed, saying 'now I see there is not the slightest difficulty.' . . . We then went on to speak about the province of Santa Fe, and here we found Cartagena which he thought to be an unsurmountable obstacle, but when I showed him the weak points of the defences, and particularly one point which makes them *most weak* (and which I did not show to him until he gave me his word of honour to reserve it for himself most sacredly) he agreed that the force would be sufficient, and the obstacles much smaller than he had imagined at first."

So far as General Abercrombie was concerned, the talk was over. As an expert in the West Indies, where he had been Commander-in-Chief, he had got from Miranda all he wanted. Yet the talk went on. The General raised the objection about the possible rebellion of the Blacks which Miranda smoothed over so easily. And now let Miranda tell the rest :

"As if he had waited for nothing else, this kind and good man broke into joy as if he had reached everything and shaking me by the hand said : ' Let us pray God that the Council says yes, and all is done ! I am going there this very moment.' We took leave in a most friendly way at about one thirty and agreed to meet again in his house after to-morrow.

" 11th.—This morning I had a note from the Aide de Camp R. [Rutherfurd] asking me at what time we were to go to Abercromby's house to-morrow and I suggested eleven in the morning.

" 12th.—I went to Rutherfurd's house, Vere st. towards eleven and found him very jovial ; but as we were leaving he had a note from Abercromby asking him to present one thousand apologies to me for he had been summoned by the Duke of York and could not spare a minute.

" Next day, or the next, we saw in the newspapers that Sir R. Abercromby had left for Scotland in a hurry—we could hardly believe it !

" 15th.—I went to see Rutherfurd and found him very shame-faced. He told me the General had actually gone and he could not understand, etc., etc."(32)

CHAPTER XXI

EPILOGUE

WE now possess a clear view of these precursors of Bolívar, a view shorn of much of its traditional glow by the study of the documents. For the most part they were idealists with no more than the modicum of personal ambition a man of action needs to carry his cause to victory. They were on the whole honest and sincere in their revolt against the antiquated system which the Bourbon dynasty had centralized to an unbearable degree. In their desire for a better government and for a better life, in their protest against the halters of Church and State officials, their eagerness to live and think, travel and talk and write freely, they felt at one with most of the enlightened men in the mother country. But owing to the all too frequent exclusion from the responsibilities of office of which they were the victims, these clever, active and restless Creoles were inclined to think that all the evil flowed from the centralized government of Spain. Circumstances both weighty and frivolous, the Terror of the French Revolution as well as the amorous affairs of a Queen of Spain, were apt to make the Government blow hot and cold, and now expel the Jesuits, now severely prohibit the books of the philosophers to whom the expulsion was due. These caprices of government did but increase the impatience of the leading Creole class, fretting under a distant, slow, often stupid Government, whose decisions, even when intelligent in themselves, were apt to be thrown out of gear and therefore made unintelligent by distance and delay. The Creoles were unable to realize how Spanish they themselves were ; how deeply rooted in their own being were the evils they revolted against. And even at the moment when, in the New or in the Old World, they were conspiring against Spain, they were not aware of the limitations due to their Spanish character which were hampering their effort and perhaps misdirecting it.

One of these limitations was a hastily conceived attitude

towards the very cause they had at heart. This was due to ignorance of both home and foreign conditions, and to a passionate rather than an objective outlook on life. Most of them were either incompletely versed in the actual life of their own continent or inhibited by colour, wealth and social traditions from facing it squarely as it actually was. Their eyes were on Paris and London rather than on their own cities and countrysides. Moreover, they did not know their Paris, or their London either. They were unbelievably green and innocent. That England which they all came to seek as the wonder-worker of liberty-miracles and as the midwife of new-born nations, that England was far and away the most progressive, the richest, technically the most advanced, intellectually the most distinguished, even morally the best balanced and enlightened nation in the world. Whatever rival claims France might have had, had been tarnished by the Terror. England was already the country of the rich, cultured, comfortable country-seats where an upper class of both urban and countryside aristocrats lived a life of luxury without effeminacy, of leadership without selfishness, of self-indulgence in drink and women without degeneracy, of patriotic insularity yet intelligently interested in foreign lands, well-travelled and generous, of educated taste in literature and the arts yet by no means intellectualist or academic— those English who were already raising the standards, and the cost, of travelling all over Europe, and attracting Haydn to London before helping Beethoven to die in comfort and peace. It was a great England.

Yet that England which was great was, above all, the upper class. These American Spaniards who flocked to London in the naïve belief that England was going to turn aside from the perfectly legitimate pursuit of her own political interests to put her might and treasure at the disposal of their dreams and passions, were so fascinated by her strength and skill, and by her success against the greatest empire the world had ever seen, that they made of her the incarnation of their dreams. For them England was not merely the great sea power of the north ; she was also the country governed according to Montesquieu, thinking as clearly as Voltaire and feeling as generously as Rousseau. They could hardly guess that most of the shortcomings and injustices which made them rant against Spain were also rampant in England. Time and again Miranda records his surprise at the things he saw in that England he admired so much.   For it was not the England of our days.   " On the road I noted a man hanged from the gallows for having murdered another one six years ago in 1784 " ; " A good road and a fine wheat country, and meadows—I observed on the road another man hanging from the gallows for having murdered."   This atmosphere is best brought out by a story told in 1792 by an anonymous author, of the time when he was a schoolboy : " A woman of the name of Moll Trotter took upon her the office of executioner to the Ulster circuit in Ireland, and regularly travelled after the Judges to execute the sentences they pronounced.   As Moll was a favourite with the schoolboys, they gave her a guard upon her arrival in every country town to protect her from the pelting of the mob ; and I happened to be appointed to that service when Moll's husband was left for execution in the town where I was at school, and I attended her into the jail to receive him.   When the husband was brought out of the cell, and he saw Moll coming up with the rope in her hand to halter him, he lifted up his hands and eyes, and exclaimed, ' My dear Molly, is it you that is going to do this to me ? ' ' Why, Phelim, *honey*,' says Moll, ' as long as the thing must be done, you know, what signifies it to you who it is that does it ; and would not you rather that your own dear wife should get the thirteen and fourpence for hanging you than a stranger ? ' Phelim acquiesced, and Moll turned him off with all the delicacy of her sex."(1)

This scene was of course rather out of the way, and moreover it hailed from Ulster.   But the setting, the mood, the executioner following the circuit, the mob pelting the executioner, the schoolboys forming a guard of honour, the tumultuous, uninhibited, coarse, boisterous, gay and, though callous, good humoured crowd, all that is true to the life of the period, and calls to mind Hogarth.   That crowd rejoiced in executions. And so, for that matter, did the upper classes.   As for freedom and equality, we know that the Jews and the Catholics had no civic rights and were barred from all public functions ; that in Ireland, where the Catholics, by far the majority, were not allowed to vote, the Protestant Parliament was bribed by Pitt into a union with England ; and that Pitt had to resign because the King would not accept even his mild plan for the gradual emancipation of the Catholics. These American Spaniards knew nothing about Warren Hastings or about the East India Company. They had not heard Burke thunder against the opium monopolists who in India, under the grim wings of Famine, had forced the peasants to plough up their green rice fields to sow opium. This same enlightened and generous Burke had drafted a Black Code to regulate the condition of slaves in British territory, improving their lot and making it more human, yet in which the master was left the right to inflict thirteen lashes without consulting the magistrate, while free negroes convicted of being " incorrigibly idle, dissolute and vicious " were liable to be sold back into slavery by the authorities. Some of them found out in time that all was not as rosy as their dreams. " I did not mean to write you till my final farewell "—wrote Caro to Miranda from Falmouth on May 11th, 1798, as he waited for the final arrangements for his ship to leave for Trinidad—" but let them tell me no more stories with their comment . . . *cosas de España !* To-morrow I shall have been here fifteen days waiting for the order for this boat to be allowed to sail. Everybody shouts ; passengers, businessmen &c. I have never seen such a thing with our mailships in La Coruña." Miranda was embittered by his repeated failures with Pitt and the gradual realization that he was but a tool in English hands.(2)

What did they expect? England's business was England, not Spanish-America—still less the hail of Spanish-American patriots which kept falling on her roof, all hard, all persistent, all noisy, all asking for rifles, ships and money to carry on while the country was saved, all falling in the same direction, but individual and unrelated, identical yet all different. How could the value of that country they wanted saved rise in the eyes of England, whose sons are past masters in the art of " hanging together," when all these leaders and

negotiators came loose, representing nothing but themselves ?
This was perhaps the worst failing of all these forerunners
of emancipation. They were patriotic, idealistic, right, all
too right, in their condemnation of the shortcomings of the
Spanish rule. But if they were in the main right as critics,
they failed in two respects. They took little or no account of
their own share in the shortcomings of the system they strove
to destroy, a share which, as we know, was considerable.
These revolutionary Creoles were widely read in generalities,
but not so widely about the actual facts of their country and
continent. Few knew the facts of the history of their own
America ; few even the lives and men of other cities. It is
no argument to say that Spain kept them in ignorance, for
they were not ignorant. They were in fact better educated,
more accomplished minds, more cultured men all round,
than any generation of Spanish Americans or of Spaniards
since then till quite late in the twentieth century.

Then again they failed, in that instead of seeking the remedy
for the shortcomings of the system in the reform of the system,
they sought it in destroying the system. No Spaniard can put
that down to them as a crime, for it is a typical Spanish
feature. These Creoles, rightly desirous of reform, did not
seek to study a programme in common with the progressive
Spaniards of their day, to strengthen the valuable forces
working at the time for reform in the mother country, and
so work out the salvation of the whole by methods inherent in,
and harmonious with, the whole. They flocked to London,
taking the short cut, making a bee line for the immediate
satisfaction of their political passion, which they saw as hunger
for national freedom, but which was also hunger for power.
Here again, though the fact must be stated objectively, no
Spaniard can reproach them for it. For the root of it is in
the Spanish character as well as in the dispersive conditions
of the immense and broken continent. Soon London was to
be invaded by a number of Spanish Mirandas seeking the
help of England against Napoleon, hardly ever on behalf of
Spain, nearly always on behalf of the particular local *Junta*
which sent them. And have we not seen in our day, in
Washington and London, a number of Mirandas begging

help to liberate their little local fatherland from a fatuously inexistent " tyranny of Castille ? "   No reproach must therefore be raised against these men who flocked to London to free themselves from " the tyranny of Spain." That there was a tyrannical element in the Spanish rule is obvious. That it was more unbearable than the tyranny of any other contemporary government is simply not true. That, under its sway, America gave forth the finest generation of wits, men of letters, thinkers and leaders it has so far produced is undeniable. That if these men and their Spanish-European friends had sallied forth into the world with less Spanish Quixotic indifference to realities, with more of the ballast of experience Sancho recommended in vain to his master, they might have rejuvenated all the Spains, the European and the American, and made of them a livable commonwealth of Spanish nations, is at least a permissible surmise. As it happened, they could not act better than they did. The sounding-box of History was not yet ready for such complex resonances. They worked with courage and good faith, and in that dispersive, disruptive, explosive way which is typical of Spain, as it is of the pomegranate. And the Empire, born as a pomegranate bursting forth and dispersing its grains of life throughout a continent, died also as a pomegranate strewing the continent with its grains in helpless dispersion, to be pecked at will by the eagles of power.

NOTES

CHAPTER I

1. *G.I.V.*, vol. VII, ch. XIII, p. 119 ; vol. VI, pp. 75, 78, 82, chs. XI and XII.
2. *G.I.V.*, vol. IX, pp. 229, 347, 374.
3. *G.I.V.*, vol. VI, p. 4. On Alvarado's misdeeds see *S.M.H.C.*, *G.I.V.*, chs. VIII and IX of vol. VII, particularly pp. 76, 77, 80, 81.
4. *Loc. cit.*, pp. 83, 84.
5. *G.I.V.*, vol. VIII, ch. V, p. 57 ; chs. XVI and XVII, pp. 183–6.
6. *G.I.V.*, vol. VI, p. 323. See also under Hojeda in *S.M.C.C.* and *S.M.H.C.*
7. *G.I.V.*, vol. VII, ch. VIII, p. 75.
8. *G.I.V.*, vol. VII, ch. XXV, p. 278.
9. *G.I.V.*, vol. VII, ch. XIII, p. 126 ; ch. XIV, p. 132.
10. *Código de las Siete Partidas*, Lib. II.
11. *G.I.V.*, vol. II, ch. XXIV, pp. 195–6.
12. *G.I.V.*, vol. VII, ch. X, p. 104.
13. *G.I.V.*, vol. IX, ch. XXXIV, p. 375.
14. *G.I.V.*, vol. VII, ch. XXIX, p. 343.

15. For these and other features of the Spanish character I refer the reader to my *Englishmen, Frenchmen, Spaniards.*
" *e el gobernador, como cualquiera orden y concierto que haya en los regimientos redunda en honra suya, e si por el contrario, en infamia, es notorio que tendrá más especial cuidado. . . .*" H.C. to Charles V, 15.x.1524 in *Gayangos*, p. 333.

16. *e paso vn buê soldado q se dezia sindos de portyllo natural de portillo e tenía muy buenos yndios y estava rrico e dexo sus yndios y bendio sus bienes e los rrepartio a pobres e se metio a frayle franco e fue de santa vida.* *B.D.C.*, ch. CII [CCV], vol. II, p. 460. He gives seven more cases of the same on this page alone. Dávila Padilla, quoted by *Ricard*, Book I, ch. VII, p. 156. Samano. *Cartas de Indias.* Quoted by *Ricard, loc. cit.*, p. 158. *Motolinia, loc. cit.*, p. 159. *Loc. cit.*, p. 159.

17. *Motolinia, Tratado II*, ch. X, pp. 140–141.

CHAPTER II

1. *G.I.V.*, vol. V, ch. VIII, p. 61.
2. Bodin-F., App., p. 51. *G.I.V.*, vol. VI, ch. XVI, pp. 107, 109.
3. *G.I.V.*, vol. V, ch. IX, p. 62.
4. *Vetancurt, Tratado de la Ciudad de Mexico*, p. 3.

" Delicacy and Slothfulness seem to be peculiar to the Country, perhaps because it is too good, for it is observ'd, that those who have been bred to Labour in *Spain*, grow idle there in a short Time, like the *Creolians*."—*Frézier*, p. 250.

5. On *encomiendas*, *S.P.* is indispensable, especially the whole of Book III. Definition in Book III, part I, p. 233 : " A right granted by royal pleasure to the well-deserving subjects of the Indies, to collect and appropriate the tribute of the Indians which might be trusted to them for their lives and for that of one heir, according to the laws of succession, with an obligation to see to the welfare of the Indians both in spiritual and in temporal matters and to

live and settle in the provinces in which they are entrusted with the grant, and to do homage and serve a special oath to fulfil this." Excellent modern treatise : *Zavala—I.J.* In English : New viewpoint on the Spanish Colonisation of America, by Silvio Zavala, Univ. of Pennsylvania (or Oxford) Press, 1943.

6. " To give these things of on high their immortality, so that they last as long as the world, it is meet that Y.M. order that the natives of these parts be given in perpetuity to the Spaniards who are in them or who might arrive later."—H.C. to Charles V in *Gayangos*, p. 330.   Date 15.x.1524.

S.P. says that had he been there " in the first days," " he would not have hesitated to advise in favour of perpetuity," though in his time it was no longer advisable owing to the way things had evolved.   *S.P.*, Book III, ch. XXXII, pars. 83, 54 and 57, vol. I, p. 432.

The reluctance of the Crown is proved in Cortés' letter to Charles V.   " And under another heading of your instructions, most unconquered Caesar Your Grace orders me not to distribute, entrust nor deposit any natives of these lands in any manner, arguing that it cannot be done with a good conscience ; and that to that effect, Your Highness ordered that lawyers and theologians should meet thereon, and they came to the conclusion that, since God our Lord had made them free, their liberty could not be taken from them." p. 328.

Quotation from *S.P.* in text, from Book III, ch. XXXII, vol. I, p. 431.

As for preference, *S.P.* says : " In the first place come those known as conquerors, and their sons and descendants, and then the settlers [*pobladores*], and thirdly, the pacifiers, who are those who in emergencies such as seditions or disorders which have taken place, followed the Royal Ensign, and those who since and nowadays rendered or render services worthy of such rewards, against outer or inner enemies, by sea and land, or in other forms, or those who have secured royal Letters enabling them to be supplied with encomiendas that are or might become vacant."—*S.P.*, Book III, ch. VIII, p. 29, vol. I, p. 271.

Cf. for instance, Book III, ch. VIII, pars. 2 and 9 amongst many others. Last quotation Book III, ch. XXXII, par. 57, vol. I, p. 432.

7. *A.B.*, pp. 290, 292, 293, 294, 306.

8. *A.B.*, pp. 314, 415.

9. *A.B.*, p. 318.

10. *A.B.*, pp. 321, 324–5.

Due note should be taken of the fact that the son of a European-born Spaniard is assumed to be a Creole.   The same feature reappears in an entry under the following year : 1601.   " This year the Captain Alonso Diburdinzo killed with one shot Nicolás de Arcos, a Creole of Potosí, son of Don Juan de Arcos, an old Castillian, who happened not to be in town ; he came back ; found the aggressor in jail, where the *Corregidor* had locked him to save his life ; Juan de Arcos got together with the Creoles, demolished the jail wall with crowbars, entered the jail and shot Diburdinzo dead, avenging his son's death."

11. *A.B.*, pp. 327, 326.

12. Festivals in *A.B.*, pp. 327–34.   Saulo's story, pp. 334–5.

13. *A.B.*, pp. 335–6, 338, 339.   In 1617 we hear of another *Corregidor* partial to the Basques, p. 342.   The author himself seems on the whole biased against the Basques.   In this case the Creoles are in alliance with Castillians.

14. The sonnet will be found in *M.P.*, vol. I, ch. I, p. 46.

15. *A.B.* , p. 443.   He quaintly adds : " I say this for those who are miserable , for there are also many Spaniards extremely vain and lavish."
U-J.J.-R.H., vol. III, Book V, ch. V, p. 316 ; vol. I, Book I, ch. V, p. 71.

16. *S.P.*, Book II, ch. XVII, par. 44, vol. I, p. 145.
Philip III's letter, *Amunátegui*, Part 3, ch. I, vol. III, pp. 68–9.

17. *U.-J.J.-R.H.*, vol. I, ch. IV, pp. 48–9.
Anonymous, pp. 286–305.

The last quotation is from *Dickson*, p. 37. It comes at the end of the following paragraph : " Men are sometimes punished in this country [*Barbados*] for cruelty to brutes ; but I am sorry to say I know of no instance of an owner having been prosecuted for abusing his slave. But no laws can reach the nameless and endless injuries which the blacks very often suffer from miscreant white men, against whom *their evidence is not in any shape, admitted.*"

Further on he explains what this means : " Many of the poor whites are disposed to take, and too many of them do take, every advantage over the Negroes which the laws leave in their power. Some of them too much depend, for a subsistence, on robbing the slaves of, or, at least, taking, at their own prices, the trifling commodities the poor things may be carrying to market, or, by seizing and *illegally* converting to their own use, articles of greater value which the slaves may have purloined from their owners. Should a slave struggle, as he often will, to retain the disputed article, a beating is, sometimes, added to the *robbery*, as it is justly called by the better sort of people. For such usage the party injured has no redress, for he often dares not complain to his owner, and, when he does, the fact remains to be proved."—p. 41.

" Mutilation is very seldom indeed inflicted by owners on their slaves, in Barbadoes. But miscreant drunkards and desperadoes, who sometimes murder slaves, do not much hesitate in committing less atrocious acts of violence on them." So says Dickson who reports two cases personally known to him : that of an elderly Negro woman who came to him, " bathed in her blood, from a very large gash in her head. [. . . .] She said she knew (and I am pretty sure, I know) the white man who cut her, and that *a great many Negroes* saw the deed done. *This was no proof.*" The other one, that of " a valuable and inoffensive negro man, belonging to an acquaintance of mine," who " was attacked, one evening, when going on his owner's business, by a white man, who, with one stroke of his cutlass, severed one of his hands from his body. His owner, who could produce no *white* evidence, was obliged quietly to put up with the damage, and the poor fellow with the loss of his *precious limb*."—p. 137.

CHAPTER III

1. Figures of high officials, amongst many others, in *Moses*, cap. V, p. 112 ; other references : *U.-J.J. N.S.*, p. 434 ; *A.B.*, pp. 470–1, *U.-J.J. N.S.*, p. 626.

2. *S.P.*, Book III, ch. VIII, vol. I, p. 267 ; Book IV, ch. XIX, vol. II, p. 163, with excellent arguments, particularly par. 25. Case of Fray Alonso de Agüero in Naples, *S.P.*, Book II, ch. XXX, par. 4, vol. I, p. 219. *Loc. cit.*, par. 7 ; and 7 to 18.

3. *T.M.I.L.*, ch. XXVI, vol. II, p. 355. *S.P.*, Book IV, ch. XIX, par. 25 vol. II, p. 167.

In 1681, Don Juan Henriquez, President of Chile, excused himself to the King for sending a list of approved candidates to a canonry, all of whom were Creoles, adding that " there is no doubt that in view of this reward, those born here will endeavour to work in learning and letters, acquiring greater merits to come by the fruit of their labours."—*T.M.I.C.*, vol. I, p. xcviii.

There is an interesting list of over 100 Chilean students of Lima University in *T.M.I.C.*, vol. I., ch. XV. Nearly all made good, and some brilliant, careers in the Church or the State or both. Pp. 433 *et seq.*

T.M. says that from the first half of the XVIIIth century, " as had been observed for some time, the Inquisitors were no longer sent from Spain but chosen among the Churchmen settled in the Indies or even born in them." He adds that the chief reason for this was to save travelling expenses. *T.M.I.L.*, ch. XXIV, vol. II, p. 355.

Feijóo. Teatro Crítico, IV, 6. *Rivadeneyra*, vol. 56, pp. 155–6.

4. *U.-J.J. N.S.*, pp. 508–12.

5. *Gage*–48, ch. XII, p. 55.

6. *S.P.*, Book IV, ch. XIX, par. 20, vol. II, p. 167.

7. On lances, etc., *S.P.*, Book III, ch. XXXIII, particularly pars. 2, 14, 19 and 20.

8. See my *Rise of the Spanish American Empire*, ch. II, section under note 13.

9. *U.—J.J. N.S.*, pp. 420, 421, 425, 419.

10. See ch. VII below.

11. *H. E.P.N.E.*, Book VI, ch. XIV, vol. II, p. 802.
U.—J.J. N.S., p. 172.
H., E.P.N.E., *loc. cit.*, p. 816.

12. *H. P.N.*, Book IV, ch. XIII, vol. II, p. 593.

13. *A.B.*, p. 344.

CHAPTER IV

1. *Breve y Sumaria Relación* to Ph. II by Dr. Alonso de Zorita, *oidor* of Mexico. *C.D.I.A.I.*, vol. II, p. 7.
G.I.V., vol. VIII, ch. XXIII, p. 267.
Cf. " and I found that the Chichimecas and the Tlaxcatecs have settled in it, though they do not inter-marry." Referring to some internal colonisation by the viceroy Luis de Velasco II in *Vetancurt, Tratado de la Ciudad de Mexico*, p. 11.
In each *pueblo*, and even in each quarter, the Indians speak a different language, belonging to that place from the days of old. They use no common language, neither the Inca nor any other ; the only one nearly all know, which is general, is Castillian. Description of the province of Guayaquil, 1608. *C.D.I.A.I.*, vol. IX, p. 260.
There are three nations of these Chichimecas, each with a different language, and with different lines and designs painted on the face and body.—Description of Tampico. *C.D.I.A.I.*, vol. IX, p. 177.
Those of this country do not agree on a common and general language and every *pueblo* speaks its own, which causes not a little discord and wars between them. [. . .] Now the language of these Indians is Castillian. They are all very much hispanified and many know reading and writing, and in every *pueblo* there are some who sing well to the organ and in church services. —Description of Puerto Viejo in Peru. *Loc. cit.*, p. 286.
The languages spoken by the inhabitants are several : the older inhabitants speak their own ; those of Tosagua, Conchipa and Toal another one, and those of Pasao have none but Castillian ; these people are more developed than other Indians and have an Indian school master who teaches them to read and write.—Description of Catarama, Peru. *Loc. cit.*, p. 301.
Similarly, p. 356, and several others.
On the Chibchas, *Restrepo–V*.

2. This generation of terrible and cruel men came from the Mexican region and peopled that of Panama, that of Darién and all those great mountains which go till the New Kingdom of Granada and on the other side to Santa Marta.— Father Valera quoted by *G.I.V.*, vol. I, ch. XI, p. 76.
On textiles and designs : *Ueber alt-peruanische Gewebemuster und ihnen analoge Ornamente der alt-klassischen Kunst* von *Dr. Alphons Stübel. Festschrift zur Jubelfeier des 25jährigen Bestehens des Vereins für Erdkunde zu Dresden*, 1888, p. 54. *Stübel–A.*, p. 76.
G.I.V., vol. II, ch. LI, p. 346. *Torquemada*, Book VI, ch. XXIV, vol. II, p. 48.

3. *G.I.V.*, vol. I, ch. XI, pp. 73–6.

4. *H.C.*, vol. I, p. 323 footnote. Humboldt holds this to castigate with it the slave owners of the Spanish Islands who asked to be allowed to reduce but gradually the number of their slaves.

5. *G.I.V.*, vol. III, ch. LI, p. 376.
Als wir in Huila ankamen, war der Gobernador (in Indianerdörfern der Ortsvorsteher) und einige andere Personen in Chicha (Maisbier) stark betrunken. Stübel-C., p. 37.

6. *Zorita, loc. cit. Vetancurt*, ch. XIII, p. 91.

7. *Manifiesto* in *Vetancurt*, pp. 96, 98, 96, 95.

Data on drunkenness are, of course, far too frequent for quotation. For instance : Martín Cortés to Philip II. *C.D.I.A.I.*, vol. IV, pp. 442–3 ; *Zorita, C.D.I.A.I.*, vol. II, p. 107 ; *Stübel* in many places ; *Rivet*, p. 79 : *On peut affirmer sans exagération que tout indien, homme ou femme, est plus ou moins alcoolique.*

8. *Manifiesto* in *Vetancurt*, p. 100.

9. Dr. Rivet, *Etude sur les Indiens de la Région de Riobamba. Journal de la Société d'Américanistes de Paris.* Pp. 75–6, 1903–4.
A curious study full of excellent observations, yet marred now and then by a supercilious and superficial attitude. Speaking of the *apegado* Indians, Dr. R. says : " *Ainsi que son nom l'indique, il ne reçoit aucune paie.*" The trouble is that even if it had been *apagado*, Dr. R.'s ethymology would not have worked. Spanish is not so simple as it looks (p. 71). Again p. 76 we read *Die Volkauberge von Ecuador*, instead of *Die Vulkanberge von Ecuador*.

10. *Der Indianer sucht bei Kirchenfesten, die oft mehrere Tage dauern, das Elend seines Daseins in einem tüchtigen Chicha-Rausche zu vergessen Die Anzüge, die bei diesen Tänzen zur Verwendung kommen, gehören nicht den Indianern, die sie angelegt haben, sondern etwas wohlhabenderen Leuten, welche es lieber sehen, wenn sie nicht zur autochthonen Rasse gezählt werden, obgleich ihr Gesicht sehr dafür sprechen mag. Stübel-E.*, pp. 313 and 308.

11. *Sie fast ausnahmslos auf der Brust ein oft fussgrosses silbernes reich verziertes Cruzifix tragen [. . .] Die nicht recht wissen ob sie ihr Vertrauen mehr dem christlichen Wunderglauben oder mehr den indianischen Geheimmitteln zuwenden sollen. Stübel-E.*, p. 316. On this point *Ricard*, ch. II. Part III is excellent.

12. This is also the opinion of Ricard who in this as in most religious matters is a shrewd and wise observer of Indian life. See, for instance, p. 324.
It is noteworthy that one often comes across cases of Indians taking part in religious services as singers or musicians without requiring a salary. For instance : " In everyone of these *pueblos* there are eight, ten or twelve Indians who sing in church and serve in the divine services, without asking for any salaries at all."—Description of Pánuco, 1608, *C.D.I.A.I.*, vol. IX, p. 155.
Similar cases of Indians who volunteer to sing in church in Nombre de Dios, Puerto Viejo, Amatlan, etc., *loc. cit.*, pp. 179, 246, 286, 316. Superstitions of Spanish origin, some in *Ricard*, p. 60. Here is another one : " Half a league from Hambato there is a very big stone and on it eight human footsteps printed. They are worshipped by the Indians, who say they are of the Apostle St. Bartholomew, of whose preachings they know from an ancient tradition." Description of the province of Villar Don Pando.—*C.D.I.A.I.*, vol. IX, p. 457.

13. " The Indians in common were poor in cattle, for not even the *curacas* had enough for themselves and for the families ; and on the contrary, the sun and the Inca had an innumerable amount of it."—*G.I.V.*, vol. III, ch. IX, p. 54.
" The poor people in general were poor in cattle, save the Collas [the Inca family] who owned much ; and therefore they suffered from want of meat, and only ate it by gift of the *curacas*, or perhaps a rabbit which on days of

great festival they killed out of those they bred at home and they called coy."
Vol. III, ch. XXV, p. 268.

"Their so high a perfection of owning nothing which was their own . . ."
says Father Acosta in high evangelical praise of the Peruvian Indians.—
Quoted by *G.I.V.*, vol. III, ch. IX, p. 56.

As for their moving about, here is what Garcilaso says : "It is true that
they never travelled for their pleasure, nor on their own business or similar
errands, for they had nothing of their own to travel for, but only on orders of
the King and of the *curacas*." *Loc. cit.*, p. 61.

14. See *Stübel–A.*, but better still *Stübel–K.I.* and in particular vol. II,
tables 13 and 12. In this last, number 2, a garment strongly influenced by
Spanish civilisation, sticks nevertheless to the stiff cross-like shape of the arms.

15. *Fragmentos de la obra general sobre Historia de los Mexicanos escrita en
lengua Nauatl por Cristóbal de Castillo a fines del siglo XVI. Los tradujo del
Castellano Francisco del Paso y Troncoso, Director en Misión del Museo Nacional
de Mexico Florencia.* 1908.
Motolinia, Tratado III, ch. XII, pp. 210, 201. See also other examples of
imitative ability in this and other chapters of Motolinia.
G.I.V., vol. II, ch. V, p. 43.

16. *G.I.V.*, vol. I, ch. XXXIX, p. 287 ; *G.I.V.*, vol. III, ch. XVIII, p. 134.
S.P., Book II, ch. XVII, vol. I, p. 42 ; *Ricard*, Part III, ch. II, p. 328.

17. *L'indien est menteur de naissance, un peu à la façon des enfants toujours
maltraîtés et battus.—Rivet*, p. 79. On the preceding page he writes : "*Descendant d'une race sans cesse opprimée, chargé d'une hérédité de trois siècles de mauvais
traîtements et de vie misérable, l'indien a l'allure et le caractère des êtres longtemps
asservis.*" As usual everything is due to those "three centuries." But all
Frenchmen are not so shallow. Here is what *Ricard* says explaining how the
Mexican Indians tried at first to resist evangelisation : "*Ils se défendirent par
l'inertie et la dissimulation. L'organisation tyrannique du Mexique précortésique
les avaient rompus à ce genre de lutte.*" *Ricard*, Book III, ch. II, p. 315.

CHAPTER V

1. *G.I.V.*, vol. V, ch. VIII, p. 49 ; vol. VIII, ch. XII, p. 133.
H.C., vol. I, p. 316.
Stübel–C., p. 60.
H. P.N., Book VIII, ch. XXIII, vol. II, p. 446.

2. *G.I.V.*, vol. II, ch. XIII, pp. 98–99 ; vol. VI, ch. XLI, p. 312. The
whole chapter devoted to this subject.
U.—J.J., N.S., pp. 312–313.

3. *G.I.V.*, vol. IV, ch. XLVII, p. 393.
Though in general I have followed Garcilaso, I am aware that there is a
school of modern Peruvian historians who believe him unduly influenced by
his mother's race into presenting the Inca régime under too rosy a colour.
See in particular Raul Porras Barrenechea, in his *Discurso de Recepción to the
Academia Peruana*, in which he contrasts Garcilaso with Sarmiento de Gamboa,
and declares his preference for Sarmiento's as a truer and more virile presenta-
tion of the facts (p. 11).—*Homenaje a Don Francisco Pizarro. Lima*, 1941.
See also my own discussion on the death of Tupac Amarú below.

4. *G.I.V.*, vol. VI, ch. XIII, p. 91.
G.I.V. says that after the Conquest the tributary Indians retained their
mother's style of dress, "thus avoiding much corruption which the showy
and proud mode of dress usually causes. But the Indians who served Spaniards
or lived in their cities went astray in this with much detriment of their estate
and conscience." Vol. IV, ch. IX, p. 75.

5. *G.I.V.*, vol. V, ch. XIII, p. 95.

6. Martín Cortés to Philip II, *C.D.I.A.I.*, vol. IV, pp. 442–441. This unfavourable opinion of Martín Cortés should be considered by those who claim the *Cajas de Comunidad* as one of the successful institutions of the Spanish rule. *Viñas*, for instance, who, p. 104, quotes the Viceroy of Peru, Marqués del Villar on " the considerable amount of money and silver which the Indians kept in their *cajas de comunidad*, coming from their lands and cattle." To be sure the idea was excellent, but it is not certain, when one reads Martín Cortés, that it was not, like many other ideas, twisted from its original intention and turned to the detriment of the Indians. Zorita to Philip II. *C.D.I.A.I.*, vol. II, pp. 82–3.

7. *Loc. cit.*, pp. 83–4, 86.

8. *H., P.N.*, Book VII, ch. XXII, vol. II, pp. 410 *et seq.*

9. *H., E.P.N.E.*, Book V, ch. XII, vol. II, pp. 666–8. Humboldt seems to call Don Luis de Velasco " *le second vice-roi de la Nouvelle Espagne*," but he means Don Luis de Velasco II, Viceroy of New Spain.

10. *Zorita, C.D.I.A.I.*, vol. II, p. 105.

11. These quotations come from the answers sent to Spain on a questionary prepared by the Council of the Indies, discussed above. (There is an error in the numbering of the pages of *C.D.I.A.I.* which makes references difficult to handle.) Texts from *C.D.I.A.I.*, vol. IX, pp. 421, 220, 244, 243, 455.

Complete home rule of the Indians and a free life based on ownership of land and free work are too frequent for quotation in these descriptions which, though official, are singularly outspoken as to abuses. " The business of the Indians is to attend to their maize-lands, which they sow twice a year in very good lands they have "—p. 159 ; " all are subject to one *cacique*, to whom they contribute nothing, and his sole authority over them is in matters of government ; the Indians appoint him every year, as well as two *alcaldes* and a chief constable and two constables and an inspector of weights "—p. 157. *Description of Tanteyac, Province of Pánuco.*

Identical cases, pp. 163, 164, 165, 174, 207, 208, 215, 218, 264 (" everyone chooses his land and sows where he likes, paying no rent "), 272, 274, 291, 292, 294, 300, 321, 327, 380–81, 456, 482, 485.

Even in mining districts, we read of free Indian labour very early. " The Indians have all come from other and different lands and they serve the miners for wages, and some come and some go every day."—*Description of Nuestra Señora de los Zacatecas.* 1608. P. 185.

We read of salaries of three to five *pesos* a month plus a ration of meat, maize and chili. P. 199.

In the few country estates, " the Indians serve of their own will and everyone earns per year fifty or sixty *pesos*." P. 188.

12. Zorita, *C.D.I.A.I.*, vol. II, pp. 113–119.

I have set down his remark about the human bones marking the road, though similar observations have been made in quite modern times by travellers who witnessed to the deadly character of some of the high passes in the Andes when nature is unfavourable. " Of which we had an ocular demonstration in the several skeletons of persons lying by the side of the road." *Hamilton–T.*, vol. II, p. 18.

13. *U.—J.J., N.S.*, pp. 289, 290, 292.

As a yardstick with which to estimate these facts, here are some paragraphs from an English officer's book of travels published in 1833 and referring to his time, just about one century later. " Let us now take a glance at slavery in other countries, and first let us make an *exposé* of an Oriental punishment which I have often been obliged most reluctantly to superintend. In the East Indies, if a person is unable to pay his debts to another, the debtor becomes the slave of the creditor until the amount is paid off.   Now, in the regiments of cavairy, there is a grass-cutter to collect forage for each horse ; these are under a head man, called on the Madras establishment a choudry ; the grass-cutters are of both sexes, but principally women, and are often slaves of the choudry.   When the bundles of grass are paraded in the troop-lines of an evening, the choudry measures them with a stick, to see that they are of the regulated height, length and thickness ; if any are deficient, the grass-cutters who brought them, whether male or female, old or young, are ordered to the front, and the choudry taking a Russian knout from his shoulders, or a short stick with a very long and heavy lash, inflicts with it such a flagellation, under the superintendence of an officer, that, compared with it, the fifteen lashes that negroes receive with a cat or cow skin are nothing.   Talk of the severity of West Indian punishment after this ! "—*Alexander*, vol. 1, pp. 116–17.

14. *U.—J.J.*, N.S., p. 292.

15. Acosta quoted by *G.I.V.*, vol. III, ch. IX, p. 58.   Numerous parallel passages in Blas de Valera, Mendieta, Motolinia, Las Casas, Torquemada and Zorita.   On the point of the impulse forward of Western history *see Berdyaev*.

16. *Sahagún*, Book X, ch. XXVII.

CHAPTER VI

1. *Labat*, vol. II, Part IV, ch. VII, pp. 39–40.

2. *Loc. cit.*, p. 48.

Captain Cazalis, of the French Company of Asiento, was accused of contra- band against his own company (1705–6) and among other things, he had sold " *les chemises et hardes destinées aux nègres, de sorte que sur cinq cents soixante-trois, dont se composait la cargaison prise en Guinée, il en était mort deux cents soixante quinze de froid et de misère.*"—*Scelle*, vol. II, p. 402.

Moreton, p. 136.

" By examples too many to be enumerated, and too shocking to be repeated, the House was constrained to admit that no savage of America ever displayed more implacable malevolence, more refined and ingenious cruelty, in tormenting his prisoner, than British captains have exhibited in the usage of the wretched slaves whom they have purchased."—Remarks on the late decision of the House of Commons respecting the abolition of the slave trade, by Thomas Gisborne, M.A., London, 1792 (*No. 6 Godwin pamphlets Bodleian* 2074), pp. 15–16.

Quelques envieux du Commerce des François, ont fait courir le bruit parmi les Nègres, que nous ne les achetions, & ne les transportions dans nos Colonies, que pour les manger.   Cette calomnie, indigne de gens qui portent le nom de Chrétiens a été cause que beaucoup de Nègres se sont désespérez pendant le voiage, & ont mieux aimé se jeter dans la mer, & se noyer, que d'aller dans un Pais, où ils s'ima- ginoient qu'on les devoient dévorer, comme ils savent qu'il se pratique en quelques lieux de l'Afrique.—*Labat*, loc. cit. 47.

He finds un-Christian this calumny against the slave traffic practised by his countrymen, but not the traffic itself.   The calumny, however, does not seem to be the actual cause of the fear of the Blacks to be devoured by the Whites ; for nearly a century later (*Labat :* 1698—*Dickson :* 1789) we read in Dickson after a description of a *scramble* or sale of Indians : " To compleat your idea, Sir, of this infernal uproar, you must be informed that some of the Africans, as is understood from those who afterwards speak English, are so possessed with the apprehension of their being bought up to be fattened and roasted and eaten, that they pine to death or commit acts of desperation, from that cause alone.   The effect of such an idea on their minds must be the same, as if the whites really fed on human flesh ; and, no doubt they look upon their purchasers as so many furious cannibals ' rushing down,' to devour them."—*Dickson*, p. 112.

3. *Moreton*, pp. 144–5.

4. *Dickson*, p. 112. The description, pp. 110–11, is perhaps even worse. Similar scenes will be found in *Pinckard's Notes on the West Indies*, particularly vol. II, p. 325.

5. *Labat*, Part I, ch. XX, vol. I, p. 149.
The story had reached the ears of *Pinckard* who in his *Notes on the West Indies*, Letter XXIV, vol. I, p. 274, tells it in his way. By then it seems to have become simpler, and the slave owner (he does not know his name) threatened only " to transmigrate with them, carrying the whip in his hand into their own country." Which seems to have sufficed.

6. *Labat*, Part IV, ch. VII, vol. II, p. 61.

7. *Labat*, Part IV, ch. VII, vol. II, p. 61.

8. *Loc. cit.*, pp. 51, 58, 60 and 59.
Cf. : Their taste for melody and harmony, if it does not demonstrate their rationality, ought at least to be admitted as an argument improving their *humanity*. The same may be said of their patriotism, a principle which glows in their bosoms, with an ardour which does them honour. That man must be callous indeed, who can remain an indifferent spectator of a meeting of two poor Africans, who may have been dragged from the same district of their native land.—*Dickson*, p. 75.

9. *Labat, loc. cit.*, pp. 58, 59 ; *loc. cit.*, p. 59.

10. *Anonymous*, p. 286.   *U.—J.J., R.H.*, vol. I, ch. IV, pp. 49–50.   Cf. *D.L.*, vol. I, p. 285, in the same sense.

11. *Labat, loc. cit.*, pp. 50, 51.

12. *Loc. cit.*, p. 50.

13. *Dickson*, pp. 73, 76.

14. *Labat, loc. cit.*, p. 53 ; *Haenke*, p. 31.

15. *Nous étions de nouveau frapppés de la gaité turbulente des noirs.* [in Venezuela].—*H., P.N.*, Book V, ch. XV, vol. II, p. 33.

16. To the numerous data already given may be added : " *Le nombre des affranchis est très considérable : les lois et les moeurs espagnoles favorisent l'affranchissement. Les exemples de personnes qui, par testament, donnent la liberté à un certain nombre d'esclaves, sont plus communs dans les provinces de Venezuela que partout ailleurs.*—*H., P.N.*, Book IV, ch. XII, vol. I, p. 572.
Haenke, p. 35.
U.—J.J., R.H., vol. I, ch. IV, Part I, p. 43.

17. *Haenke*, pp. 32–33.

18. *Labat, loc. cit.*, p. 58.

19. *Descripción de Lima*, by Father Bernabé Cobo. 1629. Quoted by *P.B.A.L.*, p. 12.
Gillespie, ch. VII, p. 84.
His allusion to the West Indies is corroborated by many passages in a number of authors, such as *Dickson, Anonymous* and singularly in *Labat : Les Anglois ménagent très peu leurs Nègres ; ils les nourrissoient [sic] très mal, la plûpart leur donnent le samedy pour travailler pour compte ; afin de s'entretenir de tous leurs besoins eux & leurs familles ; leurs Commandeurs les poussent au travail à outrance, les battent sans miséricorde pour la moindre faute & semblent se soucier moins de la vie d'un Nègre que de celle d'un cheval [. . .] Les Ministres ne les instruisent point, & ne les baptisent point ; on les regarde à peu près comme des bêtes [. . .] On souffre qu'ils aient plusieures femmes, & qu'ils les quittent quand il leur plait ; pourvu qu'ils fassent bien des enfants [. . .] On punit très rigoureusement les moindres désobéissances, & encore plus les révoltes, ce qui n'empêche qu'ils n'en arrive très souvent, parce que ces malheureux, se voyant*

poussés à bout plus souvent par leurs commandeurs yvrognes, déraisonnables &
barbares, que par leurs Maîtres, perdent à la fin patience, s'assemblent, se jettent
sur ceux qui les ont maltraîtez, les déchirent & les mettent en pièces ; & quoiqu'ils
soient assurez d'en être punis d'une manière très cruelle, ils croyent avoir beaucoup
fait quand ils se sont vengez de leurs impitoyables boureaux [sic]. *C'est alors*
que les Anglois courent aux armes, & en font de grands massacres, ceux qui sont
pris & conduits en prison sont condamnez à être passez au moulin, brûlez tout vifs
ou exposez dans des cages de fer qui les serrent, de manière qu'ils ne peuvent faire
aucun mouvement, & en cet état on les attache à une branche d'arbre où on les
laisse périr de faim & de rage.   On appelle cela mettre un homme au sec.—Labat,
Part IV, ch. XIX, vol. II, p. 134.

Les Anglois ne baptisent point leurs esclaves, soit par négligence, ou par quelque
autre motif.—Labat, Part V, ch. I, vol. II, p. 194.   He reports his discussions
on the subject with English divines. He reports a Christian atmosphere with
regard to the slaves at the house of a Mr. Vambel, director of the Danish
Company in St. Thomas Island :   *Toutes les Négresses qui servaient à table*
avaient une croix d'or au col.—Part V, ch. XIV, vol. II, p. 286.

20. *Gillespie, loc. cit.   Labat,* vol. II, pp. 43 *et seq.*

21. See, for instance, *Labat,* on the Maroons of St. Vincent :—*On a souvent*
fait des projets d'armement pour aller enlever ces Nègres et les porter vendre aux
Espagnols.—Part IV, ch. XXI, vol. II, p. 148.

Similarly, a Negro guilty of having had intercourse with a white woman,
though she honestly declared she had provoked him to it, was " *envoyé à la*
Côte d'Espagne où il fut vendu."—Part II, ch. VI, vol. I, p. 36.

This traffic of Negroes not fresh from Africa but caught somehow in the
Indies was sometimes part of the contraband or clandestine commerce then
carried on by everybody in the teeth of Spanish laws.—*Scelle,* vol. II, p. 318.

22. *P.P.*, p. 55.

D.L. provides an interesting parallel between the treatment of black slaves
in French and English territories and in Spanish and Portuguese lands which
he considers, as does Humboldt, much preferable. He writes : " *M. de*
Humboldt a prouvé, dans sa Statistique du Mexique, *que le travail des esclaves*
coûte plus cher que celui des gens libres. Etait-ce donc la peine de s'expatrier, de
transporter ses capitaux si loin, de commettre tant d'injustices et de cruautés, pour
un intérêt si ordinaire ?   On croit communément en Europe, que l'argent qu'on
emploie à acheter une bonne habitation dans les colonies, rapporte quinze pour cent
et quelquefois plus.   La chose est vraie lorsque l'habitation est bien et humainement
administrée.   Ce qui ruine la plupart des propriétaires, c'est la mortalité des
nègres.   Sur mille transportés d'Afrique, le chagrin ou une mauvaise administration
en fait périr un tiers, dans les premiers trois mois après leur débarquement ; et
au bout de six ou sept ans, les sept ou huit dixièmes des autres sont morts.   A la
Trinidad, à Tabago et à la Grenade, on calcule qu'on est très heureux, lorsque sur
trente jeunes nègres achetés dans le courant d'une année, il y en a six de bien portans
cinq ans après.   Sur la plupart des habitations, les nègres ont peu d'enfans ; le
tiers de ces enfans ne parvient pas à l'âge d'un an, et la moitié de l'autre tiers ne
parvient pas à celui de quatre, âge auquel on les regarde comme réchappés, *suivant*
l'expression du pays.   Mais il est, je dois le dire, des habitations dans les colonies
françaises et anglaises, où la population va croissant, comme dans les pays les mieux
administrés.   Elle s'accroît presqu'à l'égal de la population blanche dans les
colonies espagnoles et portugaises, parce que les nègres y sont traités avec beaucoup
d'humanité."

His impartiality is immediately established, for he goes on to praise the estate
of one Sir William Young, of Saint Vincent, as " *de toutes les habitations françaises,*
anglaises et espagnoles que j'ai connues, celle ou régne l'ordre le plus admirable."
And he develops his description of this model estate belonging to an intelligent
and humane Briton ;   a case the more remarkable since Saint Vincent was one
of the worst colonies in this respect.—Vol. I, pp. 274 *et seq.*

CHAPTER VII

1. See *Zavala I.J.* Opening chapters, for the shortlived attempt on the part of a number of settlers and even a few friars to represent the Indians as " speaking beasts." It never gained any footing in the opinion of either Church or State.

2. *G.I.V.*, vol. X, ch. XXIV, pp. 268–70 ; vol. XI, ch. XIV, p. 161.

3. *Alexander*, vol. I, p. 117. Here are more details of how Negro slaves fared in the Dutch West Indies : " The manner in which men and women are punished with the cart-whip is stated to be thus :—Both sexes are stripped entirely naked, the wrists and ankles are firmly tied together with cords ; the victims, thus ' huddled up,' are laid on the ground on their right sides ; a stake passing between their legs and arms, and driven into the ground, effectually pins them to the earth. They are flogged on one buttock till it is quite raw, and then they are turned over and unmercifully chastised on the other, by black drivers, under the eye of a Dutch overseer quietly smoking his pipe ! After one hundred and fifty or two hundred lashes are inflicted, the sufferers are lifted up, as they are unable to rise or stand alone, and it is frequently a month before they are sufficiently well to resume their work. Anyone sending a Negro to the jail may have one hundred and fifty lashes inflicted by the executioner for one dollar, and so on, pain in proportion to the number of lashes required. [. . .] There is only one doctor with a regular diploma in the whole of the extensive colony of Surinam ; ignorant Negro doctors are all the poor slaves have. The mortality is dreadful but the supply abundant. [. . .] There is a community of seven thousand lepers far in the woods of Surinam—men, women and children, cast off from all attendance, all comforts ; a Catholic priest alone volunteered to administer spiritual consolation to them and live near them."—*Alexander*, vol. I, pp. 119–120. Cf. also *Pinckard's West Indies*.

4. *Grahame*, App., p. 506. *G.I.V.*, vol. VII, ch. XXIII, pp. 255–9.

5. *G.I.V.*, vol. VIII, ch. III, pp. 30–33.

6. *G.I.V.*, vol. VII, ch. XX, pp. 207 *et seq.*

7. *G.I.V.*, vol. VIII, ch. XVI, p. 180 ; ch. X, p. 107.

8. *Descripción de la provincia de San Francisco de la Victoria de Villcapampa* by Baltasar de Ocampo, in *S.G.–C.M.*, p. 206, for Don Carlos Inca and his Spanish wife. For the other mixed marriages, there is an abundance of bibliography which need not be specified.

9. *G.I.V.*, vol. VIII, ch. XX, p. 231 ; vol. VII, ch. XXXI, p. 372

10. For battle of Salinas, *G.I.V.*, vol. VII, ch. XXXI, p. 360 ; for Chupas battle, vol. VIII, ch. XX, p. 225 ; for battle of Huarina, vol. X, ch. XXII, p. 242 ; for familiar and unfamiliar Indians, vol. VII, p. 369.

11. *G.I.V.*, vol. IX, ch. XXXIV, p. 379. *Varia. B.*, No. 1, fol. 4 and 5.

12. *G.I.V.*, vol. VI, ch. XLII, pp. 325–9.

13. *Loc. cit.*

14. *G.I.V.*, vol. II, ch. VII, p. 46 ; vol. IX, ch. XXXIV, p. 377.

15. *G.I.V.*, vol. X, ch. XXIII, p. 259 ; vol. VII, ch. XXX, p. 350.

Montesclaros to his successor. Lima, April 7th, 1612. *C.D.I.A.I.*, vol. VI, p. 224. *G.I.V.*, vol. XIII, ch. IV, p. 35.

16. *A.B.*, p. 314. Montesclaros, *loc. cit. U.—J.J.*, *N.S.*, p. 289. *S.P.*, Book II, ch. XXX, par. 26, vol. I, p. 221.

17. *S.P.*, Book II, ch. XXX, par. 21, vol. I, p. 221　*T.M.I.P.C.*, p. XLI.

18. *S.P.*, Book II, ch. XXX, par. 21, vol. I, p. 221 ; par. 31, p. 222 ; par. 29, p. 222.

19. *Crónica Mexicana de Fernando de Alvarado Tezozomoc* (probably written towards 1589) ; being vol. IX, pp. 5–196 of *Antiquities of Mexico*, edited by Lord Kingsborough. London, 1831.
Historia Chichimeca, por Don Fernando de Alva Ixtlilxochitl, same volume of same collection, pp. 197–316.
Relaciones Históricas, por Don Fernando de Alva Ixtlilxochitl, same volume of same collection, pp. 317–468.
G.I.V., vol. X, ch. XXXIII, p. 355.

20. Pamphlet by Fernando Pimentel Ixtliulxuchitl, October 25th, 1821. Mexico. Pamphlets British Museum. 9770. Bb. 9, pp. 1–45.

21. *U.—J.J.*, *N.S.*, p. 177.

CHAPTER VIII

1. *Labat*, Part IV, ch. VII, vol. II, p. 61.

2. *Anonymous*, p. 141.

3. *Gage*–48, ch. XII, p. 56.
Labat, Part II, ch. VI, vol. I, p. 33.
Moreton, pp. 105, 106.
Dickson, pp. 93, 213.
As a rider to this remark of Dickson, intermarrying between Blacks and Whites was not allowed in the Danish colonies of the West Indies until 1830. *P.-P.*, p. 53.

4. *Labat, loc. cit.*
Miranda–Archivo, vol. I, p. 200.

5. *U.—J.J., R.H.*, Part I, ch. IV, vol. I, p. 53.
Felix de Azara. *Descripción e Historia del Paraguay y del Río de la Plata*. Madrid, 1847, ch. XV, quoted in *Argentina*, vol. 4 (1), p. 527 *n*.

6. *U.—J.J., R.H.*, Part I, ch. IV, vol. I, pp. 54–6.

7. *Haenke*, p. 34.

8. Dionisio Rickel : *Compendio Breve* [. . .] *de cómo se han de hacer las procesiones. Impreso en Mexico por mandado del señor Obispo Dr Fray Juan Zumárraga.*—2nd edition with additions by the bishop himself. *T.M.I.M.*, vol. I, p. 395.
M.P., vol. I, p. xlii. Footnote.
Frézier (pp. 188–9) having described a masquerade in Pisco, in which a friar took part while a procession of the Rosary was going on, comments : " Ridiculous as this custom appeared, it may be said as great extravagancies have been seen in France on the Feast of Fools. The priests and clerks went masked to the church, and on their return thence went about the streets in carts, and mounted on stages, performing all the most impudent postures and buffooneries with which watermen are wont to divert the foolish mob." And he adds that the festival lasted from the 12th to the 15th century. A connection between dancing and Corpus Christi is of course traditional in Seville : the dance of the *Seises*.

9. *Haenke*, p. 31.

10. *Labat*, Part IV, ch. VII, vol. II, p. 53.

11. *Labat, loc. cit.*
Cf. : " In the evening entertainments they dance minuettos and dances of the Spanish school, and others which come from the Negroes. The persons of distinction learn the French school. Many ladies are outstanding in Spanish

dancing, the dancing of the common sort is little more than movements of the feet with some rhythm, and there are coming in a number of steps of the English school. In some dancing they accompany themselves with movements of the body more or less indecent according to the person who dances."—*Haenke*, p. 30.

Very much the same in *U.—J.J., R.H.*, Part I, ch. IV, vol. I, p. 5.

12. *Moreton*, pp. 125, 124.

13. *U.—J.J., N.S.*, p. 504. In the French Antilles the Mulatto born of a slave mother was a slave.—*Labat*, Part II, ch. VI., vol. I, p. 37,

There were, however, a good many regular marriages at more modest levels. In a description of Nombre de Dios (1608) we find the number of mulattas married to Spaniards to be two or three ; not many, but then the town had only 56 or 57 families in all. In Pánuco (1608) two out of five mulattas are married to Spaniards.—*C.D.I.A.I.*, vol. IX, pp. 219, 153.

14. *Gillespie*, ch. VII, p. 71. *U.—J.J., R.H.*, Part II, Book I, ch. V, vol. III, p. 71.

15. *Frézier*, pp. 186, 191.

16. *Labat*, Part I, ch. XX, vol. I, p. 150.
Sahagún, App. to Book II.

17. *Anonymous*, pp. 80, 81.

18. *H., E.P.N.E.*, Book II, ch. VI, vol. I, p. 94.

19. *Frézier* writes : " The laws of the kingdom have also provided that there should be no alliances between them [Blacks and Indians] [. . .] penalty to the black males to have their genitals cut off, and the females to be severely bastinadoed." Pp. 267–8. He is wrong. The prohibition and the penalties only applied to irregular unions but not to marriages. See texts in *Herrera*, Dec. VIII, Book VII, ch. XII, vol. IV, p. 160.
H., P.N., Book XI, ch. XXIX, vol. II, p. 573.
S.P., Book II, ch. XXX, par. 27, vol. I, p. 221.

20. *H., P.N.*, Book VI, ch. XII, vol. II, p. 135.
H., P.N., Book V, ch. XVI, vol. II, p. 127.

21. *U.—J.J., R.H.*, Part I, Book I, ch. IV, vol. I, p. 41.

22. *H., P.N.*, Book VIII, ch. XXIV, vol. II, pp. 543–4 ; Book VI, ch. XXVIII, vol. II, p. 216.

23. A curious consequence of this habit of the Mexican *peons* in Los Angeles to pass themselves as Spaniards is that the untravelled and uninformed Californian, meeting real Spaniards, often expresses surprise seeing how white they are. I was present at the 200th anniversary of the foundation of San Antonio, Texas, by the Spaniards. The authorities chose to stress the fact that the founders were Canary islanders. But though these Canarians were, of course, 100 per cent. European Spaniards in point of stock, those who had to impersonate them in the pageant painted themselves as dark as Mulattoes. In a University town of that part of the world I was informed on my arrival that I should see buildings of perfect Spanish style. They turned out to be fairly good imitations of Aztec architecture. Nevertheless one could hardly see better buildings in a handsome truly Spanish style than in some parts of California.

CHAPTER IX

1. *Herrera*, Dec. VII, Book II, ch. XII, vol. III, pp. 42–40 ; Dec. VII, Book V, ch. I, vol. III, p. 86. *Ricard*, Book III, ch. II, pp. 311 *et seq.*, with a good bibliography.

2. On the Araucanians, *Amunátegui*, Part II, vol. II, ch. III, pp. 59 *et seq*

On the Chichimecas, *C.D.I.A.I.*, vol. IX, p. 166, description of Tampico. On the Chiriguanaes, *loc. cit.* p. 338, description of Tomina.

3. On Manco Inca, *G.I.V.*, vol. VII, chs. XVII, XXII. *Herrera*, Dec. VI.

4. *G.I.V.*, vol. VII, pp. 175, 183, 186, 211, 221, 235, 192, 260, 253. *Herrera* explains the fidelity of the familiar Indians in a different way : " This Manco began to rule when eighteen years of age, and at first gave signs of being a man of good leanings, but later turned out to be very cruel : when he began the war, all the Indians who were serving the Spaniards went over to serve him : but when they saw that he had them hanged, they returned and were most useful ; and there are some who think that without these Indians the Spaniards would not have been able to defend themselves." Dec. VI, Book II, ch. I, vol. III, p. 20. And again : " The Inca, after the death of the Spaniards, ordered that many Indians should have their hands, noses and ears cut off, and their eyes gouged out, for having been friendly to the Spaniards." Dec. VI, Book VI, ch. VIII, vol. III, p. 138.

5. *G.I.V.*, vol. VIII, ch. XXXI, pp. 355–6. *Herrera* gives a different account of Manco Inca's death, in a regular battle with the Spaniards.—Dec. VII, Book VIII, ch. VI, vol. III, p. 167.

6. *G.I.V.*, vol. XIII, ch. VIII, pp. 34, 75 ; ch. X, p. 97.

7. *Y el que agora está en los Andes, que se llama Tito Cusi Yupangui, alzado, no es hijo legítimo de Mango Inga, sino bastardo y apóstata. Antes tienen por legítimo a otro, questá con el mesmo Tito, llamado Amaro Topa, que es incapaz, a que los Indios llaman* uti.—*S.G.—P.*, p. 128.

On Titu and the friars, as well as on Tupac Amarú : *Noticias Relativas al Inca Cusi-Titu-Yupanqui por el Señor D. Andrés González de Barcia, de los Consejos de Castilla y Guerra, baxo el defectuoso anagrama de D. Gabriel de Cárdenas.*—Vol. XIII of *G.I.V.*, pp. 195 *et seq.*

Also *Oviedo–G.*

Markham's attitude on Tupac Amarú's execution is biased. By all the standards of the age it was more than justified on political grounds. By the standards of our age there is at least a strong case for those who think that he was guilty. See, for instance, *Porras–F.P.*

8. As above. Also *G.I.V.*, vol. XIII, chs. XVI, XVII, XIX, XX.

9. *G.I.V.*, vol. XIII, chs. XVII, XVIII.

10. *G.I.V.*, vol. VIII, ch. XIV, p. 143.

11. On Roldán, *C.C.*, *S.M.*

Note that Holguín proceeded exactly like Cortés. The *cabildo* had to appoint him because he had resigned. " Then between those of the city and those who came there were dealings about electing a captain general ; because Pedro Alvarez Holguín, on entering the city, resigned his functions as captain." —*Loc. cit.*, p. 142.

12. *G.I.V.*, vol. VIII, ch. XXII, p. 251 and ch. XXIV.

13. *G.I.V.*, vol. VIII, ch. XXXII, p. 368.

14. *G.I.V.*, vol. XI, ch. X, p. 116.

15. *G.I.V.*, vol. XI, ch. VII, pp. 80, 81.

16. *G.I.V.*, vol. IX, ch. I, p. 7 ; ch. II, p. 17 ; ch. VII, p. 78 ; ch. VI, p. 69. Vol. VIII, ch. XXX, p. 345 ; vol. IX, ch. VII, p. 88.

17. *Loc. cit.*

18. *G.I.V.*, vol. IX, ch. X ; ch. XI, p. 23 ; ch. XIII, p. 146.

19. See these episodes in the chapters of Garcilaso already quoted in these notes.

20. *G.I.V.*, vol. IX, ch. XVI, p. 177 ; ch. XXXII, pp. 352, 355.

21. *G.I.V.*, vol. IX, ch. XXIII, pp. 369–72 ; p. 363.
On la Gasca's departure, *Alsedo*, p. 57. On his looks and character, *G.I.V.*, vol. X, ch. II, p. 15.

22. *G.I.V.*, vol. X, ch. IV, p. 46 ; ch. V, p. 58.

23. *G.I.V.*, vol. X, ch. V, p. 51 ; ch. VI ; ch. V, pp. 63, 66 ; ch. XI, pp. 135, 137–8.

24. On the battle of Huarina, *G.I.V.*, vol. X, chs. XIX–XXIII. On the battle of Sacsahuana, *G.I.V.*, vol. XI, ch. I, p. 12 ; vol. III, p. 31. Carvajal's appearance, vol. XI, ch. VIII. His attitude before defeat, vol. XI, ch. II, p. 27. Pizarro's surrender, ch. III, p. 31.

25. *G.I.V.*, vol. X, ch. XXVII, p. 292 ; vol. XI, ch. I, p. 89.

26. *Herrera*, Dec. VIII, Book VI, ch. XII, vol. IV, p. 137. Another account which seems more accurate, *Oviedo-Baños*, Book III, ch. VIII, pp. 134–5.

27. *G.I.V.*, vol. XIII, ch. III, pp. 27–29. *Alsedo*, Aviso Histórico, p. 63.
Torquemada reports two curious conspiracies which took place during the vice-regency of Don Antonio de Mendoza : one in which the Negro slaves of Mexico revolted in alliance with the Indians of Tenochtitlán and Tlatelulco (*que entonces eran muchos*), but the mutiny petered out having been found out by another Negro ; and a few years later, a conspiracy " promoted by vile and low men," including an Italian. (1549).—Book V, ch. XI, vol. I, pp. 610–11.

CHAPTER X

1. *A.B.*, p. 322. *Vetancurt, Tratado*, p. 14. *Duro-Armada*, vol. IV, ch. XVIII, p. 335.

2. *Duro-Armada*, vol. IV, ch. XVIII, p. 353 ; vol. V, ch. XVII, p. 275. Peñalosa called himself a *Mestizo*.—See papers of the Inquisition in *H.D.N.M.*, vol. III, p. 236 ; and *New Light on Don Diego de Peñalosa*, by *C. H. Hackett* ; for his character, *H.D.N.M.*, vol. III, pp. 232–69.

3. My impression on reading Torquemada is that the Martín Cortés episode was built upon scanty material by the Velasco family. There is a letter from the Provincial and Definers of the Province of New Spain to the King strongly recommending Don Luis (later Velasco II), then relatively young, to Philip II and asking that he should be allowed to remain in New Spain after his father's death ; almost asking that he should be considered for the post of viceroy (p. 627). There is this detail in the narrative : " The decapitated bodies [of the brothers Avila] were conveyed to the church of San Agustin under the guard of the Captain General Don Francisco Velasco, brother of the viceroy Don Luis, and of his nephew Don Luis (who is now viceroy of this New Spain) who was one of those who discovered this league, for he came to hear of it from some who were involved in it." P. 632. There is finally the letter of the same friars to the King, in which under a most cautious style, they repeatedly express their scepticism about the conspiracy. Pp. 632–4.—*Torquemada*, vol. I, Book V, ch. XVIII.
See also *Alamán–D.H.*, vol. II, pp. 109 *et seq.*

4. *Oviedo-Baños*, ch. IX, pp. 223–4. Letters in *loc. cit.*, Part I, Book IV, ch. III, p. 185 ; ch. VIII, p. 223 ; ch. VII, p. 206. This last also in *C.D.I.A.I.*, vol. IV, p. 274.

5. Cañete's intention, *C.D.I.A.I.*, vol. IV, p. 217. Zúñiga's text, *loc. cit.*, p. 257. On the women in the expedition, *Oviedo-Baños*, p. 222.
Date of departure 26.ix.1560 in *Means*, p. 116 ; but Zúñiga says 27th.— P. 225.

6. Zúñiga, *C.D.I.A.I.*, vol. IV, pp. 229, 272. *Oviedo-Baños*, pp. 204–5.

7. *Oviedo–Baños*, pp. 221, 222.

8. *Loc. cit.*

9. Zúñiga, *C.D.I.A.I.*, vol. IV, pp. 207, 206, 208.

10. Zúñiga, *loc. cit.*, p. 266 ; *Oviedo–Baños*, pp. 211 and 194 ; Zúñiga, p. 277 ; and *Oviedo–Baños*, p. 288.

The detail of Monteverde being German is in Zúñiga but not in Oviedo. It is typical of Aguirre's chaotic mind that when he killed Monteverde " he put on him a board which read : ' for being a servant of H.M.' " ; while in his letter to Philip II he tried to credit this death to his religious zeal.—See Murguía's record in *C.D.I.A.I.*, vol. IV, p. 202.

Between the two texts of the letter there are some differences. Zúñiga gives the list of some of Aguirre's companions ; Oviedo does not. And the ending is in Zúñiga : *Hijo de fieles vasallos tuyos en tierra vascongada, e yo rebelde fasta la muerte por tu ingratitud* ; while Oviedo says : *Y Dios te guarde, Rey excelente, muchos años.*

11. Zúñiga, *loc. cit.*, p. 238. See also p. 236 : " Some were of opinion that Aguirre should be killed since they took his office from him, because he had many Biscayan friends and was a warlike man."

12. *Oviedo–Baños*, p. 175 ; see also p. 246 in which, after a list of the men Aguirre made captains, he says : " All of which were sailors and sea carpenters whom he trusted ; he also gave posts to others all of a low class, and the captains he kept alive, he allowed them to keep their offices till he killed them off. He tried to kill gradually all the noble people, and to keep only low people, believing he would be safer with them."

On this episode I have followed Murguía, *C.D.I.A.I.*, vol. IV, pp. 191–215, and Zúñiga in the same volume, consulting also ch. II of *Humbert–V.* and ch. V of *Means*. Owing to unsurmountable obstacles I was unable to consult the recent monograph published in Spain by Don Emiliano Jos.

13. *A.B.*, p. 343.

14. *A.B.*, pp. 344, 345.

15. *A.B.*, pp. 346, 354.

16. *A.B.*, pp. 354, 355.

17. *A.B.*, pp. 351, 352, 353.

18. *A.B.*, p. 347.

19. *A.B.*, pp. 349, 350, 365, 350, 358, 360.

20. *A.B.*, pp. 365, 366.

21. *A.B.*, pp. 366, 367, 364, 370.

Alsedo (pp. 146–7) reports how on the occasion of the discovery of the mine of Puno (1668) another split occurred " which divided the kingdom in two partisanships, on the one hand Basques and men of Santander and on the other Andalusians and Creoles, this second side slaying the Corregidor and several Biscayans of his suite [. . .] they fought so bloody a battle in the plain of Icacota that to this day the field is covered with the bones of their bodies."

CHAPTER XI

1. *Wright–1932*, Doc. 4, p. 9 ; Doc. 9, pp. 20–2 ; Doc. 10, p. 25 ; Doc. 20, p. 46 ; Doc. 21, p. 49 ; Doc. 26, p. 68. The same robbery is reported as 150,000 *pesos* of which 20,000 for the Crown in Doc. 28, p. 73 ; Doc. 27, p. 71 reports the recovery of ten gold bricks worth over 6,308 *pesos* of the royal part.

2. Doc. 43, pp. 139–40 ; Doc. 41, pp. 125, 126, 127, 130 ; Doc. 42, pp. 133–5 ; Doc. 49, p. 160 ; Doc. 51, p. 66.

3. See description of their arms in "*Sir Francis Drake Revived*," *Wright*–1932, p. 295.
The necessitie, in which they stand hereof continually, causeth them to have iron in farre greater account than gold.—p. 296 ; on the two towns, Ronconcholon, 16 leagues south east of Panama, and another one Drake visited in 1573 : *loc. cit.*, pp. 299, 297.
For the religion of the Maroons, p. 298. Behaviour of Englishmen in Spanish churches, *Wright*–1932, pp. 119–21 *inter alia*.

4. *Wright*–1932, Docs. 71, 72 and p. 339.

5. *Vetancurt Tratado*, p. 13.

6. *Gage*–48, p. 130.
Embiaron a un mulato de la ciudad que se avía confederado por espía.— *Vetancurt*, on the attack of the pirates Agramont, Brown and Jacome to Veracruz, May, 1683, p. 77.
Varinas, p. 21 : "*Sobre Puertorrico se dixo que era una plaza inexpugnable con buenos artilleros, estando los soldados bien pagados y exercitados los mulatos por ser de tan buenas partes como los de Santo Domingo.*"—The meeting was attended by the Duke of Medinaceli, the ex-Viceroy Marqués de Mancera, Don Diego de Portugal and Don Joseph de Avellaneda.

7. *Alsedo*, pp. 135, 144. *Torquemada*, Book V, ch. XLIV, vol. I, pp. 690–3.
Under Velasco II, the Chichimecas were at last pacified under a *Mestizo* Captain, Caldera, son of a Chichimeca and of a Christian. *Torquemada*, Book V, ch. XXXV, vol. I, p. 669.
New Revolt of the Tepehuanes in *H.D.N.M.*, vol. II, pp. 36 *et seq.*

8. Pedro Sarmiento de Gamboa to the King, 15.iv.1581, in *Duro-Armada*, vol. II, p. 437, App. 5.
Ralegh–H 32, p. 179.
Torquemada, Book V, ch. XXI, vol. I, p. 639.

9. *Torquemada, loc. cit.*, p. 633 ; Book V, ch. LIX, vol. I, p. 727.

10. *Vetancurt, Teatro*, p. 16.

11. Father Bernabé Cobo in *Porras–Lima*, p. 12.

12. *Gage*–48, pp. 63 *et seq.*
He is most useful if his bias is carefully discounted. His epilogue is typical. He points out that Salazar and three more priests were sentenced to the galleys but fled ; that "there were not above three or four hanged of so many thousands," and that the Archbishop was made Bishop of Zamora, "so that his wings were clipt." But in this he is wrong, for it was usual to grant a Bishop's see to archbishops returning from the Indies, without in any way implying royal disfavour. La Serna's successor, Francisco Chanco y Zúñiga, became bishop of Cartagena before going to the see of Burgos (Vetancurt, p. 24) ; Mateo Zaga de Bugueiro left the see of Mexico to be also Bishop of Cartagena where he died ; Don Payo Enriquez de Ribera was offered one of the best sees in Spain and the Presidency of the Council of the Indies, but he chose a cloister (1668–81).

CHAPTER XII

1. *C.D.I.H.E.*, vol. II, pp. 133, 134, 135, 135, 135, 136, 137, 136, 137, 140, 143, 146.

2. *Varinas*, ch. X, pp. 232, 235 ; ch. XXII, p. 304.
On the sack of Veracruz and the passive attitude of Zaldivar who commanded the fleet and arrived when the pirates were still in the Island of Sacrifices : *Varinas*, ch. XXII, p. 312, and *Duro-Armada*, vol. V, ch. XVII, p. 272.

3. Mano de Relox, ch. II in *Varinas*, p. 333.

4. *Loc. cit.*, pp. 358, 359, 362.

5. *Loc. cit.*, p. 366. His ethical argument breaks down here, for we know from Sloane that the English in Belize had no better ethical basis towards the Indians than towards the Spaniards, and yet their colony *endureth*. " The Indians of this place us'd formerly to trade with them, but the English not keeping them faith, but taking and selling them, they are retired up into the country several leagues."—*Sloane*, vol. I, p. lxxxiii.

This is confirmed by the First Lord of the Admiralty, Sir Charles Wager, in several letters to Admiral Vernon : " I hear besides, that the friendship between us and the Darien Indians is broke off, by some of our traders abusing their women and carrying away some of the Indians and selling them for slaves, so that they have made peace with the Spaniards, by which they have a communication through their Country from Panama to Cartagena by which they may carry money thither without hazard. I hope this is not true, but it is so like English management, in the like cases, that I fear it is. 10.vi.1740. Original Letters to an Honest Sailor. London. 1746. Also in like terms, p. 16, July 9, 1740. See also note 2 to ch. XVII below.

6. *Macanaz–T.*, p. 10.

7. *A la Expedición Española para propagar la vacuna en América, bajo la dirección de D. Francisco Balmis.* A poem by Quintana in *Rivadeneyra*, vol. XIX, pp. 4, 5.

8. Data on Macanaz from *Macanaz–M.*
The list of his works includes the following :
No. 13. *Memorias sobre los Intereses de la Monarquía de España y Nuevo Mundo.* Paris, 1734.
No. 23. *Memorias para la Historia de España y Nuevo Mundo.*
No. 21. *Miscelaneas utiles al Bien Universal, Imperio de la España y Nuevo Mundo.*
No. 27. *Males del Perú y su remedio.*
Macanaz–M., pp. lxxi-lxxx.
He himself in a note drafted in 1739 refers to some of his works on the Indies. Apart from the one mentioned in the text, he gives : *Dos tomos en folio, sobre los vastos y opulentos reinos del Chile, Paraguay, Tucumán, Chaco, Las Guayras, Santa Cruz, los Moxos, el Marañón* [. . .] *los inagotables tesoros que encierran y las guerras que han presenciado desde el año* 1570 *hasta el día. Otro tomo en cuarto, de la guerra que los enemigos domésticos o españoles rebeldes han hecho a los españoles verdaderos del Nuevo Mundo. Loc cit.*, p. XXX.
There is the possibility of a forgery. Maldonado asserts that a number of the works published under the name of Macanaz or attributed to him are apocryphal, p. LXI. Nevertheless there is a curious clue to authenticity, though admittedly not perfect, in Macanaz's high opinion of the integrity of Spanish bishops (*Macanaz–M.*, pp. LII–III) for it tallies with what the Testament of Spain says on the subject ; the Testament, moreover, does not mention the Inquisition, and this also adds to the sense of authenticity.

9. *Macanaz–T.*, pp. 10, 21.

10. The ostensible author of this singular book is Don Cristóbal del Hoyo-Solórzano y Sotomayor, born in la Palma in 1677 ; second Marqués de la Villa de San Andrés, Vizconde del Buen Paso after 1722 when his father died ; Sargento Mayor of Cavalry, Cabo en Jefe of the arms of the district of Icod ; married in Galicia to Doña Teresa Calixta Raxo Texeiro Suárez de Deza, a daughter of the lord and lady of Argeríes in the Diocese of Lugo.—*Enciclopedia Heráldica y Genealógica of Caraffa*, vol. V, pp. 42–73. Many details in the text tally with this description of the heraldic dictionary. The author, whoever he was, is widely read in European, classical and religious literature. He is particularly strong in Hebrew literature. He is witty, licentious and often

blasphemous. It is unlikely that the Marqués himself could have written such a book.
Quotations from pp. ii, iv, 610.

11. *Loc. cit.*, pp. 25, 73, 76, 90, 94, 90.

12. *Loc. cit.*, pp. 95, 100, 214, 216, 217.

13. *U.—J.J., N.S.*, pp. 428–9, 430, 430–1.

14. *Loc. cit.*, p. 171.

15. *H., E.P.N.E.*, Book II, ch. VII, vol. I, p. 114.
Text of Macanaz and Floridablanca in *Amunátegui*, vol. III, pp. 77, 81.

16. *H., E.P.N.E.*, Book II, ch. VII, vol. I, p. 118.

17. *Loc. cit.*, pp. 114–115.

18. *Ils préfèrent aux espagnols les étrangers des autres pays.—Loc. cit.*, p. 118.
U.—J.J., N.S., p. 525.
H., P.N., Book IV, ch. XII, vol. I, p. 575.

19. *Argentina*, vol. IV (1), p. 203, ch. I, *Historia Política y Económica* by Emilio Ravignani.

20. *H., E.P.N.E.*, Book II, ch. VI, vol. I, pp. 105 *et seq.* ; also *Belaunde*, pp. 49–51.

21. On Villava, *Belaunde*, pp. 52–54 ; *Argentina*, vol. III, p. 90. I have not found any direct information on Carvajal's plan. *Belaunde* speaks about it in his first chapter. A plan of this kind is attributed to Aranda in nearly every book on the emancipation of the Spanish Empire. It is now, however, considered to have been a forgery, possibly of Godoy's. See *A. K.*, pp. 182–5, who gives the plan in appendix.

CHAPTER XIII

1. *Charlevoix–P.*, Book XVIII, vol. V, pp. 66–7 ; p. 73 ; p. 75 ; p. 54.

2. *Loc. cit.*, pp. 77–8 ; p. 80.

3. P. 172, p. 173.

4. Book XIX, p. 217.

5. The version of this episode in *Argentina*, vol. V (1), pp. 217–8, is surprisingly curt and incomplete. Mancini is both uninformed and inaccurate. The best guide is Charlevoix. True, as a Jesuit, he is biased, but he gives the original documents, provides a coherent report, often gives facts against his bias, and above all, unwittingly supplies a superb portrait of Antequera, so life-like in its fidelity to the constant features of the species from Cortés down to Bolívar, that no better, because no more automatic, proof could be given of Charlevoix's integrity.

6. For the chief facts I am indebted to *Humbert–V.* the only author who had the advantage of the narrative of Aristides Rojas in Estudios Históricos, which I have been unable to procure. With the only exception of Gil Fortoul, who though a Venezuelan historian is objective, indeed perhaps not quite fair to León, authors have tended to present this episode in a distorted light, owing to the temptation to present León as the precursor of independence. Even Humbert, who had the facts before him, and reports them accurately, is so far misled as to give (p. 111) a portrait of León which is contradicted by his own narrative.

7. *Argentina, loc. cit.*, p. 221. *Restrepo*, ch. I, vol. I, pp. 17, 36, is too generous to the Spanish authorities. *Miranda–Archivo*, vol. XV, pp. 27–68, gives a day-to-day narrative by the Protector of the Indians, showing that the behaviour of the authorities was both short-sighted and perfidious.

8. Among these risings of Indians there is one on which a ballad was published in Lima in 1750. It will be found in the B.M. under the press mark 11450 de 4, 1–7.

On Condorcanqui's rising *Argentina* V. (1), p. 212, but above all an important series of first-hand documents which make up the first part of *A.B.*

9. *A.B.*, pp. 223, 209, 211, 217, 213.

10. *Loc. cit.*, p. 211.

11. *Loc. cit.*, p. 211.

12. *Loc. cit.*, pp. 242, 246.

13. *Loc. cit.*, pp. 311, 313.

14. See the reports of Segurola in *A.B.*

15. *Loc. cit.*, p. 256. " *usuras de extrangeros* " (*A.B.*, p. 243) can only mean usury dealings by Spaniards, in view of p. 242 : " *los europeos de negociaciones y tratos usurarios* " and " *las usuras perjudiciales de los europeos.*"—P. 238.

16. *Loc. cit.*, pp. 240, 246–7, 263 ; Book IV, ch. XII, vol. I, p. 574.

17. *Loc. cit.*, pp. 240, 244, 247, 262, 248, 263.

18. *H., E.P.N.E.*, Book II, ch. VI, vol. I, p. 112.

CHAPTER XIV

1. *Montesquieu n'a pu se résoudre à traîter sérieusement la question de l'esclavage.*—*Feugère*, p. 164.

On the institution of slavery in French opinion, *loc. cit.*, p. 161.

Il n'est pas de bourgeois ni d'ouvrier qui n'ait son nègre esclave.—Quoted, *loc. cit.*, p. 162.

The French author advocating slavery was Melon : *Essai Politique sur le commerce.*

Montesquieu on slavery : *On ne doit point souffrir que le citoyen puisse augmenter le tribut de l'esclave.*—Book XIII, ch. IV.

S'il veut lever des tributs en argent sur les esclaves de sa noblesse, il faut que le seigneur soit garant du tribut. And in a footnote : *Cela se pratique ainsi en Allemagne.*—Ch. V.

Chapters III–VI of Book XIII deal with the tribute of taxes to be paid in countries in which slavery prevails. They assume tacit acceptance of slavery. Books XV and XVI deal with slavery in general. Book XV, ch. I, condemns it and notably says : " *Dans le gouvernement monarchique, où il est souverainement important de ne point abbattre ou avilir la nature humaine, il ne faut point d'esclave.*

Ch. IV consists of two short, superficial and ill-informed paragraphs on the causes of slavery in the Spanish Indies, and an equally ill-informed and superficial paragraph on slavery in the French colonies. The pearl is ch. V, the recondite irony of which is referred to in the text. It begins with a downright untruth : " *Les peuples d'Europe ayant exterminé ceux de l'Amérique, ils ont du mettre en esclavage ceux de l'Afrique.*" It is then that he enumerates the arguments he would use for slavery if he were required to defend it : " *Ceux dont il s'agit sont noirs depuis les pieds jusqu'à la tête, et ils ont le nez si écrasé qu'il est presque impossible de les plaindre.* [. . .] *De petits esprits éxagèrent trop l'injustice que l'on fait aux africains. Car si elle étoit telle qu'ils le disent, ne seroit-il pas venu dans la tête des princes d'Europe, qui font entr'eux tant de conventions inutiles, d'en faire une générale en faveur de la miséricorde et de la pitié ?* "

Among those who were taken in by this irony was *Dickson*, who after refuting these arguments, writes in his footnote : See Montesquieu's *Apology* for Slavery, commonly called the Spirit of Laws, Book XV, ch. 5."—p. 82.

Montesquieu was very well versed in classical authors and the facts of antiquity, but very ignorant of Spanish texts, laws and practices. Quotations from the Geneva 1748 edition.

2. On Colón's and Peter Martyr's ideas see *C.C.*, *S.M.*

Narrant Hispani nautae, esse in novo isto Orbe, quem repererunt, insulas quasdam, inter quas si bellum incidat, honestissimus & sit, & habeatur qui pacem ab hoste roget : alterum scelestum, & omnibus in commune hostem, qui rogatum neget : & indignissime eos ferre, quorum hostes in postulanda ipsos anteverterint, officio pulcherrimo ad illorum sentenciam, atque amplissima. Quid nobis literae ? quid humanitas prodest ? quid tot artis vitae ? tanta educatio ? [. . .] *Illi rudes & Barbari populi, citra literas, citra cultum omnem, & pietatem, veras sanasque opiniones a recta & pura natura edocti sunt.* Bruges. 8th July, 1524, to the Archbishop of Lincoln.—*Epistolarum Philippi Melanchthonis Libri Iv. Quibus, Auctarii loco, accesserunt Thomae Mori et Ludovici Vivis Epistolae,* Londini MDCXLII, p. 70.

3. Saavedra Fajardo goes as far as to say that the book of Las Casas was actually an invention of the powers jealous of Spain. Envy, he writes in his *Empresa XII,* "broadcast a faked book on the ill-treatment of the Indians, under the name of the Bishop of Chiapa, letting it run first in Spain as printed in Seville the better to accredit the lie, and translating it afterwards in all languages."

4. *Naturam appello docilitatem et propensionem insitam ad res honestas. De pueris . . . instituendis* quoted by Americo Castro, *El Pensamiento de Cervantes,* p. 167n.

Good discussion on golden age and good savage in these pages, particularly 183. On Montaigne and other influences on Rousseau see *Influence des Récits de Voyages sur la Philosophie de J.J. Rousseau,* Gilbert Chinard, in Publications of the Modern Language Association of America, vol. XXVI, p. 477.

5. *Emile,* Book IV, vol. 9, p. 54.

All quotations from Rousseau in : *Oeuvres de J.J. Rousseau. Nouvelle édition avec des notes historiques et critiques ; augmentées d'une appendice aux Confessions* par M. Mussay Pathay. Paris, 1834.

6. *Emile,* Book II, vol. 8, pp. 101, 104.
Emile, Book I, vol. 8, p. 20.
Discours sur l'Inégalité parmi les Hommes, vol. 4, pp. 221–22.
Emile, Book V, vol. 9, p. 383.

7. *Narcisse.* Préface, vol. 11, p. 234n.

8. *Rousseau Juge de Jean Jacques.* 3e Dialogue, vol. 16, p. 414.

9. Vol. 11, pp. 435 *et seq.*

10. *Narcisse.* Préface, vol. 11, p. 227n.
Emile, Book I, vol. 8, p. 56.
Contrat Social, Book III, ch. XIII, vol. 5, p. 207.
Rêveries d'un Promeneur Solitaire, 7e Promenade, vol. 3, p. 333.
Narcisse. Préface, vol. 11, p. 228 ; vol. 11, p. 229.
Contrat Social, Book I, ch. IV, vol. 5, pp. 109–108.
Discours sur l'Economie Politique, vol. 4, p. 393.

11. *Contrat Social,* Book I, ch. VI, vol. 5, p. 111.

12. *Contrat Social,* Book III, ch. VIII, vol. 5, p. 191.
Contrat Social. Cf. : ch. II, vol. V, p. 170 ; ch. III, p. 172 ; ch. VIII, p. 190.
Lettre à Mirabeau (26.vii.1767), vol. 19, p. 481.
Contrat Social, Book II, ch. VIII, vol. 5, p. 265. Note that it fits the Inquisition perfectly.

13. *Discours sur les Sciences et les Arts,* vol. 4, p. 15.
Quoted in *Spell,* p. 15.
Emile, Book V, vol. 9, p. 397.
Considérations sur le gouvernement de la Pologne, ch. III, vol. 5, p. 293.

Aranda to Floridablanca, 7.vi.1786. *M.P.-H.* quoted by *Spell*, p. 50.—
Quoted by *Spell*, p. 50.

Rousseau's ignorance of Spain as well as his debt to her are well illustrated
by the following words from his *Lettre à D'Alembert sur les Spéctacles*, vol. 11,
p. 47 : " *Vous pouvez avoir vu à la Comédie Italienne une pièce intitulée La Vie
est un Songe. Si vous vous rappelez le héros de cette pièce, voilà le véritable
misanthrope.*" Mussay Pathay thinks this was an Italian play produced in
1717. But Zeek rightly points out that Rousseau was five then and therefore
he must be thinking of another play under the same title by Louis de Boissy.
(See *Louis de Boissy. Auteur Comique*, 1694-1758, par. C. F. Zeek,
Jr. Grenoble, 1914.) Zeek observes that no Frenchman of the period mentions
Calderón at all. It is, nevertheless, curious to trace the devious way from
Calderón's great monologue :

> *Y yo con más albedrío*
> *Tengo menos libertad*

to : " *L'homme est né libre et partout il est dans les fers,*" of the *Contrat Social*,
through the Italian play and particularly Boissy :

> *Tout est né libre et je porte des fers.*
> *Oh Ciel ! Unique auteur des tourments que j'endure,*
> *Fais partager mes fers à toute la nature*
> *Ou donne moi la liberté*
> *Dont jouit, en naissant, la moindre créature.*
> *Acte I, scène IV.*

Boissy's play was first produced on 12.xi.1732.

14. *Spell*, p. 22.

15. Conseil de Genève.

16. François Grasset, Lausanne, 8.iv.1765 to Rousseau. Quoted in *Spell*,
p. 39.
Il faut de la force pour percer les barrières de la bigoterie en Espagne ; Emile
l'a fait.—Keith to Rousseau, 1764. Quoted by *Spell*, p. 42.
Quotations from *Mercurio*, p. 44.

17. *Nouvelle Héloise*, vol. 6, p. 431.
*El Pensador Matritense. Discursos Críticos sobre todos los Asumptos que
comprehende la Sociedad civil.* V vols. Barcelona, vol. III, pp. 31, 77 and 78.

18. *El Pensador Matritense*, pp. 100, 105, 107.

19. *Spell* and *M.P.-H.* are good references for this. Quintana's line from
the above quoted poem in *Rivadeneyra*, vol. 19, p. 5.

20. *Spell*, pp. 34, 130 ; *Argentina*, vol. 5 (1), ch. I, p. 14 ; p. 17.
Spell, p. 136.
*The Lamento Métrico General, Llanto Funesto y Gemido Triste que a el sensible
y nunca bien sentido doloroso Ocaso de Nuestro Augusto Católico Monarca el
Señor Don Carlos III produxo Don Estevan de Torralla y Landa, natural de los
Reynos de España y Minero de S.M. en las provincias de Caxamarca y Huamachuco*,
printed in Lima in the Royal Press of the Foundlings in the year 1790 will be
found in the British Museum under 11450 de 4.

21. *Contrat Social*, Book IV, ch. III, vol. 5, pp. 263, 257.

22. On V.'s dealings with S. America, *Ricardo R. Caillet-Bois. Las Corriente,
Ideológicas Europeas del Siglo XVIII y el Virreinato del Río de la Plata*, ch. I
of vol. 5 (1) in *Argentina*, p. 5.

23. Quotations from Act I, scene V, scene I and V ; Act II, scene IV and V
and Act V, scene VII of the play. *Theatre de Voltaire*, Paris, 1861. It is
strange indeed to read on *Alzire* over the signature of a present day English
Roman Catholic : " The spirit of the play was so far in advance of its time

that when the critical reaction came against the drama of the XVIIIth century, the peculiarly vital interest of Alzire still lay in the future." " It is doubtful whether any play on that scale, had ever before been so directly concerned to elucidate the essentials of the Christian religion." *Voltaire*, by Alfred Noyes, pp. 222, 224.

24. Ferney, 15.vii.1768, vol. 54, p. 515.
Vol. 55, p. 112.
All quotations from *Oeuvres Complètes de Voltaire*. A Paris, chez. Antoine-Augustin Renouard. 1819–21.

25. *Miranda-Archivo*, vol. IV, pp. 129, 130.

26. On Raynal's collaborators see *Feugère*.
Book XIX, ch. II, p. 46, vol. 4.

27. On the Archbishop's story, *Feugère*, ch. VIII, p. 271.
Loc. cit., p. 278.

28. *Bourgoing*, vol. II, p. 221 ; vol. I, pp. 304–5.
Raynal, Book XI, ch. XXXI, vol. 3, p. 228.
Cumaná, 17.x.1800. *L.A.H.*, p. 87.

CHAPTER XV

1. According to J. Loeb (*Revue des Etudes Juives*, vol. XIV, p. 161) there were 235,000 Jews in Spain. Acc. to Vincenzo Quirini, Venetian Ambassador, they amounted to one third of the population of Spain. (*Alberi. Relazioni degli Ambasciatori*, vol. I, p. 29.) Both quoted by *Goris*, p. 554. Quirini's figure is far too high, and in any case all figures of population for those days are hazy.

Graetz, that most intemperate historian of the Jews, is incoherent on Ferdinand and Isabel. He speaks of " Isabella the bigot " (vol. IV, ch. X, p. 333) and heaps abuse on the King and Queen, yet is bound to acknowledge that both before and after the expulsion and the setting of the Inquisition in full sway, the household of the King and Queen swarmed with converted Jews, who held such posts as gave them control over the financial and the military establishments of the country, and that both Ferdinand and Isabel stood up to the Inquisition in favour of some Jews (see for instance under Abarbanel). The Jews he says (vol. IV, ch. XI, p. 361) " loved Spain too dearly to part from her without bitter pangs of regret, and the King and Queen had often protected them from oppression." See also pp. 416, 422, 361, 362, 782. Nevertheless, Graetz exaggerates somewhat because he concentrates on the rich Marranos. For the lamentable ignorance of the poor Marranos arriving in Antwerp : *Goris*, ch. VI, pp. 572–3.

2. This was stated in an article in the London Monthly Review in which Pinto's letters to Voltaire were discussed soon after their publication. In this article the treatment meted out to the Jews in Spain, where it is said they were " *fort à leur aise & fort considérés* " was contrasted with their lot in the whole of Europe, where even in the XVIIIth century, says the author of the article, they were " *dans l'oppression et dans la misère, réputés esclaves et traîtés inhumainement.*" *Lettres-Juifs*, p. 51.

Graetz, vol. IV, ch. XIII, p. 415.
" The Jews were not indeed admitted in triumph through the great portal but they were let in by Cromwell through the back door and got a firm footing in the house. [. . .] Luis Nobles, an immigrant Marrano merchant, was accused of illegally engaging in business through a Portuguese papist, but he was acquitted by the Protector on the ground that he was not a Catholic but a Jew." This indirectly established the fact that one could be a Jew and be admitted to England.—*Graetz*, vol. V, ch. II, p. 52.

3. *Graetz*, vol. IV, ch. XIII, p. 429.

4. Dr. Blas Gonzalo de Ribero, of the Holy Office, arguing in a paper to the King against the removal or relaxation of the rules on " blood-cleanliness," explains that the Jews, in the days when they were the chosen people of God, never allowed equality to gentiles converted to Judaism whom they never described as Israelites, but only as Proselytes. Now, he goes on, when " the Spanish Gentile Republic, a nation loved by God, which seems to have subrogated to itself as to honours in the place of the Israelite [. . .] the same rule should be applied [. . .] the same difference between the Christians, old Gentiles, and the Jews and Moors newly come to it." *Varia-B.*, No. 71, fols. 19, 20.

Graetz, vol. IV, ch. XIII, p. 423.

5. *Ceverio De Vera (Juan) Viaie de la Tierra Santa y Descripcion de Jerusalem . . . con relacion de cosas marauillosas assi de las prouincias de Leuante como de las Indias de Ocidente.* Pamplona. Mathias Mares, 1598, ch. XXI, fol. 94.

6. On Conversos and Lutheranism, *Goris*, ch. VI, pp. 553 *et seq*. *Quando Cesar hara facto bruggiar una mezza dozzena di vivi Lutherani et li bene confiscati.—Loc. cit.*, p. 559.

Gracia Mendes in *Graetz*, vol. IV, ch. XVI, pp. 610 *et seq*.
Miques, *loc. cit.* and ch. XIII. Also for both *Grosse Jüdische National-biographie*, vol. IV, pp. 495-6.

7. Marco Pérez and Antonio Pérez related : *Goris* (p. 582) says so, though he gives no authority. It is known that Antonio was accused by the Inquisition of being a secret Jew. He hailed from Zaragoza, or rather his father did ; and so did Marco. The sentence against A.P. read in the auto de fe of 19.x.1592 when he was burnt in effigy, accuses him of wishing " to uproot the Inquisition, for he is a descendant of Jews and a great grandson of one Antón Pérez, a Jew who after conversion relapsed and was burnt, of whose *sambenito*, at present in the main church of Calatayud, the prosecutor gave witness in his statement." But at the request of Gonzalo, Antonio's son, the Holy Office revoked this sentence on 16.vi.1615 : " and we declare that his memory and fame must be absolved and that the trial and sentence should be no obstacle for his sons and heirs [. . .] nor should what was said and alleged by the prosecutor of this Inquisition against their blood-cleanliness stand in the way of the said sons and heirs."—Summary of the trial of A.P. by B.L. de Argensola, chronicler of Aragón, in *C.D.I.H.E.*, vol. XII, pp. 565, 569.

No conclusions should be drawn in haste, for there are grounds for thinking that the first sentence calumniated A.P., but also for suspecting that the second sentence was merely due to friendship and a desire to let the family off. The speed with which the Holy Office swallowed its own words after less than four years of work by Gonzalo-P. (1611-15) is suspect.

The *G.J.N.B.*, vol. III, gives Pérez as *eine Marannenfamilie in Cordova oder Kastilien, welche aus Spanien vertrieben, sich in der Türkei und Amerika niederliess. Der älteste Sprosse dieser Familie, Antonio Pérez, ein reicher Kaufmann aus Saragossa rettete sich 1487 vor der Inquisition.*

On Juan Baptista P. : *T.M.I.L.*, vol. II, ch. XVIII, p. 150. He was burnt in 1635 and not in 1610 as printed in *G.J.N.B.*, vol. III.

8. *T.M.I.L.*, vol. II, ch. XVIII, p. 150.
G.J.N.B., vol. III.
Goris, ch. VI, pp. 579-80.

9. *T.M.I.Cg.*, App. XII, p. 435.
Royal Cédula 1534 : *C.D.I.A.I.*, vol. XLII, p. 476.

Jewish authors on staunch loyalty of Conversos : for instance, Graetz and Roth in many passages. So : *Graetz*, vol. IV, ch. X, p. 333. On this point agreement is complete on both sides. Thus : " The descendants of this lineage [the Jewish] have no limit as to the hardness and pertinacity of their

faith, as shown in Portugal, Castille and other parts, where though the ancestors
converted are already back in the sixth or seventh generation, they have not
yet forgotten the law of their sires."—P. 17. Memorandum on *Estatuto de
Limpieza* by Blas Gonzalo de Ribero, no date [Philip IV], *Varia-B.*, No. 71.
And on the other side : " *Les théologiens chrétiens* [. . .] *ne purent* [. . .]
*jamais convertir un seul homme de cette Religion. On a vu, il est vrai, quelques
juifs feindre d'abjurer, tantôt par avarice, tantôt par terreur ; mais aucun n'a
jamais embrassé le Christianisme de bonne foi* [. . .] *Orobio parle de quelques
rabins espagnols et arabes qui abjurèrent et devinrent Evêques en Espagne, mais il se
garde bien de dire qu'ils eussent renoncé de bonne foi à leur religion. Lettres-Juifs.*
Catalogue Raisonné, pp. 90–1.
On Portuguese conspiracy in Lima, *T.M.I.L.*, vol. II, ch. XVIII, p. 163.
Carvajal's case in *Publicaciones del Archivo General de la Nación*. Mexico, 1932.
Los Judíos en la Nueva España.
Roth, The Jews in the Defence of Britain, Reprint from *Transactions of the
Jewish Historical Society of England*. 1940, vol. XV, pp. 9, 10, 11
It is well understood and held in no doubt that foreign merchants well
versed in Spanish affairs gave intelligence to the enemy, both in Cadiz and in
Jerez.—Fray Pedro de Abreu. *Historia del Saqueo de Cádiz por los Ingleses en
1596.* Cadiz 1866, p. 71. Quoted by *La Fuente*, p. 95.

10. *Roth, loc. cit.*, p. 18. *Graetz*, vol. V, ch. II, pp. 32–4.
France seems to have been more generous than England to the Spanish Jews :
*La nation portugaise : on nomme ainsi les Juifs Portuguais & Espagnols :
ils sont établis en France & y jouissent, depuis* 1550, *des mêmes privilèges que les
autres sujets du Roi, en vertu de Lettres Patentes renouvelées de regne en règne.—
Lettres-Juifs*, vol. I, pp. 2–3n. As for the other Jews, *Graetz* (vol. V, ch. VIII,
p. 364) says " It was forbidden to Jews to settle anywhere in France."
Despite these privileges granted to the Portuguese Jews, when the Jews of
Amsterdam compiled this set of letters to Voltaire in self defence, they were
made to affix the following P.S. to their preface :—*P.S. Nous n'avons pu
obtenir la permission de publier ce Recueil, qu'à condition qu'un Chrétien y mettroit
les notes qu'il jugeroit à propos. Nous y avons consenti, sans adopter ce qu'il
pourra dire, & sans en répondre ; nous aurons soin de distinguer les notres et
celles de nos auteurs d'avec les siennes, par les mots abrégés Chrét Aut. Edit.*
p. viij.

11. The Bordeaux exodus is in *Graetz*, vol. V, ch. VIII, and with more
details in *Lettres-Juifs*, vol. I, opening pages.
Pinto reproaches Voltaire that he does not manage to " *distinguer les
autres Juifs des Espagnols & Portuguais, qui jamais ne se sont confondus de la
foule des autres enfants de Jacob.*" " *Leur divorce avec leurs autres frères est à
tel point que si un Juif Portuguais en Hollande & en Angleterre éspousoit une
Juive Allemande, il perdroit aussitôt ses prérogatives ; il ne seroit plus reconnu
pour membre de leur synagogue ; il seroit séparé du corps de la nation.*" Vol. I,
pp. 10–17.
T.M.I.Cg., App. XVI, p. 438.

12. On Jewish origins of Freemasonry from the Catholic angle see in particular W. T. Walsh's *Philip II*, London, 1937, ch. XVI. On German Fm
and the Jews, *Gould*.
On the Avila buildings, *Tirado*, vol. I, pp. 213 *et seq.*

13. Beginnings of F.M. in Spain, *La Fuente*, vol. I, pp. 101 *et seq.* ; *M.P.–H.*,
vol. III, ch. I, pp. 74 *et seq.* ; *Juan Canter. Las Sociedades Secretas y Literarias*,
Ch. IX, vol. 5 (1) of *Argentina*, pp. 259 *et seq.* Quotation from *Tirado*, vol. 263.

14. On Althotas and Ximenes, *Vie de Joseph Balsamo connu sous le nom de
Comte Cagliostro, extrait de la procédure instruite contre lui à Rome en* 1790.
A Paris, 1791, pp. 6–7, 126–131.
On Martínez Pascual Cagliostro, *La Francmaçonnerie et l'Occultisme au*

XVIIIème siècle by Henri D'Almeras, Paris, 1904. Also *Cagliostro in his Egyptian Rite of F.M.* by Henri Ridgely Craus, Washington, 1919, p. 14. See also under these names in *M.P.–H.*

On the meaning of L.P.D. the Masonic authors are not agreed. Trowbridge (p. 108) says the interpretation given in the text is an invention of the priests ; but he gives no other. Evans, a 33 Degree, accepts it.

15. *Torrubia*, last page of preface. There seems to be no foundation for the view expressed by some Masonic authors that he was a Catholic spy in their ranks.

Letter to Holy Office of Lima, *T.M.I.C.*, vol. II, ch. XVI, pp. 500–7, and *T.M.I.L.*, vol. II, p. 26, pp. 360–1.

16. Lagrange case, *loc. cit.*, p. 362–7.
T.M.I.L., vol. II, ch. XVI, pp. 362–4 ; *T.M.I.C.*, vol. II, ch. XV, p. 508.

17. *P.A.G.N.*, *M.*, XXI, p. VIII.

18. *Loc. cit.*, pp. IX–XXVIII. The case is curious also because not a few of the statements made by the witnesses allow the suggestion that Fabris was a Jew.

19. On Burdales, see the proceedings in detail and the preliminary pages. The Mexican authors of the book are of the opinion stated in the text about the Viceroy-Archbishop (p. XXX).

20. B.'s lubricity, p. 183 ; on regicide, p. 187.
On Branciforte as instigator, *loc. cit.*, p. 209. On Laussel's carnal tendencies, p. 218. On regicide, pp. 214, 217, 224. Sentence, p. 412.

21. *T.M.I.L.*, vol. II, ch. XVI, p. 367.
The standard English, American and German books on Fm. are practically useless for the Spanish-speaking world. Their information is scanty, faulty and even at times untrue. The Masonic Cyclopedia does not even mention Aranda.

CHAPTER XVI

1. *Schlosser*, p. 281 ; *Schoell*, Book VIII, ch. XI, vol. 39, p. 50.

2. *H.*, *P.N.*, Book VII, ch. XIX, vol. II, pp. 245, 274. *U.—J.J.*, *N.S.*, pp. 528, 529.
Las Misiones Jesuíticas, by Father William Furlong Cardiff in *Argentina*, vol. III, pp. 595 *et seq.*
Juan Canter. *Le Imprenta.* In *Argentina*, vol. 4 (2), ch. I, p. 19.

3. Data from Father Furlong Cardiff, *loc. cit.*, pp. 596, 597, 601. *Loc. cit.*, pp. 605, 608, 610, 614.

4. The 4 letters : vol. II of *Memoires Secrets du Marquis de Louville*, Paris, 1818, pp. 247–317. The most useful is the second.

5. Texts from *Voltaire–R.*, 1829. Letter no. 100, Paris, 4.v.1762, vol. LXII, p. 193. Same idea, p. 209. Also Letter 99, pp. 186–7. " *Plus nous sommes attachés à la sainte religion de notre Sauveur Jésus Christ, plus nous devons abhorrer l'abominable usage qu'on fait tous les jours de sa divine loi.*" So Voltaire to D'Alembert from Ferney in 1762 (No. 96, p. 180). The next paragraph, with its sudden dirty obscenity almost in the same breath with the deity, shows that religion in Voltaire was but an idea and not a feeling. " *Philosophe par opinion, elle se nombrait religieuse par politique* "—wrote Ségur on Catherine the Great (*Schoell*, vol. 44, p. 377). Note the antithesis in the language of the period between the terms philosophe and religieux. The letters of Voltaire to D'Alembert always begin : *Mon cher philosophe.* D'Alembert wrote to Voltaire : " *Je ne sais ce que deviendra la religion de Jésus, mais sa Compagnie est dans des mauvais draps.*"—P. 187.
Les Jésuites commencèrent. Ils avaient voulu travailler aux articles sur la

théologie [for the Encyclopædia] *et ils avaient été refusés.*—Lettre 8e, p. 86.
*Catalogue Raisonné des Esprits Forts depuis le Curé Rabelais jusqu'au Curé
Jean Mester par M.P.V. Professeur en Théologie.* Londres, 1788.

See a repulsive example of cold inhumanity in the humanitarian D'Alembert
in the obscene remarks on Malagrida, 31.x.1761, p. 174, n. 94. On his religion,
Letter 105, p. 208.

That Voltaire aimed at religion itself seems to me clear. "*On n'a coupé
qu'une tête de l'hydre. Je lève les yeux au ciel et je crie : Ecr : l'inf*" :—
Lettre à Damilaville, 4.iii. 1765, vol. 53, p. 40. He was not very optimistic
about the result of the expulsion, for he wrote an epigram later to show that
kings and Jansenists remained on top and understood each other very well :

SUR L'EXPULSION DES JÉSUITES

*Les renards et les loups furent longtemps en guerre ;
Les moutons respiraient : nos bergers diligens
Ont chassé par arrêt les renards de nos champs ;
    Les loups vont désoler la terre :
    Nos bergers semblent, entre nous,
    Un peu d'accord avec les loups.*

Vol. XII, p. 353.

Facing the series : Fanaticism-Superstition-Bigotry-Religious persecution-
dogma-Church-Religion-God, it is my opinion that Voltaire wanted to get rid
of everything but God and possibly Religion very generally understood, and
D'Alembert of everything without exception.

6. Lettre 44, Voltaire to D' Alembert, vol. 62, p. 76, 25.ii.1758.
On Pompadour and Jesuits and Pope, *Crétineau-Joly*, ch. II, pp. 103 *et seq.*

7. *Gondomar*, vol. III, pp. 145, 171, 200.

8. *Crétineau-Joly*, ch. I, pp. 18 *et seq. Schoell*, vol. XXXIX, Book VIII,
ch. XI, p. 46.
*On sait que le Duc de Cumberland s'était flatté de devenir roi de Portugal.
Je ne doute pas qu'il n'eût réussi, si les Jésuites, confesseurs de la famille royale ne
s'y fussent opposés. Voilà le crime qu'on n'a jamais pu leur pardonner.*—*Testament
Politique du Maréchal de Belle-Isle*, quoted by *Crétineau-Joly*, p. 42.
Schoell, loc. cit. ; Crétineau-Joly, loc. cit. Picot, vol. IV, pp. 9 *et seq.* The belief
that gold was abundant in the lands controlled by the Jesuits in Paraguay turns
up frequently in the letters from the Director of the *Asiento* Company mentioned in note 4 above, and the fact is even said to be one of the causes of the
secrecy the missions kept about their activities, and of the difficulty for strangers
to be admitted in them.

9. Siècle de Louis XIV quoted by *Crétineau-Joly*, p. 77.

10. *Voltaire-R.*, vol. 62, p. 174, 31.x.1771. He refers to Malagrida. See
Voltaire's letter to Damilaville, 2.iii.1763 (wrongly set down March 3rd in
Crétineau-Joly, p. 102). There is a curiously ambiguous sentence in this
letter : *Il ne faut pas calomnier les malheureux, surtout quand on n'a pas besoin
de leur imputer des crimes.*—Vol. 52, p. 71.
Crétineau-Joly, pp. 108 *et seq.*

11. *Crétineau-Joly*, pp. 125, 101, 133. That Choiseul used the Jesuits to
divert attention from Martinique is explained by D'Alembert himself, quoted
by *Crétineau-Joly*, p. 138.

12. *Voltaire-R.*, vol. 62. Lettre 354, p. 640 ; vol. 55, Lettre 420, p. 589.
Picot, vol. IV, pp. 45 *et seq.*

13. "The influence of the Jesuits on Spanish morals, from everything I
have learned, was undoubtedly favourable." *Doblado*, p. 87. See his outspoken defence note D, p. 474. On Roda and the Colleges, *Doblado*, pp. 102
et seq., Letter III and app., pp. 447 *et seq.*

14. *Doblado*, App. to Letters III and VII by an English Peer, pp. 454–8 ; also Letter Vii itself.

15. I follow *Coxe*, vol. III, ch. LXIV ; *La Fuente*, vol. I, pp. 113, 119. *Alamant-D.H.*, vol. III, pp. 315–17 ; *Crétineau–Joly*, ch. III, p. 167 ; *Doblado, loc. cit.*

Au moment de mourir le Duc d'Albe déposa entre les mains du Grand Inquisiteur, Philippe Bertram, Evêque de Salamanque, une déclaration portant qu'il était un des auteurs de l'émeute des Chapeaux ; qu'en 1766 il l'avait fomentée en haine des Jésuites. Il avouait aussi avoir composé en grande partie la lettre supposée du Général de l'Institut contre le Roi d'Espagne. Il reconnaissait encore avoir inventé la fable de l'Empereur Nicolas I et d'être l'un des fabricateurs de la monnaie à l'effigie de ce monarque. Crétineau–Joly, vol. III, p. 321. This Emperor Nicolas I, an invention of Pombal, was said to be a Lay Jesuit who crowned himself Emperor in Paraguay, commanded 150,000 soldiers and sent home 3 million *pesos* a year to the Jesuit Order in Rome. The pamphlet was burnt in Madrid as a libel by order of the Crown under Ferdinand VI. *La Fuente, loc. cit. Alaman–D.H.*, p. 319.

16. Same sources and *M.P.*, *H.*, vol. III, pp. 139 *et seq.*

17. See Letter from the Marquis D'Ossun, French Ambassador, to Louis XV, as quoted by Rochford to Lord Shelburne, Paris, 6.v.1767, in *Coxe*, vol. III, ch. LXV, p. 332n.
Schoell, Book VIII, ch. XII, vol. 39, p. 163, says of this letter " *que le Duc de Choiseul est accusé d'avoir fait fabriquer* " *;* but see also note 15 above on the Duke of Alba's share in this machination. On the authenticity of this piece, *M.P.*, *H.*, vol. III, p. 143n. Though not scientifically ascertained, the balance of evidence is in favour of it. *Coxe* says the Jesuits were allowed to take other conveniences and even their money on specifying the amount in writing.—Vol. III, p. 328.
Crétineau–Joly, p. 178.

18. *M.P.*, *H.*, p. 144. *Argentina*, vol. 5 (1), ch. VIII, p. 222. *Coxe*, vol. III, ch. LXV, p. 329.

19. *Crétineau–Joly*, pp. 194–6. *Coxe, loc. cit.*, p. 337. History of this Conclave in *Crétineau–Joly*, pp. 214–68. Ganganelli's statement to Charles III reads : " *Il reconnait au Souverain Pontife le droit de pouvoir éteindre en conscience la Compagnie de Jésus, en observant les règles canoniques, et il est à souhaiter que le future Pape fasse ses efforts pour accomplir les voeux des couronnes.*"—P. 260.

20. On Moñino : Charles III to Tanucci, quoted by *M.P.-H.*, vol. III, p. 159.
" *Les membres de cette Compagnie avaient mérité leur ruine par l'inquiétude de leur esprit et l'audace de leurs menées.*"—*Crétineau–Joly*, p. 293.

21. *M.P.* as usual swells the merit of the Jesuits Spain lost. Some of these men were, nevertheless, of outstanding capacity.

22. On Vizcardo see *Argentina*, vol. 5 (1), p. 224 ; *Miranda–Archivo*, particularly vol. XV ; and *Spell*.
Miranda–Archivo, vol. XV, pp. 320, 321.

CHAPTER XVII

1. *Miranda-Archivo*, p. 340.
Lansdowne in debates on Nootka Sound in the House of Lords : *The parliamentary History of England from the earliest period to the year* 1803, Vol. XXVIII. London, 1816. Columns 914–18 and 937 *et seq.* Quotations : col. 945.
Varinas, Mano de Relox, ch. X, p. 367 ; *Walpole*, vol. I, pp. 133–4, 135.

2. *Coxe*, vol. III, ch. LX, pp. 261–2. *Walpole*, vol. I, pp. 558, 560, 618 ; Burke, *Thoughts on a Regicide Peace* ; quoted by *Walpole*, vol. I, p. 684.

A New Ballad on the taking of Porto Bello by Admiral Vernon. London, 1740. Bodleian Library. 85b, 29. *Original Letters to an Honest Sailor*. London, 1746, pp. 46, 27, 51, 58, 46. *Short Verses in Imitation of Long Verses in an Epistle to W—m P—tt*. London, 1746.

Coxe is curiously inconsistent about this war. He endeavours to put the blame on Spain, yet once the war has begun, he forgets and naively declares: " As the plans of aggression against Spain had been already matured, the rupture of the negotiation was the signal for immediate hostilities."—P. 261.

3. On Manila, *loc. cit.*, p. 274. The fact that these " 26 English ships richly laden " were caught in Sacramento explains who it was who carried on contraband, and who it was who instigated trouble between Portugal and Spain, though in the following sentence, Coxe writes : " Spain endeavoured to cut off the obnoxious colony of Sacramento from the bank of the Río de la Plata [. . .] while the Portuguese laboured to extend their limits in order to preserve the advantages of a port and to continue the contraband traffic with Buenos Aires." —*Coxe*, vol. III, ch. LXIX, pp. 385–6.

4. *Coxe*, vol. III, ch. LXX, p. 396.
Franklin's text from *History of the Dispute with America from its origin in 1754*. Written in the year 1774, by John Adams Esq. London, 1784. Pp. 5–8.

5. *The Rights of Great Britain asserted against the Claims of America ; being an Answer to the Declaration of the General Congress. The ninth Edition. To which is now added a further refutation of Dr. Price's State of the Nation's Debt*. London, 1776.

6. From Adams' *History* as in note 4 above, pp. 77–80.

7. *Loc. cit.*, pp. 29–30 ; 77–80.

8. Adams' *History*, pp. 82–3. *The Rights of Great Britain*, p. 83.

9. *Coxe, loc. cit., A.–K.*, pp. 85 *et seq.*

10. Aranda–Grimaldi : *A.–K.*, p. 94.

11. *Coxe* : " While the French Court fomented the rebellious spirit of the colonists, they instigated Spain to increase the embarrassments of England by an attack against Portugal."—Vol. III, ch. LXVIII, p. 381.
He is, of course, wrong. It was the other way about.—Grimaldi : p. 114, ch. LXIX.

12. *A.–K.*, p. 144. Kalb : *Argentina*, vol. 5 (1), p. 156. Quotation from *Cool Thoughts on the Consequences of American Independence*, written in 1783 against a pamphlet by the Dean of Gloucester presenting the loss as beneficial to Great Britain. Bod. Godwin Pamphlets, 308 (9).

13. *A.–K.*, pp. 129–148. *Argentina, loc. cit.*, pp. 160, 158 ; *Schoell*, vol. XL, ch. XIII, p. 136.

14. *Rights of Great Britain*, p. 93. Paine's letter to Raynal, p. 50.
Godoy.—C.D., vol. II, p. 68 note.

15. On Vergennes and Gibraltar : *Coxe*, ch. LXXV, vol. III ; but also : " In the afternoon I had the visit of [. . .] Mr. Fitz-Herbert, who among other things told me that during the negotiations for the last Peace our *good allies* were on no account ready to accept that the English should cede Gibraltar to Spain. . . . Let us keep the secret."—1.iii.1787.. Miranda.—*Miranda-Archivo*, vol. II, p. 271.
Aranda and Vergennes : *A.–K.*, pp. 166–7.

16. *Schoell*, Book VIII, ch. XIII, vol. XL, pp. 136–7.

17. *Argentina*, vol. 5 (1), pp. 179n *et seq.*

18. *Raynal*, Book XI, ch. XXXI, vol. III, p. 231.

19. *The Declaration of Independence. An Interpretation and an Analysis*, by Herbert Friedenwald, New York. 1904. Ch. IX.

20. *Miranda–Archivo*, vol. VIII, p. 9.

CHAPTER XVIII

1. *Spell*, pp. 143 *et seq.* for a good summary of these measures. *Argentina*, vol. 5 (1), pp. 27 *et seq. M. P.-H.*, vol. II, pp. 246 ; 204. *Godoy C.D.*, vol. I, p. 95.

2. *Argentina*, *loc. cit.*, p. 29. *T.M.I.C.*, vol. II, ch. XVI, p. 529. *T.M.I.L.*, vol. II, ch. XXVII, p. 381. The Inquisitor Abarca " ordered the volume of the Methodical Encyclopædia to be returned to Dr. Rozas and to take from him the work of Raynal."—*T.M.I.C.*, *loc. cit.*, p. 533. The Supreme Council of the Inquisition, however, allowed Raynal in Almodóvar's translation " because it is not so much a translation as an extract in which the useful has been separated from the harmful."—*The Lima Inquisition* 1802 in *T.M.I.C.*, *loc. cit.*, p. 532.

3. *Spell*, p. 144. *Godoy C.D.*, vol. I, p. 51. *M.P.–H.*, vol. II, p. 254.

4. *Godoy C.D.*, vol. II, ch. XLII, p. 169. *M. P.-H.*, vol. II, p. 246, 254. *M. P.-H.*, vol. II, p. 260.

5. *Godoy C.D.*, vol. I, ch. VII ; ch. X, vol. I.
On the popularity of the war in Spain see *Godoy C.D.*, vol. I, p. 112n, and in particular his quotation from de Pradt to the effect that while the French Assemblée Constituante had received gifts to the value of 5 millions, and England in 1793 to the value of 45, gifts for the war against France in Spain reached 75 millions and even beggars offered them. P. 139. On Aranda's arguments against the war, see ch. XVIII.

6. *Miranda–Archivo*, vol. VIII, pp. 7, 10.
Kersaint's plan : Caillet–Bois in *Argentina*, *loc. cit.*, p. 34.

7. *Argentina*, *loc. cit.*, p. 35. *Miranda–Archivo*, vol. XV, p. 351.

8. *Miranda–Archivo*, vol. VIII, p. 11 ; vol. XV, p. 153.

9. *Miranda–Archivo*, vol. VIII, p. 11 ; *Argentina*, *loc. cit.*, p. 34.
Miranda–Robertson, vol. I, p. 130, 13.iii.1799. *Miranda dans La Révolution Française* by Rojas, pp. 2, 4.
Miranda–Archivo, vol. VIII, pp. 11, 15.

10. *Godoy C.D.*, vol. I, pp. 268–9. On Roncesvalles, *Godoy C.D.*, p. 262
See also Vol. II, pp. 32, 37.

11. *Miranda–Robertson*, vol. I, p. 137. *Spell*, pp. 217 *et seq.*
Argentina, 5 (1), pp. 38 *et seq.* ; 39.

12. A good analysis of the Negro-French combination in the Rio de la Plata in *Argentina*, *loc. cit. Amunátegui*, vol. III, pp. 117 *et seq. Miranda–Archivo*, vol. XV, pp. 421, 420. On Mallet, *H.D.N.M.*, vol. 3, p. 391.

13. *Vi sono molti Spagnuoli, che tengono per cosa certa, che quest' Isola (San Dominico) in breve tempo sera posseduta da questi Mori di Guinea—Historia del Mondo Nuovo*, 1572, p. 65, quoted by *H., P.N.*, Book IV, ch. XII, vol. I, p. 571. *Hazard*, pp. 103, 107 and others.

14. This narrative is a summary of ch. VIII of *Hazard*.

15. *H., P.N.*, Book IV, ch. XII, vol. I, p. 570.

16. *Miranda–Archivo*, vol. XV, p. 207.

17. *Miranda–Archivo*, vol. XV, pp. 272–3 ; 228 ; 233 ; 344, 350 ; 403–4.

CHAPTER XIX

1. *Argentina*, vol. 5 (1), ch. VIII, p. 228, in which it is wrongly assumed that Walpole was still in office in 1743.

2. See some of these plans such as Kaye's (1776) and Hippisley's in *Argentina* 5 (1), p. 227. Best source for Aubarède : *Miranda–Archivo*, vol. XV, pp. 5 *et seq.*, whence quotations. The brief summary in *Argentina* 5 (1), pp. 228–9, is incorrect in at least one point, the date ; and the name of the Marquess is given as Aubarde.

3. *Miranda–Archivo*, vol. XV, p. 24.

4. *Argentina*, 5 (1), pp. 231–3.

5. On Vidall, *Argentina, loc. cit.*, pp. 233–5 ; *Miranda–Archivo*, vol. XV, pp. 177, 272, 283. On connection with Socorro, Briceño quoted by *Mancini*, p. 43. On Miranda–Dalling, see next chapter.

6. Signatories : Don Juan Vicente Bolívar, Don Martín de Tovar and Marqués de Mixares. *Miranda–Archivo*, vol. XV, p. 68.

7. On Olavide, abundant bibliography. Much useful material in *M.P.–H.* On Thürriegel–Miranda, *Miranda–Archivo*, vol. IV, p. 327. Miranda's views on La Carolina, *loc. cit.*, vol. I, p. 124.

8. Summary in *M.P.–H.*, vol. III, pp. 211–12.

9. *Passant dans de justes angoisses le temps à jamais mémorable de la Terreur il a appris ce qu'il ne soupçonnait pas quinze ans auparavant, qu'il y avait sous le ciel quelque chose de plus redoutable que l'Inquisition.—Bourgoing*, vol. I, p. 386.

10. *Argentina*, 5 (1), pp. 232 *et seq.*

11. *Restrepo*, vol. I, p. 38. His narrative differs in some important details from *Argentina, loc. cit.*, and from *Biografía del General Antonio Nariño by Soledad Acosta de Samper*, Pasto, 1910.

12. Earlier, about October of last year there had been in London a person from Santa Fe de Bogotá (D. Antonio de Nariño, alias D. Palacio Ortiz), a man of rank, talent and good sense ; who also had to go away without being able to obtain a hearing.—José Caro, London, October 15th, 1797. *Miranda–Archivo*, vol. XV, p. 185.
Cf. *Restrepo*, vol. I, p. 40, and *Argentina, loc. cit.*

13. *Miranda–Archivo*, vol. XV, p. 378. Proclamation in *Gil Fortoul*, vol. I, pp. 122, 127.

14. *Gil Fortoul*, vol. I, p. 134. He adds that the Captain General did not think their offers very sincere.

CHAPTER XX

1. *Archivo–Miranda*, vol. I, p. 14 ; p. 13 ; p. 16.

2. On his titles of Colonel and Count see note 18, below.

3. On M, the "scion of a noble family " *Miranda–Robertson*, p. xiii. On coat of arms *Miranda–Archivo*, vol. I, p. 20. Quotation from *Miranda–Archivo*, vol. I, p. 4.

4. *Miranda–Archivo*, vol. I, p. 37, p. 43, p. 135, p. 39, pp. 76, 91, 104 ; vol. V, p. 142 ; vol. I, pp. 128, 122, 124, 123 ; 133, 135, 134.

5. *Miranda–Archivo*, vol. IV, pp. 330, 334, 356, 350, 386.

6. See explanation of these charges in *Miranda–Archivo*, vol. IV, pp. 403 *et seq.*; protectors, p. 371 ; orders, p. 346 ; transfer to the Navy, p. 350, p. 351 ; vol. I, pp. 141–91, on Pensácola.

7. Vol. V, pp. 201, 200 ; vol. XV, p. 394. Cf. Dalling to Germain, 10.x.1781 and 15.xi.1781 in C.O. 137/82 quoted by *Robertson–Miranda*, vol. I, p. 23n.
Miranda–Archivo, vol. VIII, p. 9. See below special note on Miranda's stay in Jamaica and dealings with General Dalling.

8. *Miranda–Archivo*, vol. V, p. 142 ; vol. VII, p. 9 ; vol. VIII, p. 9 ; vol. VII, p. 17 ; vol. I, p. 222 ; vol. VII, p. 8.

9. Vol. V, p. 147 ; vol. I, pp. 231, 326, 251–2, 227, 299.

10. Vol. I, pp. 212, 260, 226, 230.

11. Vol. I, pp. 238, 286.

12. Vol. I, pp. 235, 250, 232.
Of General Knox he says that he was " one of the best educated soldiers in the theory and practice of the art of war of the many leaders I have known in this continent, including the *Idol*."—P. 315 ; vol. I, pp. 317, 291, 314.

13. Vol. I, pp. 223, 214, 210, 246.

14. Vol. I, pp. 346–7, 342–3, 357, 352, 353.

15. Vol. II, p. 282.   See also, for Catherine, pp. 275, 291, 298, 300, 308.

16. Texts of the two letters in vol. II, p. XIII.   Macanaz was not Minister but Chargé d'Affaires.

17. See Smith's letter 26.iii.1788, vol. XV, p. 86–91, also vol. XII, pp. 182–3n. On Cambridge, vol. IV, pp. 313–316.

18. As it has sometimes been argued that Miranda personally did not dub himself a Count, it may be useful to record a number of cases in which he unmistakably does it, and those in which he is addressed as such by others with a frequency which would be impossible were it not accepted by him and in fact expected.   References to volumes and pages of his *Archivo*.

Date	Miranda himself		Others	
23.vii.85		vol.	V, p.	298
12.ix.86		,,	VII, ,,	194
22.ix.86 (1)	vol. VII, p. 326			
87		,,	II, ,,	289
87		,,	VII, ,,	207
87		,,	VII, ,,	106
18.v.87 (2)	vol. VII, p. 101			
10.viii.87		,,	VII, ,,	196
18.viii.87		,,	VII, ,,	123
18.viii.87		,,	VII, ,,	103
4.ix.87	vol. VII, p. 202			
10.x.87 (3)	,, VII, p. 260			
21.xii.87	,, VII, p. 35			
10.i.88 (3)	,, VII, p. 260			
2.ii.88		,,	VII, ,,	327
8.ii.88		,,	VII, ,,	326
21.iv.88		,,	VII, ,,	111
88		,,	VII, ,,	257
22.v.88		,,	V, ,,	378
12.vi.88		,,	VII, ,,	123
26.viii.88		,,	V, ,,	396
8.ix.88 (4)	vol. V, p. 399			
30.ix.88 (4)	vol. VII, p. 196			
4.x.89		,,	VI, pp.	5–7
7.v.90		,,	VI, p.	46
15.viii.90		,,	VI, ,,	70
9.viii.90		,,	VI, pp.	68–69
90		,,	VI, p.	63
93		,,	XIII, ,,	233
23.xii.99		,,	XV, ,,	406

(1) This is a passport granted by the Imperial authorities obviously on his instructions.   (2) A tailor's bill which would not be addressed to a Count if

the person concerned did not wish it so. (3) Contracts for personal servants evidently drafted by Miranda himself. (4) Letters of recommendation in which " *le porteur de la présente* " is not only described as Count Miranda but as " *noble méxicain* " obviously at Miranda's suggestion.

19. Vol. VII, p. 45 ; 20.vii.89, p. 45, pp. 52, 54.

20. Though Spain gave up Nootka Bay, her studies of the coast did not cease. Elice and Fidalgo explored the coast up to 60°50′ ; and the two finest expeditions from the scientific point of view, those of Malaspina (1791) and Galiano–Valdés (1792) took place after Spain had given up her rights. Of the last, Humboldt writes that it confirmed the discovery of the mouth of the Columbia river made in 1775 by another Spaniard, Eceta, and he adds : " *Cette reconnaissance étoit d'autant plus importante que Vancouver, qui avoit déjà suivi cette côte de très près, n'avoit pu apercevoir aucune entrée depuis les 45° de latitude jusqu'au Canal de Fuca, et que ce savant navigateur doutoit même alors de l'existence du Río de Colombia ou de l'Entrada de Eceta.*" P. 341.—The Encyclopædia Britannica mentions no one but Vancouver in its article on British Colombia. Humboldt's study : *H., E.P.N.E.*, Book III, ch. VIII, vol. I, pp. 328–350.
Vol. VII, p. 383. See also ch. XVII, n. 2, above.
Vol. VII, p. 54 ; vol. XV, p. 110.

21. Vol. XV, p. 113.
Some of the papers listed vol. XV, p. 110, were not delivered by Miranda to Pitt till May or even October, particularly the list of the Jesuits, to which Pitt attached so much importance. (121).

22. Pitt crawling on maps, vol. XV, p. 121.
Miranda–Life, vol. I, p. 106 ; p. 112.

23. Note 28.i.91 : vol. XV.
Pp. 128–9. Pitt's promises, p. 134, 8.ix.91, Miranda to Pitt. Mistrusts Pitt : Letter to Smith, Pitt's secretary, 6.vii.91, p. 130. Catholic disqualification, p. 136. Other details, Miranda to Pitt, 18.xi.91, pp. 139–40.

24. Vol. XV, pp. 142, 111, 143.

25. Vol. XV, pp. 264, 265. See about Miranda's intentions, p. 144, footnote.

26. Moscoso *Godoy–C.D.*, vol. I, p. 374, chs. XXX, XXXI, XXXVIII of vol. I for this period, and ch. XXXVIII, vol. II, for the war. Quotations from *Miranda–Archivo*, vol. XV, p. 171, 176.

27. In the list of Jesuits, vol. XV, p. 98–102, can be found a José Pozo and even a Francisco Miranda, but I see no Salas. On the other hand there is a Manuel de Salas *tesorero propietario* who with Bolívar's father, D. Juan Vicente, as accountant *ad interim*, signed together a paper for Miranda's father on 5.i.1771 (vol. I, p. 10) and vol. V, p. 111, a Captain of Engineers, D. Joseph del Pozo y Sucre, signs on March 1st, 1783, a certificate on oath and in his favour in connection with some accusations made by the authorities against Miranda. While the first belongs to a previous generation the latter is very likely to be the Pozo y Sucre described often as a Jesuit. He had fortified Trinidad under Chacon, the excellent Governor of that island till it was lost in 1797. On Olavide, see above and also Adams to James Lloyd, March 26, 1815, John Adams, Works, vol. X, pp. 141–3, Boston 1856.

28. Vol. XV, p. 202.

29. Vol. VII, p. 136 ; vol. III, p. 88 ; vol. XV, p. 400.

30. Vol. XV, p. 267.

31. Vol. XV, pp. 277–8. *Miranda–Life*, vol. I, p. 172. *Miranda–Archivo*, vol. XV, pp. 343, 342, 374, 375, 378, 381.

32. Vol. XV, pp. 397, 398, 399.

NOTE ON MIRANDA'S GUILT

In his introduction to Miranda's Diary Prof. W. S. Robertson writes : " The injustice of this sentence is shown by the fact that in 1799 the Council of the Indies completely exonerated both Cagigal and Miranda " (p. xv).   Let us see. The charges against M. were 4 : He was " passionately parcial to the English " ; he had granted them a clause *ultra vires* and contrary to Spanish policy, he had engaged in contraband ; and he had allowed General Campbell to visit the forts of Havana (vol. V, p. 75).

The last charge was a calumny.   It was easily rebutted (vol. V, pp. 79 ss.). The ease with which M.'s innocence triumphed here should have advised caution on the other points.   The facts are complex as they emerge from the tomes of M.'s archives and from the papers in the P.R.O., notably F.O. 72 (1 and 2, pp. 97, 113–114, 77–8 and C.O. 137/84, notably fols. 77, 80).

Was there animus and ill will against M. ?   Probably yes.   Miranda complains to Charles IV of José de Gálvez' *malevolence* (VII, 53).   It was believed that Bernardo de Gálvez had resented an article published in the *Providence Gazette*, attributed to Miranda, in which clause 1 of the capitulations was criticized because the British garrison which had surrendered to the Spaniards was to be sent to England.   (V, p. 119 for text of article ; V, pp. 200, 201, 213 for rumours attributing to this article Miranda's troubles, p. 223 for detailed explanation).   But even Miranda's agent wrote to him referring to Gálvez : " It is true the article stung the said person a good deal and that he could not hide it ; but it is also true that he has in his hands three orders, the first of March 11, to send you to C., who has also order to arrest you and keep you in the port of Cabaña [Havana] at the disposal of the Court " (V, p. 200). And there is no question that the Spanish Government had every reason to feel concerned about Miranda.

The facts are put by Cagigal in a letter marked " secret " and addressed on 22.i.82 to José de Gálvez, Minister for the Indies (V, pp. 61–69).   A decision was taken to send an officer to Jamaica to arrange for an exchange of prisoners. C. chose M. and gave him instructions to gather military information, for which he put 4,000 *pesos* at his disposal, ostensibly for his subsistence and that of three servants.   C. mentions no other money save " the few *reales* to help the many war prisoners in Jamaica."   But the English were not caught napping.   When M. arrived in Bluefields a British coast guard boarded his flag of truce and in complete disregard of M.'s diplomatic privileges, searched her.   The story is told by M. in vol. V, pp. 8 and 20.   But let us listen to the story as reported in the P.R.O. papers :

" In the beginning of September 1781 Don Francisco de Miranda Aid de Camp to General Cagigal, then Governor of the Havannah, was sent to Jamaica in a Flag of Truce, on the ostensible pretext of settling a Cartel between Jamaica and Cuba, but who, from confidential intelligence afterwards received, came for the express purpose of learning the state of our military Force and preparations for defence ; The Armies of France & Spain having then in contemplation to attack Jamaica early in the following Spring.   This Flag of Truce was boarded by one of His Majesty's Cruizers on her approaching the coast, & seized on account of Thirty or Forty Thousand Dollars being found on board of her ; But upon Mirandas asserting that this Specie was sent for the purpose of discharging the Debts and relieving the necessities of the Spanish Officers Prisoners of War in Jamaica, the money and Vessel were released. It is however worthy of notice, that the Spanish officers declared on their being exchanged, that Miranda had absolutely refused them any part of this Cash, and that they were therefore under the necessity of borrowing a very considerable sum from a Merchant in Kingston."   (C.O. 137/84).

This fact that Miranda refused to help the Spanish prisoners is confirmed in a letter from J. de Gálvez to the Governor of Havana as well as by the complaints of some of the prisoners themselves in M.'s archives (vol. V, pp. 75 and 18).

Now then : how did 4,000 *pesos* and " a few *reales* " for the prisoners of war become 30 or 40,000 dollars ? And what was that money doing in Jamaica if it was not helping the prisoners ? For it was not paying for information either. C. says so. M. suggested to him " to cover the acquisition of news with the veil of business " (V, 62) and he, Cagigal, extols the information brought over by M. as being far better than that procured by " anyone who would acquire it for money " (V, 83). The information, say M. and C., was provided by one Philip Allwood in exchange for the right to " introduce," i.e., to smuggle 6 or 7,000 *pesos* worth of linen goods into Cuba. On 1.ix.1783, about two years later, the Captain of H.B.M.'s *Fox* wrote from Havana to Lord Mountstuart :

" Philip Allwood Esqr. a very considerable Merchant of the Island of Jamaica who came down here since the Peace to recover a large Sum of Money that he in the course of the war had advanced in trade and other ways to different Spanish prisoners who were carried into that Island was on the 20th of last Month seized, all his papers taken from him and his person thrown into prison without any cause whatever assigned him for such extraordinary proceeding ; nor can I altho twelve days have since elapsed either from the Governor Don Luis Unzaga or the Judge Don Juan Antonio de Vruñuela by whose authority I find Mr Allwood was arrested procure any reason whatever for such an extraordinary stretch of power against a subject of my Royal Master.

" He was taken out of the House of Brigadier General Ezpeleta the Commander in chief of His Catholic Majesty's Forces in the West Indies with whom he lived, and who is as much astonished and as ignorant of any reason for such an act of Violence and Injustice as I am.

" To give your Lordship the most perfect Idea in my power of this Business I have taken the liberty of inclosing you a copy of my Correspondence with the Governor on the subject, and by the advice of General Ezpeleta I have done the same to General Gálvez the late Commander in chief here, to whom General Ezpeleta has also wrote *supposing* the cause of Mr. Allwood's imprisonment to have originated in the time of his Command here at which time General Cagigal, now also at Madrid, was Governor and no stranger to the supposed matter.

" About two years ago General Cagigal then Governor here sent a Captain Miranda to Jamaica to settle a cartel ; while at Jamaica Miranda bought two vessels and loaded them with different goods for the Havana market great part of which goods were bought from the Copartnership of Mr. Allwood who speaking Spanish was pitched upon by Governor Dalling of Jamaica and Sir Peter Barker as a proper person to accompany Miranda back to the Havana [*sic*] to compleat the business of the Cartel upon their parts.

" On Miranda's arrival with whom Allwood came passenger at this Island the vessels and cargoes were seized as contraband by order of the Intendant, and repleven'd [*sic*] by Governor Cagigal, which brought on a dispute between the Governor and Intendant that was carried to their Court, and ended in the removal of the Governor with an order from Court at that time (now near two years ago) to arrest both Miranda and Allwood in hopes as they say here that the latter would be an evidence against the former ; however before that order arrived Mr. Allwood had compleated his Mission here and returned to Jamaica, and Miranda had saved himself by flight to America. It is therefore *supposed* that it is by virtue of that order given against him in the hight of the War, that he is now arrested." (F.O. 72/2, p. 97.)

Allwood, however, was but a façade for the real business man : Eliphalet Fitch. This shady character became M.'s companion as soon as he landed in Kingston ; to such an extent that the Governor of the Island, General Dalling, invited him to dinner " in the company of Mr. Fitch," an invitation which M., in a manner most indiscreet for a friendly guest on a diplomatic mission, declined for himself on the excuse of being indisposed, and on behalf of Fitch on the ground that his friend was too busy ! Not unnaturally General Dalling rebuked Miranda in a stern note dated 28.ix.81 (V, pp. 12, 13). The report in the P.R.O. says : " Eliphalet Fitch became the early companion and confident of Miranda, in consequence of Letters received by him from certain Friends at the Havannah, and it was publickly noticed, that Fitch travelled more about with this Officer, than propriety or even common decency could then well justify." Then it adds :

> " By the Custom House Books of Kingston, it is well established, that on the 2ᵈ of October 1781, Arthur Bold cleared out the schooner Flora John Goff Master for New York, with 253 Coils of rope, 800 pieces of Canvass, 3 luncheons of Hardware, 104 Casks of Nails, 1 Trunk of Dry Goods, 1 luncheon of Black pepper, and 41 Kegs of White lead ; and it likewise appears by Affidavits, that the Flora instead of proceeding to New York, went directly to the Havannah, and had her cargo sold to the Spaniards. (*loc. cit.*)
>
> " Miranda & Fitch worked together in the project. They obtained permission from the Governor and Admirals to make further purchases under pretext that the vessels were wanted to carry off the Prisoners. They told the Admiral that the Governor had consented if the Admiral did not object, and the Governor that the Admiral was willing if *he* would agree.—The account continues, of the duplicity in arranging the smuggling."

There is little spying in this, and much business. In vain does Cagigal swell the importance of M.'s services (V, 83 ss.). The English were fully aware of what M. was after in Jamaica ; or they would not have searched him. Moreover, an American accomplice of M.'s contraband dealings was sentenced to 3 years' imprisonment in Veracruz as late as 1784. (*New York Gazetteer*, April 19, 84 ; in VII, 323.) The conclusion is obvious. M. took his opportunity to make money and so did Cagigal, Allwood and Fitch, all at the expense of the Spanish Treasury and none with a bad conscience, since such transactions were made respectable by custom. M., moreover, was pro-English and (rightly) suspected by the Spanish Government on the score of his loyalty. And that explains part of the situation.

But in M.'s case, as the papers here quoted show, there evidently was something else. He had received from C. money, if not much, to help the Spanish prisoners ; he did not help them ; they borrowed from an English merchant of Jamaica ; who was Allwood ; precisely the man who came with Miranda to Cuba and, with M's. and C.'s protection, tried to make money out of the Spanish State. Does not that suggest that M. induced Allwood to lend money to the Spanish prisoners and the Spanish prisoners to borrow from him, with the lure of good business to be done in Cuba, and the whole obviously to the advantage of M. and, it would appear also, of C. ? The papers do not lend themselves to any other interpretation.

C.'s complicity is evident. He liked and admired M. But a fidelity which survived even M.'s anti-Spanish dealings much later, becomes suspect. There may have been a touch of Freemasonry about it. The phrase " Eliphalet Fitch became the early companion and confident of Miranda, in consequence of Letters received by him from certain Friends at the Havannah," to be found in the P.R.O. papers is suggestive. I fancy that there may be a quiet hint at some Masonic meeting in the following note : " Lord Henry Fitzgerald presents his Compliments to Mr. Nevil, begs he will acquaint the Spanish Gentleman, that there is no play to-night, and that he is sorry he shall not have the pleasure of introducing him there, as he had propos'd.—Saturday morning." (V, 189.) This paper refers to M.'s stay in Kingston. Moreover, Aranda, supreme Pontiff of Spanish Masonry, was one of the men appealed to on behalf of Miranda, as M. himself writes to C. : " With great pleasure I enclose a copy of the letter which our good friend Rodriguez wrote to Count Aranda,

Floridablanca, Lozada, Pini &c. . . ." Note "our good friend" (V, p. 13).
C.'s letters in favour of M. when M. left for U.S.A., fleeing from the Spanish
Courts whose authority C. was paid to uphold, also smack of Masonic brotherhood. It is curious that Miranda wrote to C. : " Ever united to the Party
in all these emergencies, both by choice and by justice, I shall remain steadfast
to the end " ; and the letter is marked *confidential*. (16.iv.83, vol. VII,
p. 9.)

As for M.'s sense of his own guilt, he writes to C. : " Without an extraordinary endeavour of your protection my ruin is inevitable. I shall never,
however, break my promise to you " ; which can only be one of silence over
a common fault. This is confirmed by the humility with which C. answers
an imploring note from M., on the run : " Decide whatever you please and I
shall at once carry it out." M. in the above quoted note adds : " I only entreat
you for your honour to tell me what I must do in the present circumstances
to take (if such a thing is possible) the decision which may be less ruinous for
my honour and my subsistence." And later : " I hope that you realise the
ingenuity, friendship, frankness and fidelity with which I speak in this letter,
and how much I risk in it, and that you will keep it adequately secret." This is
the language of a man who holds his chief as an accomplice. To wit : " If
I am to speak out, what I think about your affairs and mine, I am expecting
a tragedy any day." (Vol. V, p. 131.) Moreover Bernardo de Gálvez, Commander in Chief, in a letter to C. (8.viii.82), excusing himself for having had
to send M. to Havana from Guarico, where he kept him in the hope that
Madrid would cancel the orders for imprisonment, adds a *post scriptum* which
speaks for itself : " Friend, though pro forma it was found necessary to lay
hands on M.'s papers ; since I shall be the only one to see them, I assure you
that if by chance I found one which might tell against you [or it might mean
him ?] I shall burn it or it will never be found." Gálvez was as good as his
word. Rodríguez wrote to M. : " It seems that G. . . . has read and burnt
several papers belonging to you and which could do nothing but injure you
most gravely."[1] (V, 202.) There is, moreover, in all this letter an obvious
sense that the man to whom it is addressed has much to hide.

And, of course, there was a secret. A correspondent signing J.M.P. wrote
to C. on 1.viii.82 that So-and-so was " the rascal who has revealed to *the man*
all the secret which M. had entrusted to him." (V, 93.) And that this secret
may well have been more injurious to C. than to M. would appear from a
curious passage in a letter from M. to C., Philadelphia, 11.i.84 (vol. VII, p. 12) ;
M. explains that all went well in Philadelphia till someone wrote all kinds of
ill reports about him from Havana, and goes on : " And here I am in the most
unpleasant circumstances a man of honour may ever find himself ; for if I
try to vindicate myself I break the secret I have promised you on my honour
to keep till you hear from the Court, and if I keep silent, there goes my esteem
and my honour in the eyes of these people who have received me so well from
the first to the last."

Finally there is that exoneration by the Council of the Indies towards the
end of 1799. By then the man who was being exonerated had been for years
negotiating with the British Government in what, for official Spain, was treason.
And, moreover, the Spanish Government knew all about it. Godoy was in
office—a freemason. It is reasonable to argue that the sentence of the Council
of the Indies aimed at reconquering Miranda or getting hold of him with the
bait of rehabilitation. On 10.xii.99, C. wrote to M. (vol. XV, p. 392) imparting
the news of the sentence which washed them both clean and urging him to
come to Barcelona and Valencia so that they both could proceed to Madrid
to claim their right to an indemnity. The situation for C. may have been
simpler, for he probably had no inside knowledge of M.'s treason. But the

(1) The original Spanish contains a negative which makes its sense absurd, particularly in
relation with the superlative " gravísimo " " which could not inflict on you a very great
injury ". It may be an erratum. At any rate R. confirms that G. burnt papers " which might
have been useful against you " (p. 200).

Government that absolved him had probably other views, and Miranda also, for of course he did not come to Spain.

CHAPTER XXI

1. *Miranda–Archivo*, vol. IV, pp. 313, 316.
On Moll Trotter : *Farther Reasons of a Country Gentleman for Opposing Mr. Wilberforce's Motion on the* 15*th day of May last for prohibiting British Subjects trading to Africa to procure Negroes for the British Colonies.* London. 1792. Bodleian. *Godwin Pamphlets.* 2074. No. 7.

2. Burke's Black Code, pp. 262–89, vol. VI of *The Writings and Speeches of Edmund Burke.* London. No date. Clauses 35, p. 287, and 41, p. 289.
Miranda–Archivo, vol. XV, pp. 256–7.

BIBLIOGRAPHY

The following list is limited to the books actually quoted in the text. They are printed in the alphabetical order of the short names adopted in the notes. In a number of cases a comment has been added on some point of interest referring to the book in question.

A.B.—*Archivo Boliviano. Colección de Documentos Relativos a la Historia de Bolivia,* edited by Vicente de Ballivian y Roxas. Paris, 1872.

A.K.—*Die Politik des Grafen Aranda.* By Dr. Richard Konetzke. Berlin, 1929.

A.M.—*Examen Crítico-Histórico del Influjo que tuvo en el Comercio, Industria y Población de España su Dominación en América.* By D. José Arias y Miranda. Madrid, 1854.

Alaman-D.H.—*Disertaciones sobre la Historia de la República Megicana, desde la época de la Conquista* [. . .] *hasta la Independencia.* By Don Lucas Alamán. Mégico, 1844. 3 vols.

Alaman-H.M.—*Historia de Méjico desde los primeros movimientos que prepararon su independencia en el año 1803 hasta la época presente.* By Don Lucas Alamán. Méjico, 1849. 4 vols.

Alarcón-Guerra.—*D. Juan Ruiz de Alarcón y Mendoza.* By D. Luis Fernández-Guerra y Orbe. Madrid, 1871.

Alexander.—*Transatlantic Sketches comprising Visits to the most interesting Scenes in North and South America and the West Indies. With Notes on Negro Slavery and Canadian Emigration* by Capt. J. E. Alexander. London, 1833. 2 vols.

Alsedo.—*Piraterías y Agresiones de los Ingleses y de otros Pueblos de Europa en la América Española, desde el siglo XVI al XVIII deducidas de las obras de* D. Dionisio de Alsedo y Herrera. Published by D. Justo, Zaragoza. Madrid, 1833.

Altamira-H.—*La Huella de España en América.* By Rafael Altamira y Creves. Madrid, 1924.

Amunátegui.—*Los Precursores de la Independencia de Chile.* By Miguel Luis Amunátegui. Santiago, 1872.

Anderson.—*Tales of Venezuela illustrative of revolutionary men, manners and incidents.* By John Anderson. London, 1838. 3 vols.

Anonymous.—*Six Months in the West Indies in* 1825. London, MDCCCXXVI.

Antipatía.—*Antipatía de los Franceses y Españoles. Obra apacible y curiosa Compuesta en Castellano* por el Doctor Carlos García.
   Antipathie des François & des Espagnols. Œuvre Curieuse & agréable composée en Espagnol par le Docteur Charles García & mis [sic] en François R.D.B. A Rouen, chez Jacques Caillove, dans la court du Palais, MDCXXXVIII.
   There is a certain mystery over this Franco-Spanish author known in the literature of national character and psychology under the mixed name of Charles García, though there is no doubt that he was a Spaniard.

Argentina.—*Historia de la Nación Argentina.* Edited by Ricardo Levene. Buenos Aires, 1936–9.

B.A.H.V.—*Boletin de la Academia Nacional de la Historia*. Tomo XXII, No. 87. Caracas, 1939.

B.D.C.—*Historia verdadera de la Conquista de la Nueva España, por Bernal Díaz del Castillo, uno de sus Conquistadores*. Edited by Genaro García. Mexico, 1907. 2 vols.

Balbuena.—*Grandeza Mexicana*. By Bernardo de Balbuena. Madrid, 1821. (Siglo de Oro en las Silvas de Erífile.)

Barclaii.—*Icon Animorum*. Ioannis Barclaii. Londini, Ex officina Nortoniana apud Iohannem Billium. MDCXIV. Cum Privilegio.

Belaunde.—*Bolívar and the Political Thought of the Spanish American Revolution*. By Victor Andrés Belaunde, Member of the Peruvian Academy, Corresponding Member of the Spanish Academy. Baltimore, 1938.

Berdyaev.—*The Meaning of History*. By Nicolas Berdyaev. London, 1936.

Beristain.—*Biblioteca Hispano Americana Setentrional* by Dr. D. José Mariano Beristain y Souza. Second edition. Edited by Dr. Fortino Hipólito Vera. Amecameca, 1883. 3 vols.

Bernardo.—*El Bernardo, Poema Heroyco* by Dr. Don bernardo de Balbuena. Madrid, 1808.

Bodin-E.—*The Six Bookes of a Common-Weale written by I. Bodin, a famous lawyer, and a man of great experience in matters of State*. Out of the French and Latin Copies, done into English by Richard Knolles. London, 1606.

Bodin-F.—*Les Six Livres de la Republique de Iean Bodin Angevin auec un discours & responses du mesme autheur aux Paradoxes du Sieur de Malestroit sur le rehaussement & diminution des monnoyes, & le moyen d'y remédier*. A Lyon, MDXCIII.

Bodin-L.—*Io. Bodini andegavensis de Republica Libri Sex, Latine Ab Autore Redditi Multo Quam Altea Locupletiores*. Lugduni Et Venundantur Parisis, MDLXXXVI.

Bourgoing.—*Tableau de l'Espagne Moderne*. J Fr. Bourgoing. Quatrième édition. Paris, 1807. London, 1808. 3 vols.

Bourne.—*Spain in America*. By Edward Gaylord Bourne. 1904.

British Guiana Boundary.—*Appendix to the Case on behalf of Her Britannic Majesty*. 1898–9.

C.C. S.M.—*Christopher Columbus. Being the Life of The Very Magnificent Lord Don Cristóbal Colón*. By Salvador de Madariaga. London, 1939.

C.D.H.M.—*Colección de Documentos para la Historia de Mexico*, edited by Joaquín García Icazbalceta. Mexico, 1858. 2 vols.

C.D.I.A.I.—*Colección de Documentos inéditos relativos al descubrimiento, conquista y colonización de las posesiones españolas en América y Occeania* [sic], *sacados, en su mayor parte, del Real archivo de Indias*, bajo la dirección de los Señores D. Joaquín F. Pacheco y Don Francisco de Cárdenas, miembros de varias reales academías científicas, y Don Luis Torres de Mendoza, abogado de los Tribunales del Reino. Madrid, 1864–84. 42 vols.

C.D.I.H.E.—*Colección de Documentos Inéditos para la Historia de España*. Por el Marqués de la Fuensanta del Valle y D. José Rayón. Madrid, 1875.

C.M.H.—*The Cambridge Modern History*. Planned by the late Lord Acton, L.L.D. Regius Professor of Modern History. Edited by A. W. Ward, Litt.D., G. W. Prothero, Litt.D., Stanley Leather, M.A., University Press, Cambridge, 1907.

Cagliostro-V.—*Vie de Joseph Balsamo connu sous le nom de Comte Cagliostro, extraite de la procédure instruite contre lui à Rome en* 1790, traduite d'après l'original italien. Paris, 1791.

Calef.—*More Wonders of the Invisible World, etc. collected by Robert Calef, Merchant of Boston, in New England.* London, 1700.

Carande.—*Carlos V y sus Banqueros.* By Ramón Carande. Madrid, 1944.

Charlevoix-P.—*Histoire du Paraguay* par le P. Pierre François-Xavier de Charlevoix de la Campagnie de Jésus. Paris, 1757.

Cockburn.—*The Unfortunate Englishman or a Faithful Narrative of the Distresses and Adventures of John Cockburn and five other English Mariners. Containing a Journey over Land, from the Gulph of Honduras to the Great South Sea.* London (*circa* 1730).

Cortes-M.M.—*Teoría de las Cortes.* Por Martínez Marina. 1820.

Crétineau.—*Clément XIV et les Jésuites.* Par J. Crétineau Joly. Paris, 1847.

D.L.—Voyage aux Iles de Trinidad, etc. Par M. Dauxion Lavaysse. Paris, 1812. 2 vols.

Depons.—*Travels in South America during the years* 1801, 1802, 1803 *and* 1804. By F. Depons. Printed for Longman, Hurst, Rees and Orne, London, 1807. 2 vols.

Desologuren.—*Letter from Don Juan Desologuren On Defence of the Indies against the Dutch.* November 19th, 1637. App. of British Guiana Boundary, vol. I, p. 77.

Dickson.—*Letters on Slavery* by William Dickson, formerly Private Secretary to the late Hon. Edward Hay, Governor of Barbadoes. London, MDCCLXXXIX.

Doblado.—*Letters from Spain* by Don Leucadio Doblado. London, 1822. [Blanco White]

Draper.—*An Address to the British Public on the Case of Brigadier-General Picton.* By Lieut.-Col. Edward A. Draper. London, 1806.

Duro-Armada.—*Armada Española desde la Unión de los Reinos de Castilla y de León.* By Cesareo Fernández Duro. Madrid, 1895–1903. 9 vols.

E.H.R.—English Historical Review.

Ercilla.—*La Araucana. Dirigida Al Rey Don Felipe Nuestro Señor. Su autor Don Alonso de Ercilla y Zuñiga, Caballero del Orden de Santiago, Gentilhombre de la Cámara de la Magestad del Emperador.* En Madrid por D. Antonio de Sancha, MDCCLXXXVI.

*Esquemeling-*1891.—*The Buccaneers and Marooners of America, being an account of the famous adventures and daring deeds of certain notorious freebooters of the Spanish Main.* Edited by Howard Pyle. London, 1891.

*Esquemeling-*1898.—*The Buccaneers of America, a true account of the most remarquable Assaults committed of late years upon the coasts of the West Indies by the Buccaneers of Jamaica and Tortuga (both English and French) wherein are contained more especially the Unparalleled Exploits of Sir Henry Morgan, our English Jamaican Hero, who Sacked Porto Bello, burnt Panama, etc., by John Esquemeling, one of the Buccaneers who was present at these tragedies now faithfully rendered into English.* London, 1898.

Estrada.—*Guerras de Flandes.* Escrita en Latín por el P. Famiano Estrada, de la Compañía de Jesus y traducida en Romance por el P. Melchor de Novar de la misma Compañía. En Colonia, MDCLXXXII.

Feijóo.—Obras. Biblioteca de Autores Españoles (Rivadeneyra), vol. 56. Madrid.

N*

Feugère.—L'Abbé Raynal (1713–1726) *Documents Inédits.* Anatole Feugère Angoulème, 1922.

Fischer.—Viceregal Administration in Spanish America. By L. E. Fischer. Berkeley (California), 1926.

Frézier.—A Voyage to the South Sea and along the Coasts of Chili and Peru. In the Years 1712, 1713 *and* 1714. *Particularly Describing the Genius and Constitution of the Inhabitants, as well Indians as Spaniards, etc.* By Monsieur Frézier, Engineer in Ordinary to the French King. London, MDCCXVII.

Frézier-F.—Relation Du Voyage De La Mer Du Sud Aux Cotes Du Chili Du Perou, Et Du Brésil. Fait pendant les années 1712, 1713 & 1714, par M. Frézier, Ingenieur Ordinaire du Roi. Amsterdam, MDCCXVII. 2 vols.

Fullarton.—Substance of the evidence delivered before the Lords of His Majesty's Most Honourable Privy Council in the case of Governor Picton under the statute 23d *of King Henry VIII which relates to treason and murder* submitted [. . .] by Colonel Fullarton of Fullarton. F.R.S., 1807.

G.B.A.W.—Opere di Giordano Bruno Nolano. Ora per la prima volta raccolte e pubblicate da Adolfo Wagner Dottore. Lipsia, MDCCCXXX.

G.F.—The History of Freemasonry, its antiquities, symbols, constitutions, customs, etc. By Robert Freke Gould. London, 1884–87. 6 vols.

G.I.V.—Historia General Del Perú o Comentarios Reales de los Incas por el Inca Garcilaso de la Vega. Madrid, 1800. 13 vols.

Gage-48.—The English-American his Travail by Sea and Land or a New Survey of the West-Indies, etc. ; by the true and painfull endeavours of Thomas Gage, now Preacher of the Word of God at Acris in the County of Kent. London, Anno Domini 1648.

Gage-77.—A New Survey of the West-Indies or the English American his travel by Sea and Land. By Thomas Gage. London, 1677.

Galvez-P.—José de Gálvez Visitor General of New Spain 1765–1771. By J. Priestley. Berkeley, 1916.

Gayangos.—Cartas y Relaciones de Hernán Cortés al Emperador Carlos V colegidas e illustradas por Don Pascual Gayangos. Paris, 1866.

Gide-Congo.—Voyage au Congo. Carnets de Route. André Gide. Paris, 1934.

Gil Fortoul.—Historia Constitucional de Venezuela. By José Gil Fortoul, Caracas, 1930.

Gillespie.—Gleanings and Remarks collected during many months of residence at Buenos Aires and within the Upper Country etc. By Major Alexander Gillespie of the Royal Marines. Leeds, 1818.

Godoy-C.D.—Cuenta dada de su vida política por Don Manuel Godoy, príncipe de la Paz, o sean Memorias Críticas y apologéticas para la Historia del Reinado del Señor D. Carlos IV, de Borbón. Madrid, 1836.

Gondomar.—Documentos Inéditos para la Historia de España Publicados por los Señores Duque de Alba y otros. Madrid, 1943.

Goris.—Etude sur les Colonies marchandes Méridionales (Portugais, Espagnols, Italiens) à Anvers de 1488 à 1567, par J. A. Goris. Louvain, 1925.

Gracián.—El Criticón. Por Baltasar Gracián. Philadelphia, University of Pennsylvania Press, Oxford University Press, 1938.

Graetz.—History of the Jews. By Professor H. Graetz. Specially revised for this English edition by the author. London, 1891. 5 vols.

Grahame.—The History of the United States of America, from the Plantation of the British Colonies till their Revolt and Declaration of Independence. By James Grahame. London, 1836. 4 vols.

Guiñazú.—La Magistratura Indiana. Por Ruiz Guiñazú. Buenos Aires, 1916.

Gunther.—Inside Latin America.—By John Gunther. London, 1942.

H.C.—Essai Politique sur l'Ile de Cuba. Alexandre Humboldt. Paris, 1826. 2 vols.

H.C. S.M.—Hernán Cortés. Conqueror of Mexico. By Salvador de Madariaga. Buenos Aires, 1942.

H.D. N.M.—Historical Documents relating to New Mexico, Nueva Vizcaya and Approaches thereto, to 1773. Collected by F. A. Bandelier and Fanny R. Bandelier, etc. Washington, 1923. Ed. by C. H. Hackett.

H. E.P.N.E.—Voyage de Humboldt et Bonpland. Troisième partie. Essai Politique sur le Royaume de la Nouvelle Espagne. Paris, 1811. 2 vols.

H. P.N.—Voyage aux régions équinoxiales du Nouveau Continent, fait en 1799, 1800, et 1804 par Alexandre de Humboldt et A. Bonpland, rédigé par Alexandre de Humboldt avec deux atlas. Paris, 1814.

Haenke.—Descripción del Perú. Por Tadeo Haenke, Socio de las Academias de Ciencias de Viena y de Praga. Lima, 1901.

Hakluyt.—The Principal Navigations Voyages Traffiques & Discoveries of the English Nation Made by Sea or Overland to the Remote & Farthest Distant Quarters of the Earth at any time within the compasse of these 1600 years. London.

Hall.—Extracts from a Journal written on the Coasts of Chili, Peru and Mexico In the Years 1820, 1821, 1822 by Captain Basil Hall. Royal Navy. Edinburgh, 1825. 2 vols.

Hamilton.—American Treasure and the Price Revolution in Spain 1501-1650, by Earl J. Hamilton, Ph.D., Cambridge (Mass.), 1934.

Hamilton-T.—Travels through the Interior Provinces of Columbia. By Colonel J. P. Hamilton. London, 1827. 2 vols.

Haring.—Trade and Navigation between Spain and the Indies in the time of the Hapsburgs. By Clarence Henry Haring. Cambridge, Mass., 1918.

Harlow-Jackson.—The Voyages of Captain William Jackson (1642-1645), edited by Vincent T. Harlow, B.A. Litt., F. R. Hist.S. Camden Miscellany, vol. XIII. London, 1923.

Hazard.—Santo Domingo Past and Present with a glance at Hayti. Samuel Hazard. London, 1873.

Herrera.—Descripción de las Indias Occidentales de Antonio de Herrera Coronista Mayor de Su Mag^d de las Indias, y su Coronista de Castilla. En Madrid en la Oficina Real de Nicolás Rodriguez Franco. Año de 1730.

Humbert-C.V.—Histoire de la Colombie et de Venezuela. Jules Humbert. Venezuela, 1921.

Humbert-V.—Les Origines Venezueliennes. Essai sur la Colonisation Espagnole au Venezuela. Bibliothèque des Universités du Midi, Bordeaux-Paris, 1905.

Humbling.—A Proposal for Humbling Spain. Written in 1711 By a Person of Distinction. And now first printed from the Manuscript etc. London, [1714].

I.M.—Documentos Inéditos o Muy Raros para la Historia de Mexico publicados por Genaro García y Carlos Pereyra. Tomo V. La Imprenta de Mexico. Mexico, 1906.

Icaza.—*Sucesos Reales que parecen Imaginados de Gutierre de Catina, Juan de la Cueva y Mateo Alemán.* Los refiere y comenta Francisco A. de Icaza. 1919.

Keynes.—*A Treatise on Money* by John Maynard Keynes. London, 1930.

L.A.H.—*Lettres Américaines d'Alexandre de Humboldt* 1798–1807 *précédées d'une notice de J. C. Delamétherie et suivies d'un choix de documents en partie inédits, publiées avec une introduction et des notes* par le Dr. E. I. Hamy. Paris, 1905.

L. Cartas.—*Cartas del Libertador.* Publicadas por Vicente Lecuna. Tomo IV. Caracas, 1929.

La Fuente.—*Historia de las Sociedades Secretas en España.* By Vicente de La Fuente. Lugo, 1870–1. 3 vols.

Labat.—*Nouveau Voyage aux Isles de l'Amérique contenant l'Histoire Naturelle de ces Pays etc.* Père Labat. A la Haye, MDCCXXIV. 2 vols.

Lea.—*The Inquisition in the Spanish Dependencies.* By Henry Charles Lea. New York, 1908.

Leonard.—*Romances of Chivalry in the Spanish Indies with some registers of Shipments of Books to the Spanish Colonies.* In University of California Publications in Modern Philology, vol. XVI, 1932–1933. By Irwing A. Leonard. Berkeley, California, 1933.

Lettres-Juifs.—*Lettres de quelques juifs portugais, allemands et polonois à M. de Voltaire. Avec un petit commentaire.* 4ᵉ édition. Paris, 1776. 3 vols.

Leys-Kenya.—*Kenya with an introduction by Professor Gilbert Murray.* By Norman Leys, M.B., D.P.H. (Fulani ben Fulani) 3ᵈ edition. London, 1928.

Lozano.—*El Maestro del Libertador.* By F. Lozano y Lozano. Paris, 1913.

M. P.—*Historia de la Poesía Hispano-Americana.* By Don Marcelino Menéndez Pelayo. Madrid, 1913.

M.P.-H.—*Historia de los Heterodoxos Españoles.* By Dr. D. Marcelino Menéndez Pelayo. Madrid, 1880. 3 vols.

Macanaz-M.—*Regalías de los Señores Reyes de Aragón, por D. Melchor de Macanaz.* Publícalas [. . .] D. Joaquín Maldonado Macanaz. Biblioteca Jurídica de Autores Españoles. Madrid, 1879.

Macanaz-T.—*Testamento de España* por el Excmo. Sr. D. Melchor de Macanaz, Ministro que fué de Estado en la Corte de Madrid. Mexico, 1821.

Macaulay.—*The History of England from the Accession of James II.* London, 1906.

Madrid-Corte.—*Libro Histórico Político, Solo Madrid es Corte, y El Cortesano en Madrid etc.* Por Don Alonso Núñez de Castro, Coronista de su Magestad. En Madrid, Año de MDCLXXV.

Mancini.—*Bolívar et l'Emancipation des Colonies Espagnoles des Origines à 1815.* Jules Mancini. Paris, 1912.

Mariana-H.E.—*Historia General de España* que escribió el P. Juan de Mariana. Valencia, MDCCLXXXIII. 9 vols.

Mariana-R.—*Joannis Marianae Hispani, e Societate Jesu, De Rege et Regis Institutione.* Libri III. Maguntie, 1605.

Mariana.—*Obras del Padre Mariana.* Rivadeneyra, vol. 31.

Maroons.—*The History of the Maroons From their Origin to the Establishment of their Chief Tribe at Sierra Leone : Including the Expedition to Cuba For the Purpose of Procuring Spanish Chasseurs ; and the State of the Island of Jamaica.* By R. C. Dallas, Esq., London, 1803. 2 vols.

Means.—History of the Spanish Conquest of Yucatán and of the Itzas, by Philip Ainsworth Means, in Papers of the Peabody Museum of American Archæology and Ethnology, Harvard University, vol. VII. Cambridge, Mass., 1917.

Mendieta.—Historia Eclesiástica Indiana, obra escrita a fines del siglo XVI por Fray Gerónimo de Mendieta, de la Orden de San Francisco. La publica por primera vez Joaquín García Icazbalceta. Mexico MDCCLXX [misprint for MDCCCLXX].

Miranda-Archivo.—Archivo del General Miranda, 1750–1810. Caracas, Venezuela, 1929. 15 vols.

This is an invaluable collection not only for American but for European history as well. It deserves a better edition with adequate indexes, notes and explanations. There are at times curious errors on the part of the editors. For instance vol. IV, p. VI, the editor says : " With the Prince of Darmstadt he [Miranda] converses on travel and letters ; and of a Charity Asylum visited, he says : ' It is one of the Probation Houses well organised though tyrannical I have seen—compare with the prison at Madrid ! ' Then adds : ' No people without philosophy and much education can preserve its liberty '." But if one reads Miranda's own text, p. 11 of the same volume, one finds this last phrase : " No people without philosophy and much education can preserve its liberty," refers to Switzerland and not to Spain.

Miranda-Life.—The Life of Miranda. By W. S. Robertson. Chapel Hill, 1929. 2 vols.

Miranda-Robertson.—Diary, tour of the United States 1783–1784. By William Spence Robertson. New York, MCMXXVIII.

Moreton.—West India. Customs and Manners containing strictures on the soil, cultivation, produce, trade, officers and inhabitants ; with the method of establishing and conducting a Sugar Plantation, in which is added, the Practice of training new slaves. By J. B. Moreton, Esq. London, 1793.

Moses.—South America on the Eve of Emancipation. By Bernard Moses. New York, 1908.

Moses-L.—Spanish Colonial Literature in South America. By Bernard Moses. 1922.

Motolinia.—Historia de los Indios de Nueva España by Fray Toribio Benavente o Motolinia, in *C.D.H.M.* vol. I, pp. 1–249.

Oviedo-Baños.—Historia de la Conquista y Población de la Provincia de Venezuela escrita por D. Joseph de Oviedo y Baños, vecino de la ciudad de Santiago de León de Caracas, quien la consagra y dedica a su hermano el Señor D. Diego de Oviedo y Baños, Oidor de las Reales Audiencias de Santo Domingo, Guatemala y Mexico, del Consejo de S.M. en el Real y Supremo de las Indias. Madrid, 1723.

Oviedo-G.—A narrative of the Viceregal embassy to Vilcabamba, 1571, *and of the execution of the Inca Tupac Amaru, Dec.* 1571 *by Friar Gabriel de Oviedo, of Cuzco,* 1573. Translated by Sir Clements Markham, K.C.B., President of the Hakluyt Society, 1908. Published as a suppt. to *S.G. C.M.*

P.A.G.N. M.—Publicaciones del Archivo General de la Nación, Mexico, 1932. XX. Los judíos en la Nueva España, XXI. La vida colonial. Los precursores ideológicos de la Guerra de la Independencia. La Masonería en Mexico en el siglo XVIII. Tomo II.

P-P.—El Regimen Español en Venezuela. Estudio Histórico. By Dr. C. Parra Pérez. Madrid, 1932.

Paine.—A Letter addressed to the Abbé Raynal on the Affairs of North America in which the mistakes in the Abbé's Account of the Revolution of America are corrected and cleared up by Thomas Paine, M.A. of the University of Pennsylvania, and author of a tract entitled *COMMONSENSE*. Philadelphia, Printed, London, reprinted MDCCLXXXII.

Parra-León.—Filosofía Universitaria venezolana 1788–1821. Discurso y estudio histórico. By Dr. Caracciolo Parra-León. Caracas, 1933.

Poinsett.—Notes on Mexico made in the Autumn of 1822. By J. R. Poinsett. London, MDCCCXXV.

Porras-F.P.—Francisco Pizarro. (Discurso de Recepción a la Academai Peruana Correspondiente de la Real Española de la lengua). By R. Porras Barrenechea. Lima, 1941.

Porras-Lima.—Pequeña Antología de Lima. By R. Porras Barrenechea.

*R.A.B.M.—*Revista de Archivos, Bibliotecas y Museos. Madrid.

R.C.—Historia de la Revolución de la República de Colombia en la América Meridional. By José Manuel Restrepo. Besanzon, 1858.

R.P.T.P.—Tradiciones Peruanas. By Ricardo Palma. 1924.

Ralegh-H. 28.*—The Discoverie of the large and beautiful Empire of Guiana by Sir Walter Ralegh* edited by V. T. Harlow, M.A., B.Litt. London, 1928.

Ralegh-H. 32.*—Ralegh's Last Voyage, being an account drawn out of contemporary letters* and selected by V. T. Harlow, M.A. London.

Raynal.—Histoire Philosophique et Politique des Etablissements et du Commerce des Européens dans les Deux Indes. Guillaume-Thomas Raynal. Geneva, MDCCLXXX.

Rein.—Der Kampf Westeuropas um Nordamerika im 15 *und* 16. *Jahrhundert. Allgemeine Staatengeschichte.* Adolf Rein, 1925.

Restrepo-V.—Los Chibchas antes de la Conquista española. By Vicentè Restrepo. Bogotá, 1895.

Ricard.—La " Conquête Spirituelle " du Mexique : Essai sur l'apostolat et les méthodes missionnaires des Ordres Mendiants en Nouvelle Espagne de 1523–24 *à* 1572. Robert Ricard. Paris, Institut d'Ethnologie, 1933.

Rights G.B.—The Rights of Great Britain Asserted against the Claims of America, being an Answer to the Declaration of the General Congress. The Ninth Edition. Godwin Pamphlet 308, no. 14. London, MDCCLXXVI.

Rippy.—Historical Evolution of Hispanic America. By J. F. Rippy. Blackwell, Oxford, 1932.

Rojas-E.H.—Capítulos de la Historia Colonial de Venezuela. By Aristides Rojas. Madrid, 1919.

Rojas-L.H.—Lecturas Históricas. By Aristides Rojas. Caracas, 1927. 2 vols.

Rousseau.—La participation de l'Espagne à la guerre d'Amérique. Revue des Questions Historiques 72, p. 488. Fr. Rousseau, 1902.

S.G. C.M.—History of the Incas by Pedro Sarmiento de Gamboa and the execution of the Inca Tupac Amaru, by Captain Baltasar de Ocampo, translated and edited by Sir Clements Markham, K.C.B., President of the Hakluyt Society, Cambridge, MDCCCCVII.
    Markham's introduction to *S.G. C.M.* is typical of his incapacity to achieve an impartial outlook ; p. xiii in particular is lamentable. He decides that all he does not like in Sarmiento's History has been interpolated by the viceroy in order to blacken the Incas ; and calmly adds that these interpolations " are so obvious that I have put them in italics within brackets." There is not a shred of a documentary proof, as is pointed out by Steffen, otherwise none too favourable to the viceroy. (Anotaciones a la Historia Indica del Capitán Pedro Sarmiento de Gamboa,

por el Dr. Hans Steffen, tomo CXXIX, p. 1130, nota 2 de Anales de la Universidad de Chile, 1911.) Steffen (p. 1129) adds moreover that " Pietschmann, having examined the matter reaches the conclusion that Sarmiento has fulfilled his purpose without in any way doing violence to either the sources or the tradition."
Markham himself feels bound to declare that " the History of the Incas by Sarmiento is without any doubt the most authentic and reliable that has yet appeared," p. xii.

S.G.-P.—*Geschichte des Inkareiches von Pedro Sarmiento de Gamboa,* Herausgegeben von Richard Pietschmann. (Abhandlungen der königlichen Gesellschaft der Wissenschaften zu Göttingen). Neue Folge, Band VI Berlin, 1906.

S.P.—*Politica Indiana compuesta por el Señor Don Juan de Solórzano y Pereyra Cavallero del Orden de Santiago, del Consejo de Su Magestad en los Supremos de Castilla e Indias etc.* Corregida e ilustrada con notas por el Lic.do Don Francisco Ramiro de Valenzuela etc. en Madrid. Año de MDCCLXXVI.

Sahagún.—*Historia Universal de las cosas de Nueva España* por el M.R.P. Fray Bernardino de Sahagún. Vol. VII de Antiquities of Mexico, edited by Lord Kingsborough, London, 1831. 9 vols.

San Andrés.—*Carta DEL MARQUES DE LA VILLA DE S. ANDRES, Y VIZCONDE DE BUEN-PASSO, respondiendo à un Amigo suyo lo que siente de la Corte de Madrid. DEDICADA A LA MUY ILUSTRE SEÑORA DOÑA MARIA THERESA VELEZ DEL HOYO, y SOTOMAYOR.* Y DADA A LUZ POR EL M.R.P. Fr. GONZALO GONZÁLEZ de SAN GONZALO, Lector Jubilado, y Padre más antiguo en la Provincia de San Joseph en el Reyno del Perú.
The author of this curious book is supposed to be Don Cristóbal del Hoyo-Solórzano y Sotomayor, born in La Palma (Canary Islands) in 1677 ; second Marquess de la Villa de San Andrés, Viscount del Buen Paso from 1722, when his father died ; a prominent figure in the islands. He married in Galicia Doña Teresa Calixta Raxo Texeiro Suárez de Deza, a daughter of the lord of Areríes, in the bishopric of Lugo.—Enciclopedia Heráldica y Genealógica of Caraffa. Vol. V, pp. 42–73. There are many details in the book which tally with these data. Whoever he was, the author reveals a vast European, classical and theological culture, including a fair knowledge of Hebrew. He was ingenious, licentious and blasphemous. It is most unlikely that the author was the Marquess himself. The friar who on the first page assumes editorship for the book says in the introduction that he had 500 copies printed. The Inquisition, though fairly mild in those days, can hardly have allowed many to slip through its fingers. It is to be found neither in the British Museum nor in the Bodleian library.

Sánchez.—*La Literatura del Perú.* By Luis Alberto Sánchez. Buenos Aires, 1939.

Sandoval.—*Historia de la Vida y Hechos del Emperador Carlos V Maximo, Fortissimo Rey Catholico de España, y de las Indias, Islas, y Tierra Firme del Mar Oceano, &c. Por el Maestro Fray Prudencio de SANDOVAL* Su Coronista, Obispo de Pamplona. Nueva Impression, enriquescida con lindas Figuras. En Amberes. Por Geronymo Verdussen, Impressor, y Mercader de Libros. Año, MDCLXXXI.

Sandoval-A.—*De instauranda Ethiopicum salute.* Alfonso de Sandoval. Sevilla, 1678.

Sarmiento-Markham.—*History of the Incas.* By Pedro Sarmiento de Gamboa Translated by Sir Clemens Markham. London.

Sarmiento-Steffen.—Anotaciones a la Historia Indica. Por M. Steffen. Anales de la Universidad de Chile, 1911–12. Tomo 129.

Scelle.—Histoire Politique de la Traite Négrière aux Indes de Castille etc. par Georges Scelle. 2 vols. Paris, 1906.

Schlosser.—Histoire des Révolutions Politiques et Littéraires etc. Fr. Ch. Schlosser, 1825. 2 vols.

Schoell.—Cours d'Histoire des Etats Européens depuis le bouleversement de l'Empire Romain d'Occident jusqu'en 1789 par Max Samson—Fred Schoell. Paris, 1833.

Sidney Smith.—The Spanish Guild Merchant. By Robert Sidney Smith. Duke University Press, 1940.

Simon.—Primera Parte de las Noticias Historiales de Tierra Firme, por Fr Pedro Simon. Madrid, 1625.

Sloane.—A Voyage to the Islands Madera, Barbados, Nieves, S. Christopher's and Jamaica with the natural History [. . .] *of the last of those Islands,* to *which is prefixed an Introduction wherein is an Account of the Inhabitants, Air, Waters, Diseases, Trade, &c.* by Hans Sloane, M.D., in two vols. London, 1707.

Spell.—Rousseau in the Spanish World before 1833. By Jefferson Rea Spell. Austin, 1938.

Stübel-A.—The Necropolis of Ancon in Peru. By W. Reiss and A. Stübel. Translated by Professor A. H. Keane, 1880–1887. Berlin. 3 vols.

Stübel-C.—Die Vulkanberge von Colombia. Geologisch-topographisch aufgenommen und beschrieben von Alphons Stübel. Nach dessen Tode ergänzt und herausgegeben von Theodor Wolf. Dresden, 1906.

Stübel-E.—Die Vulkanberge von Ecuador. Geologisch-topographisch aufgenommen und beschrieben von Alphons Stübel. Berlin, 1897.

Stübel-K.I.—Kultur und Industrie Südamerikanischer Völker. Von A. Stübel, W. Reiss und B. Koppel. Text und Beschreibung der Tafeln von Max Uhle, Leipzig. Berlin, 1889. 2 vols.

T.M.I.C.—Historia del Tribunal del Santo Oficio de la Inquisición en Chile. Por José Toribio Medina. Santiago, MDCCCXC. 2 vols.

T.M.I. Cg.—Historia del Tribunal del Santo Oficio de la Inquisición de Cartagena de las Indias. Por José Toribio Medina. Santiago de Chile, 1899.

T.M.I.L.—Historia del Santo Oficio de la Inquisición de Lima. Por J. Toribio Medina. Santiago, 1887.

T.M.I.M.—La Imprenta en Mexico (1539–1821). Por José Toribio Medina. Santiago de Chile, MCMXII.

T.M.I.P.C.—La Instrucción Pública en Chile. Por José Toribio Medina. Santiago de Chile, 1905.

Tenison.—Elisabethan England. Survey of Life and Literature. By Eva Mabel Tenison. London, 1933–40. 7 vols.

Tirado.—La Masonería en España. Por M. Tirado y Rojas. Madrid, 1892–3.

Toreno.—Historia del Levantamiento, Guerra y Revolución de España por el Excmo. Sr. Conde de Toreno, precedida de la Biografía del Autor, escrita por el Excmo. Sr. Don Leopoldo Augusto de Cueto. Madrid, 1872.

Torre-Imprenta.—Orígenes de la Imprenta en España y su desarrollo en América Española. By José Torre Revello. Buenos Aires, 1940.

Torrubia.—Centinela contra francmasones. Discurso sobre su origen, Instituto

Secreto y Juramento. Descúbrese la Cifra con que se escriben, y las acciones, señas y palabras con que se conocen. Por Fray Joseph Torrubia. Madrid, 1752.

Trowbridge.—Cagliostro. The Splendour and Misery or a Master of Magi by W. R. H. Trowbridge. London, 1910.

Tryals.—The History of the Most Remarkable Tryals in Great Britain and Ireland in Capital Cases etc. Faithfully Extracted from Records, and other Authentic Authorities as well Manuscript as Printed. London, 1715.

U.-J.J. N.S.—Noticias Secretas de America sobre el Estado Naval, Militar, y Político de los Reynos del Perú y Provincias de Quito, Costas de Nueva Granada y Chile : Gobierno y Regimen Particular de los Pueblos de Indios : Cruel Opresión y Extorsiones de sus Corregidores y Curas : Abusos Escandalosos Introducidos Entre estos Habitantes por los Misioneros : Causas de su Origen y Motivos de su Continuación por el Espacio de tres siglos. Por Jorge Juan y Antonio de Ulloa. Londres, 1826. The authenticity of this Noticias Secretas of Ulloa and Jorge Juan is discussed by *Altamira* in his *Huella*, pp. 101–5. He explains that the first to raise doubts on this remarkable book was Professor William R. Shepherd, of Columbia University. Altamira himself in 1913 raised the matter in the Congress of London. Later Don Carlos Pereyra discussed it in an article published by the Unión Hispano-Americana on Novembre 11th, 1920. It seems to me that though the obvious bias of the English editor may have induced him to some infidelities of detail, it would be difficult to consider the whole of this report as otherwise than genuine and, for the time being at any rate, I have taken it as such.

U.-J.J. R.H.—Relación Histórica del Viage a la América Meridional hecho de orden de S. MAG. para medir algunos grados de Meridiano terrestre etc. Por Don Jorge Juan etc. y Don Antonio de Ulloa. Impresa de orden del Rey en Madrid, año de MDCCXLVIII. 4 vols.

Usigli.—Mexico en el Teatro. By Rodolfo Usigli. Imprenta Mundial, Mexico, 1932.

*Varia-B.—*A Collection of printed and MS Material on Spain and the Indies. Bodleian : Arch Seld. A. subt. 11.

Varinas.—Colección de Documentos Inéditos relativos al Descubrimiento, conquista y organización de las antiguas posesiones de Ultramar. Segunda serie publicada por la Real Academia de la Historia. Tomo 12. Vaticinios de la Pérdida de las Indias. Madrid, 1899.

Vetancurt.—Teatro Mexicano. Descripción Breve de los Sucesos exemplares históricos, políticos, militares y religiosos del Nuevo Mundo Occidental de las Indias [. . .] dispuesto por el R. P. Agustin de Vetancurt, Mexicano, hijo de la misma provincia. Mexico, 1698.

Viñas.—España y los Orígenes de la Política Social.—Las Leyes de Indias. Por Carmelo Viñas y Mey. Madrid, 1930.

Viñas-E.—El Estatuto del Obrero Indígena en la Colonización Española. Por Carmelo Viñas y Mey. Madrid, 1929.

Viñas-P.S.—La Política Social y la Política Criminal en las Leyes de Indias. Por Carmelo Viñas y Mey. Madrid, 1922.

Viollis.—Indochine S.O.S. Andrée Viollis. Paris, 1935.

W.H.—Witch Hunting and Witch Trials. The Indictments for Witchcraft from the Records of 1373 Assizes held for the Home Circuit A.D. 1559–1736. Collected and edited by C. L'Estrange Ewen. With an introduction. London, 1929.

W.P.—The Witch Persecutions. Edited by George L. Burr. *A.B.* Translations and Reprints from the Original Sources of European History. Published by the Dept. of History of the University of Pennsylvania. Philadelphia, Pa., 1897.

W.R.—A History of the Witches of Renfrewshire who were burned on the Gallow-green of Paisley. Paisley 1809. (*Beginning with*) *A Treatise on Witchcraft by Sir George Mackenzie of Rosehaugh who was King's advocate and one of the Lords of the Privy Council in Scotland. From his " Laws and Customs of Scotland in Chancery Criminal."* Printed in 1678.

Walpole.—Memoirs of the Life and Administration of Sir Robert Walpole, Earl of Orford, by William Coxe, M.A. London, 1798. 3 vols.

Wesley.—The Journal of the Reverend Charles Wesley, M.A. Sometime Student of Christ Church, Oxford. London, 1849. 2 vols.

Witchcraft-Hutchinson.—An Historical Essay concerning Witchcraft. With Observations upon Matters of Fact etc., by Francis Hutchinson, D.D., Chaplain in Ordinary to His Majesty and Minister of St. James' Parish in St. Edmund's Bury. London, MDCCXX.

Wood-Oxford.—The History and the Antiquities of the University of Oxford in two books. Oxford, 1796.

*Wright-*1928.*—Spanish Documents concerning English Voyages to the Caribbean* 1527–1568.—The Hakluyt Society, second series no. LXXI. London, 1932.

Wright-J.—The English Conquest of Jamaica by Irene A. Wright, B.A., Camden Miscellany vol. XIII. London, 1923.

Woodward.—A New American History. By W. E. Woodward, New York, 1936.

Zavala-M.—La Utopia de Tomás Moro en la Nueva España y otros estudios con una introducción, por Genaro Estrada. Por Silvio A. Zavala. Mexico, 1937.

Zavala E.I.—La Encomienda Indiana, por Silvio A. Zavala. Madrid, 1935.

Zavala I.J.—Las Instituciones Jurídicas en la Conquista de América, por Silvio A. Zavala. Madrid, 1935.

INDEX

O